Please remember that this is a library book,
and that it belongs only temporarily to each
person who uses it. Be considerate. Do
not write in this, or any, library book.

Social Work with Groups

Social Work with Groups

Third Edition

Helen Northen
Roselle Kurland

COLUMBIA UNIVERSITY PRESS   NEW YORK

Columbia University Press
Publishers Since 1893
New York, Chichester, West Sussex
Copyright © 2001 Columbia University Press

Library of Congress Cataloging-in-Publication Data

Northen, Helen.
   Social work with groups / Helen Northen, Roselle Kurland. — 3rd ed.
     p.   cm.
   Includes bibliographical references and index.
   ISBN 0-231-11632-2 (cloth : alk. paper)
   1. Social group work. I. Kurland, Roselle. II. Title.
HV45 .N6 2001
361.4—dc21
                                                    00-066042

♾

Casebound editions of Columbia University Press books
are printed on permanent and durable acid-free paper.
Printed in the United States of America

c   10 9 8 7 6 5 4 3

Contents

Preface

Social work practice with groups is a positive and optimistic way of working with people that draws out and affirms the very best in them. In fact, the very act of forming a group is a statement of belief in people's strengths and in the fact that each person has something to offer and to contribute to the lives of others. Effective group work, in which people interact personally to support and challenge one another as they consider, understand, appreciate, respect, and build upon each other's experiences, situations, problems, dilemmas, and points of view, is needed today more than ever in our increasingly depersonalized world. But effective group work requires a considerable body of ethical principles, knowledge, and professional skill. This new edition of *Social Work with Groups* aims to address the complex requirements of effective group work practice by setting forth a comprehensive framework that can be applied differentially to diverse populations and situations.

The second edition of *Social Work with Groups* continues to be used widely by students, faculty, and practitioners. Its theoretical base and applications to practice have stood the test of time. Yet practice has accelerated rapidly in the last dozen years, as has the knowledge about human behavior, social policy, and social environments that informs good practice. This edition provides new and updated information about the theory and practice of social work with groups. Its readers will gain understanding not only of what to do but also of how and why to do it at a given time.

The book's first several chapters present a substantial core of values, purposes, knowledge, and skills that are generic to work with groups of varied types and diverse memberships in a range of settings. The next several chapters examine the ways in which the social worker uses the knowledge base in actual practice to address group issues and content in a sequence from initial contacts with prospective clients through four stages of group development. A chapter on evaluation concludes the work. The book demonstrates the integral interrelationship between theory and practice. A particular contribution is that concepts and principles of practice are illustrated by examples from diverse groups in diverse settings and communities. The content is buttressed by findings from research.

Practice in this book is based upon an ecosystems orientation that takes into account the biological, psychological, and social functioning of the members, the development and social processes of groups, and environmental forces. Practice is goal directed and process oriented, with mutual aid as a primary dynamic for change. Practitioners help groups to form for particular purposes and facilitate the development of relationships among the members through which they become able to provide mutual aid and support in working toward their personal and social goals.

This third edition of the book has an additional author—a unique pairing of writers. As a student at the School of Social Work of the University of Southern California, Roselle Kurland sought out Helen Northen as her mentor, with the result that the two became friends and associates in efforts to advance social work practice and education. At times, the former student became the mentor to the former teacher. Helen Northen wishes the readers to know that she is grateful for the outstanding contributions made by Roselle Kurland to this book. And Roselle Kurland wants readers to know that she is even more appreciative now, after working on this book, of the depth of knowledge and understanding contained in the work of Helen Northen. Mutual respect is, indeed, the foundation of what has now become a collegial relationship in the best sense. Both authors acknowledge the numerous students, colleagues, and friends who have supported them in their search for the best ways to enhance the lives of people through meaningful experiences in groups.

Social Work with Groups

1 Groups in Social Work Practice

Enhancement of the psychosocial functioning of people and improvement of their environments are the primary concerns of social work. The profession has a rich heritage of activities directed toward reforming conditions that degrade the human personality, providing services and resources to meet basic needs, and improving people's capacity for more effective interpersonal relations and functioning in social roles. As people's problems in meeting their basic needs, coping with stressful situations, and developing satisfying social relations have become identified and understood, so, too, has need for knowledge and skill on the part of those persons who are in helping roles.

Historical Highlights

Social work with groups is now an integral part of practice within the profession of social work. Groups of all kinds are ubiquitous in American society. The famous Frenchman, Alexis de Tocqueville, writing about democracy in America in 1832, explained that

> the most democratic country on the face of the earth is the one in which men have, in our time, carried to the highest perfection the art of pursuing in common the object of their common desires and have applied this new science to the greatest number of purposes. Among

democratized nations, people become powerless if they do not learn voluntarily to help one another. Feeling and opinions are recruited, the heart is enlarged, and the human mind is developed only by the reciprocal influence of men one upon another. As soon as several of the inhabitants of the United States have taken up an opinion or a feeling which they wish to promote in the world, they look out for mutual assistance; and as soon as they have found one another, they combine into groups. From that moment, they are no longer isolated men.[1]

In that one paragraph, Tocqueville captured the essence of group membership. Meeting the need to belong and using mutual aid for empowerment are still the raisons d'être for the use of groups in social work practice. The vast world of groups generally operates without professional leadership, but on an autonomous or self-help basis. The history of social work with groups deals with the recognition that some groups require professional help to achieve certain purposes not often attainable only through mutual aid between the members.

Early Developments

The use of groups in social work today is built on firm foundations. By the time that group work was introduced into social work education in the early 1920s, many social agencies were serving groups.[2] The Young Men's Christian Association had been introduced into the United States from England in 1851 and the Young Women's Christian Association in 1866. The Young Men's Hebrew Association was organized in 1880 and the Young Women's Hebrew Association in 1902. In the first two decades of the twentieth century, several youth-serving agencies were founded to enrich the lives of children and "build character." These included the Boy and Girl Scouts, Boys Clubs of America, Camp Fire Girls, B'nai B'rith, and the National Jewish Welfare Board.

Social settlements were the best known of the agencies associated with group work. The first settlement, Toynbee Hall, was founded by Samuel Barnett in the Lower East Side of London in 1884. Students from Oxford University, influenced by the social gospel, took up residence in a large house in that neighborhood. It was believed that, in order to understand and help poor people, the helpers needed to live among them as neighbors and learn about the environment in which they lived. The residents were the first volunteers, later joined by others who provided services and resources to meet the needs of their neighbors.

The first settlement in the United States was the Neighborhood Guild in New York in 1886, now called University Settlement, followed by Hull House in Chicago and College Settlement in New York, both in 1889. Hull House, founded by Jane Addams, became the most famous of the settlements. In addition to their fame in achieving social reforms, the residents organized clubs, recreational and cultural activities, citizenship classes, and other educational groups to meet the interests of their neighbors. Many of the neighbors were recent immigrants from Europe; later, they were poor people of color who were moving into industrial jobs in the North. In the preface to Jane Addams's most famous book, *Twenty Years at Hull House*, Henry Steele Commager wrote:

> The opening of Hull House was the beginning of what was to be one of the great social movements in modern America—the Settlement House movement: here in a way was the beginning of social work. As yet there was no organized social work in the United States—the beneficent program of Mary Richmond was still in the future—and as yet there was not even any formal study of Sociology. It was no accident that the new University of Chicago, which was founded just a few years after Hull House, came to be the center of sociological study in America and that so many of its professors were intimately associated with Hull House.[3]

We have inadequate knowledge of early social work practice with groups, but there is evidence that social work with groups was recognized quite early. For example, in 1915, Zilpha Smith said that "the brands of social work which do not, in the long run, require both the family and the group work method are few."[4] Further, she recommended that all social work students should have field work for one year in a casework agency and one year in a settlement. Five years later, in 1920, Mary Richmond, regarded as the founder of social casework, expressed her knowledge of groups and their values. She observed that

> there was a tendency in modern casework which I have noted with great pleasure. It is one full of promise, I believe, for the future of social treatment. I refer to the new tendency to view our clients from

the angle of what might be called small group psychology. . . . Halfway
between the minute analysis of the individual situation with which we
are all familiar in casework and the kind of sixth sense of neighborhood
standards and backgrounds which is developed in a good social settlement, there is a field as yet almost unexplored.[5]

She was referring to the small group. By 1922, there was sufficient recognition of group work for Richmond to write that case workers needed to have
a sense of the whole of social work and of each of its parts. "The other forms
of social work," she said, "are three—group work, social reform, and social
research."[6]

It was in the next year that the first specialization in group work called
the "Group Service Training Course" was established at Western Reserve
University. Three years later, the name of the program was changed to "Social Group Work" to ally it to social casework, the other specialization in
the school. Wilber Newstetter, the director, recognized that there was a great
need to develop a scientific knowledge base that could be applied to practice
and to distinguish the use of groups in social work from their use in education and recreation. That took a long time.

A Knowledge Base Develops

Efforts to develop a scientific knowledge base for group work came later
than for casework. It gradually occurred with a melding of concepts from
sociology and psychology, combined with knowledge of group discussion,
adult education, and problem solving. Conferences, seminars, and committees were established to study work with small groups. These included,
for example, a committee on group work of the Chicago chapter of the
American Association of Social Workers, regional conferences of the YMCA
and YWCA, and The Inquiry. The Inquiry, organized in 1923, undertook
the task of formalizing discussion as a method, using Alfred Sheffield's book,
Creative Discussion, and the contributions of social philosophers and adult
educators.[7] Grace Coyle, who was then employed by the YWCA, was a
participant. Later, she reminisced, "Looking back, it was for those involved
a period of excitement and ferment, of social discovery, and of deepened
insight as we tried to clarify both our philosophy and its aims and values and
our methods of dealing with groups.[8] Mary Parker Follett, a participant in

The Inquiry, believed that small groups are essential to democracy. She wrote, "The group process contains the secret of collective life, it is the key to democracy, it is the master lesson for every individual to learn, it is our chief hope for the political, the social, the international life of the future."[9]

John Dewey made a major contribution to group work theory.[10] His philosophy of education and studies of the problem-solving process provided essential knowledge for understanding how to work with groups. His educational philosophy emphasized the need to individualize each child, view the child as a whole person, use social experiences as part of the educational process, employ nonauthoritarian discipline, and focus on learning through cooperative effort. His formulation of the problem-solving process with both individuals and groups has stood the test of time.

Newstetter's interest in developing a scientific knowledge base for group work was carried out in 1926 when he, with Mark Feldstein and Theodore Newcomb, began a research project at Camp Wawokiye.[11] It was a study of the interpersonal relations between boys who were referred to the camp from a child guidance clinic for the purpose of improving their peer relationships. Based on this study, the researchers developed concepts about the acceptance-rejection process that occurs in group interaction. They found that the children's needs could be met and their relationships improved through group associations. They demonstrated that experimental research on groups could be conducted in natural settings.

During the time that Newstetter was conducting his research, other early educators were developing knowledge of groups through preparing and analyzing records of practice. The first major contribution was made by Clara Kaiser, who had been on the staff of the YWCA of Chicago and joined the faculty of Western Reserve University in 1927. She taught group work and developed field work placements for students. One of her major projects was to analyze process records of groups prepared by students to discover values, concepts, and principles of practice. That work resulted in the publication of *The Group Records of Four Clubs* in 1930. In that same year, Grace Coyle's book, *Social Process in Organized Groups*, was published. It was her doctoral dissertation in sociology from Columbia University. It was not a book on practice, but it offered a framework of concepts for understanding the formation, structure, composition, and decision-making processes in groups and the interrelation of groups with their environment.

When Kaiser left Western Reserve University in 1934 to pursue advanced studies, Coyle was appointed to her position. One of her first projects was a follow-up of Kaiser's work on records of practice, resulting in the publication of *Studies of Group Behavior* in 1937.

Drawing much of their knowledge from the social sciences, early group workers emphasized the need to understand and respect the cultures of the people who participated in groups. Addams and other social workers sought to preserve the values and traditions of the ethnic groups that comprised the populations of their neighborhoods. A related goal was to improve relationships between individuals of different racial, ethnic, and economic backgrounds. That theme continued to be prevalent in the literature of the post-Depression years. Coyle, for example, recognized the prevalence of stereotyping, intolerance, and prejudice and thought that "we can often break through such barriers to produce an appreciation of people as they become known to each other."[12] In the classic text, *Social Group Work Practice*, Gertrude Wilson and Gladys Ryland gave considerable attention to knowledge about cultural, social class, and gender differences and how to use that knowledge in helping members of groups to understand and relate effectively to each other. That is still one of our profession's most urgent needs.

As was true in social casework, knowledge about the behavior and development of individuals was early applied to work with groups. The major focus was on the development of personality and the nature of relationships between people. Coyle had referred to the use of psychoanalytic theory, but it was Wilson who was the first to integrate appropriate knowledge from Freudian theory, and more especially from ego psychology, into group work practice. Margaret Hartford noted that when Wilson joined the Western Reserve University faculty in 1936, her knowledge of psychoanalytic theory made a major contribution to the knowledge of group work.[13] Her ability to integrate that content with knowledge from the social sciences and from practice theory was evidenced in her major book with Ryland, *Social Group Work Practice*. During this period of time—the 1940s—the application of psychoanalytic theory to groups was furthered, especially by the work of Gisela Konopka, Fritz Redl, Samuel Slavson, and Saul Scheidlinger.

Beginning in the late 1950s, systems theory was introduced into social work by Gordon Hearn, who was a professor of group work at the University of California at Berkeley. He wrote the definitive book, *Theory Building in Social Work*, using knowledge of social systems. He followed through on this theme by editing a book that demonstrated the application of systems theory to practice in varied situations.[14] Now, more attention is being given to ecological-systems concepts, individual-group-environment interaction, and ways in which gender, race, ethnicity, sexual orientation, and health affect group purposes and development.

Fields of Practice

Until about the mid-1950s, most practice was with children and youth in community agencies. Coyle formulated this practice in her book, *Group Work with American Youth*, published in 1948. It seems strange, but that was the first book on the practice of social group work. It was followed quickly by Harleigh Trecker's *Social Group Work: Principles and Practice*, which covered services to all age groups in community settings. It was the book by Wilson and Ryland, *Social Group Work Practice*, that made the transition to the use of groups in all fields of practice and was much broader in scope than the others. Gisela Konopka's *Therapeutic Group Work with Children* was the fourth book published at the end of the decade. Social group work was now being practiced in many fields beyond group services.

As it demonstrated its usefulness in military services during World War II, group work for therapeutic purposes spread rapidly. Neva Boyd had earlier conducted socialization groups with mentally ill patients at Chicago State Hospital in the mid 1930s, using a variety of social experiences for therapeutic purposes.[15] So far as is known, the first field work placements in schools of social work in psychiatric settings were arranged by Wilson at the University of Pittsburgh in 1939, first in a child guidance clinic and then in mental hospitals. Other schools soon followed suit.

The use of groups for therapeutic purposes was accelerated by the arrival in the United States of refugees from Germany and Austria. In their European practice, groups had played an important part in education and therapy. Konopka noted that "their own painful experiences in Nazi Germany or Austria . . . intensified their motivation to work on improving social relations."[16] The group was viewed as the means for achieving that goal. These persons included Walter Friedlander, whose book identified common elements between social casework, social group work, and community organization, Konopka, who has written numerous books and articles on group therapy, adolescence, and social group work practice, Henry Maier, whose major work has been in theories of human development and group work as part of residential treatment, and Fritz Redl, whose major contribution has been the development of therapeutic group work with emotionally disturbed children in both community and residential settings.[17]

The use of groups in mental health settings was strongly supported by the National Institute of Mental Health, which financed two national invitational conferences on the use of groups in such settings in the 1950s.[18] The participants were about equally divided between those primarily identified with casework and those involved with group work. By that time, many caseworkers were adding work with groups to their practice.

Although group work was used in medical settings as early as 1905, it took longer for it to take hold there than it had in psychiatric settings. By 1959, however, interest in the use of groups in health settings had advanced sufficiently for the National Association of Social Workers (NASW) to appoint a committee to study groups in medical hospitals and clinics. In the resulting publication, Louise Frey reported twenty-three articles on the subject.[19] The rapid increase since that time was documented by Northen who, in 1983, found 249 publications.[20] Therapy groups predominated, followed in frequency by support groups, psychosocial education, crisis resolution, socialization, training, and mediation. Notice the large number of types of groups that had been described. A biopsychosocial theoretical orientation provided the foundation knowledge used by a large majority of the writers.

Today, groups are used for a variety of purposes in all fields of practice — family-child welfare, industrial social work, gerontology, health, mental health, and education.

Defining Social Group Work

In the late 1920s, the American Association of Social Workers, one of the predecessor organizations to the National Association of Social Workers, was interested in discovering a common base for social work practice. It appointed Margaretta Williamson to ascertain the generic elements of group work. She concluded that "there was evidence of a common professional ground—recognition of a similar philosophy, a convergence of training and technique, some interchange of personnel, and a tendency toward exchange of experience." She described the importance of voluntary and democratic participation and the leader's use of problem-solving processes with members of the group, colleagues, persons in community services, boards, and committees. The purpose of group work was to "seek the development of the individual to his fullest capacity and to encourage more satisfactory relations between the individual and his environment."[21] That concept of person-environment interaction has stood the test of time.

Work on defining and describing social group work continued at a rapid pace. A major definition was provided by Newstetter in a paper presented at the National Conference of Social Work in 1935:

> Group work may be defined as an educational process emphasizing (1) the development and social adjustment of an individual through voluntary group association and (2) the use of this association as a means of furthering other socially desirable ends. It is concerned therefore with both individual growth and social results . . . The underlying philosophical assumption is that individualized growth and social ends are interwoven and interdependent, that individuals and their social environment are equally important.[22]

He, like Williamson, place importance on person-environment interaction.

The development of group work was fostered by several organizations. A section on social group work was included in the National Conference of Social Work in 1935 for the first time where several papers were presented, including Newstetter's definition. The National Association for the Study of Group Work was founded a year later. The word *National* was changed to *American* in 1938 to accommodate Canadians. The purpose of the AASGW was to clarify and refine the philosophy, knowledge, and practice of work with groups. Members included recreational leaders, educators, and social workers. It published the journal *Group Work* and annual reports of its activities. Based on the work of a committee, chaired by Kaiser, the aim of group work was found to be "the development and adjustment of the individual through voluntary group association."[23] In 1946, members of the study group voted to become a professional organization, the American Association of Group Workers, which, in 1955, became integrated into the new National Association of Social Workers.

An early project of NASW was to formulate a working definition of social work practice that would set forth the common base of practice for work with individuals, groups, and communities. The first sentences of the definition prepared by the commission were: "The social work method is the responsible, conscious, disciplined use of self in a relationship with an individual or group. Through this relationship, the practitioner facilitates interaction between the individual and his social environment with a continuing awareness of the reciprocal effects one upon the other."[24] Like earlier definitions, that one emphasizes the person-environment concept. Members of a subcommission on group work participated actively in developing the definition.

NASW, in addition to the commission, had membership sections, including one on group work. The national group work section, chaired by Hartford, undertook to develop a detailed definition of social group work.[25] It asked ten educators to prepare their definitions, following a common outline. Within many common concepts, the definitions described different objectives. There was disagreement, for example, about whether education, social action, social growth, citizen participation, and therapy were all to be included in social group work.

While NASW was studying practice, the Council on Social Work Education was conducting a major study of curriculums, published in thirteen volumes in 1959. Marjorie Murphy was full-time director of the project on social group work. As a result of her work with an advisory committee, chaired by Paul Simon, group work was defined as "a method of social work whose purpose was the enhancement of persons' social functioning through purposeful group experience."[26] She described in detail the objectives and content essential for developing competence related to that definition. The resulting book seemed to be fairly well accepted among educators and, along with the other curriculum areas, became a basis for accrediting programs in schools of social work.

Clarifying Theories

Incorporation of findings from research in the social sciences continued to enhance knowledge of the dynamics of group process and its use in practice. Building on Coyle's work, Hartford published *Groups in Social Work*, in 1971, in which she summarized the burgeoning mass of knowledge and indicated its use in practice. Since then, other educators, such as Charles Garvin, have traced the application of psychological and sociological knowledge to practice.[27]

By the mid-1970s, books on social work practice with groups increased. It was time to make a major effort to clarify variations in values, purposes, and theories. Earlier, Catherine Papell and Beulah Rothman had proposed three theoretical models of group work, labeled social goals, reciprocal, and remedial.[28] Robert Roberts and Helen Northen invited Wilson to review the history of social group work and ten educators to prepare essays about their theories of practice, following a set of guidelines. In a concluding chapter to the book that resulted, the editors analyzed the common and divergent components of the theories.[29] The major conclusion was that the ten position papers did not represent ten distinct and mutually exclusive approaches to practice. All authors subscribed to the basic values of the profession; they described an interactional process between the social worker and members through three or more stages of group development; they used small group theories; they accepted the concept of psychosocial functioning but put greater emphasis on the social than the psychological; most often, they described the purpose as being the enhancement or improvement of social functioning and viewed the role of the worker as facilitator of the group process. The essays gave strong evidence of a move away from specialization based on practice methods. Only Emanuel Tropp took a strong stand, arguing that social group work should continue as a distinct specialization. Since then, writers have continued to develop new or modified models of social work practice with groups.

Emergence of a New Organization

Two interrelated events occurred in the late 1970s to advance the practice of social work with groups. NASW had not had any program devoted specifically to work with groups since the mid-1960s, nor any journal of group work. The first event was the founding of a new journal, *Social Work with Groups*, edited by Catherine Papell and Beulah Rothman, now edited by Roselle Kurland and Andrew Malekoff. The second was the formation of a committee to organize a symposium on group work practice, held in Cleveland, Ohio in 1979 to honor the memory of Grace Coyle. That there was a groundswell of interest in group work was evidenced by the unexpectedly large attendance at the symposium, leading to the decision to have annual meetings. In 1985, the committee was transformed into a membership organization, the Association for the Advancement of Social Work with Groups. The symposiums and resulting publications have contributed substantially to the writings on practice with groups.

Major Issues

Casework-Group Work Relationships

Almost from the time that group work was identified as a method within social work, there was interest in understanding its relationship with social casework. In the late 1930s, Wilson conducted a survey of this issue under the auspices of the Family Welfare Association of America. She found that group work had spread from the youth services and settlements to many social agencies that had previously given help only to individuals one by one. She identified a core of values, knowledge, and techniques that are generic to both methods. She found that there were some differences and distrust of each other's methods that blocked progress toward easy and complete cooperation. The major difference was found to be in the nature of the one-to-one relationship in casework and the worker's relationship with each member and the group as a whole in group work. In spite of differences, the conclusion was that "the poles of thinking are today reaching toward each other."[30] Interest in this subject has continued throughout the years.

Beginning in the 1950s, evidence mounted that many social workers who had majored in a social casework sequence were working with groups for therapeutic purposes. A study by the psychiatric social work section of NASW indicated that many of its members were engaging in services to groups.[31] Further evidence was obtained by Guido Pinamonti, who reviewed the literature on work with groups by caseworkers in many types of agencies.[32] He found that many practitioners were using groups for purposes of orientation, education, and therapy.

Toward Integrated Practice

The history so far presented has indicated a clear trend toward recognition of the common base of social casework and social group work. In his early paper defining group work, Newstetter described the broadening base of social work, an emphasis on generic concepts, and many similarities in techniques of practice. Increasingly, since that time, several leaders in the profession have questioned whether, in fact, casework, group work, and community organization were separate methods. These persons included Bertha

Reynolds, Marion Hathway, and Arlien Johnson.[33] It was Johnson who traced the evolution of social casework, social group work, and social community organization work. She noted that these methods had become independent of specific agencies and fields of practice; they have generic content and are adaptable to many situations and settings. She predicted that "in the future, all social workers will have basic skills in both individual and group relationships and that the present specializations will disappear in favor of a social work method."[34] Her article was written in 1955, the year that the NASW was founded in a major effort to establish a unified profession.

Johnson's prediction became partially true in the 1960s, when a strong trend was evident toward viewing work with individuals and work with groups as one social work method. It was thought that practitioners should become competent in providing services through individual, family, and group modalities, depending upon the needs of clients. The first school of social work to be accredited by the Council on Social Work Education for such a program was the University of Southern California, in 1964.[35] Word of the changes spread rapidly, with the result that the council now expects schools to have a generalist foundation. That does not mean that courses or concentrations in work with groups or families, fields of practice, or social problems cannot be included in curriculums.

The rationale for the integration of modalities is the view that social work practice is an entity made up of several approaches, sometimes calling for work with an individual, sometimes for work with a family or one of its subsystems, and sometimes for work with a small group or with organizations in the community. It recognizes that the choice of a unit of service should be based on the needs of the client system. A social worker may use a combination of modalities, depending upon the situation. Social workers should have at their disposal a repertoire of means to be drawn upon selectively in given circumstances. Many educators and practitioners who believe strongly in the value of group work are advocates for the integrative practice position.

By 1980, at least ten books had been published on the generic or generalist base of social work practice. The books dealt with group work as a component of social work practice, either treating it in separate sections or integrating it into the whole. It should be noted that some of these works were authored or coauthored by writers originally identified as having a primary interest in groups.[36] Many of the authors, however, believe that practice courses need to be improved to assure that the specific, as well as the generic, aspects of work with groups are taught adequately. Some educators, however, who formerly taught or now teach a full sequence of courses in group work are firmly convinced that adequate learning about groups does not occur in integrated curriculums. They believe that the amount and quality of teaching of the special aspects of group work are not possible in integrated courses. They agree with Ruth Smalley that "sufficient difference has been identified for each of the methods to suggest that a two year process concentration in one method, class and field, would ordinarily be necessary to produce even a beginning practice skill."[37] That became the minority view. Obviously, research is necessary to answer this question.

Purposes of Practice

A third major issue that has been perpetuated over many years concerns the breadth of purposes included in social work practice with groups. In addition to some concerns that attention to social action is inadequate, the debate concerns the emphasis that should be given to prevention of problems and enhancement of social functioning as contrasted with group therapy. Ted Goldberg reviewed a large sample of the periodical literature in which the words *treatment* or *therapy* were used. The results indicated that a large majority of writers included therapeutic groups within the province of social work practice, but a minority took strong exception to that view.[38] Hans Falck, for example, took the position that "social work is not a therapy."[39] That is far different from Konopka's view that "when the group worker uses his professional training and skill to work with groups of individuals who have problems in personal and social functioning, he enters the practice of group therapy."[40]

A more recent statement broadens the use of the term. Mary Woods and Florence Hollis state that the term *therapy* refers to "work in which social and psychological means are used to enable individuals (singly or in family or formed groups) to cope with environmental, interpersonal, and/or intrapsychic dilemmas—and the interaction among these—that are causing personal distress."[41] Some of the differences seem to occur because the proponents define such terms as treatment and therapy differently, resulting in different attitudes toward the words.

What Helen Perlman wrote in 1965 in her article, "Social Work Method: A Review of the Past Decade," is still true today.

When one looks at the range of practice embraced by group work, it is easy to understand the run of high feelings in its ranks, about the definition and identity and the push by its leaders and formulators to develop further its practice models and principles. In the examination of its writings, one sees some internecine struggles over whether its commitments should be on a continuum of education to therapy or education to socialization.[42]

In today's world, these struggles continue. Perhaps, the continuum should be from education to socialization to therapy.

A Theoretical Approach to Practice

As variations in purposes and knowledge of practice with groups continue to be developed, this book sets forth the values, knowledge, theory, and skills that are essential for competence in working with groups for the basic purpose of enhancing the psychosocial functioning of individuals and improving their environments. It is an ecosystems orientation.

Values

Values are an important determinant of the social worker's selection of knowledge for use in assessment, planning, and treatment. They are ideas about what is worthwhile or useless, desirable or undesirable, right or wrong, beautiful or ugly. They include beliefs and ideologies, appreciative or aesthetic preferences, and moral or ethical principles. Translated into ethical principles of conduct, values guide the practice of any profession. They derive from a few fundamental beliefs and attitudes about people and society.

The ultimate value of social work is that human beings should have opportunities to realize their potentials for living in ways that are both personally satisfying and socially desirable. Ashley Montagu has written, "the deepest personal defeat suffered by human beings is constituted by the difference between what one was capable of becoming and what one has in fact become."[43] Most social workers would agree with this statement. Underlying the value of realization of potential are many more specific ones that elaborate its meaning. Implied in the basic value is simultaneous con-

cern for personal and collective welfare for the mutual benefit of all concerned. As Samuel Silberman has pointed out, "Successful social work service should benefit the child and the family, the patient and the hospital,
the employer and employee, the member and the group; not one at the
expense of the other, but for the benefit of both."[44]

A conviction that each person has inherent worth and dignity is a basic
tenet of social work. A practitioner who has this conviction holds dear certain
specific values. All people should be treated with respect, regardless of their
likenesses or differences in relation to others. The principle of individualization is deduced from this value, as are acceptance and self-direction. People should have opportunities to grow toward the fulfillment of their potential, for their own sakes and so that they may contribute to building a society
better able to meet human needs. They should have the right to civil liberties
and to equal opportunity without discrimination because of race, age, social
class, religion, nationality, state of health, sexual orientation, or gender. They
should have access to resources essential to the fulfillment of their basic
needs.

A conviction that people should have responsibility for each other is another basic value of social work. It is the democratic spirit in action. This
value leads to the view that all people should have freedom to express themselves, to maintain their privacy, to participate in decisions that affect them,
and to direct their own lives, with an accompanying responsibility to live
constructively with other people. People are interdependent for survival and
for the fulfillment of their needs. Mutual responsibility, rather than rugged
individualism, should prevail. Individuals and groups should assume social
responsibility in small and large ways, according to their capacities to do so.

People are interdependent. Konopka eloquently reminds us that "all lives
are connected to other lives. . . . It is the vital interrelationship of human
beings that is the heart of social group work. The focus is on *freeing* individuals while helping them to support each other."[45]

Social workers appreciate the diversity of groups and cultures that comprise society. American society, as is also true of many other societies, is
made up of a network of ethnosystems, each sharing some common values
and characteristics and each having some values unique to members of that
group.[46] Each individual, family, and group needs to be particularized so
that there can be opportunities for each social unit to maintain its own
culture and to make a contribution to the whole. A democratic philosophy,
according to Kenneth Pray, rests upon a deep appreciation of the validity
and the value to society as a whole of these individual differences in human

beings. It conceives of social unity and progress as the outcome of the integration, not the suppression or conquest, of these differences. Accordingly, it tests all social arrangements and institutions by their impact upon human lives, by their capacity to use for the common good the unique potentialities of individual human beings through relationships that enlist their active and productive participation.[47] Group, as well as individual, differences should be accepted and used for the welfare of all.

The ideology of social work from a broad psychosocial perspective views individuals as whole persons, interacting with others in the systems and the subsystems in which they find themselves. It is humanistic, scientific, and democratic. It is humanistic in its commitment to the welfare and rights of clients and the social systems of which they are a part. It is scientific in that it prefers objectivity and factual evidence over personal biases. It emphasizes that the practitioner's judgments and actions are derived from a reasoning process, based on scientific knowledge to the extent that it is available. It embodies the great idea of democracy, not as a political structure, but as a philosophy governing relationships between people, based on reciprocal rights and obligations, and directed toward the welfare of the individual, family, group, and society.

Professional Ethics

The values of social work are operationalized into ethical principles regarding social workers' conduct in their relationships with individuals, families, groups, and organizations. The *Code of Ethics* published by the National Association of Social Workers, alerts practitioners to principles that need to be taken into account in every phase of their work. The major ethical principles are concerned with the relationship between the worker and the client system, competent practice, integrity, propriety, commitment to the welfare of clients, and protection of the rights and prerogatives of clients. These rights include self-determination, confidentiality, and social justice. The code gives scant attention to specific ways that the principles are applied in groups. Attention to this matter will occur throughout the book.[48]

Purpose

The purpose of social work is improvement in the relationship between people and their environments. That purpose encompasses the achievement of positive changes in the psychosocial functioning of individuals, families, and groups and in the conditions in the environment to lessen obstacles and provide opportunities for more satisfying and productive social living.

Within that general purpose, social work with groups may be directed toward helping the members to use the group for coping with and resolving existing problems in psychosocial functioning, preventing anticipated problems, or maintaining a current level of functioning in situations in which there is danger of deterioration. Further, it may be directed toward developing more effective patterns of group and organizational functioning and removing environmental obstacles. With any group, the specific outcomes sought vary with the desires, needs, capacities, and situations of the members who comprise the group and with the purpose and nature of the group itself.

In assisting persons to enhance their psychosocial functioning, individual, family, group, or community modalities may be used, depending upon assessment of the person-environment situation. The practitioner also performs a variety of other roles: work beyond the group is often essential. These roles include advocate, case manager, broker of services and resources, educator, or collaborator. In this book, however, the focus is on the use of the group as the means and context for helping people to prevent or solve problems, within a person-environment perspective.

An Ecosystem Approach

The practice described in this book is within a contemporary ecosystem approach that takes into account the multiple and complex transactions that occur between persons within their families, other membership and reference groups, and organizations. An ecosystem approach is relevant to social work because social work situations involve people's coping with changing environments or with changes in their own capacities to deal with their surroundings. Henry Maas notes that these situations "call for altered patterns of interaction between persons and their social contexts."[49] The changes that can be made depend in part on the options and responsiveness of environments and on people's capacities and developmental potentials. Knowledge about the interrelationships between people and their environments has been a major theme in group work throughout its history, as was noted in the historical section of this chapter.

Ecology is the study of the relationship of plants and animals to one another and to the biological and physical environment. In the words of Robert Cook, "The study of the interrelationship of living things with one another and with the basic natural resources of air, water, and food is called ecology, after the Greek *oikos* for house."[50] Ecologists use the term *ecosystem* to refer to a community of associated species of plants and animals together with the physical features of their habitat.[51] The essence of ecology is that no organism can live alone: there is a web of interdependence among all living things and between these organisms and the physical environment in a given habitat. The environment provides the conditions and nutrients essential to survival and growth or it provides obstacles to survival and growth. It has been remarked by Henry and Rebecca Northen that "the capacity of living things to adapt to new environments and conditions is one of the marvels of nature. The wonder is not only that so many forms of life have evolved but also that the forms are so neatly suited to all the available niches that earth offers."[52] Organisms change, and are changed by, aspects of their physical and social environments. A neat fit between the organism and its environment is essential to survival and satisfactory development.

The ecosystem approach is a form of practice based on understanding the needs, problems, and strengths of individuals and their families; the characteristics of the group; and the resources and obstacles in the environment. It is based on knowledge that individuals, families, and groups develop and change over their life spans. It is a form of practice in which leadership is primarily facilitative, through the "creative use of the social process,"[53] supportive social relationships, and mutual aid in problem solving for the purpose of enhancing the psychosocial functioning of the members and reducing environmental obstacles.

Psychosocial is not a precise term. According to a survey by Francis Turner, it has been used since 1930 to refer to the feelings, attitudes, and behavior of persons in their relationships with others.[54] Coyle emphasized that the term also refers to the social conditions and situations that influence human well-being.[55] That view is consistent with social work's long interest in people as social beings who have social connections in their families, various groups, social networks, and organizations and who live in natural and social environments.

In enhancing social functioning, one goal is to empower clients, especially those who feel powerless, to achieve mastery over self or aspects of their environments. Barbara Simon, tracing the history of empowerment in practice, asserted, "That has long been a purpose of social work practice but it only came to be called empowerment when Barbara Solomon published *Black Empowerment: Social Work in Oppressed Communities.*[56] Solomon wrote that "empowerment refers to a process whereby persons who belong to a stigmatized social category throughout their lives can be assisted to develop and increase skills in the exercise of interpersonal influence and the performance of valued social roles."[57] Judith Lee used that definition in her recent book on empowerment.[58] Ruby Pernell, writing specifically about group work, explained that "empowerment requires the ability to analyze social processes and interpersonal behavior in terms of power and powerlessness. . . . It consists of skills to enable group members to influence themselves and others, and to develop skills in using their influence effectively."[59]

Enhancement of functioning includes functions of both prevention and treatment. The small growth-oriented group is the appropriate modality of practice when a person's needs can be met through interaction with others, as distinguished from help apart from others.

This approach to practice differs from models that are based solely on behavioral or cognitive theories, are highly structured, emphasize the achievement of concrete tasks or changes in habits, and in which leadership is largely directive.

Supports for Practice

Social workers derive sanction to practice from governmental bodies, the profession of social work, the clients themselves, and, except in private practice, a social agency or organization. Governmental bodies sanction practice in a variety of ways. They establish legislation and appropriate funds for specified services, provide a legal base for the operation of voluntary agencies, grant special privileges such as tax exemptions to charitable organizations, and determine whether or not practitioners should be licensed or registered. Through its organizations, the profession of social work sanctions practice by defining standards for and conditions of practice. It has programs that certify competence, accredit professional education, establish codes of ethics, provide channels for complaints against members, and encourage the development of theory and research. Social agencies also authorize particular forms of practice. Kaiser has explained how the nature and quality of practice is "profoundly affected and to some extent determined by the purpose, function, and structure of the institution in which it is carried on."[60]

The social agency's influence on service may enhance greatly the ability of practitioners to meet the needs of their clientele or it may impede them from giving appropriate and qualitative service. Agencies have criteria for determining eligibility of clients and the characteristics of people they serve in terms of their needs and problems: age, gender, race, ethnicity, sexual orientation, social class, and health. They may or may not provide adequate facilities, resources, access to transportation, personnel policies, work loads, and patterns of communication between personnel and with the network of external resources. For private practitioners, the specific conditions for the provision of services are set by their perceptions of the needs of certain potential clients and their professional interests and competence, within the standards set by certification and accountability to funding sources. Ultimately, the sanction comes from the people who use the services, for social workers cannot perform their roles unless the participants grant them the necessary status. The knowledge about sanction is generic to social work with individuals, families, groups, and organizations.

Common Principles of Practice

In the provision of direct services to people, social work practice consists of a constellation of activities performed by a practitioner in a planned and systematic way. The plan is designed to lead toward the achievement of the purpose for which service to a particular person or group is initiated. The common characteristics of the practice of social work are many and inter-related. They have been stated in different forms by different writers, in either a few abstract generalizations or in specific terms. Some of the essential characteristics of social work practice that apply to work with individuals, families, and other small groups are the following:

1. Social workers recognize that practice is purposeful. The specific purposes toward which the service is directed are determined by the needs of the persons being served within the purpose of the profession. Purposes are defined through a process in which both the worker and the clients participate, and they change as do the needs of the clients.

2. Social workers develop and sustain collaborative professional relationships with individuals, families, and groups. Acceptance, genuineness, empathy, power, and self-awareness are components of the social work relationship.

3. Social workers engage in the interrelated processes of social assessment, formulation of plans for service, social treatment, and evaluation of outcomes.

4. They identify and support the strengths of clients: enhancing self-esteem, nourishing hope, and encouraging high and achievable expectations.

5. They individualize their clients, which occurs when a person's needs and capacities along with the unique qualities of the environment are understood and taken into account by the practitioner.

6. They center their attention simultaneously on process and on the verbal and nonverbal content of the interview or group session.

7. They select and make flexible use of procedures and skills to meet the needs of clients or members, with sensitivity to both commonality and diversity.

8. They, through the purposeful use of verbal and nonverbal communication, enable their clients or members to express feelings, attitudes, and opinions and to contribute knowledge that enlightens the content.

9. They facilitate the participation of clients or members in all aspects of the service. The rights of people to self-determination are respected within certain understood limits.

10. They participate collaboratively with individuals and groups in decision-making processes that empower them to use the resources in the social environment to improve their life situations.

11. They make use of agency and community resources, contribute their knowledge to help develop new or improved services, collaborate with others who are serving clients individually and/or in groups, and participate in efforts to influence desirable changes in policies and procedures.

12. They make flexible use of individual, family, group, and community modalities from whatever the initial point of contact with a person, moving from an individual to a group or wider community or from the community to a small group or individual, on the basis of the needs and the availability of appropriate services.

Selection of Groups as Units of Service

A small group is a particular kind of social system produced by persons in interaction with each other and with other social systems. As Earle Eubank has defined it: "A group is two or more persons in a relationship of psychic interaction, whose relationships with one another may be abstracted and distinguished from their relationships with all others so that they might be thought of as an entity."[61]

A small group, normally consisting of two to twenty people, is usually thought of as one in which members are able to engage in direct personal relations with each other at a given time. The essential emphasis is pithily stated by George Homans, "small enough to let us get all the way around it."[62] The idea is for every member to be able to relate face to face with every other member. Mark Davidson explains that the group is greater than the sum of its parts because "a system consists of the interdependent parts plus the way the parts relate to each other and the qualities that emerge from these relationships."[63]

The burgeoning of electronic media in the past decade is resulting in the broadening of this concept of the face-to-face group. Increasingly, telephone groups and computer groups, where members are not physically present in one room at the same time, are taking place.[64] Such groups make possible interaction with others who have similar issues for those who are geographically distant or homebound.

Within a generic or integrated approach to social work practice, groups may complement or supplement individual, family, or community modalities, and they can be supported by these other modalities. Individual and group formats may be combined or used in sequential order, depending upon the needs of the particular clients at a given time. The dimension of mutual aid operates in groups, which is one primary factor that differentiates group work from other modalities of practice. Mutual aid goes beyond self-help and help from others. It is people helping each other. People grow and change through their relationships and interactions with others. The fact that people need people is the raison d'être for social work practice with groups. The need is presented dramatically by William Schutz in his introduction to *The Interpersonal Underworld*.

Laurie was about three when one night she requested my aid in getting undressed. I was downstairs and she was upstairs, and . . . well. "You know how to undress yourself," I reminded. "Yes," she explained, "but

sometimes people need people anyway, even if they do know how to
do things by theirselves."

As I slowly lowered the newspaper, a strong feeling came over me,
a mixture of delight, embarrassment, and pride; delight in the realization that what I had just heard crystallized many stray thoughts on
interpersonal behavior, anger because Laurie stated so effortlessly what
I had been struggling with for months; and pride because, after all,
she is my daughter.[65]

People need people, as Laurie said. But they need people who are supportive and helpful, not destructive. Within supportive relationships, the
mutual aid process is the essence of a successful group experience that contributes to self-fulfillment and effective psychosocial functioning.

Dynamic Forces for Change

When the mutual aid process operates successfully, dynamic forces are
released that are often referred to as change mechanisms or as curative or
therapeutic factors. These forces make the group the preferred modality
under certain circumstances. Unlike the one worker to one client system,
there are multiple relationships and interactions to be understood and used
for particular purposes. To make viable decisions about the appropriate use
of groups, the practitioner needs knowledge about the unique processes that
operate therein and the goals that can best be reached through a group
service.

Contributions to clarifying the dynamic forces in small groups have been
made by social psychologists, psychiatrists, and social workers. The first major research was conducted by Raymond Corsini and Bina Rosenberg in
1955.[66] These authors analyzed 300 articles, from which 166 different statements about change mechanisms were identified. They classified these statements into 9 categories: ventilation, acceptance, spectator therapy, intellec-
tualization, universalization, reality testing, altruism, transference, and
interaction.

In 1970, Irvin Yalom reported on what he called the curative factors that
operate in long-term psychotherapy groups for adults and tested these factors
against the members' views of how they were helped through the group
experience.[67] The factors are as follows: instillation of hope, universality,
imparting of information, altruism, the corrective recapitulation of the pri-

mary family group, development of socializing techniques, imitative behavior including modeling and vicarious learning, cohesiveness, catharsis, and interpersonal learning. Yalom emphasized that interpersonal learning is a particularly important force in groups. It involves "the identification, the elucidation, and the modification of maladaptive interpersonal relationships."[68] In 1975, he added existential factors to the list.[69]

The first major social work contribution was made by Malcolm Marks, who described why groups are the preferred means of help for emotionally disturbed boys in residential treatment.[70] Another major report was the result of deliberations at a conference on the use of groups, primarily in adult psychiatric settings.[71] Several similar dynamic forces were identified in these major reports and in subsequent writings. The dynamic forces that have been most frequently identified as applicable to the practice of social work with groups may be summarized as follows.[72]

1. **Mutual support**. A climate of peer support, in addition to support from the worker, reduces anxiety and facilitates self-expression and willingness to try out new ideas and behaviors.

2. **Cohesiveness** — the group bond. The mutual acceptance of members and commitment to the group make the group attractive to its members. When members feel they belong to a group that has meaning for them, they are influenced by other members and by the norms of the group. When the members provide mutual support, the group fulfills the basic human need to belong, sometimes referred to as social hunger.

3. **Quality of relationships**. When the relationship with the worker and between the members provides a blend of support and challenge, Howard Goldstein saw that "there is the relative safety of controlled intimacy."[73] These positive relationships can serve as a corrective emotional experience.

4. **Universality**. The realization that similar feelings and difficulties are common among the members lessens the sense of being unique and alone. Self-esteem and mutual esteem are enhanced by the recognition that others have difficulties, too, and yet are likeable and worthy people. Members discover the reassuring fact that they are not the only ones with troublesome emotions and experiences. Such discovery makes such feelings and events less frightening and controlling of behavior.

5. **A sense of hope**. By identifying with the group and perceiving the

group's expectations of positive outcome, members may become influenced by optimistic goals of others and move toward them. They perceive how others have endured similar problems and coped with them successfully.

6. **Altruism.** Self-esteem and personal identity are enhanced as members learn that they can extend help to others and get something helpful back. People relate better to others who appreciate and use what they can contribute. Many members may have been devalued so often that their self-esteem is very low.

7. **Acquisition of knowledge and skills**. The group is a safe place to acquire needed knowledge; to risk new ideas, efforts, and behaviors; and to learn valued social skills. Opportunities afforded for self-expression and for trying out and mastering social skills have a beneficial effect upon the members' self-esteem and enjoyment of being with others.

8. **Catharsis.** Expression of feelings and disclosure of ideas and experiences, as these are accepted by others, lessen anxiety and free energies for work toward the achievement of desired goals.

9. **Reality testing**. Groups provide a dynamic environment in which multiple perspectives are shared. Members use each other as sounding boards for comparing feelings, opinions, and facts. Feedback from peers is often more candid and explicit than are responses offered by the worker. The group becomes a protected reality in which to try out different ways of dealing with relationships and other psychosocial problems.

10. **Group control**. Through behaving in accordance with the group's expectations, members reduce their resistance to authority, suppress inappropriate behavior, endure frustration, and accept necessary and fair limitations. Temporary group controls serve as a means toward the goal of appropriate self control.

These are the dynamic forces of mutual aid. Findings from research generally support the importance of these forces in positively influencing the members' group experience. Findings also suggest that some factors are more important than others for different types of groups and even for different members of the same group. By which of these means particular members are helped depends upon interpersonal needs, environmental resources, and the purposes, structure, and composition of a particular group. Furthermore, these dynamic forces need to be viewed as potential benefits; they are not present automatically in groups but need to be fostered by the practitioner.

Criteria for Selection of a Group Modality

Through understanding the dynamic forces that can be mobilized in groups, it is possible to develop criteria for selecting a group experience for a given person or category of people.

Enhancement of relationships   When the purpose of service is some form of enhancement of social relationships, the group is usually the preferred modality. In a study of definitions of group work from the first one in 1920 up to 1964, Hartford concluded that there was consensus: one important purpose of group work was to help people to resolve problems in social relationships and also to help "normal people to grow socially."[74] Sonia and Paul Abels stated this purpose in another way—work with groups "ought to be directed toward the strengthening of mutual and reciprocal relationships";[75] and Goldstein's formulation is that "groups often aim to correct maladaptive patterns of relationships."[76]

The particular dynamics of groups, as described previously, make them ideal social contexts for coping with deficits or difficulties in social relationships. A small group in which these forces operate affords an ideal environment in which people can be helped to work on dependence-independence conflicts, sibling rivalries, conflicts with authority, violence, rejection, withdrawal, loneliness, and loss. Even when the major problems are in the functioning of the family system, usually indicating a service to the family unit, a member of the family may benefit from a group experience. Some people may not be able to bear the anxiety of family sessions or may not be able to overcome a fear that other members will retaliate for their disclosure of previously unexpressed feelings and ideas. When the boundary of the family is quite closed to new inputs, multiple family groups may stimulate the members to new ways of expressing feelings, assigning roles, communicating with each other, and making decisions.

Social competence   A second purpose of social work service that usually calls for the use of a group is the enhancement of social competence. For purposes of preventing problems in social functioning, the group is clearly the predominant modality, according to Frances Caple's research.[77] The goals are to help the members to function more adequately in their vital social roles and to cope with changes in role expectations as they move through life transitions.[78] The need for services stems from lack of adequate knowledge, social experiences, and skills for coping with an anticipated event or situation, usually a new phase of psychosocial development or a transition to a new or changed role. Examples are prospective adoptive parents who may not have accurate knowledge about the many considerations that ought to go into making an appropriate decision, or children moving into a new developmental phase or educational level. Other clients may lack skills in applying for jobs, being appropriately assertive, or using available community resources. Many patients and their relatives need to learn new or changed roles that accompany physical disability or they need to be resocialized into changed role expectations.

On the basis of extensive study of socialization theory, Elizabeth Mc-Broom concluded that a group is the most effective and natural modality for intervention in enhancing social competence because social competence can be developed only through relationships with other people.[79] Similarly, Carel Germain and Alex Gitterman assert that when there is a common set of life tasks, groups provide multiple opportunities for human relatedness, mutual aid, and learning task-related coping skills.[80] And Solomon states that group methods provide rich opportunities for empowering clients who belong to stigmatized minority groups. Competence is power: empowerment is a process whereby people are enabled to enhance their skills in exercising interpersonal influence and performing valued social roles.[81]

Coping with stress   A third interrelated purpose for which a group is often the preferred modality is the development of capacities to cope effectively with stress, occasioned by such situations as a life transition, cultural dissonance, a life threatening illness, divorce, rape, or physical violence. Support and stimulation from peers aid members to disclose and manage emotions, release tension, enhance damaged self-esteem, and discover new ways of coping with stress and with the reality of the situation. Some research indicates that people who have had traumatic experiences often feel isolated, lonely, and depressed. Such people are more likely to have serious difficulties in coping realistically with the consequences of the event than those with supportive social networks.[82] Such people are particularly suitable for a carefully planned therapeutic group experience.

Indirect services   Groups are also, of course, the modality of choice for services aimed primarily, not toward helping clients within direct service, but toward staff training, collaboration, planning, and social action.

The following chapters set forth the knowledge and skills essential for the development of groups in which the dynamic forces operate and in which the members work toward the purposes of enhancing social relationships, developing social competence, coping with transitions and role changes, and improving environments. In developing effective groups, practitioners make use of the generic values, knowledge, and skills of social work, adapting them to the needs of particular members and to varied group situations.

2   The Knowledge Base for Practice

In social work practice, the small group is both a social context and a means through which its members modify their attitudes, interpersonal relationships, and abilities to cope more effectively with their environments. As Mary Louise Somers put it, the social worker recognizes "the potency of social forces that are generated within small groups and seeks to marshall them in the interest of client change."[1] A group can become a powerful growth-promoting environment, with power to support and stimulate its members toward the accomplishment of individual and corporate purposes. Positive results are not, however, assured. Quite the contrary, a group may have very little influence on its members, or it may have a potent influence that is destructive for its members or for society. The development of a group must not, therefore, be left to chance. To make effective use of groups, social workers require a body of knowledge about individuals, small groups, and environments, and how to influence them.

Understanding Psychosocial Functioning

In this chapter, concepts from the behavioral sciences have been selected for their pertinence to the effective use of small groups for the achievement of some purpose or goal within the realm of enhanced psychosocial functioning. Human beings are open systems involved in dynamic, changing transactions with their environments throughout life. Psychosocial functioning is concerned with the complex gestalt of emotion, cognition, and action, motivated by both conscious and unconscious forces in the personalities of the persons involved, and the resulting pattern of relationships between people in defined environments. It may be desirable to improve the person's coping and social skills, the functioning of systems of which they are a part, or both. The hoped for change may be in a person's attitudes, emotions, thoughts, or behavior, in the group's structure or process, in the environmental situation, or, most commonly, in the interaction involving person-group-environment. Psychosocial functioning is a key construct for understanding human behavior.

Major Concepts

Several major content areas have been selected to describe and explain an individual's psychosocial functioning.

1. **Ego functions.** Ego psychologists give central importance to the functions of the ego—a dynamic force for understanding, coping with, adapting to, and shaping external environments.[2] Stress, coping and adaptation are essential concepts. When stress upsets a person's steady state, the ego responds through the use of protective defenses or problem-solving efforts. Significant experiences from the past, conscious or unconscious, may influence a person's capacity to cope with stress and to relate effectively with other people. Adaptation occurs through changes in health, self-understanding, interpersonal interactions, or the environment. In problem-solving efforts, cognition, affect, and behavior are all involved. As Howard Goldstein expressed it, "Emotions are incomprehensible without some kind of cognitive designation, vague though it may be; cognitions are empty of meaning without reference to the emotional energies; and behavior would appear random if its cognitive motives and emotional forces were absent."[3] Human beings are resilient; they have "self righting tendencies," including "both the capacity to be bent without breaking and the capacity, once bent, to spring back."[4] Resilience is a relational dynamic nurtured by a two-way process of mutuality and empathy—a process of mutual aid.

2. **Human development.** Psychosocial development, according to Erik Erikson, occurs sequentially, typically proceeding in a fairly orderly fashion through stages that describe successive experiences

in mastering developmental tasks and relating to other people.[5] Erikson notes that relationships are essential to giving purpose and meaning to life. His model of development sets forth the tasks to be mastered in each of eight stages in the life span, with special emphasis on relationships in the family and other social networks. He takes into account biological, psychological, and sociocultural determinants of behavior and development and interrelates individual and group identity. The sequence of stages is thought to be universal, but the typical solutions to master expectations of each stage vary from culture to culture and by populations within a given society. For every maturational stage, there appears "a radius of significant relations who aid, abet, or hinder the organism's coping with and resolving life tasks."[6] People react to developmental changes and the stress that accompanies them through the process of adaptation.

3. **Biophysical factors**. Psychosocial functioning is influenced not only by the strength of the ego and the developmental process, but by other factors. These include biophysical factors that are essential for the person's survival and health. Changes in physiological conditions may lead to alterations in cognition, affect, and behavior. Evidence from research suggests that there is a close interconnection between emotion, thought, action, and physiological processes.[7] Biophysical factors include genetic endowment, physiological maturation, biological factors in mental illness, the use of drugs, and illness and disability.

4. **Cultural influences**. The United States, according to Barbara Solomon, "is an ethnosystem that is a composite of interdependent groups each in turn defined by some unique historical and/or cultural ties and bound together by a single political system."[8] Ethnic groups differ in terms of values, norms, and traditions and in race, religion, and social class. Stereotypes about gender and differences in status between males and females also have an impact on personal behavior, group interaction, and environmental opportunities.[9] Through both individual and institutional racism, many members of minority groups face prejudice and discrimination and feel powerless to achieve their desired goals. Lorraine Gutiérrez and Edith Lewis remind us that power provides ability to influence one's life, to participate in efforts to control aspects of

public life, and to have access to means of making decisions.[10] They also remind us that power may be used to block opportunities, exclude others from decision making, and control others.

5. **Environmental influences**. Families and other reference groups to which a person belongs are the context and means for changing attitudes, interests, and behavior. Social and physical environments interact with individuals, families, and groups to enhance or inhibit effective social living. Availability of and access to health and welfare resources, support networks, employment, education, and recreation influence psychosocial functioning. So do environmental hazards, such as poor housing, lack of green space, and availability of drugs, alcohol, and guns. Environments may provide support or they may present obstacles to the achievement of personal and social goals.

Groups as Social Systems

Knowledge of groups as social systems, including families, comes primarily from social psychology and sociology, supplemented by psychoanalytic theory.[11] Such knowledge is of special value to social workers in understanding the formation, developmental processes, and relationships between the members who comprise the group and in understanding the group's interaction with its environment.

Major Small Group Theories

The approaches to the study of small groups that are most widely known have developed since 1930. They are field theory, sociometry, and interaction process analysis.

Field theory   Perhaps the best known theoretical approach to the study of small groups is field theory, associated with the work of Kurt Lewin and his associates. Its basic thesis is that an individual's behavior is a function of the life space or field, which consists of the person and environment viewed as one constellation of interdependent factors operating at a given time. The focus is on the gestalt, the totality of factors as they interrelate in a defined situation. Behavior is a function of the interaction of personality with the environment. The personality includes the psychological and physical systems. The environment includes the immediate social group, the family, work group, and other groups to which the person belongs. It also includes the cultural system made up of the tradition and norms of the person's nationality, racial, religious, and other reference groups. Lewin developed the equation "B F (P,E)." Behavior is a function of person-environment in continuous reciprocal interaction. He emphasized that "to understand or to predict behavior, the person and his environment have to be considered as one constellation of interdependent factors."[12] With a group, regarded as a system, there is a continuous process of mutual adaptation of members to each other, labeled "dynamic interaction." Lewin's conceptualization is, indeed, in harmony with the intersystem, ecological, and biopsychosocial perspectives that are prevalent in today's direct service practice.

Sociometry   As individuals come together in a group, an intricate network of interpersonal relationships gradually develops. Each member has emotional reactions to the other members, being attracted to some and rejecting others. These feelings may or may not be reciprocated. Sociometry, a method for depicting and measuring interpersonal attraction in groups, was developed primarily by Jacob Moreno and Helen Jennings.[13] It builds on field theory, with special emphasis on small groups as networks of affective relations, as these relations are identified by the stated choices of persons for others with whom they would like to associate in defined situations. It deals with the reciprocity of positive choices that bind members of a group together and with individual differences that account for a member's acceptance or rejection by others. Its major thesis is that the full realization of the individual's personality and the effective functioning of social groups depend upon the spontaneity with which given individuals accept others as co-participants in specified activities. As a device for ascertaining the quality of the relationships between members of a group, Moreno and Jennings developed the sociogram, a scheme for assessing the acceptance-rejection process. This graphic representation of the pattern of relationship in a group will be presented in more detail in the next chapter.

Group interaction   Group interaction itself is the focus of the research conducted by Robert Bales and his associates, referred to as interaction process analysis.[14] The group is viewed as a system of individuals in interaction for the purpose of solving some problem. The focus is on patterns and sequences of communicative acts of members. To solve problems related to the achievement of the task of the group, members either seek or give information, suggestions, or opinions. Members also deal with the socioemotional problems of managing tension and maintaining an integrated group.

Groups are never in a state of static equilibrium; they swing back and forth between the emotional and task realms. The problem-solving process has certain sequential phases that follow each other in a fairly regular manner, each phase being dependent upon the preceding one and each influencing those that follow.

Within the interactional analysis approach, George Homans's work had as its objective the development of a set of concepts drawn from observations of groups.[15] The concepts he described were group formation, patterns of relationships, verbal and nonverbal communication, development of norms and roles, and cohesion. The essence of Homans's theory is that the group is an adaptive social system, surviving and evolving in an environment. The whole is determined, not only by its constituents, but also by the relation of the parts to one another and to the environment.

In these theories—field theory, sociometry, and interaction process analysis—there is considerable overlapping in the concepts described. From these concepts, a conceptual framework for the analysis of the dynamics of groups has been formulated. The framework contributes to understanding the group as a social system in which there is interdependence between the parts and the whole and that is in continuous interaction with its environment.

A Conceptual Framework for Understanding Groups

Assessment of Groups

Understanding individuals who comprise a group requires knowledge of psychosocial functioning and development through the life cycle, but it also requires knowledge of the impact of the group's structure and process on the members' behavior. In turn, a group cannot be understood accurately without knowledge of the members and their social contexts. The structure and processes of small groups influence and are influenced by the members of the group and the members' and the group's environments. The parts of a group are, in one sense, its members. In another sense, the parts are the interrelated group processes that influence the members' behavior and the group's operations and development.

Social Interaction — Communication

Social interaction is a term for the dynamic interplay of forces in which contact between persons results in a modification of the attitudes and behavior of the participants. In a study of fifteen formulations of group process by social workers and social scientists, Tom Douglas concluded that interaction is the basic process.[16] Through verbal and nonverbal symbols, people react to each other. The meaning of any act becomes human by the response of others to it.

Communication is the very essence of social interaction.[17] It is a complex social process through which information, feelings, attitudes, and other messages are transmitted, received, interpreted, and responded to. It consists of the verbal, explicit, and intentional transmission of messages between people. It consists also of all the nonverbal processes by which persons influence one another. Ideas are exchanged primarily by verbal means; emotional content is expressed by such nonverbal means as facial expression, posture, gestures, silence, and actions.

An open system of communication, based on the right of each member to be recognized and heard, increases the chances that members will face and solve their own problems and the problems of the group. Within the system, the worker's role is to behave in ways that will facilitate the group's effort to achieve its purpose. Positive change is facilitated by interaction that is honest, sincere, and meaningful to the participants. That is more likely to occur when an individual is involved in the group and has responsibility for some part of the group's effort to realize its purpose. Thus, each member shares some information and attitudes with others. He or she does not feel the need to withhold information owing to fear of reprisal or lack of confidentiality concerning what is shared.

The desired pattern of communication is one that is group-centered as contrasted with a leader-centered pattern in which all communicative acts are channeled through the worker or particular members of the group. Instead of using a formal structure, members communicate with each other and with the worker. With genuine involvement in the process, new ideas, experiences, points of view, and emotional responses may become incorporated into the personalities of the members. Although the particular pattern of communication will shift as the group deals with varied situations, the social worker's efforts are directed toward the achievement of a pattern that is predominantly one of integrated interaction. In this pattern, there is reciprocal interplay between the members—a cross-influencing of each person by each other that is often referred to as mutual aid. Palassana Balgopal and Thomas Vassil define the term: "a web of interdependent and resonating aspects of parts in a system."[18] Any part can be understood only by viewing it in the context of interrelationships with other parts.

Within the interactional process, purposes are defined, a pattern of relationships develops, members acquire differential status, personal roles emerge, values and norms are clarified, conflicts occur, and cohesion develops.

Purpose

Every group has a purpose, that is, an ultimate aim, end, or intention. In the family, purposes are established by society's expectations concerning such functions as the care and socialization of children and the maintenance of certain cultural values and norms. In addition to these general purposes, each family has its own set of goals, the more specific ends that are instrumental to the purpose. So, too, do other types of groups. The goals of a group influence the selection of members, the patterns of communication that develop, the group's norms, the activities of the group, and the criteria by which the members and the group will be evaluated. But these processes also influence the ways in which motivation toward the achievement of goals will develop, and the goals themselves become clarified, strengthened, modified, or abandoned.[19]

Bernard Berelson and Gary Steiner and Marvin Shaw report that some evidence from research supports the proposition that harmony between the purposes of individuals and the group purposes enhances both the satisfaction of the members and the effectiveness of the group.[20] The perception that one's personal goals are being advanced within the general purpose of the group provides motivation for the achievement of goals. The social worker needs, therefore, to help the members to identify and clarify the varied goals of the individuals who comprise the group and to find the common ground within these particular goals. If a group sets its own goals, they will tend to be progressive, so that the members move from one to another under their own motivation. Achieving clarity of purpose will be discussed in chapter 7.

Interpersonal Relationships

Fundamentally, the purpose of the group and the compatibility between persons determine what the nature of the group is and often, in fact, whether or not a group will develop. This fact points to the necessity for concern with the affective forces of attraction and repulsion among members of a group that comprise the emotional bond between the members.[21] Acts of communication in a group convey positive and negative expressions of emotion as well as of opinions and facts. Both in verbal and nonverbal ways, the members communicate their feelings toward each other. Helen Phillips notes that in every human relationship, there are "emotional reactions to one's self, to the other person, and to the specific content of the material expressed."[22] The varied responses of persons toward others are means through which they attempt to satisfy their own needs for relationships with others and to avoid threats to self.

Groups require that members be able to give to others and to receive from them and that they be interested in and concerned for each other. In many groups, members do not have the ability to perceive other members as distinct personalities and to be concerned about them. Mature object relationships, characterized by love of others, are in contrast to the immature, narcissistic relationships of some group members, whose needs are expressed by the phrase "I want what I want when I want it."[23] In such narcissistic relationships, the orientation is toward the self rather than toward give and take with others. The behavior toward another person is motivated primarily by the individual's own needs and impulses. Other persons are used primarily for self-gratification. In any group, there will be variations in the members' abilities to relate to others in ways that are fairly realistic, that indicate mutuality of concern for and interaction with each other, and that tend toward identification with the positive values and norms of the group. For a collection of individuals to become a group, or for an existing group to survive, the positive unifying forces must predominate over the negative, divisive ones.

Status and Role

Status refers to a person's position relative to others in a hierarchy of statuses in a given group.[24] Through a process of evaluation in a group, the members rank each other, with or without awareness of the process. The basis for such rankings depends upon the values and aspirations of the members. People have a different status in each group to which they belong or, for that matter, at different times in the same group. They also have generalized status in the community, which may be achieved through such means as education, income, or competence. Or this status may be ascribed to a person on the basis of certain factors other than achievement: color, ethnic origin, money, age, gender, physical condition, ancestry, or style of living. Members bring this status with them into the group. Depending upon the agency, members may already have a status that labels them a leader or expert, for example, or a deviant, such as an offender, school dropout, foster child, or patient. The bases for members' ratings of each other are thus brought with them into the group from earlier life experiences, their current membership and reference groups, and their cultural values. But that status changes as members interact and as socioemotional and task roles emerge.

The concept of role is one of those most frequently referred to in the literature on small groups; yet there is no single agreed upon definition of the term. Many definitions of role are similar to the one proposed by Urie Bronfenbrenner: "A role is a set of activities and relations expected of a person occupying a particular position in society, and of others in relation to that person."[25] As Herman Stein and Richard Cloward point out, whenever the question is asked "What is the proper way to behave in this situation?" or "What is really expected of me?" there is an implied problem of role definition.[26] People tend to organize their behavior in terms of the structurally defined expectations assigned to each of their multiple social roles. Each position or status has its organized role relationships that comprise a role set, "that complement of role relationships which persons have by virtue of occupying a particular social status," as defined by Robert Merton.[27] This idea of role set emphasizes the importance of relationships among and between members of a group. Members' positions in the group both influence and are influenced by the roles to which they are assigned or those they achieve. Status and role are inextricably interrelated. Practitioners need knowledge about, and skills in affecting, the roles of members, which is the subject of chapter 10.

Values and Norms

A distinctive culture, consisting of values expressed through a set of norms, is a property of any stable social system. Once a set of norms is accepted, they influence the goals toward which members strive, the ways members relate to each other and to significant persons in the environment, the nature and operation of the content of the group, and the means for resolving problems.[28]

A norm is a generalization concerning an expected standard of behavior in any matter of consequence to the group. It incorporates a value judgment. A set of norms defines the ranges of behavior that will be tolerated within the group and introduces a certain amount of regularity and predictability in the group's functioning because members feel some obligation to adhere to the expectations of the group, which they have had a part in developing. Norms serve as the principal means of control within a group. They provide pressures toward conformity. As stated by John Thibaut and Harold Kelley, "They serve as substitutes for the exercise of personal influence and produce more economically and efficiently certain consequences otherwise dependent upon personal influence processes."[29] Since they are usually based on agreement between members, the need for personal power to enforce the norms is reduced and responsibility for enforcement is shared among the members. Norms that are accepted and complied with will become intrinsically rewarding and thus reduce the need for external control. They thus provide a means for regulating behavior without entailing the costs and uncertainties involved in forcing conformity to imposed rules through use of interpersonal power.

In effect, then, norms suggest what a group sees as important and what it dismisses as insignificant, what it likes and dislikes, what it desires, and what it objects to or is indifferent about. The constellation of norms, based on a group's perception of what ought to be, provides weak or strong motivation for its members to use the group for their mutual benefit. One of the most important tasks of the practitioner, therefore, is to facilitate the creation and management of norms.

Tension and Conflict

The sociologist Charles Cooley wrote, "The more one thinks of it, the more he will see that conflict and cooperation are not separable things, but phases of one process which always involves something of both."[30] Tension, or the threat of it, is essential for human development. According to Walter Buckley, "Tension is seen as an inherent and essential feature of complex adaptive systems: it provides the go of the system, the force behind the elaboration and maintenance of structure."[31]

The word *conflict* tends to elicit frightened or hostile responses, yet conflict itself is an important ingredient in development and change. It can be destructive in its impact on the self, other members of the group, or society. Yet it can also be a constructive building force in group relations. It is a natural and necessary component of group process, created through the ways people communicate with each other.

Conflict is simply behavior in which there is disagreement between two or more persons. It encompasses a wider range of behavior than its usual images of violent struggle and war. Conflict occurs when at least one person feels obstructed or irritated by one or more others. Three basic elements characterize the conflict situation: there are two or more identifiable parties to the conflict, the parties perceive incompatible differences that create frustration, and there is interaction between the parties around the differences. Conflict is the behavior as contrasted with the emotions, such as fear or hostility, that are often connected with it. At the intrapersonal level, conflict refers to contradictory, incompatible, or antagonistic emotions and impulses within a person. At the group level, conflicts arise out of the intrapersonal conflicts of the members, misinformation about the objective state of affairs, or differences in goals, values, and norms between the members. At times, conflict has its source in the divergence between the values and norms of the group and those of certain segments of the community of which the group is a part. Differences in goals, values, and norms are due to differing life experiences and socioeconomic resources.

The view of conflict espoused here is a sociopsychological one, consistent with an ecosystem approach to practice. It recognizes the need to understand the persons involved, the nature of the issues, the responses of others to the conflict, the social environment in which the conflict occurs, and the consequences of the conflict for all who are affected by it. Numerous social scientists agree that conflict is inevitable and has potentially functional and constructive uses, as well as dysfunctional and destructive ones.[32]

People who have learned to manage their internal conflicts may well be what Nevitt Sanford has called more fully developed individuals than those who have never dealt with serious intrapersonal conflicts.[33] Such persons' range of coping mechanisms and adaptive behavior may be broader and more flexible, and their capacity for empathy may be greatly increased. Conflict prevents stagnation, stimulates interest and curiosity, and makes possible the recognition of problems and the consequent rethinking and assessment of self. Conversely, however, conflicts that are too long lasting, too severe, or too basic to personality structure may lead to severe intrapsychic disintegration and breakdown in psychosocial functioning.

Group Cohesion

Concern with the cohesion of a group is based on the results of studies that indicate that cohesion has an important influence on the group. Cohesion is a group property with individual manifestations of feelings of belongingness and attraction to the group. The concept refers to the attraction that members have for each other and for the group as an entity.[34]

Research indicates that the more cohesive the group, the greater its influence on the members. To the extent that a group is highly attractive to its members, it has the ability to produce changes in attitudes, opinions, and behavior. There tends to be greater satisfaction with the group, higher morale, less internal friction, and greater capacity to survive the loss of some of its members. In groups of high cohesion, the members may disagree with each other, but they also tend to find solutions to problems and conflicts more quickly. In general, groups with high degrees of cohesion are more effective than those with low cohesion in achieving their respective goals. The outcome for the members is better.[35]

When a group becomes a cohesive one, according to research by Avraham Levy, the following indications will usually be evident: (1) Regularity of attendance and punctuality predominate, especially in groups in which membership is voluntary. (2) Members feel that they belong, as evidenced by knowing who are members and differentiating themselves from nonmembers. (3) Members increase their expressions of "we" feelings, symbolizing identification of members with each other and with the group entity. (4) Relationships between members become accepting, interdependent, and intimate. (5) Members become highly invested in their participation in the content of the group experience. (6) Members express verbally their satisfaction with being a members of the group and with the way it operates.

(7) The social climate is characterized by spontaneity, informality, and appropriate self-disclosure. (8) The group's norms provide pressures toward uniformity. (9) A system of ritual has developed that distinguishes the group from other groups and social networks.[36]

Strong cohesion may have negative as well as positive consequences for the members of a group. Members who are highly attracted to a group may have difficulties in recognizing the negative aspects that should be changed, or they may be unduly influenced by the other members. Overdependency on the group for basic satisfactions may limit the members' involvement in activities in the community. Strong identification with the group, an aspect of cohesion, simultaneously carries the potential for loss of individuation and personal identity. A cohesive group may protect itself against new inputs of information from the external environment; the boundary becomes relatively closed to new ways of thinking, feeling, and behaving. New ideas may threaten the existing satisfaction with the group. In such instances, Nancy Evans and Paul A. Servis note that cohesion becomes the ends, not the means, toward achieving other goals.[37] The need, then, is to develop a cohesive group through which all members can benefit without loss of their own identity, so that they can function effectively when the group is discontinued. The type of group that is developed cannot be left to chance. It should become one in which the relationships and norms are those that promote growth toward more effective psychosocial functioning.

A social worker makes efforts to direct a group in which (1) there is a shared purpose; (2) the role of member is defined as a collaborative one; (3) relationships are characterized by a preponderance of positive ties and interdependence between the members; (4) communication is characterized by freedom of expression, openness, and mutual aid; (5) the values and norms of the group support healthy growth toward adaptive behavior; (6) conflict is acknowledged and coped with through appropriate decision-making processes. Such a group will be a cohesive one in which the dynamic forces for change are apt to operate, resulting in positive results for the members.

In one sense, as George Homans wrote, "There is still only one sufficient reason for studying the group: the sheer beauty of the subject and the delight in bringing out the formal relationships that lie within the apparent confusion of everyday behavior."[38] But, for a professional practitioner, the shift out of confusion to understanding is translated into an accurate assessment of the group for use in helping that group to achieve its goals.

Group Development

It takes time for a collection of people to develop into a group that becomes an instrument through which positive gains may be achieved by its members. As a group develops, noticeable differences occur in the behavior of the members and in the structure and functioning of the group. Although change in any group is a continuous, dynamic process, it is useful to think of a group as moving through a number of stages characteristic of its life cycle. The identification of stages in a group's development provides clues for assessing individual and group functioning and for selecting appropriate content and interventions. This enables a worker to ascertain where a given group is in its development and then plan what needs to be done to help it move forward toward the achievement of its purpose.

Studies of Group Development

Social scientists as well as social workers have been interested in studying the process of group development. The first major study was published in 1965 by Bruce Tuckman, who derived a model from a comprehensive review of fifty publications that described stages of group development in training, therapy, task-oriented, and laboratory groups.[39] Using Robert Bales's concept of socioemotional and instrumental or task realms, he concluded that four analogous stages occur within each realm.[40] He labeled these as forming, storming, norming, and performing.

In social work practice, interest in group development occurred as early as 1949, when Gertrude Wilson and Gladys Ryland wrote that the worker "affects the social processes for the purpose of helping the action to move forward, but is also concerned with the quality of the action and its relation to the real interests and needs of the members."[41] But they did not identify stages. The famous article by James Garland, Hubert Jones, and Ralph Kolodny was the first in social work to identify and describe stages in group development.[42] The groups studied were composed of children and adolescents in community agencies. The central theme of their model is closeness. The focus in each stage is on the socioemotional issues facing the members. A list of the group development stages they identified is as follows.

1. **Preaffiliation.** The characteristic patterns of members' behavior are approach-avoidance to determine whether the group will be safe and rewarding.
2. **Power and control.** Resolution of the issues of the leader's power and control gives members freedom for autonomy and readiness to move toward intimacy.
3. **Intimacy.** Intensification of personal involvement in the group occurs as members become more intimate with each other.
4. **Differentiation.** Mutuality and interdependence predominate. Mutual acceptance of varied personal needs brings freedom and ability to differentiate and evaluate relationships and experiences in the group on a reality basis.
5. **Separation.** A number of emotional reactions are set off in the members when they become aware of separation. Various defensive and coping devices are used to avoid and forestall termination and to face and accomplish it.

In 1969, Helen Northen's *Social Work with Groups* was the first book to conceptualize theory and practice according to stages of group development. Since that time, almost all of the authors of books have given attention to that subject. Three stages of group development have been used by several authors, referred to simply as beginning, middle, and ending stages. The rationale for a three-stage model is that there is greater agreement on the issues to be addressed at the beginning and ending of a group than there is in intermediate stages. On the other hand, some authors assert that two- or three-stage formulations are oversimplified. Arthur Cohen and Douglas Smith argue that "this reduction of a highly complex process of group interaction to two or three phases, as reflected in the literature, may be due to an inability to deal with group phenomena because of inadequate methodology. However, oversimplification represents a disservice."[43] They based their judgment on an analysis of 144 characteristics of member behaviors, taken from critical incidents throughout the life of the group.

In 1980, Roy Lacoursiere reviewed slightly more than one hundred studies of group development, covering varied types of groups.[44] He concluded that there are five stages: (1) orientation, a period when members are concerned about what it will be like to be in the group and are oriented to the experience, (2) dissatisfaction, when members realize the reality that seldom lives up to their hopes and fantasies, (3) resolution of conflicts, (4) production, characterized by mutuality, enthusiasm, learning, and working toward goals, and (5) termination, when there is a sense of loss over the anticipated end of the group.

Any division of group life into stages is somewhat arbitrary, for indeed there is a continuous flow of interaction that shifts and changes throughout the group's duration. Just as one stops the camera to take a still picture, it is evident that a group is different at that moment from what it was earlier. The group has changed.

Linda Schiller has recently developed a model that is applicable to women's groups. She refers to this formulation as a relational model.[45] It emphasizes the idea that members "must first have established a sense of safety in their group affiliations and connections before they are able to take on and challenge each other." Her stages are preaffiliation, establishing a relational base, mutuality and interpersonal empathy, challenge and change, and separation and termination. She notes that "the therapeutic relationship and an empathic attunement is of critical importance for both men and women," but the "timing of the attention to the relationship may have greater primacy to women."[46] Sylvia Zamudio found that closed, time-limited groups for bereaved children, composed of both boys and girls ages eleven to fifteen, develop similarly to Schiller's model.[47]

A Model of Group Development

To develop a useful model of group development, two facets need to be considered: (1) the predominant patterns of behavior related both to socioemotional issues and to tasks, and (2) typical characteristics of group structure and process. Each stage has its own developmental issues that must be attended to and at least partially resolved before the group can move into the next stage. What happens in a particular stage influences the processes and content of the next one. Although there is always some distortion of reality in attempts to integrate and combine findings from diverse sources, certain trends seem to emerge from the major studies. Because of the complexity of the problem and variations in types of groups, a four-stage model, in addition to the process of planning, seems adequate if short-term, as well as longer-term, groups are to be taken into consideration.

Stage I: Inclusion-orientation   The title of this stage conveys the socio-emotional and task issues that concern members of the group. In the initial stage, the predominant socioemotional issue is inclusion, similar to what Garland, Jones, and Kolodny refer to as approach-avoidance behaviors, and what K. Roy MacKenzie and W. John Livesley refer to as engagement.[48] Members act in many ways to decide whether or not they will be included in the group's membership. In the task area, orientation predominates. Members seek and receive information from the worker and other members and search for the common ground and the potential meaning of the group for them. As they become oriented to the new situation, the members arrive at a tentative contract or working agreement.

Stage II: Uncertainty-Exploration   The title of this stage indicates that the members are uncertain about many aspects of the group's operation, particularly concerning who has power to do what and whether they can find acceptance in the group. The members explore these matters. The predominant socioemotional theme is conflict and difference, particularly in relation to the authority of the social worker and the distribution of power among the members. The typical patterns of behavior are expressions of uncertainty and anxiety about mutual acceptance and group identity, competition for power, and development of satisfying roles in the group. The predominant task is exploration of the situation in relation to its hoped-for benefits, acquisition of realistic mutual expectations, and interpersonal relationships based on mutual trust and acceptance. The group becomes a system of mutual aid.

Stage III: Mutuality-Goal Achievement   The title indicates that the predominant socioemotional theme is interdependence and the task is work toward achieving goals. The typical socioemotional patterns of behavior are intensification of personal involvement, seeking or avoiding intimacy, and enhancing personal identity, along with group identity. Interpersonal relationships tend to be characterized by mutual acceptance, empathy, self-disclosure, and respect for differences; conflict tends to be recognized and dealt with in functional ways; the group is an appropriately cohesive one that allows for differentiation as well as integration. Members tend to cooperate and participate actively in the group's work. The major task is the maintenance and enhancement of the group as a means for social growth and problem solving. Mutual aid is at its peak.

Stage IV: Separation-Termination   This title indicates that the predominant social emotional issue is separation and the task is termination. The members are ambivalent about separation from the worker, the group, and other members. They prepare to leave the group and make transitions to other relationships and activities. They work to complete unfinished business, review and evaluate the experience, stabilize gains that have been made, and transfer these gains into situations in the community.

Recurrent Issues and Variations

Several authors have noted that there are issues in interpersonal relationships that recur, but in different ways, throughout the life span of the group, for example, intimacy, control, and power.[49] The model of stages described here does not deny the presence of these recurrent issues. They are often evident in the dynamic interactions of members as the group moves toward a new stage. The concept of stages emphasizes the points at which particular issues predominate. A group may simultaneously have characteristics of more than one stage at a given time. These formulations of recurrent issues are indications of the complexity of the group process, varying with the purpose and structure of the group.[50] Paul Ephross and Thomas Vassil describe how stages of group development that are similar to the ones described here are applied to task or work groups.[51] And Jacqueline Mondros and Toby Berman-Rossi describe the relevance of stages of group development to community organization.[52]

A group is composed of individuals, each unique in some ways. People progress at different rates, in different ways, and in relation to different needs. A group tends to move irregularly, not uniformly, on all the relevant dimensions of group structure and process. That does not deny the fact, however, that there is a fundamental core of movement, with variations along both individual and group dimensions, that can be thought of as the development of a group. Knowledge of developmental stages is central to group work practice. It enables workers to better understand the behavior of members as it occurs in the group and even to anticipate behavior that might take place. Such knowledge also has a vital impact upon the ways in which workers intervene in the group. Their interventions are shaped by their understanding of the group's stage of development and the consequent needs of its members at that stage.

Groups in Environments

Person-group-environment is a construct that emphasizes the interdependence of individuals in their families and other groups and in their relationships with the broader environment. The nature of the environment has a tremendous influence on the well-being of individuals and groups.

The environment is simply defined as the objects, conditions, or circumstances that influence the life of an individual, group, or community. The term refers to physical or to social and cultural surroundings or both. Susan Kemp, James Whittaker, and Elizabeth Tracy define the environment as a multidimensional entity that includes the following dimensions:

1. the perceived environment, i.e., the environment as constructed in individual and collective systems of meaning and belief,
2. the physical environment, both natural and built,
3. the social/interactional environment, comprised largely of human relationships at various levels of intimacy, and including family, group, and neighborhood networks and collectivities,
4. the institutional and organizational environment,
5. the cultural and sociopolitical environment.[53]

Urie Bronfenbrenner has emphasized the importance of the environment as perceived by a person.[54] He describes the environment as a nested arrangement of contexts, including the microsystem or person, the mesosystem of interpersonal relations within families and groups, the exosystem of social structures and institutions, and the macrosystem of political and legal influences and cultural patterns. Each of these contexts has potential effects on health, illness, and social well-being. When working with groups, social workers need to understand the impact of the members' environments on the use they make of the group.

Early leaders in the development of group work paid attention to the interaction of the group with its environment, even before contemporary knowledge about complex adaptive systems and human ecology had been conceptualized. In *Social Process in Organized Groups*, Grace Coyle analyzed the literature on all kinds of groups and larger organizations. The first chapter is titled "The Organized Group in its Social Setting." Groups are viewed as forms of reciprocal relations. Internal group influences interact interdependently with influences from other social systems. Characteristics of the community milieu, such as ethnic stereotypes, social class differences, dislocations of families, and the pluralistic nature of society, affect individuals and the groups to which they belong. A major theme is that a group must be viewed within the multiplicity and complexity of organized life. Coyle wrote: "The nature and quality of the community life . . . permeate the life of all the associations within it. The reciprocal action of individuals, groups, and the total milieu creates each organization and determines its functions and processes."[55]

Neighborhoods and Communities

Members of groups live in neighborhoods that influence their perceptions of the world, their access to opportunities, and their sense of safety and well-being. The neighborhoods in which people live are characterized by their social history and cultural traditions. They vary in terms of the diversity of ethnic and religious populations, the presence and extent of social problems, and the availability and accessibility of physical and social resources. Each neighborhood has a distinctive physical environment in terms of geography, climate, flora and fauna, parks, mountains, beaches, or deserts that influence the quality of living for its residents. The climate, geography, and scenery mean many things to different people. John Shimer, a geologist, said that "each part of this sculptured earth has its own characteristic flavor and its own special type of landscape, and each arouses unexpected and varied reactions in the observer."[56]

People of similar ethnicity, race, or religion tend to cluster in a particular neighborhood or larger geographical area. By doing so, they are assured of living near people who share their traditions and customs and provide mutual support and a sense of belonging. The sense of fit between people and their environments is enhanced.

People of fairly similar social class status also tend to cluster in particular areas—the rich in the most desirable neighborhoods in terms of beauty and amenities and the poor in the most dilapidated and oppressed communities. The tendency of people to move out of slums as they acquire higher incomes creates stark problems for those remaining behind and for those who take their place.

Cultural Diversity

Cultural diversity is a fact of life in the United States and in many other countries today, making it essential that social workers practice with sensitivity and competence to meet the needs and build on the strengths of the varied groups that comprise our population.

To understand diversity, Solomon introduced the concept of ethnosystem, as defined earlier. Within a given race, there are many ethnic groups. Japanese, Koreans, Vietnamese, and Chinese are all Asians, but their histories, place of residence, values, major interests, and customs differ widely. White people do not comprise a homogeneous category: the tendency to label all whites "Anglos" hides the significance of varied ethnic groups who differ from each other in many ways and differ from persons of English ancestry. Among black people, African Americans come from different countries and may be ethnically quite different from those who come from the West Indies. Native Americans belong to hundreds of tribes and prefer to be identified by the name of their tribe, rather than as Indian or Native American.

Knowledge about ethnic groups is expanding rapidly. To be effective in serving any category of people, it is essential that practitioners acquaint themselves with the latest knowledge about the population. Major books have been produced concerning social work practice with diverse populations, for example, with black people, subgroups within Latino communities, Chinese Americans, and they contain bibliographies for further reference.[57]

Ethnicity refers to a sense of peoplehood and belonging, based on a common culture.[58] The common factors include language or dialect, physical features, religion, kinship patterns, nationality, and contiguity. Everyone is a member of at least one ethnic group and increasing numbers of Americans belong to two or more because they have mixed ancestry. Ethnicity is an important component of both individual and group identity and serves as a reference group for its members. It may even be a critical lifeline for new immigrants, providing some point of connection in an otherwise confusing and uncertain environment.

The ethnic groups that comprise the population of the United States and Canada are diverse in terms of their histories, needs, and resources. People in every subpopulation may have many needs and serious psychosocial problems, but members of some groups are in more dire circumstances than are those of the dominant white group. These tend to be those populations whose race, color, language, and physical appearance set them apart from

European Americans. They tend to be subjected to prejudice and discrimination. Prejudice is an unfavorable attitude toward individuals or groups, based on stereotypes and faulty perceptions that obscure the ability to view others as they really are in all their likenesses and differences from others. Discrimination is an act that is taken against a person on the basis of the category to which the person belongs. Prejudice defines an attitude: discrimination defines behavior.[59] Discrimination continues to be part of the everyday lives of oppressed people. Through both individual and institutional racism, oppressed people tend to feel powerless to achieve their desired goals. Other ethnic groups that are devalued have also found it hard to achieve the "American Dream." Many of them are poor, live in crowded or dilapidated housing, and in neighborhoods that lack adequate health, educational, and welfare resources. They have not had equal opportunities in education and employment.

Social class interacts with race, ethnicity, and gender to influence a person's opportunities for a satisfying life. Research on social class in the United States identifies different numbers of social classes, ranging from three to six.[60] The criteria for assigning social class status also vary, but it is clear that some people have higher incomes, more education, more prestigious jobs, greater access to resources, and more power than do others. Rather than rigid boundaries, there is a continuum from highest to lowest status. Social class exerts a profound influence on life styles and opportunities for finding satisfaction in living.

Understanding social class is necessary, but there is a danger that poor people will be stereotyped. Many people are resilient. They are able to achieve upward mobility and have great capacity to pursue their desired goals in spite of obstacles. It is a responsibility of social workers to help them achieve power to be able to do that.

Referring to prejudice and discrimination, Elaine Pinderhughes believes that, no matter the level of oppression and who is identified as minority or majority, the key issue appears to be that of power.[61] Stereotypes can be considered as rationalizations to maintain the status quo and justify domination on the part of persons in power. People are oppressed when power is exercised in a cruel or unjust manner. Discrimination is disempowering, denying social justice to those who are the objects of discrimination. Powerlessness stems from a complex and dynamic relationship between people and a relatively hostile environment.

Kemp, Whittaker, and Tracy point out that perceiving environments as "a locus of oppression and inequality must be balanced by the equally valid understanding that they are also a vital source of support and opportunity."[62] The strengths within the environment can be harnessed to improve the quality of life for individuals, families, and groups.

The Institutional Environment

The institutional environment includes the network of health, education, recreation, and welfare organizations with which people must deal in their communities. The organizations in which work with groups is practiced have a profound influence on that practice, owing to the kind of services they provide and the criteria they use for accepting clients. They may provide adequate or inadequate resources, including space, furnishings, equipment, funds for programs, access to transportation, and workloads. They have policies, rules, and procedures that have an impact on the structure, composition, and duration of groups, and patterns of communication between personnel that facilitate or interfere with planning and treatment.

Paul Glasser and Charles Garvin observed that central to the criteria that govern the use of groups "is the worker's power within the organization."[63] Workers' legitimate power, based on their positions in the institutional structure, and their informal professional influence are crucial factors in facilitating the quality of their work.

Social Networks and Social Support

Members of groups are parts of one or more social networks in their communities. The group to which they belong is one part of that network. With many members having difficulties in some aspect of their psychosocial functioning or environmental stress, social support outside of, as well as inside, the group is essential to their well-being.

Support is an interactional process of giving and receiving help. According to Gregory Pierce, Barbara Sarason, and Irvin Sarason, "social support refers to social transactions that are perceived by the recipient or intended by the provider to facilitate coping in everyday life and especially in response to stressful situations."[64] It is a product of interacting influences among persons, their personal relationships, and the situations they both create and to which they respond.[65] In social work groups, support is given through the process of mutual aid.

In everyday life, social support is generally received through relationships with members of a social network, which is defined as a social system composed of people who are interconnected with others in some way—through family ties, friendships, acquaintances, colleagues at work or school, and organizations.[66] Among these, research indicates that "kinship and friendship are the most important types of primary social relationships which can be used as support systems."[67] These informal support systems, however, need to be supplemented by formal ones. When a group becomes a cohesive one, it can be a major source of support for its members and can help members to enhance their overall network in the community. Well-being depends upon having an adequate network, and people vary greatly in needs and preferences for larger or smaller networks. It is not the size of the network alone that matters most: it is the quality of relationships. Truly supportive relationships are those characterized by close proximity, frequency of interaction, mutual trust, similar norms, and reciprocity.[68]

Studies have also given attention to negative aspects of social networks.[69] They may create tension and conflict between some of the members. They may reinforce deviance as in drug-oriented networks or delinquent gangs. They may force conformity to their norms through peer pressure. Some members may be rejected by others or feel overwhelmed by what others expect of them. The characteristics of other people in the network may not fit with a particular person's needs and interests.

In social work with groups, it is important for the practitioner to assess each member's social network and direct appropriate attention to means for enabling members to strengthen, expand, or change them. Knowledge of individuals, groups, and environments is clearly interconnected and used by social workers for purposes of assessment, planning, treatment, and evaluation.

3   Relationships: The Heart of Practice

"One of the most striking features with regard to the conscious life of any human being is that it is interwoven with the lives of others. It is in each man's social relations that his mental history is mainly written and it is in his social relations that the causes of the disorders that threaten his happiness and his effectiveness and the means for securing his recovery are to be mainly sought." Mary Richmond, quoting the physician James Putnam, wrote that in 1917.[1]

People's lives are enriched when the need for a strong human connection is met—one that is accepting, genuine, and empathic. Perlman noted, "The emotional bond that unites two or more people around some shared concern is charged with enabling, facilitative power toward both problem solving and goal attainment . . . An understanding, empathic relationship contributes to a person's sense of inner security and alliance with his fellow men."[2] Fisher said it this way: "Individual bonds to one another are the essence of society."[3] People need people; they are social organisms from birth on.

It was stated in the last chapter that Erikson's formulation of human development was based on changes in the capacity for relationships with other people from initial trust in infancy to integrity in old age. John Bowlby's work on attachment theory made clear that the infant's propensity for attachment to other persons is a genetically endowed capacity.[4] Carol Gilligan reported that contemporary studies reveal the "intensely social and moral nature of the young child's relationships with others."[5] These findings do not mean, however, that the environment is not important: it greatly promotes or impedes the development of that capacity.

Gisela Konopka traced the development of relationships from the primary tie to the mother, who is usually the primary caretaker, to early interactions with peers. She emphasized the interrelatedness of family and peer relationships. The child's sense of self-esteem, for example, "develops through the influence of these two sets of relationships: relationships with family members and relationships with contemporaries outside the family group."[6] At each stage of development, people find fulfillment through supportive relationships with others in pairs, triads, larger subsystems, groups, and associations. The quality of these relationships is influenced by the opportunities and obstacles in the environment and by the values and norms of the groups or associations to which a person belongs. A social work group then can become a major source for the enhancement of capacity to develop satisfying and socially constructive relationships with other people and for the correction of relationships that are destructive to self or others.

When people's relationships are destructive, something has gone wrong in the interaction of feelings, thoughts, and actions of a person and events in the environment. Too often, there are instances of child neglect, as in the case of a mother who leaves her fourteen-month-old child alone for days on end, or of physical abuse by roughly shaking and causing a baby to die because he cried too much. And it is no longer unheard of to learn of children killing children or even adults with guns. Neglect, abuse, and violence occur too frequently. In most cases, studies reveal that the perpetrators have long-standing problems in relationships. Social workers, particularly in work with groups, need to pay more attention to preventing such problems as well as to providing therapy for persons with problems in social functioning.

Peer Relationships

Relationships with peers become increasingly important as children mature. In childhood, play is the primary means of relating to others; later, conversations predominate. There is some evidence that "peer relationships may be as important to social development as association with adults, perhaps more so."[7] Through relationships with peers, children have a wider variety of social experiences than adults can offer and basic social skills are learned. These skills include such everyday ones as how to make a friend, how to let other people know you like them, how to join a group, how to keep secrets, how to negotiate effectively with an adult, how to defend one-self without fighting, and how to manage conflict. In play, the experiences that children share and the support they give to another frequently result in friendships.[8] Friends are important to personal emotional stability and the adequacy of social functioning. But the development and maintenance of friendships require social competence.[9] A close relationship, such as friend-ship, is initiated and developed jointly. The participants have to test the likelihood that it will be beneficial to them, assess each other's needs, meet mutually agreed upon expectations, adopt appropriate styles of communi-cation, and come to trust each other. The skills involved in providing mutual support and mutual aid are crucial to friendships of high quality.

Variations in the pattern of relationships in a group occur owing to dif-ferences in capacities, goals, and needs. Considerable research, for example, reports that girls and women prefer close, confiding relationships.[10] Gilligan has found that "the central theme of girls and women's own stories is an intense concern and a persisting quest for authentic relationships and gen-uine connection."[11] For men, on the other hand, shared activities seem to have priority, although there are many variations in preferences among both genders.

Cultural factors are also important. Attitudes toward members of diverse racial, ethnic, and social class backgrounds influence the ease with which supportive relationships develop in a group. Differences in language, physi-cal features, religion, and family structure may limit the development of self-disclosure and intimacy between the members. But when these differences can be understood and appreciated, close relationships may develop for the benefit of all. Peer relationships thus offer valuable learning about a wide variety of people, so necessary in our complex, multicultural society.

People need to form close relationships with others for their own well-being, but many individuals are lonely, isolated, or rejected. Or their rela-tionships do not meet their needs for the degree of intimacy and affection, inclusiveness, and power they desire. Poor peer relationships in childhood have been found to be connected with subsequent social difficulties in ad-olescence and adulthood.[12] Children's friendships are thought to facilitate the development of a good sense of perspective, interpersonal sensitivities, companionship, and social competence. Children with poor peer relation-ships have troubles. They perform poorly in school, experience learning difficulties, and drop out of school more often than other children do. They are more likely to become delinquent. In adulthood, they are more likely to be discharged dishonorably from the armed services and have higher rates of physical and mental health problems. They are at high risk for developing mental disorders. These problems are created by the interaction of personal, interpersonal, and environmental factors. They are not solely caused by the person: a relationship always involves two or more persons who influence each other in a particular situation. Michal Mor-Barak describes numerous studies that "indicate, quite unanimously, that social relationships are beneficial to health in a number of groups of people and in varying life situations.[13]

Supportive Relationships

William Schutz has postulated three basic interpersonal needs: inclusion, control, and affection.[14] People indicate a desire to have others initiate interaction toward them or to leave them alone: they express behavior toward others in terms of inclusion or exclusion. People differ, too, in their need to control others and in preferences for being controlled by others. The balance of power may be stable or shift in different situations. Again, persons behave toward others and prefer that others behave toward them in certain ways with respect to affection, even though everybody needs to love and be loved. The responses of persons toward others and of others toward them may or may not be reciprocated. Urie Bronfenbrenner has a similar formulation of interpersonal needs, but places greater emphasis on reciprocity.[15] He identifies the basic needs as reciprocity, balance of power, and affective ties.

Supportive relationships have six basic dimensions, according to research by Robert Weiss.[16] These dimensions are

1. attachment provided by relationships from which a person gains a sense of security and place;
2. integration into a social network provided by relationships in which concerns are shared, companionship is provided, and opportunities for exchange of services are offered;
3. opportunities for nurturance of others that develop into a sense of being needed;
4. reassurance of worth through relationships that attest to one's competence in a social role;
5. a sense of reliable alliance in which a person expects continuing assistance when needed, primarily from kin;

6. help in stressful situations through the receipt of emotional and instrumental support.

Characteristics of Relationships

Ambivalence

The way in which persons relate to each other is the heart of the group process. The attitudes that people have toward each other are naturally somewhat ambivalent. Human relationships are characterized by various positive ties—love, affection, empathy, cordiality, and identification. These are associative and tend to unite people. Relationships are also characterized by various negative ties—hatred, hostility, repulsions, fears, prejudice, and indifference. These are dissociative, separating in their effect. When persons come together, they may accept each other, reject each other, or be indifferent to each other. They may seek to establish intimate, personal relationships or behave in an impersonal manner. They may prefer that others respond to them with a particular degree of closeness or distance. A positive orientation to other persons is often reciprocated by the other, but not necessarily. There may or may not be compatibility between the needs of persons for relative intimacy or distance. The extent to which persons find acceptance in a group depends upon the complex interaction between their own needs and attributes, those of other individuals, and the social climate of the group. Individuals are like all others in many ways; they are also unique human beings. Each member of a group has many things in common with other members, but is different in many ways as well. Similarities and differences in such characteristics as age, gender, religion, race, nationality, education, and economic status are influential in determining the place a person will find in a group. Other important factors are the similarities and differences in the members' goals and aspirations, the nature of their needs and problems, their capacities, achievements, and interests, the opportunities and deprivations of their environments, and the groups to which they belong and those to which they aspire.

The combination of affectionate or hostile feelings between members is very subtle at times. It is difficult to know the reasons for liking or not liking others. Positive or negative feelings may be based on distortions in interpersonal perception. A person may have false perceptions of another owing to ineptness in communicating intent. A child, for example, tries to express

friendly interest in another child through a push, but the gesture is misinterpreted as one of hostility. Ignorance of the nuances of language of various
subcultural populations often leads to the use of words that hurt, when no
hurt is intended. People tend to stereotype others, that is, to perceive them
according to preconceived notions about what they will be like or how they
will behave, representing failure to individualize them and to recognize
them as they really are. There is a tendency to stereotype persons who differ
from oneself in such characteristics as race, religion, gender, social class,
appearance, or age. Certain distortions in perception of other people are
connected with mental illness as part of a constellation of serious problems
in the perception of reality.

Transference

A person may have a false perception of another based on transference
reactions.[17] Many relationships have within them feelings, attitudes, and
patterns of response transferred from other, earlier relationships, particularly
those with parents. Persons can misunderstand the present relationship in
terms of the past. They tend to relive earlier attitudes with the persons in
their present situation and react in ways that are not logical or appropriate
to the current relationship. A transference reaction may be functional or
dysfunctional to a relationship. Emotional attitudes and behavioral patterns
evolved in the course of family living and other meaningful earlier groups
are subject to transfer in various degrees in subsequent group relationships.
In a group, transference reactions may be enacted toward the worker, who
may represent a parental or other authority figure to the members. Such
reactions may also be directed toward other members of the group who have
the emotional significance of siblings to the member who distorts the current
relationship. Only by observing both the transference and the reality characteristics of a relationship, and by noting how they contrast, overlap, and
interact, is full justice done to the process of assessment. Positive transference
occurs in groups of young children, as illustrated by a social worker's visit to
a member of her group in a hospital who was to have surgery the next day.

When I entered the room, Catherine saw me and burst into tears. I approached her with a smile but with concern, too. I put my hand gently

on her shoulder. She looked up and said tearfully, "I'm going to surgery tomorrow." I said that I knew and that she is worried about it. She started to shake her head negatively but then slowly changed and said, "Yes, I am." I asked if she wanted to tell me about it. She said, "There's a sticker up my spine and it hurts a whole lot." I said I knew it hurt and asked if she was afraid of what would happen tomorrow. She nodded her head. There was silence, during which time she stared intently at my earrings. She asked, "May I see your earring?" I took one off and gave it to her. She patted it very lovingly and said, "My mother has a lot of earrings." This was the first time she had ever mentioned her mother. I said it must be hard for her not to be able to have her mother here when she goes into surgery. She agreed but said she understood. Then she asked if she could touch the pretty buttons on my blouse. She touched them slowly, each one. I knew she was grasping for every bit of security she could find and that I was in a mother role with her. While she was playing with my buttons, she began to cry again softly and said, "I can't be in the play group any more." I said she certainly could. She couldn't be there tomorrow or perhaps for several days, but then she'd be able to come. She said she really could not come, because she would have to be lying on her bed. I said I knew that, but it didn't matter because we could move her bed or have the meeting around her bed. This pleased her very much and she relaxed visibly.

In groups, transferences are not always of a member to the worker; they often occur between the members, as in this example.

In a group of women, Mrs. J. glowered at Mrs. P. when the worker asked Mrs. J. to wait until Mrs. P. had a chance to speak. Mrs. P. asked Mrs. J. why she was angry with her. Mrs. J. looked startled and then said, "Well, I've a right to be angry—you cut me off." Mrs. B. said, "But the rest of us have a right to talk, too." Mrs. P. said she could not understand why Mrs. J. acted so strongly against her. Mrs. J. did not reply. There was a silence, which I did not interrupt. Mrs. J. broke the silence, saying that she did react too strongly; Mrs. P. had done nothing to her. I commented that I was the one who had requested that Mrs. P. be given a chance to speak. Mrs. B. asked Mrs. J. if she might be jealous of Mrs. P. because the worker had turned her attention away from Mrs. J. and toward Mrs. P. Mrs. W. said she agreed with that idea, commenting that it was natural to be jealous of the attention that another member receives, "just like children who want the mother's attention all to themselves." The members all laughed at this, including Mrs. J. Mrs. W., in a light manner, said that the group sometimes acted like a family of kids who get jealous of each other. Mrs. J. thought it was natural for kids to feel this way but not for adults. The members continued to talk about the incident and reassured Mrs. J. that other adults often reacted as she had done.

That illustration shows clearly the way in which the use of group process enhances the members' understanding of relationships.

Identifications

As members interact with each other and with a professional practitioner, identifications may be formed. Identification is one form of imitation whereby a person feels like another person. It is a process through which a person adopts some real or imagined attitude, pattern of behavior, or value of another person and through which the desired aspect becomes integrated into the ego. It becomes a part of a person's sense of identity. It is largely an unconscious process, for the person is seldom aware that he or she is modifying some aspect of self to be like another person. Positive identifications are based on admiration of another person, but there can also be negative identifications based on fear. In the latter instance, identification is a defense; Anna Freud demonstrates how anxiety may be warded off through identification with an aggressor.[18] This often happens when a group is influenced by one member who initiates behavior that immediately stimulates the others to participate in similar ways. As a group develops cohesiveness, positive identification takes place also with the group as an entity. The values and norms of the group then become incorporated into the personalities of the participating members.

Group Acceptance

As described earlier, a feeling that one is accepted in a group and that one, in turn, accepts other members is a powerful therapeutic factor. Acceptance denotes the quality of being regarded favorably by the group to the extent that continued interaction with others is possible without undue stress. As members feel accepted, their self-esteem rises. They become more open to new ways of feeling and thinking and feel comfortable enough to reveal some of their feelings, aspirations, and concerns to others. They can dare to look at the unacceptability of some of their behavior, using that knowledge for growth and change. As they feel accepted, members tend to enhance their identification with the group which, in turn, enhances the group's impact on their attitudes and behavior.

Mutual Aid

One major reason that the group can become a potent force for development and change is that group practice builds on the powerful interdependency of people. This is mutual aid. To be sure, it is mutual aid in a group with a professional worker who has a distinctive role in the group. The group provides a give-and-take situation that may reduce feelings of inadequacy or difference and of dependency on the worker. In any healthy relationship, each participant carries a contributing, as well as a taking, role. Alice Overton and Katherine Tinker emphasize that "shrinkage in self-esteem and resentment occur when people are only the recipients of help — they relate better to people who use and appreciate what they can contribute."[19] Altruism is one of the therapeutic forces. This very potential poses problems, however, for many persons who are inadequate in their abilities to enter into the give and take of group participation. The potential value of the group will depend upon whether a member can be helped to find acceptance and to move into interdependence with others. This process results in a feeling of belonging to the group, another of the major dynamic forces for change in groups.

Subgroup Alliances

As members of a group come to discover what they have in common, various subgroups and alliances develop that express common interests, mutuality of feelings of attraction or repulsion, or needs for control or inclusion. These subgroups reflect the personal choices, interest, and interpersonal feelings of the members, not always on a conscious level. Members with reciprocal interpersonal needs tend to find each other. Isolates, pairs, and triads combine to form a pattern, often described as the interpersonal structure of a group.[20]

The smallest subgroup is the pair or dyad, which is the most intimate and personal of all patterns of relationships. Dyadic relationships include mutual pairs in which the give and take between the members is about equal, courtship pairs in which one person is seeking and the other being sought after, dominant-dependent pairs in which one tends to control and the other to defer, sadist-masochist pairs in which one is attacked by the other but seems relieved by it, and complementary pairs in which the qualities and needs of one supplement those of the other. In the pair, harmony brings greater advantages than in any other relationship, and discord brings greater disadvantages.

The triad, or group of three persons, is another subgroup to be understood. It is famous in fiction as the love triangle for the reason that a third person has an effect on the pair; in a group of three, there is often the rivalry of two for the affection or attention of one. The triad may consist of a mediator and two others between whom there is conflict. There may be a two-person coalition against one. A third person may increase the solidarity of the pair or may bring discord into the relationship. Often a triad evolves into a pair and an isolate, or, through the addition of another person, into a double pair. Larger subgroups comprise various combinations of isolates, dyads, and triads. As the group increases in size, subgroups tend to become more prominent.

In the formation of subgroups, the generalization that "birds of a feather flock together" is contradicted by the equally accepted idea that "opposites attract." There are indications, however, that proximity in school, work, or residence, the presence of similar individual characteristics such as age, gender, race, and ability, common interests and values, and complementarity in patterns of needs influence the differential degree of intimacy between members of a group. The more lasting subgroups often stem from strong identifications or similarity of symptoms. In evaluating the emergence of subgroups, the basic questions concern the way in which they relate to the group as a whole, whether there is cooperation or conflict between the subsystems, and whether they are functional for the particular tasks of the group at a given time. Subgroups may at times interfere with the group's effectiveness and cohesion, but they may at least as often contribute to individual and group development.

Sociograms are schemes for depicting the subgroups and alliances that emerge in a group. They show the web of socioemotional ties between members of a group.[21] Originally, the sociogram was constructed from the confidential responses of members to requests that they choose which members they like and which ones they dislike or with whom they would or would not choose to participate in a given activity. More recently, they have been constructed from the leaders's own observations of the interactions between members at a given time. When these attractions and repulsions are charted, the status of each individual and subgroup is revealed, which may assist leaders in their assessment of the strengths and problems in intermember relationships. By comparing sociograms of a group constructed at different times, the stability and shifts in patterns become clear. An example of a sociogram is presented below.[22]

This sociogram reveals the composition of the group in terms of gender; a complex pattern of attractions and repulsions between the members and whether these are mutual or one way; the lack of a strong leader among the members; a member who is a near isolate having a positive reciprocated tie with only one member; pairs and triads; and the relationships between male and female members.

Sociograms can be used to indicate different aspects of relationships. Instead of gender, for example, the symbols may be race, religion, education, or experience. Or it can chart more than one variable by using additional symbols or colors to give a quick snapshot of the group at a given time.

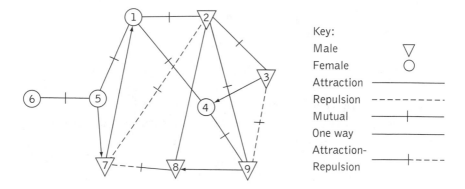

FIGURE 3.1 Typical Sociogram

Helping Relationships

The nature and quality of social workers' relationships with groups, sub-groups, and individuals have an important effect on the achievement of goals and the development of the group. Social workers develop a unique relationship with each member and of equal importance with the group. That relationship may call for interviews with members individually, outside the group, as well as giving them differential attention within the group. As stated by Helen Phillips:

> The worker's relation to each member is important, but if he is to accelerate the group relations and help members to use them, he will need to modify the many diverse, individual strands of his relationship with the members so that they will be in process with each other and so that he will have a connection with the group as a whole.[23]

Within the group, whatever the worker does that is directed toward a particular member influences the group as a whole. Grace Coyle said it this way:

> It seems to me that the primary skill is the ability to establish a relationship with a group as a group. This involves the capacity to feel at ease, in fact, to enjoy the social interplay among members and to be able to perceive both individual behavior and its collective manifestations . . . as well as to become a part of the relationships and to affect them.[24]

If social workers have a connection with the group system, they also simultaneously view the individuals, the network of relationships, and the environment. The complexity makes special demands on workers who seek to develop and sustain a relationship that is sensitive to the feelings of members toward them and toward each other as these influence the climate of the group. Within these expectations, there is ample room to respond appropriately to different members in different ways at different times.

The Fiduciary Relationship

The social work relationship, according to Herb Kutchins, is a fiduciary one—that is, it is based on trust and used only for the benefit of others.[25] Ethically, practitioners should act in accordance with the highest standards of integrity, without discriminating against anyone. They act in the best interests of the members and should not take advantage of them to promote their own needs and interests. They may not use their power to exploit or harm clients. The relationship between the worker and each member is a crucially important component of practice.

It may seem strange that a practitioner in a helping profession would need to be reminded of the ethical principle of honesty. Yet there are times when, unwittingly perhaps, the principle is violated. Workers have been known to deceive their members by promising confidentiality beyond their power to guarantee it. They have withheld information from members, attempted to cover up mistakes they have made, or lied about their feelings toward certain members. They need to find ways to recognize their feelings and mistakes and then disclose them in a way that enhances, rather than detracts from, the member-group-worker relationship.

Characteristics of Helping Relationships

A supportive helping relationship requires a set of values, attitudes, and interpersonal skills that reflect social workers' concerns for their members. Understanding the importance of supportive relationships was enhanced by Carl Roger's famous research on what he called the "therapeutic triad" that comprised the necessary and sufficient conditions for the success of counseling.[26] These conditions were designated as empathic understanding, unconditional positive regard, and congruence. Later, these were renamed accurate empathy, nonpossessive warmth, and genuineness or authenticity. The results of many studies indicate that there is a positive relationship between these attributes and positive outcomes of treatment. In social work, Baruch Levine describes the practitioner's role as a nurturer of these qualities in the initial phase, gradually moving to the facilitation of these qualities among the members as the group develops.[27]

Acceptance

Nonpossessive warmth is a term that indicates a practitioner's acceptance of, or love for, a client. It means caring for clients as unique persons with a right to have their own feelings and thoughts. This quality is similar to what social workers usually call acceptance. Mary Woods and Florence Hollis defined acceptance as "the maintaining of an attitude of warm goodwill toward the client, whether or not his or her way of behaving is socially acceptable and whether or not it is to the worker's personal liking."[28]

Evidence of an attitude of acceptance include showing genuine interest in members, giving them recognition, listening sensitively to what they say, paying attention to what they do, communicating a desire to be helpful, and really caring about them. It is indicated by many small actions of courtesy, greeting members in ways appropriate to their cultural traditions, and calling them by their preferred form of address. Acceptance of members requires self-awareness concerning differences in values, tendencies to stereotype, and being able to care about clients who have engaged in violence, child or spouse abuse, neglect of children or older adults, for example. Acceptance does not mean approval of behavior. Where behavior is hurtful to self or others, the message is clear: "I accept and care about you as a person, but I cannot accept that behavior."

Empathy

An anonymous English writer is credited with the statement that empathy means "to see with the eyes of another, to hear with the ears of another, and to feel with the heart of another."[29] Rogers defined empathy as "the ability of the therapist to perceive experiences and feelings accurately and sensitively and to understand their meanings."[30] It has both affective and cognitive aspects. David Berger reported that the term *empathy* first appeared in a literary context in 1903 as the "English equivalent of the German *einfuhling,* 'to feel with' or 'to feel within.' "[31] People are empathic if they are sensitive to the needs and feelings of others. In social work, Mary Woods and Florence Hollis have a similar definition. They define empathy as "the capacity to enter into and grasp the inner feelings or subjective state of another person."[32] Thomas Keefe also describes the use of empathy in social work practice.[33] Saul Scheidlinger has related these ideas to groups.[34] A person's intimate feelings and concerns can be discovered and evaluated only if the worker and the members are involved in the same situation. When the worker can feel with the members and communicate that understanding to them, then members tend to feel free to explore their feelings and concerns. When members sense that the responses to their messages are attempts to understand, rather than to judge, it is not necessary for them to cling to defensive distortions of communication. James Raines has reminded us that "empathy can never be stated; it must also be demonstrated."[35]

Empathy in work with groups is a process that involves several sets of behavior:

1. Accurate understanding of each member's strengths and problems in group participation.
2. Based on that understanding, sensitive anticipation of the feelings and concerns that members may bring to the group, referred to by William Schwartz as "tuning in."
3. Facilitation and acceptance of members' expressions of positive and negative feelings.
4. Imaginative reflection on the particular member's or group's messages, feeling what it might be like to "walk in their shoes."
5. Awareness of one's own feelings toward members and reactions to what is going on, being able to separate one's feelings from those of members. That lessens the likelihood of imposing one's own values and emotions on others and making faulty judgments about others.
6. Accurate reception of messages sent by members, based on sensitive observation and listening.
7. Accurate feedback to the members, necessitating the verbal facility to communicate understanding in language that can be grasped by recipients of the message. Also involved is the use of paraverbal messages and nonverbal acts, which convey a desire to understand.
8. Involvement of members in learning to empathize with one another by asking questions and making comments that focus on their feelings as like or different from the feelings of others.

In groups, it is not just the social worker who exhibits empathy but, more important, the members who become able to empathize with each other. In their article on work with groups of women who have been sexually abused, Linda Schiller and Bonnie Zimmer give a clear example. Stated one survivor:

> I was alternatively enraged and saddened by what I was hearing from the other group members about their abuse as children. I was so struck by the innocence and helplessness of Sally when I looked at the pictures from her childhood which she brought in to show the group when it was her week to tell her story. And then it suddenly hit me for the first time ever . . . that I, too, was once a little girl, and that if it wasn't Sally's fault that she was abused, then maybe it wasn't mine either. I flashed back to a picture of myself in my green plaid jumper and white blouse with the Peter Pan collar, and thought, "My God, I was only five years old then."

"Through extending compassion and empathy to others, and by seeing the similarities between themselves and others in the group, the survivor can then move to a place of self-forgiveness."[36] The authors refer to this phenomenon as the concept of self-empathy.

Authenticity

Authenticity or genuineness is the third ingredient of a helping relationship. The words *authenticity* and *genuineness* are synonymous, defined as not false or copied, agreement with known facts or experiences, reliable, sincere, trustworthy. Effective practitioners do not present a facade. To be genuine does not mean that the workers disclose their own feelings, problems, and experiences to the members, except for a carefully thought through purpose. It does mean that workers do not deceive the members about self or situations. Genuineness requires considerable self-awareness so that the workers' verbal messages become consonant with their feelings and they are able to control their negative or defensive responses so that they will not be harmful to others. What is effective is the absence of phoniness and defensiveness. Honesty and freedom from defensiveness provide a model for the members to emulate.

Authentic social workers admit their mistakes, fulfill the conditions of their contracts, provide rather than withhold knowledge, and answer members' questions according to their assessment of the meaning of the question and the members' needs. Telling the truth is an ethical principle: it is the essence of authenticity. Yet the quality of the relationship in which truth is told is crucial. Norman Cousins, in writing about medicine, said that "certainly the physician had the obligation to tell the truth but he also had the obligation to tell it in a way that did not leave the patient in a state of emotional devastation—the kind of emotional devastation that could compromise effective treatment."[37] The same is true for social work.

A common concern of practitioners is how to respond to personal questions from members about their age, ethnicity, marital status, religion, or life experiences. There is not a simple answer. For example, a member of a group composed of married couples asks the worker, "We wonder if you are married." The response depends upon the worker's understanding of its meaning to the questioner and other members. An authentic response might be, "No, I'm not," and then wait for verbal or nonverbal responses from members. Or, the worker might add, "But maybe you wonder if that will affect my ability to help you." The worker's next message would depend upon the members' response to the statement. Members might ask questions that the worker prefers not to answer, thinking that to do so would not be in the best interests of the group. The response to the question, then, might be to convey the meaning, "I really don't want to talk here about that; sometimes a person wants to keep some things private," or, "Rather than answer that question, I'd like to try to understand what it would mean to you to know that." There should be no glib response to such questions.

The importance of authenticity to the members is indicated by statements in evaluations such as, "You kept your word," "We knew you wouldn't lie to us—we could trust you," or "As I look back, I'm glad you really leveled with me." The skills that contribute to the development of authenticity, based on professional ethics, include truth telling accompanied by empathy, examination of one's own feelings and biases in order to prevent them from harmful expression, and creation of a social environment that reduces social distance between the practitioner and members of the group.

Research on Relationships

Considerable evidence from counseling, psychology, and psychiatry indicates that the quality of the relationship is a necessary condition for positive outcomes. In a review of seventeen studies on relationship variables in groups that incorporated the qualities of acceptance, empathy, and genuineness, Robert Dies concluded that the results "generally demonstrate that the quality of the therapist-client relationship is important for group process and therapeutic outcome."[38]

Within social work, too, there is evidence that these qualities are primary factors in both continuance of treatment and positive outcomes.[39] That these qualities are important to outcome, even when distinctly different theoretical models are used, was supported by Arthur Schwartz's comparative study of behavior and psychodynamic approaches with two matched groups of clients.[40] The major finding was that successful patients in both groups rated "the interpersonal interaction with the therapist as the single most important part of their treatment."

In a more recent review of research in clinical social work, Mary Nomme Russell reported, "The conclusion reached by a majority of the studies has been that a positive relationship exists between these clinician attributes and client therapeutic gain."[41] She points out that the qualities can be viewed as independent variables of the practitioner or as a product of the client-worker relationship, to which both clients and workers contribute, referred to as "the therapeutic alliance." A positive alliance contributes to positive outcomes. From a systems perspective, it is clear that the attributes of clients and practitioners are interdependent. But it is the worker who is primarily responsible for influencing the process.

Evaluative research continues to support the importance of these qualities to successful outcomes. In his review of many studies, Nick Coady concluded that the therapeutic alliance was one of the best predictors of outcome, regardless of the therapeutic approach used. He noted that success involves collaboration between worker and clients and suggested that the helping process be reconceptualized along "empathic-collaborative lines."[42] Thomas Young and John Poulin reviewed three additional major studies of this subject in the 1990s, all with the same findings, even when the help given was limited to clinical management, as contrasted with treatment.[43] Research also provides evidence that, in spite of the importance of the qualities of acceptance, empathy, and authenticity in determining outcome, many practitioners do not have high levels of these qualities.[44] When they lack these qualities, they may be ineffective or even harmful to clients. Fortunately, there is evidence that these qualities can be learned. Supportive relationships are not inherited and their lack is not an unchanging aspect of personality, even though some people actually seem to have more of them than others do. These ingredients of effective relationships can be learned through training and education. That is the good news.

Use in Practice

A group is a "relationship laboratory." When there is a common purpose, the members talk, engage in activities, and relate to each other with a range of positive and negative feelings. Workers focus on both the content of the group and the ways members are relating to them and to one another. For, as expressed by Helen Perlman, "even when people are drawn together because of a like felt problem and are bent on investing themselves in its solution or mitigation, they have difficulty in holding to their tasks and purpose unless they are sustained and nourished in their group relationships."[45] That applies to task groups as well as support or therapeutic groups.

Supportive relationships in groups are a source of gain because the members have a sustained relationship with others without getting hurt; the relationships provide a safe environment. A person's intimate feelings and concerns can be discovered and evaluated only if there is mutual trust between the worker and each member and between the members. When the worker is genuine, empathic, and accepting, the members feel free to communicate their feelings, concerns, and ideas. When members perceive that the worker is attempting to understand, rather than to judge, it is not necessary for them to cling to dysfunctional defensive maneuvers. Group workers, however, often need to attend to members whose role functioning is destructive to other members or the group process while still demonstrating their caring and concern for them.

With some members, the relationship itself is a corrective emotional experience. It does not repeat the condemnations, abuse, rejections, or misuse of power that have characterized one or more of their significant relationships. These members often expect that practitioners will respond to them as they feel others have done. Through the worker's consistent attitudes, members are able to change those feelings and behaviors that have a destructive influence on their well-being.

Some social workers find it difficult to initiate and sustain effective relationships in groups because they become overwhelmed by the intensity and multiplicity of feelings and problems expressed. The intricacies of the relationships create challenges for the worker. To be able to accept, empathize

with, and communicate authenticity is not easy; the need for these qualities
may strain the capacities of the worker. Awareness of one's own responses is
essential in order to avoid distortions of perceptions to the extent that this is
possible. When it is the worker who transfers feelings and reactions from
earlier relationships onto one or more members, the term *countertransference* is used. Countertransference components of the relationship need to
be recognized, and if they are inimical to the progress of an individual or
the development of a group, they need to be understood and controlled.

Essential to the development of supportive relationships is intervening
with cultural sensitivity. As Charles Garvin pointed out, these interventions
are guided by values and ethics and by belief in the strengths of members.[46]
Continuing in this vein, Alicia Lieberman points out that cultural sensitivity
is not a general quality, owing to the large number of cultures and different
value systems within each culture. She stated that essential is

> interpersonal sensitivity, an attunement to the specific idiosyncrasies
> of another person. This has two major components: (1) knowing about
> the specific content of these idiosyncrasies, and (2) an attitude of open-
> ness about finding out about what we don't know. That means discov-
> ering and appreciating the values, beliefs, and traditions of a particular
> group, individual differences within that group, and awareness of one's
> own culture.[47]

Within the many commonalities between people of a particular culture,
attention to individual differences is fundamental. After all, individualization
is a basic principle of social work practice with groups. Acceptance of and
feeling empathy with a member require that workers be aware of the meaning of their own culture to them in order to avoid stereotyping members.
Flexibility is essential. According to Elaine Pinderhughes, it is demonstrated
when one has "general knowledge about a cultural group and sees the specific way in which knowledge applies, or does not apply, to a given client.[48]

Understanding and coming to terms with the values of their own important reference groups is necessary for those who hope to understand the
values of other people. Konopka points out that the worker needs "to realize
that he sees others through the screen of his own personality and his own
life experiences. . . . This is why a social worker must develop enough awareness of at least the make-up of his own particular screen."[49] Fortunately,
workers may correct this screen through careful analysis of their own be-

havior in relation to others and through the use of supervision or consultation. Such efforts help them to take into account their own biases, even though they cannot completely eliminate them, and thus make it possible to understand better the persons with whom they work.

If social workers can come to accept, empathize with, and be genuine with the persons with whom they work, they will not need to worry about using the professional relationship for purposes inimical to the well-being of the members. To relate to others with these qualities is not dependent upon long duration of the relationship. The workers' attributes can be conveyed in short-term, as well as long-term, involvement. Workers can communicate these intentions to the members of the group only if they truly possess the qualities.

Power

A professional relationship conveys acceptance, empathy, and genuineness. It also carries authority in that the social worker assumes some degree of leadership in influencing the initiation and development of the group. Paul Pigors explains that this authority is vastly different from the exercise of authoritarian power over others for personal gratification or for the achievement of one's own ends.[50] The authority is derived from knowledge, professional skill, and power invested in the worker by the agency or other institution. It is also derived from the power the members give the leader to influence them. The nature and degree of the worker's influence on individuals and the group process vary with the capacities of the members to cope with the demands of group life, to participate in the group, and to make their own decisions. When members are unable to cope with a situation, then workers actively use their authority. On the other hand, when the members are able to participate responsibly, workers support the group's autonomy. When, on rare occasions, workers must use coercive authority because members are hurting each other, destroying property, or engaging in such behavior as child abuse, which must by law be reported, the coercive authority is vested in the professional role and in its legal sanctions.

Social workers do not first form a relationship and then get to work. The relationship develops as workers help the members to work on the socio-emotional and problem-solving tasks of each stage of group development.

Relationships Beyond the Group

Social workers are concerned not only with the relationships with and between members but also with the relationships that the members have with their significant others. The term *significant others* refers to any person or group who has a strong influence on the clients' psychosocial functioning and the opportunities in the environment that are available to the client. In addition to the clients' relationships with significant others, the social worker often has relationships with such significant persons as well. The nature and quality of the social workers' relationships with such persons may hamper or facilitate the effectiveness of their service. The purposes for which supportive relationships are developed with significant others may be to exchange information about the members and their situations in enhancing joint understanding, to influence the attitudes and actions of the others toward the member or group, to develop a plan for working together for the benefit of the members, and to secure access to essential services and resources.

Members of groups belong to families, each with its own particular physical and social environment. When social workers have contacts with members' families, supportive relationships are important, but often more difficult. In work with children, for example, workers may tend to blame the parents for the child's difficulties rather than strive to understand their feelings and situations. Practitioners who accept and empathize with members of the family will recognize and focus on the strengths in the family and relate to each member differentially, based on their understanding of the family's goals, culture, and roles. They will focus on strengthening the relationship of the member of their group to the family and of the family to other social institutions.

Collaboration

Social workers seldom operate autonomously; rather, they collaborate with colleagues and members of other disciplines. It is clear that many members of groups have multiple needs; therefore, multiple services are required. The group experience is one part of a larger multimodality plan of services for a given member or family, making it necessary to develop and sustain working relationships with the other persons involved in providing the services.

In the field of health, for example, group workers collaborate with physicians, nurses, physical and occupational therapists; in mental health, with psychiatrists and psychologists; in schools, with principals, teachers, and guidance counselors; in family and children's services, with foster and adoptive parents, attorneys, residential treatment personnel; and in occupational social work with employers, job specialists, and colleagues.

Successful collaboration requires that social workers develop accepting and genuine relationships with other personnel, respecting the special expertise of colleagues in their own and other disciplines. It requires that social workers be able to communicate clearly the purpose of their own profession and the place of group work within it, without defensiveness.[51]

An example is of a social worker who met with an influential physician who, in a meeting of the interdisciplinary team, had strongly objected to the organization of a parent's group in a children's hospital. In the meeting, the worker stated her desire to understand his point of view. Through listening to him, she learned that he thought positive parent-child relationships were important to the child's treatment. The worker expressed full agreement with this position. The physician then went on to explain his opposition to the group. She learned that he feared that the meetings would be gripe sessions that would undermine his relationships with parents. Expressing understanding of this concern, the worker was able to explain the purpose of the group as being in harmony with his view of the importance of relationships between parent and child and between them and the hospital staff. She described the anticipated content of the group, and responded to his comments and questions in language appropriate to the situation. The physician said he was satisfied and would let the team know that he approved of the group. He offered to help make it a success.

To achieve effective collaborative relationships, Bess Dana has proposed several principles to guide practitioners:

1. Acceptance of the need to begin where one's colleagues are.
2. Respect for differences in values, knowledge, and problem-solving styles and capacities.
3. Willingness to share one's own knowledge, values, and skills, even when they may conflict with the knowledge, values, and skills of others.

4. Willingness to work through, rather than avoid, conflicts.
5. Willingness to change or modify the definition of the problem to be addressed, or the means of addressing it, on the basis of new understanding derived from the perceptions and interpretations that other practitioners hold of both the problem and the ways of dealing with it.
6. Ability to use group process as a means for meeting the salient demands of collaborative practice.[52]

The social worker with a group may be the person who has responsibility for integrating appropriate resources in the organization or community as an important component of the plan of service for one or more members. The plan then becomes a community-based approach to providing multiple services to persons with special needs. The quality of relationships between the persons who participate in the endeavor will make a difference in the failure or success of the plan.

4   Intervention in Groups

The role of the social worker in reciprocal interaction with the members of a group consists of a sequence of patterns of behavior and attributes expected of the practitioner by the profession of social work, employers, licensing organizations, and the persons who are served. The social worker's is an achieved role, earned through education and experience. Within the group, actual behaviors are influenced by the group's purpose, content, and structure and the members' needs and expectations. One of the advantages of the use of groups in social work is that stimulation toward improvement of social functioning arises from a network of interpersonal influence in which all members participate. Thus, the practitioner is one important influence, but so too is each member of the group.

Through mutual aid, the dynamic forces emerge and facilitate the positive use of the group by its members. These factors, presented in the first chapter, are what make the group the modality of choice in many situations in which people need help in improving their interpersonal relationships, combating low self-esteem, coping with life transitions and traumatic events, and developing skills essential for satisfactory role performance. These forces do not operate automatically; far from it, the worker's major task is to facilitate their development and use in relation to the group's goals. Social workers influence the quality of group interaction. They cannot fail to influence the group's patterns of communication, norms, roles, subgroups, and problem-solving processes. The focus on individual needs of members is important as well, but cannot in reality be separated from what is going on in the group as a system. What goes on in the group is dependent upon interactions between the members and the impact of environmental forces on individuals and the group. In providing service to a group, social workers do not limit their focus to the internal workings of the group. They often engage in conferences with the families of group members, briefly or as part of a treatment plan. They are continuously engaged with the organization that sponsors the group and with numerous systems in the community. Thus, they have a constellation of subroles to fulfill: counselor or therapist, resource provider, educator, liaison or broker, collaborator, and consultant.

The primary task of the social worker is to facilitate the group process, so that the group truly becomes a prime influence on the behavior of its members. A committee of psychiatrists wrote:

> The key question, we believe, is whether we therapists can become completely aware of the ever changing and flowing reality of this process, and then conceptualize from our awareness. . . . Process may be viewed as the dynamic interaction of all the phenomenological aspects of the therapy, encompassing all overt as well as covert interactional expressions of feelings, thoughts, and actions occurring over time. . . . We need to appreciate what went before, what is happening now, and dimly what is portended in the future.[1]

Facilitating the process of the group toward achievement involves motivating and assisting members to participate actively and collaboratively in the process. The worker is concerned with participation in the process because the primary means of help when using a group are the support and challenge that members give each other, supplemented by the worker's direct contributions to the work of the members. Changes in attitudes and behavior occur when members are actively involved in the group—when they are able both to give and to take from others. They benefit from perceiving both their likenesses to and differences from others. Thus, the focus is on the development of meaningful group interaction without losing concern for individuals. Sharing of feelings, thoughts, and experiences is necessary so that all of the members can become aware of what others are feeling and thinking and use this knowledge for appraisal of their own feelings, thoughts, and actions. The satisfaction of each member is essential to the development of cohesive groups that influence their members positively.

Social workers need, therefore, to make sure that the group becomes a mutual aid and mutual need-meeting system. As Joseph Anderson has pointed out, "The essence of group process . . . is mutual aid."[2] Workers attempt to maximize the dynamic forces so that the group becomes the primary instrument of help. Focus on the group does not negate the importance of the individual. When the focus is on interpersonal interaction, neither the individual nor the group is submerged: both are viewed as equally important. Neither can be fully understood without the other.

Clusters of Interventive Skills

Relationships, as discussed in the preceding chapter, are crucial elements of practice with groups, but effective problem-solving requires that social workers make other contributions to developing and intervening in the group interaction. How to describe the complex constellation of means by which workers use their personalities, values, knowledge, and skills to help a group is a thorny problem. Writers use different terms to describe the set of interventions from which practitioners select a particular one, according to their cumulative understanding of the person-group-environment situation at a given time. These clusters of interventions are often referred to as procedures, techniques, or skills. In spite of the different terms that are used, there is considerable agreement about types of interventions to achieve particular goals. The major clusters of skills are structuring, support, exploration, information-education, advice-guidance, confrontation, clarification, and interpretation.

This typology of interventive acts is based on Marian Fatout's content analysis of major books on practice and on the research of several other social group workers, including Anne Marie Furness, Frank Peirce, and Lynn Videka-Sherman.[3] The formulations of techniques of skills that are most similar to the one offered here are those of Pallassana Balgopal and Thomas Vassil, Thomas Carlton, Paul Ephross, and Alex Gitterman.[4] Other writers' inventories of skills, including those by Harvey Bertcher, Ruth Middleman and Gale Goldberg Wood, and Lawrence Shulman have been incorporated, when possible, into the categories used here.[5] These skills are used in work with various types of groups, although the frequency of their use may vary and some may be emphasized more than others. It is interesting that, in a comparative study of socialization and treatment groups, Gideon

Horowitz found that the same skills are used with both types of groups: they are generic.[6]

The social worker's actions or use of skills are viewed as a reflection on instrumentality of the worker's intentions. Each major action is based on an intent. William Gordon referred to this notion of intent as "the concrete ends toward which daily social work practice is directed."[7] These intents reflect workers' values, goals, and understanding of individuals, the group, and the environment at a given time.

Structuring

People are influenced to move toward achievement of their goals through participation in a group whose structure meets their needs and provides direction for their interactions. The objective of structuring is to create an optimal environment for work. Structuring includes techniques to assure the flexible use of policies and administrative procedures, preparation for sessions, the use of space and time, the definition of limits, selection of a pattern of communication, and focusing discussion and activity.

Policies and procedures   Flexible use of policies and ways of work of an agency provide a framework within which the worker and the members operate. The agency is one social system in a network of interlocking systems that comprise the institutional/organizational environment as conceptualized by Susan Kemp, James Whittaker, and Elizabeth Tracy and by Charles Garvin.[8] The environment has a profound influence on the agency's program, policies, and resources. To work together effectively, the worker and members need to be clear about the policies and procedures concerning purposes of service, use of time, duration and frequency of sessions, fees, principles of confidentiality, and the major focus and content of the group. Such agreements provide a boundary within which the worker and members are free to operate. These policies and procedures should be used flexibly and changed in accordance with the needs and capacities of the members. Achieving clarity about the structure of the service reduces ambiguity and confusion and thereby provides support so that energies can be released for working toward the agreed upon goals. Within the requirements, the plan for a particular group provides the framework for the group's operations.

Preparation for meetings   Before each group meeting, workers prepare in an effort to enhance its value for the members. They review pertinent records or other data to clarify the direction of their efforts. They follow up on members who might have been absent the time before. They make decisions about whether new members should be admitted or visitors allowed to attend. They secure the necessary equipment and supplies to be used by the group and set the stage by arranging the physical environment, because space carries psychological meaning for those who use it. It provides a boundary and anchor for a given set of actions.[9]

Definition of limits   Limits, restrictions on behavior, are important forms of structuring. They provide outer boundaries or parameters for behavior. Fatout described how providing limits is an empowering process. Within realistic boundaries, members are able to discover the power and control that is available to them.[10] They need to learn to meet realistic demands and to be protected from the destructive tendencies of self and others. Limits provide a sense of safety, diminishing fears of going too far and losing control of oneself. Initial rules are replaced by the group's own norms as sources of limits. Such limits are more acceptable than the use of power by the worker in the form of punishment or negative criticisms. Some people need to learn to overcome excessively rigid conformity to policies and rules so as to develop spontaneity in relationships and to use their capacities in more creatively adaptive ways. They need permission to try out different modes of behavior. The social worker needs to balance the use of permissiveness and limits, based on differential assessment of the individuals and the group as a whole. Structural controls are not ends in themselves but serve as a means to the goal of self-control and self-direction.

Selecting a pattern of communication   Social workers strive to influence the structure of communication that evolves in a group. Middleman and Goldberg Wood have described several patterns used in groups.[11] In the round robin, each member takes a turn in presenting certain information to the group, a useful way to make introductions or to secure a variety of facts, ideas, or feelings quickly. In an individual-centered pattern, one member engages with the worker in an extended back and forth discussion while other members watch and listen. In a leader-centered pattern, all messages are sent through the leader. An agenda-controlled pattern is most frequently used in task or educational groups. In formal organizations, such as boards of directors, *Robert's Rules of Order* determine when, how, and to whom participants may speak about what.

The usual pattern of communication in support and therapeutic groups is a group-centered one, referred to as free-floating. This open system, based on the right of each member to be recognized and heard, increases the likelihood that members will help each other to achieve individual as well as group goals. Positive changes are facilitated by interaction that is honest, clear, sincere, and related to the needs of members. Workers promote such a system of communication through the quality of their relationships and through encouraging participation and involvement of members in the group's activities, with sensitivity to each member's capacities and needs.

Focusing   One important skill of structuring is focusing, that is, guiding the flow of verbal communication or the sequence of an activity toward content that is relevant to the group's purpose at a given time. The intent is to maintain the focus of attention, bring it back to a previous situation, or move to a new issue. Workers monitor the pace of the group so that the members do not become confused or lose interest. They try to ensure, for example, that each member has an opportunity to participate so that domination by one member or a subgroup does not persist, agreed upon norms are not violated, and situations detrimental to one or more members are recognized and dealt with. Members do expect practitioners to provide guidance so that the most productive use is made of the time available. When members do not use time productively, workers comment or ask questions that focus the members' attention on an issue of importance to their use of the group. Workers may reinforce the importance of continuing further with what is going on, call attention to the observation that one member's contribution has not been picked up on, comment that the group seems to have shifted its attention, or request that the group stay with the discussion longer. Whatever the comment or question, they seek responses from members to it and may need to elaborate on the reason for the concern.

Support

Support is a basic form of human interaction and is perhaps the most essential of the psychosocial skills. Support is defined by Steve Duck, a psychologist, as "those behaviors that, whether directly or indirectly, communicate to an individual that he or she is valued and cared for by others."[12] Gregory Pierce, Barbara Sarason, and Irvin Sarason state that support "is perceived by the recipient or intended by the provider to facilitate coping in everyday life, and especially in response to stressful situations."[13]

In everyday life, social support is generally received through relationships with members of a person's social network. A network is a social system composed of people who are interconnected with others in some way— through family ties, friendships, acquaintances, colleagues at work or school, and organizations. In a network, there is an exchange of emotional and material resources to meet human needs.[14] Many members of groups lack an adequate social network, in which case the group can become one important component of the members' networks and can help members to develop more adequate networks.

Types of support   Emotional and instrumental support are the two forms of support. Emotional support is the major form, within which four types have been identified.[15] The first is comfort and security given during a time of stress, resulting in the feeling of being cared for. The second form of emotional support is integration that results in a sense of belonging, gratifying basic affiliation needs. The third form is esteem support, that is, communication that bolsters a sense of competence and self-worth through emphasizing strengths and giving encouragement and realistic reassurance. The fourth type is altruism—the opportunity to provide nurturance to others, leading to the feeling of being needed by others, thereby enhancing self-esteem and motivation. There are indications that these forms of support are highly correlated with each other.

Instrumental support is the second form. One type of instrumental support is the provision of essential knowledge for understanding stress and problems and how to cope with them. The second form is tangible or material aid through the provision of goods, services, and other resources.

Literally hundreds of studies have been conducted that suggest that support from others improves people's abilities to cope with stress in their lives and also enhances their psychological well-being.[16] It is clear that within a supportive relationship the members of a group are enabled to feel secure, reassured, accepted, less anxious, and less alone. What is supported are the strengths and constructive defenses of persons in order that they may maintain a level of functioning or attain a better one. The aim is to support the ego in its efforts to cope with new or difficult situations. In systems terms, the steady state needs to be maintained in reasonable balance so that stress is not beyond the members' coping capacities.

The relationship between the worker and the group is itself a means through which the members are supported in their efforts to use the group for their mutual benefit. Workers set the tone for mutual support through expressing their own caring and the expectation that members will become able to do this too. To a large extent, the members support each other as they become aware of their common purposes, aspirations, interests, and needs and as they work out the positive and negative feelings toward each other. They become supportive of each other as they feel security and trust in the workers, as they come to identify with them and later integrate some of the worker's patterns of supportive behavior into their own personalities. In addition to relationship, the primary skills involved in support are the appropriate use of attending, realistic reassurance and encouragement, setting realistic expectations, and use of environmental resources.

Attending   Attending is essential in supporting one member, a subgroup, or the group as a whole. It is the ability to pay undivided attention to what is being said or done. Its purpose is to convey a message of respect and a feeling that what is being said or done is important. While essentially silent, workers are actively observing, listening sensitively, and following the flow of verbal and nonverbal communication. They note not only the manifest content but also the feelings behind it. They send back cues that they are interested in and understand the information through such nonverbal means as head nods, leaning toward the speaker, murmurs, and occasional paraphrasing or requests for elaboration. They involve the group in whatever is going on, even while paying attention to one member, through scanning the responses of all to the comments of one member.[17]

Encouragement   Encouragement is another powerful means of support. Many members need considerable encouragement to participate actively in the group. Workers encourage members to do so through such means as inviting participation or recognizing a particular contribution made by one member to another member or to the group as a whole. They express confidence that improvement in some area of concern to a member is possible and that they can be counted on to do their part to bring it about. They share their belief that participation in the group will be beneficial. Some realistic hope is necessary to develop and sustain motivation to enter into a group, remain in it, and make optimal use of the opportunities it provides. Hope is one of the dynamic forces that facilitate positive changes in individuals and the group's development. Members develop positive motivation when they are encouraged to remain in the group and to participate in varied discussions and social experiences in which they can feel success.

Realistic reassurance   Provision of realistic reassurance is an important skill in the use of support. Reassurance tends to reduce feelings of insecurity and anxiety. Persons often come into a new group, especially if they have been referred to it for help with a problem perceived by a relative or person in a position of authority, with feelings of stigma, abnormality, or guilt. A moderate level of stress may motivate a person to attain a goal, but when it is extreme it is disruptive and incapacitating. Workers provide reassurance through encouraging disclosure of feelings, accepting the feelings, and noting the universality of them when this is so. They encourage or limit the extent of the expression of feelings so that those expressed can be coped with at a given time, and thus they reassure members that the group is a safe environment. When realistic reassurance cannot be given, it is often helpful to acknowledge the difficulty and to suggest that ways can be found to improve the situation. False reassurance is not helpful; it usually stems from the worker's need to make things better or to deny the reality of the problematic situation. Along with encouragement, realistic reassurance instills hope that things can be better and thereby enhances motivation for trying to change oneself or one's situation.

Defining realistic expectations   Defining realistic expectations provides support to members. When they are clear about what is expected, the energies of members can become mobilized around the accomplishment of goals, rather than be tied up with anxiety and uncertainty about their own capacities, rights, and responsibilities in the situation. One realistic expectation is that members will become able to support each other, building upon the basic need of people to give to, as well as to take from, others. The question is how to set realistic expectations without arousing the members' fears that they will disappoint the worker or fail in the tasks. Workers need to demonstrate that they will continue to accept the members, regardless of their performance. Setting high expectations is a major contributor to positive outcomes, according to findings in a study of practice with overwhelmed clients by June Hopps, Elaine Pinderhughes, and Richard Shankar.[18]

Judicious use of humor   "Laughter is essential to life," wrote Alex Gitterman.

> Humor puts people at ease during initial contacts, as they enter un-
> familiar situations and meet professional strangers for the first time.
> Shared laughter serves as a social bridge and facilitates engagement
> and rapport. . . . It provides people with a common experience, akin
> to breaking bread together. It provides a commonality—a shared mo-
> ment.[19]

Humor, however, is too often used to ridicule or stereotype people who differ
from the humorist in some important respect. Gitterman goes on to inform
us that "effective humor is spontaneous, gentle, and well timed and requires
the capacity to laugh at oneself," not others.

Securing environmental support   Support from the social worker and
other group members needs to be augmented by support from parents,
spouses, or other relatives and from other social systems that directly influence the members and their use of the group. Since a group is a social
system that is connected with other social systems, it is influenced by and,
in turn, influences these other systems. Interviews with family members and
other significant persons in the members' social orbit may result in encouragement for the member to remain in the group and in the provision of
whatever resources are necessary for that to happen. When a child is the
group member, the minimal involvement of the parents is that of granting
permission for the child to be served for a particular purpose. Relatives may
be helped to consider how they can alter some of their behavior toward the
child. Married persons may support or sabotage the group treatment of their
partners. Joint or family interviews may often result in an increase of supportive behavior. The focus should be on strengthening the relationship of
the member to the family and of the family to other social institutions. In
residential settings, the attitudes of other social workers and members of
other professions likewise may or may not provide support for the clients'
use of a group service.

A complex process   Giving and receiving support sounds simple, but it
is a complex process. Not all attempts to offer support are successful: members may not be able to believe that someone can care about them and want

to be helpful or that they deserve to receive support. Workers' behaviors may be perceived as, and actually be, demeaning, intrusive, or insensitive.

Many times, what support a person has had may be eroded: the difficult behavior of one member makes it difficult for others to offer support. An example is of an adolescent whose delinquent behavior contributes to her parents' feelings of embarrassment and shame; the parents then do not try to elicit support from others. Some friends tend to avoid being around the child and family and often blame the parents for the child's difficulties. Parents of such children may earlier have had little support, and tend to become more isolated as their child's difficulties escalate. It becomes a vicious circle. A group may become an essential modality for helping such parents cut through this isolation and find support and appropriate help.

Support is a crucial component of the helping process in groups, whether the major purpose is socialization, psychoeducation, crisis intervention, or therapy. But support also applies to task or work groups, as discussed by Ephross and Vassil and Ronald Toseland and Robert Rivas.[20] Some groups are labeled "support" groups because they aim to have members support one another in their efforts to cope with a common problem.

Exploration

Exploration is one of the dominant sets of skills used in social work practice with groups. Exploration is used (1) to elicit information, feelings, and thoughts about the circumstances relevant to each member and to the group, the members' understanding of the group's purpose, goals, and ways of work, and (2) to ascertain the feelings and patterns of behavior of individuals and the relationships between the members of the group. In most exploratory work, there is almost simultaneous effort to obtain information to increase the worker's understanding of the members in their environments and to direct discussion or activity into productive channels for understanding self, other people, and situations.

Exploration of feelings   Exploration of feelings has been given much attention in practice theory. Support is an essential condition for the expression of genuine feelings and concerns. When they feel supported, members find courage to express feelings and thoughts that would be suppressed in usual situations, to expose some of their vulnerabilities, and to dare to risk trying new things. As feelings of love, satisfaction, competence, and happiness are expressed, these feelings are reinforced if the responses to them are supportive. Feelings of anger, sadness, hopelessness, hostility, and fear are also often expressed, usually leading to a reduction in anxiety. If persons can recognize the universality of these feelings, as well as their unique meaning to them, their anxiety tends to lessen. Feelings often lose some of their intensity and hold on a person once they are expressed to and accepted by others. But, more important, once expressed, feelings are open to examination and clarification. By being able to identify and describe a feeling, for example, a child may learn to substitute verbal symbols for harmful action. Ability to associate emotions with words supports the ego's capacity to cope with them.

Exploration includes, but goes beyond, ventilation. Irvin Yalom, in writing about therapeutic factors in groups, has observed that "the open expression of affect is without question vital to the group therapeutic process; in its absence a group would degenerate into a sterile academic exercise. Yet it is only a part process and must be complemented by other factors." He suggests that it is the "affective sharing of one's inner world and then the acceptance by others" that seems of paramount importance.[21] Not merely releasing the feelings but also exploring them with the other members is important.

Purposeful inquiry   Purposeful inquiry constitutes another of the skills within the category of exploration. Through it, workers give direction to the members' efforts to ascertain, expand, and clarify information. They ask questions and make comments to guide the members in providing essential information, referred to as the skill of probing.

Questioning   Questions asked by social workers tend to fall on a continuum from closed to open-ended. Closed questions are asked when specific information is sought about a member, the group, or situation. They are as simple as "Have you decided to join the group?" "Is that time satisfactory for all of you?" or "In what grade is Megan?" They require specific answers.

Open-ended questions are asked to seek description or elaboration of events, experiences, problems, and situations. They optimize self-determination in that they give the members the power to find their own style of communication and the content to be covered. The members can reveal their own subjective frames of reference and select those elements of their situations that are of greatest concern to them. The form might be "Could each of you tell us what you hope to get from being in this group?" or "How did we happen to get off of the subject of discipline?" or "What seems to be contributing to the difficulty?"

Open-ended questions may be used to test the perceptions that members have of their problems or the nature of the treatment. In a group of young children in a hospital, for example, the worker asked a five-year-old boy how come he had an IV on his arm. He said it was to keep him puffed up so he'd look normal—without it, he'd go down like a balloon. Another boy said he was in the hospital because his mother had just come home with a new baby that she liked better, so she traded him in. Another said that it was because "I peed too much." The perceptions may be accurate or distorted, a necessary piece of information for the worker.[22] The challenge for the worker is to explore in ways that do not feel like cross-examination, as often happens when one question after another is asked.

Commenting   Comments are usually more effective than questions in encouraging members to give information on pertinent matters, allowing for freedom to decide what to present and how to do it. The specific skills include (1) reflecting back, as when a social worker comments, "You said it was scary to come here at night all alone" (2) requests for elaboration such as "How were you able to convince your husband about that?" (3) sharing an observation, as when a worker says, "I noticed that you were listening intently when the videotape showed," (4) restating an idea to clarify a member's message, as "You were saying that . . . " (5) summarizing the theme, for example, "Today we talked about the divorce and its influence on your children," or "Perhaps you could add other things to what I've said."

Purposeful silence and sensitive listening   Purposeful silence and sensitive listening are powerful aids to self-revelation and examination of self and situation. Purposeful silence often indicates that a worker is listening and following what is being said. Such a stance tends to induce talkers to continue in the same vein. In other instances, purposeful silence indicates that clients are expected to mobilize their thoughts and then express them. A worker's personal need to fill in a short period of silence with words often interferes with members' efforts to get ready to share pertinent information.

Values of exploration   Exploration is one of the most frequently used clusters of techniques in work with groups and is an essential part of problem solving. When the practitioner gives inadequate attention to exploration of the nature and meaning of problems and alternative solutions, the results are often less than those desired. Inadequate consideration of alternative explanations and solutions leads to faulty assessment by the worker and the members and, therefore, to poor solutions or decisions. Barbara Solomon has shown how lack of attention to alternatives impedes the empowerment of oppressed populations; her warning is applicable to work with any group.[23] Some practitioners tend to shortcut exploration out of a desire to reach a resolution to a problem quickly. They accept a member's or the group's first proposal: the focus is on action—"What are you or we going to do?"—rather than on the means to achieve the best possible action—"How can we make a good decision?" "What is really going on here?" "What seems to be contributing to the difficulty?" as perceived by all of the members. Some practitioners may also be uncomfortable with the ambivalence, differences, and uncertainties that exploration often accelerates. So, in a rush to bring certainty to an issue or get busy with a task, workers may avoid or shortcut exploration. The process of exploration furnishes a necessary foundation for moving beyond eliciting and elaborating information to using the information for other helpful purposes.

Information-Education

The purpose of education is to provide new knowledge and skills required for coping with a particular situation. People often change if they know what is desirable and effective with respect to rational self-interests. Lack of knowledge contributes to ineffective functioning. Assimilation of information from the social environment is central to the process of problem solving in a group. Positive change may be influenced by an educational process that offers tools and resources useful to the members. One of the major tasks of the social worker, according to William Schwartz, is to contribute data—ideas, facts, and value concepts—that are not available to the members and may prove useful to them in attempting to cope with the part of the social reality involved in the problems with which they are working.[24]

Providing information   Knowledge is one road to ego mastery; it provides security and is a source of power. Sharing information, rather than withholding it, provides the best safeguard against dependency upon the worker. Knowledge is provided or new skills taught when the material is clearly relevant to the members' situations and when they do not have ready access to the information. The information that is shared needs to be accurate: the worker needs to know the facts and how they relate specifically to a particular member's or the group's needs.

People often need new information or reinforcement of knowledge to make sound decisions about themselves and other persons who are significant to them. They often need specific details about community resources and their use. They often need to understand general principles of human growth and development or the implications of an illness or physical handicap for themselves or their families. They need information about laws that affect them concerning such events as abortion, marriage, adoption, divorce, discrimination in housing or jobs, and consumer protection. They need to know about expectations for effective performance of such social roles as parent, marriage partner, friend, student, employee, or patient.

Information is given in ways that relate clearly to the purpose of the group and the goals of the members. Workers do not rigidly follow a fixed agenda or outline. They pay attention to the psychosocial and cognitive needs of the members at a given time. They offer the information briefly in language that can be understood by the members, and in a tentative manner, making clear that it is open to examination by members who may question and refute it. They clarify to what extent the information given is based on facts or opinions. When workers observe nonverbal cues that indicate doubt or skepticism or disagreement with the information, they seek feedback and encourage expression of feelings and alternative ideas. "You look puzzled," "You may not agree with that," "That seems to upset you," or "How do you see it?" are comments and questions that stimulate the members to come to grips with the issue being addressed. There may be a need to go beyond imparting information to assisting members to recognize and cope with their emotional reactions to the information through the use of exploration and clarification. Rosalie Kane has reminded us that education and therapy are closely akin.[25] Emotions and relationships can obscure educational messages, and members need help to bridge the cognitive and affective aspects of learning.

Modeling   Modeling is simply providing an example for imitation or comparison. The worker or a member demonstrates how to do something or communicate a message in an appropriate manner. The modeling may demonstrate an action-oriented experience or be part of role playing a situation of concern to members. The members then attempt to copy the modeled behavior through rehearsal. Modeling is not always a planned activity. It occurs as members observe the worker or a particular member and, through the process of identification, incorporate the behavior they desire to emulate into their personalities.

Summarizing   To summarize is to make a statement that draws together and briefly restates the essence of a particular presentation or discussion. It is often used at the beginning of a session so members can recall what happened at the last meeting and to orient new members, or those who were absent, to the group's work. It is often used to review the major points made about an issue to move discussion ahead or to remind the members of the progress made when ending a session. It is often preferable to have members, rather than the worker, summarize and seek responses from others. It reinforces what was previously learned. It has a bridging effect, suggesting what lies ahead.

Advice-Guidance

Advice is a form of direct influence that suggests or recommends a particular course of action. Suggestions or recommendations, if carried out by the members, may further the attainment of the members' goals and provide an important source of emotional and cognitive stimulation.[26] Social workers share opinions, based on knowledge, and explain the reason for the advice, a form of information giving. They offer advice cautiously, so as not to hamper the members' efforts to arrive at their own decisions. They offer such advice as tentative ideas for consideration by the members rather than as commands. Although workers are often hesitant to give advice for fear of encouraging dependency, they probably do so more often than they acknowledge. Members resent advice at times and do not use it, but this is most often true when advice was not sought or when it was inappropriate to their needs.

Members often want and need advice from workers. They may perceive lack of advice as lack of interest in helping them. In a study of groups by Morton Lieberman, Irvin Yalom, and Mathew Miles, it was found that the members valued direct advice or suggestions given by the practitioner or other members of the group about how to deal with some life problem or important relationship. Those who made large gains in treatment marked this item as important significantly more often than did those who made few gains.[27] In another study, by Eric Sainsbury, it was indicated that clients tended to reject advice when it was perceived as an order to do something, but it was accepted when perceived as a suggestion for their consideration.[28]

This finding suggests that it is the way advice is given that makes a difference in its usefulness. In still another study, on the use of advice by eight social workers in a parent-counseling program, Inger Davis concluded that working-class parents received more advice than those of middle-class status did, all of the social workers gave some advice, and parents' reactions to advice tended to be more negative than positive. Parents also said, however, that they liked the workers to give advice and none wanted less advice than they received. This paradox may be resolved, according to Davis, by realizing that advice may serve an important therapeutic function other than guiding actions. It may stimulate a person to think of alternative ways for dealing with problems.[29]

Advice is generally accepted by, and useful to, members if it is what they really need, if it is presented in a way that connects it to the current life situation, if it is ego syntonic, if it is presented in a manner that conveys genuine interest in the person's welfare, and if the person's own decision-making processes are engaged in responding to the advice.

Suggesting and recommending   Tentative suggestions by the social worker in the form of either questions or comments are frequent in practice with groups. Examples of suggestions might include such phrases as "Some members have found it helpful to . . . " "Could we review what you have been saying to find out if it applies to others?" "Have you thought of getting some care for your husband?" The response of the members determines what happens next. Such messages often stimulate further work on a particular issue. There are times when advice is given in the form of a definite recommendation, as, for example, "You really must tell your partner that you are HIV positive," or "Remember that it's necessary to keep your appointments with your probation officer," or "Could you talk to your teacher this way?" Whatever advice is offered needs to be grounded in knowledge and based on a sound rationale.

Securing feedback   Seeking feedback from members about the advice offered will help both the worker and the group to discuss the suitability of the advice and alternative ways of solving the problem. The giving of advice usually is woven into the discussion going on in the group at a given time. It is offered after members have tried to find solutions to the issues or problem and are unable to proceed further without help from the worker.

Confrontation

The purpose of confrontation is to interrupt or reverse a course of action. It is a form of statement that faces a person or a group with the reality of a feeling, behavior, or situation. Its dictionary meaning is to face boldly, to bring a person face to face with something. It is a form of limiting behavior that faces members with the fact that there is some inconsistency between their own behaviors or between their own statements and those of other sources, that their behavior is irrational, or that it is destructive to self or others. It is concerned, not with the meaning of the behavior, but with stopping it or redirecting the course of the discussion or activity.

Challenging obstacles   Confrontations usually challenge a client's defenses, such as denial, rationalization, projection, or displacement, or they challenge unacceptable behavior. They upset the person's emotional balance, creating temporary discomfort or anxiety, and thus unfreeze the system and make possible a readiness to change in order to reduce the discomfort. A confrontation disconfirms the acceptability of what is happening. It provides information that contradicts distortions or blindness to facts, directly and openly. It provides a force that challenges obstacles to the achievement of goals, and stimulates self-examination. Some clients may interpret it as criticism, verbal assault, or rejection. To avoid these responses, it needs to be accompanied by empathy.

Alice Overton and Katherine Tinker say that confrontations are direct statements, but they need not be harsh: the firm challenge should be "with an arm around the shoulder."[30] There is a vast difference between confrontation that is accusatory, such as "Stop lying to me" and one that deals with denial by such a statement as "I know it's hard for you to tell me, but I already know that you are in serious trouble with the police," accompanied by a gentle tone of voice, or "Whenever you start to talk about your sexual abuse, you change the subject: that won't help you."

Confrontation is not synonymous with punishment or demolishment of someone. It is often a precursor to positive change. One example would be saying to Jim, a father, who covered up for his son's stealing, "I feel angry with you because you've said over and over again that you want to help your son, but by covering up for him you are contributing to his delinquency instead of helping him to get along better." Another member said, "Jim, you know that's true, face it." Jim pleaded, "But what can I do differently to make it better?" That led to a productive discussion in the group of ways the members could improve their parenting. The focus of confrontation is on one aspect of a person—not on the total personality.

Values of confrontation   Confrontation is an essential skill in helping members to develop power to control their behavior and achieve their desired goals. Solomon wrote forcefully of its importance in helping oppressed populations. A major criterion of a nonracist practitioner, she wrote, "is the ability to confront the client when true feelings of worker empathy and genuineness have been expressed but have been misinterpreted or distorted by the client." Confrontation is combined with the "ability to feel warmth, empathy, and genuine concern for people regardless of race, ethnicity, or color."[31] There is support from empirical research for the principle that when it is accompanied by a high degree of empathy, confrontation is an effective ingredient in practice. When employed by practitioners with little empathy, it is not.

Member-to-member confrontation   Confrontation may be of a person's verbal or nonverbal behavior or of the interactional patterns between members of groups. It needs to be based on sound assessment of both individuals and the group. It is not the worker alone who uses confrontation. The members confront each other, often quite bluntly, requiring that the worker evaluate the impact of confrontive statements on particular individuals and on the group, following up in whatever way seems necessary. The worker may ask the group itself to evaluate the consequences of such confrontations on the progress of individuals and the movement of the group. To find patterns of behavior, the worker may comment on omissions and contradictions in the descriptions of the members. A comment that seeks to understand what happened tends to be more effective than questioning why it happened. It tends to focus on the chain of events, and this makes clear the nature of the behavioral pattern to the members.

Clarification

Clarification simply means to make understandable. It is used to make a statement clear, free from ambiguity. It frees the mind from confusion. Its purpose in practice is to improve cognitive understanding of an experience, emotion, pattern of behavior, or environmental situation. It brings vague conversations into clear focus.

Social workers often want to help the members of a group to recognize and identify the various aspects of a social situation, then extend or elaborate on that understanding, and move ahead to clarify the problems and the situation. Three major aspects need clarification by the members of a group: the social situation, which includes the outer environment, the agency, and the group, the patterns and content of communication, and the attitudes and behavior of the members in various social situations.

Members of groups often do not have adequate understanding of situations in the community that influence their attitudes and behavior. A lack of resources, presence of a gang culture, racist or sexist attitudes, substandard housing, and lack of public transportation are examples of community conditions that negatively influence their daily lives. Some members may have distorted or one-sided views of varied institutions and groups in the community or of the legal requirements for certain privileges, such as driving a car, remaining on probation or parole, using public buildings, or providing day care for children. When they can distinguish between problems within themselves and those occasioned by conditions over which they have little control, they can focus their energies on coping with these matters. When such distortions are corrected, the members can then move to learning how to use the available resources to meet their needs.

Members often need help to correct their misunderstanding of the agency as it influences the service given, or they may need help to clarify their perceptions of the group itself. The members may simply need information about these matters or may have misperceptions about some aspect of the agency or the group that require clarification as a prelude to correction. Attitudes and responses to the social worker may be brought into the group's discussion, as may attitudes and responses to each other. Clarification of such matters tends to remove obstacles to a sound relationship between the worker and the group and between the members. It makes it possible for members to turn their attention to working on other problems of concern to them. Clarification of the nature of the group and agency is predominant during the early stage of the group's development, as will be seen in chapter 12.

Clarification of distortions in communication is often essential. In a group, the network of communication is more complex than in a one-to-one relationship. Each member's messages need to be understood by all and to be responded to in appropriate ways. Within the interacting processes of the group, corrections of distortions in the intent and content of communication may be delayed. Some messages may get lost in the welter of competing messages so that responses are missing. Lack of a core of common experiences may make communication difficult, requiring considerable clarification of the intent and meaning of any message.

There is often a need to help persons to check out the intent of a message with the way in which that message was perceived by others, through such means as questioning others about what they understand and requesting restatement of the message sent. When a person has expressed an emotion or an idea, a reaction is expected that contributes to the extension, clarification, or alteration of the original message. When a person is aware of the results produced by his own actions, his subsequent actions are influenced by this knowledge. Some members of groups need to be asked to listen to others, to indicate when a message is not clear, and to offer correction of messages, when requested. There may be double-bind messages, those in which one set of words contradicts another. Words may convey one attitude or request, and tone of voice a different one. In double binds, there is often no right response, so that the person is caught in a dilemma and may become anxious, inactive, or withdrawn.

Forms of Feedback

A major set of skills is used to clarify the person-group-environment configuration. They are often referred to as forms of feedback.[32]

Reflection on feelings   Going beyond the acceptance of expressed feelings to provide support, social workers often reflect feelings. Ability to associate emotions with words and actions supports the ego's capacity to cope with them. Feelings may be denied or their expression may be out of proportion to the reality of the situation. By being able to identify and describe a feeling, for example, a child may learn to substitute verbal symbols for harmful actions. Practitioners encourage reflection of feelings by making comments to elaborate and understand the feelings. To reflect feelings accurately, workers need to feel empathy to connect with the member's emotional experience and offer a congruent statement. For example, prior to surgery a woman said, "I may even die—I'm scared." "Going into surgery is scary," the worker responded. Another worker, speaking to a mother, commented, "You're troubled about Jennifer, aren't you, and angry with her too."

In one study of clients' reports on their experiences with therapists of different theoretical orientations, there was considerable consensus that the most helpful procedure, in addition to the worker-client relationship, was the recognition and clarification of feelings that clients had been approaching hazily and hesitatingly.[33]

Paraphrasing   Paraphrasing is a way of mirroring behavior as it is observed by another. Workers or other members may rephrase persons' statements so that they can see their problem and situation more clearly or in a new way. Sometimes persons are not sure what they have said, because there were so many confused thoughts and feelings connected with the words. When workers or members of the group can express what they heard, the sender of the message can decide whether this is what was really meant. Members who did not clearly hear another person may respond with a request for clarification. It may then be possible for members to pursue the subject in more depth. Such an act may also enlist the participation of other members, since the worker's reflection of client activity is like an invitation to react further to what is being said. Some examples might be, "In other words, did you say that you are afraid to see your doctor about the infection?" or "Would another way of saying that be . . . ?" or "Was the main point you wanted to make that you can no longer tolerate your son's behavior?"

Reframing   Reframing or recasting problems is a cognitive skill that is used to help members to view problems or situations from a different perspective that accords with the facts. The range of alternative actions is thereby increased.[34] Toseland and Rivas give an example of a group in which one member is a scapegoat. Through an explanation by the worker, the issue is reframed from the scapegoat as the problem to an interactional problem shared by all of the members. That reformulation of the problem led to discussion of what the members do in their relationships with the scapegoat and what they, including the scapegoat, might do differently.

Making connections   Another skill of clarification is to make a statement that connects two events that are obscure to one or more members so
as to help them understand logical connections between aspects of their
own behavior or emotions or between their behavior and that of others. The
worker may offer a comment that identifies the common ground between
people. Such statements may call attention to the common needs, problems,
or interests of two parties who may be in conflict. They may call attention
to common feelings that underlie apparent differences. Connections may
be suggested to tie some members' memories of their past experiences to
the present situation. Reviewing past situations is a tool for helping people
to learn from experience. Reviewing patterns of experience and behavior
may make it possible for a member to take a different turn, based on evaluation, toward more effective functioning. Joan Hutten has stressed that
"allowing clients to talk with feeling about past traumas when they are re-
evoked by present experiences is one of the opportunities we do have to
intervene 'preventively' in relation to the future." She notes that the discovery of continuities of experience can reopen a person's potential for further
development. Coping capacities can be released when past experiences can
be integrated into the personality "instead of having to be cut off or kept at
bay by heavy psychic expenditure."[35]

Illumination of group process   Many specific skills are used to clarify
the process that is going on in the group at a given time, referred to by Yalom
as process illumination.[36] Workers ask the members to reflect on what has
happened in their relationships with each other in order to understand their
patterns of feeling, thinking, and doing. They ask them to reflect on the
consequences that the behavior has for them and for others and to discover
discrepancies between attitudes and behavior or between past and present
experiences. To help members examine their own process, workers have to
assess the process and request that the members look at what has been going
on between them: what happened in what order, what they are thinking and
feeling about what happened, and what alternative explanations they can
give about the process. There may be initial resistance to a request to work
on understanding the process. Examination of the behavior of self in relation
to others may create anxiety because it reminds them of earlier criticisms
about their behavior. Such discussions are usually taboo in most social situations: there may be fears of retaliation for feelings expressed toward another or fear of disrupting the existing power structure. Once the members

find acceptance for their thoughts and feelings, however, they become able to engage in such discussion and find it helpful. These discussions are a form of reflective thinking about the process going on between the members at a given time. It is important to remember that the understanding about one's relationships gained in the group needs to be generalized to relationships with people in the environment.

Principles of clarification   A number of principles govern the use of skills aimed at clarification:

1. Clarifying skills should be based on sound assessment, yet offered in a tentative manner so that workers can check their observations against the members' own views and invite feedback from the group. Workers need to share the basis for reaching a particular generalization.
2. Usually, the briefer and more concise the comments, the better. It is important to present only one fact or thought at a time and to express oneself clearly, simply, and directly.
3. Workers need to follow through with considerable exploration of the reactions of the member who is the target of a particular intervention and of the other members to the clarifying message. Furthermore, whatever understanding had developed needs to be repeated in different forms over a period of time, if it is to result in more adaptive behavior.
4. Workers find the thread of connections between one individual's need and the needs of others. There is a tendency to direct clarifying statements to individuals rather than to the group system. Directing more comments to the group leads to a greater sense of relatedness and cohesiveness.

Interpretation

To carry understanding further, when the worker judges it to be desirable, interpretation of the underlying meaning of behavior or its roots in the past may be used. An interpretation is a statement that explains the possible meaning of an experience or motivation for behavior or searches for reasons for a particular difficulty. Its purpose is to bring into conscious awareness such feelings, ideas, and experiences as are not readily acknowledged or verbalized and to help the person to integrate these new understandings. It is through finding meanings that a person makes sense of this world.

Some examples illustrate the nature of interpretation. A mother in a child guidance clinic was upset because her four-year-old son said, "I wish Tommy was dead. I hate him." After a brief silence to learn what other members might say, the worker explained, "When a person feels angry or frustrated, he may have violent thoughts. But there is a difference between a wish and an action in carrying it out. One can both love and hate the same person at different times." After a thoughtful silence, she asked, "Does what I said make sense?" Another mother said, "It sure does to me." She then told a story about her son. Tommy's mother said, "I'm beginning to see that now."

In another example, a worker said to a fourteen-year-old girl, "I've noticed, Betty, that when the group is talking about their mothers, you remain silent and look sad. Is that because it's hard for you to accept the fact that your mother is no longer alive?" Even young children can understand an interpretation. To a five-year-old girl, a worker said, "I think you might be scared to go to school because you think your mommy won't be home when you get back from school."

In making interpretations, workers need to assess the obstacles and capacities of the ego of the member to use such explanations. The worker considers the readiness of the members to participate in relation to the common and unique needs in the group, mutuality of acceptance and empathy, and the potential effect on each member. It is futile and may be hurtful to present information about the underlying meaning of behavior before it can be comprehended or related to the current situation. Working toward such understanding should be a natural process, with members participating and the worker supplementing or affirming what the members are able to do. When members think about the worker's explanation, that can help them to find their own meanings.

An illustration is from a group of patients in a mental hospital. One member, Mrs. J., was hiding under a blanket. The worker commented on this, saying that the members might like to discuss the idea of using physical hiding to shut out reality. One member suggested that Mrs. J. was hiding behind the blanket so she would not need to admit that she was daydreaming. Mrs. J. came out from under the blanket. She said she wanted to shut out her problems from the view of others. The worker said, "I wonder if you might want to shut out problems from your view, too." Mrs. J. did not respond verbally, but other members acknowledged that this could be so. Two members gave examples from their own experiences. At the next meeting, Mrs. J. freely brought out deep feelings of hurt and said she no longer needed to hide behind her blanket.

Seeking for the meaning of behavior or underlying emotions may help persons to make connections between various aspects of problems, as they appear in current functioning, or to make connections between the past and the present. The focus is on bringing to conscious awareness such feelings and experiences that are not readily verbalized and acknowledged but that can be recalled, verbalized, and acknowledged with some assistance from others. At times, the past must be dealt with.

As an example, Fatout reviewed research indicating that severely abused children were damaged in many ways, often resulting in being unable to develop and sustain relationships in varied life situations. She pointed out that such children need to understand what happened, their feelings about what happened, and its impact on their present behavior.[37] In another example, an adult member of the Snohomish Indian tribe recalled vividly her first day in school. She was dressed up and eager to learn; the teacher went around the room to show the children how to hold a pencil, touching all of their hands, except her own. She was the only American Indian in the class. A deep feeling of hurt and difference persisted through the years. She needed to recall it and integrate it into her personality.

As Gisela Konopka said, "This does not mean that the past serves as an excuse, but even Freud never thought of it that way, nor that it suffices to dwell on the past. Looking at the past may help to work through present problems and to prepare for the future."[38] Many members of groups suffer from the memories of earlier traumatic experiences such as the Holocaust, rape, sexual molestation, parental divorce, or a murder or suicide in a family. The ghosts of the past must often be brought into the present and coped with.

The worker may ask the group to consider connections between feelings, behavior, or events, or point up the consequences of behavior. When members or the worker suggest explanations, these are related to the particular situation. There is general agreement with Grace Coyle's view that the worker refrains from "interpretations of unconscious mechanisms to individuals in the group, although he may help group members to deal with conscious or preconscious material."[39] Probes for connections and interpretations of meaning are likely to be more effective with members who have fairly good ego integration than with those who are more emotionally disturbed.[40] Interpretations must be attuned to the particular perspectives of the members and timed in accordance with their readiness. That is a general principle, applicable to all groups.

Another example of the use of interpretation is taken from Judith Lee and Danielle Park's record of a group of depressed adolescents in foster care.[41] Cherise is the member of the group with the most severe depression.

> After a round of work on accepting natural mothers for what they were, Cherise said her foster mother was old and didn't care much about her. She felt she had no family to talk about here. Her natural mother is dead, they don't know where her natural father is, she's never met her brother, and on top of all that, she doesn't feel she belongs in her foster family. The other girls were overwhelmed by this and saddened. They looked at me. I said that Cherise feels that everything has gone wrong for her. Let's help her to take one part at a time. The members asked different questions about what she had said. After Cherise told her story, I said that I think she feels particularly upset today because each of you has a living mother to talk about. She feels left out. (Interpreting and pinpointing the immediate provocation for her depression.) Cherise nodded in agreement. The girls were very supportive, but Leticia added, "Yeah, but with or without mothers, dead or alive, we all wound up in the same boat anyway—foster care, and none of us got fathers." They all laughed lightly, including Cherise. The work continued on a new level about foster families, and Cherise was with it.

Principles of interpretation   All the principles used in clarification are also used when interpretations of the meaning of behavior are made, but there are some additional principles.

1. In interpreting meaning, workers usually offer these comments as impressions, suggestions, or opinions. They encourage the members to test out the applicability of the comments to their situations and to respond to them.
2. Workers avoid generalizations that deal with the total person. Rather, they partialize them to a particular feeling, idea, behavioral pattern, or situation.

3. Interpretations are usually directed to the conscious or preconscious levels of personality. Usually, the focus is on the present.
Recall of the past is facilitated and past events are interpreted when
such recall helps the person and other participants to cope with
the past as it has an impact on the present.

4. Offering interpretations that explain the underlying meaning of
behavior may threaten the ego's defenses; children and adults with
weak egos need considerable support and empathy as they attempt
to deal with understanding and coping with their difficulties.

5. The worker's aim, as with any other technique, is to help the members do as much as possible for themselves. Hence, questions that
help members to explain feelings, behavior, and situations may be
more effective than interpretations given by the worker because
those contribute to a sense of power over their lives. But when
meaning eludes members and is considered by the worker to be
important to progress, the worker's interpretations may be very useful and sometimes essential.

6. A special characteristic of the use of interpretation in a group is
that, to be useful, it need not be directed specifically to a person.
During a period when a problematic situation develops, various
members may present experiences, feelings, and make relevant
comments. To the extent that the underlying theme of the content
is relevant to particular persons' concerns, they may derive understanding of themselves and their experiences. Often, when feelings
or explanations are universalized, they touch closely on some
members' particular concerns. This dynamic is what Konopka refers to as anonymity of insight.[42]

   Much of this formulation of interpretation is based on the empirical research of Robert Brown.[43] Moreover, in a review of several studies on the
use of interpretation in short-term groups, Robert Dies concluded that "the
accumulated evidence, then, strongly supports the values of interpretation
as a vehicle for therapeutic change."[44] Another study, by Lieberman, Yalom,
and Miles, also found that the qualities of relationship were necessary ingredients in successful outcome, but only when combined with work toward
improved cognitive understanding.[45] That is what clarification and interpretation provide.

These skills involve give and take between the members and with the worker in providing mutual support and mutual help for the benefit of all. The selection of skills is always specific to a situation. No one skill results in positive changes; rather, a constellation of skills is used to meet the particular needs of members and groups at a particular time.

In summary, social workers with groups use the categories of intervention to

1. develop and use structure to create an optimal environment that meets the needs of members and provides direction for their interactions;
2. develop supportive relationships between worker and members, and between members, and between members and others that are characterized by acceptance, empathy, and genuineness;
3. support members emotionally with a sense of security and caring, gratifying their basic need for belonging, bolstering a sense of self-esteem, and providing opportunities to give to others, and use instrumental supports to provide essential knowledge and material and social resources;
4. explore for the purpose of eliciting facts, thoughts, feelings and concerns to secure understanding of the problem and the member-group-environment situation as a basis for working toward achievement of goals;
5. inform and educate members with facts, ideas, values, and social skills that are useful to them in acquiring competence, making decisions, and coping with problems;
6. offer advice and guidance cautiously to suggest or recommend a course of action when members have been unable to find their own solutions to problems of individuals or in the functioning of the group;
7. confront a member or the group with the reality of a feeling, behavior, or situation in order to interrupt or reverse a course of action that is inimical to the welfare of the person or group, accompanied by an accepting, empathic relationship;
8. clarify feelings, experiences, patterns of behavior, or environmental obstacles in order to improve cognitive understanding as a basis for adaptive coping and decision making;

9. interpret the possible meaning of an experience or underlying motivation by bringing into conscious awareness feelings, ideas, and
experiences that are not readily acknowledged or verbalized;
10. apply these actions selectively regardless of whether the content of
the group is primarily discussion- or action-oriented.

Social workers need to be reminded that there is no single way to say or
do something; it depends upon the particular situation. So perhaps the most
important skill is actually the reflection-in-action that goes on in the worker's
mind continuously. As the members are engaged in activity or discussion,
workers observe and listen, become aware of their own feelings, biases, and
values, reflect on what they perceive to be the quality and meaning of the
interchanges between the members, and then act to support what is going
on or add something new to the group's activities. This thought process,
combined with action, makes work with groups an especially challenging
and exciting modality of practice.

5   Planning

Many complex forces determine the meaning and value a group will have for its members. For people to be served effectively in a group, sound preparation for the initiation and subsequent development of that group is essential. Yet, practitioners often neglect or give only cursory attention to the planning process.[1] Perhaps this is because they do not appreciate the importance of planning. Or perhaps they feel pressured and in a rush to get a group going. But thorough and thoughtful planning contributes mightily to the success of a social work group. It is an important part of social group work practice.

Planning comprises the thinking, preparation, decision making, and actions of the social worker prior to the first meeting of a group. Between the time an idea for a group is conceived and the time there is readiness to actually have the first meeting of that group, a complicated range of decisions must be made. As Max Siporin notes, the planning process is deliberate and rational, designed to assure the achievement of specific objectives.[2] The social worker, often in collaboration with others, needs to make choices about the nature of the group that is being formed. The worker's decisions are based upon knowledge of social contexts, group processes, agency policies and procedures, and assessments of clients in their networks of interacting social systems.

For decades, no comprehensive model of planning was presented in the literature on social work with groups. In fact, the literature gave little attention to planning even though it was said to be important. Some of the profession's most basic writing included planning as a key social work activity,[3] but the literature provided little direction or guidance for practitioners about the actual planning process. Instead, different authors emphasized discrete elements that they viewed as important to group formation.[4] That is no longer true today. In the past decade, much of the writing on social work with groups has given substantial consideration to the planning process.[5]

Thoughtful pregroup planning is beneficial because it contributes to the creation of groups that meet the needs of their members, groups whose purposes are ones that their members are invested in and want to achieve. As a result, such groups are more likely to have regular attendance, few dropouts, and high cohesiveness.[6] Thoughtful pregroup planning also benefits the worker who engages in it by enhancing the worker's knowledge of members' goals and expectations, understanding of group interaction,[7] and ability to make appropriate use of self with the group.[8]

For the worker with a group, planning has two other benefits that might not be immediately obvious.[9] First, planning increases workers' self-confidence. Workers who have given substantial thought to a group they are forming enter that group feeling more sure of themselves and what they are about. As a result, they are able to listen better to clients, to be more responsive to them, to be less rigid and more flexible. Second, planning helps workers—almost forces them—to obtain a better understanding of individual group members, their environments, contexts, backgrounds, communities, cultures, attitudes, points of view, and concerns. The workers' immersion in planning leads to their enhanced comprehension of group members and the worlds in which they live. Such understanding on the part of workers is crucial to good group work practice.

A Model of Planning[10]

Within the social and agency contexts of service, six areas need to be considered in planning for the formation of a group:

Need. What are the problems, issues, and areas of concern of the prospective group members?

Purpose. What ends and objectives will the group pursue collectively? What are the goals of the group members individually? What is the nature of the interrelationship between the collective and individual ends and goals?

Composition. How many group members will there be? What are anticipated to be some of the important areas of commonality and difference between them? Who will be the worker(s) with this group?

Structure. What specific arrangements need to be made to facilitate the conduct of the group, particularly in regard to time and place?

Content. What means will be used to achieve the group's purpose? What will actually take place in the group?

Pregroup contact. How will members be secured for participation in the group? How will they be prepared for their participation in the group?

Conceptions in each of these six areas are made within the **social** and **agency contexts** that surround them. Beliefs and conditions that exist in the culture, the community, and the agency environments will impact upon the group and need to be considered in the pregroup planning process.

The relationships between the elements of planning is shown in figure 5.1.

Need is the first area to be considered. The determination of purpose then emanates directly from need. The four other areas—composition, structure, content, and pregroup contact—flow directly from need and purpose and are considered simultaneously. The social and agency contexts surround and influence all the planning components.

At times, a worker forms a group in which there is no choice in composition because membership is predetermined. In a school setting, for instance, a group may be planned for all the boys in a particular classroom, or, in a residential setting, a group may be formed for all who reside on a particular floor. In planning such a group, as indicated in figure 5.2, the relationship between the elements of planning is similar to that in a group that is begun from scratch.

The difference is that the process begins with composition. The worker needs to ascertain the needs of the particular persons who are to become group members. Then, as when composition is *not* predetermined, purpose emanates from need, and structure, content, and pregroup contact follow. Once again, all the planning components are impacted upon by the agency and social contexts.

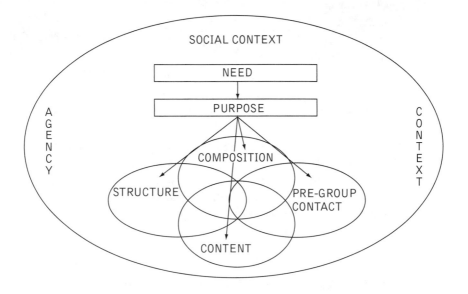

FIGURE 5.1 Pregroup Planning Model (for use when group composition *is not* predetermined)

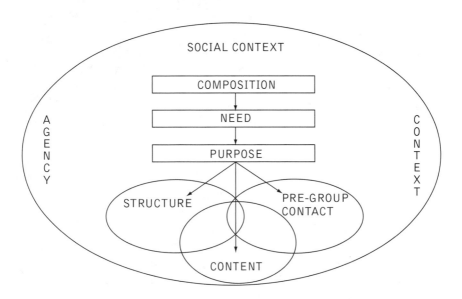

FIGURE 5.2 Pregroup Planning Model (for use when group composition *is* predetermined)

Social Context

A group does not exist in a vacuum. It is influenced and affected by the community in which it is located and by the range of communities of which its members are a part and that serve as reference points for them. There are many different kinds of communities: geographic areas or neighborhoods, service areas, such as hospitals or schools. Other important communities are social in nature—those based on race, ethnicity, religion, and/or age, for example, whose members may share values, norms, and worldviews. The immediate and extended family is yet another potent community. As Hans Falck emphasizes, an appreciation of clients' many memberships is essential.[11]

In some communities, many institutions and organizations address health, education, and welfare needs, while in others such institutions and agencies are few. In some communities, a range of services and resources exist, while in others scant services and resources are available to address people's needs and issues. The availability of and access to services need to be considered by the worker who is planning a group. Cognizance of existing community services and resources provides the worker with clues about gaps that exist and also about other resources that might be used in conjunction with the group that is being planned.

Attitudes toward social work services in general and toward groups in particular in the social community of potential group members are also important for the worker to consider in the planning process. Such attitudes are strongly influenced by cultural norms and beliefs. For example, in some cultures the need to go outside one's immediate family for help with a problem is an indication of personal failure and inadequacy. To talk with a "stranger," i.e., a social worker, individually is difficult, but to talk in public with a number of strangers, i.e., other group members, is even more onerous.[12]

Knowledge of such attitudes helps the worker in planning, particularly in considering the areas of pregroup contact and content. How to present the group service and how to talk with potential members about the group that is being offered need to be thought through by the worker. In the pregroup contact, the worker needs to invite potential group members to express and then to really listen to the reservations they may have about group participation. The worker also needs to be prepared and able to articulate the potential benefits of small group participation. Similarly, in thinking in advance about the group's content, the worker needs to consider the level of interpersonal demand that will be asked of group members and whether that level is in harmony with the cultural environs.

In thinking through the social context of the group that is being formed, the practitioner needs to consider many questions:

- What are the important communities—geographic, service, social, familial—of which potential group participants are members?
- What are the services and resources and what are the gaps in service that exist in these communities?
- What will be the relationship of the group that is being planned to the services that exist?
- Who are the important persons in the social and familial communities of potential group members?
- What are their attitudes about social work services and about their participation in a group?
- What are the attitudes toward groups that potential group members are likely to hold?
- What are the implications of those attitudes for planning, especially in regard to pregroup contact and content?

Agency Context

Groups are usually formed within a social agency or multidisciplinary organization where social work is one component, as in schools, hospitals, clinics, prisons, residential institutions, businesses, and industries. Such organizations are comprised of complex networks of people in interlocking social systems, such as boards of directors, advisory committees, administrative, clerical, professional, and paraprofessional staff. Within the organization, certain persons have the authority to define the parameters and conditions of service to be given. Some practices are sanctioned by the organization, while others are not. Organizational policies exist concerning preventive, developmental, or rehabilitative functions, eligibility requirements, including fees for service, the types of clients to whom service will be offered, the resources available to client and practitioner, and even the theoretical base to be used by practitioners. The agency's structure, policies, and procedures influence matters of access, continuity, equity, and quality of services. Many of the agency's functions and policies may, in turn, be defined partially by laws, governmental regulations, and/or external financial arrangements and funding sources.

The effect of agency context on the planning of a group is pervasive, for the conditions that exist within the agency strongly impact upon group formation efforts. Thus, the social worker needs to be cognizant of agency functions, practices, and policies that may be relevant to group formation. Policies in regard to reporting, accountability, evaluation, confidentiality, informed consent, intake, eligibility, fees, and staff workloads may have particular impact. Efforts may be necessary on the part of the worker to combat those agency policies and practices that get in the way of the formation of needed groups.

Attitudes about groups that exist in an agency, especially those held by persons in positions of influence and authority, can have substantial consequences for the formation of groups. Unless group services are a well-established part of an agency program, their presence tends to disrupt organizational arrangements, for they require a new stance toward clients and a shift from the familiar and comfortable one-to-one style of work. The use of groups may create a subtle redistribution of power and control between staff and clients.[13] Thus, some staff may see bringing clients together in groups as threatening.

Sometimes, negative attitudes about groups can result from the agency's history of experience with groups. For example, if past efforts to reach out to and recruit group members were inadequate and group attendance was low as a result, generalizations may be made that clients "don't like" or "won't come" to groups. That conclusion may not be at all valid. Similarly, generalizations about the inevitability of disruptive behavior of members in all groups may be made on the basis of one agency experience with a group whose members were noisy and boisterous. It is a good idea, therefore, for the worker who is attempting to form a group to find out about the agency's history of experience in work with groups, especially if there is a sense that negative attitudes toward groups exist within the agency. Knowing about the agency's history enables the worker to address the negative attitudes to which past experiences may have contributed.

Negative attitudes may also be influenced by some common and persistent myths that exist about groups. One such myth is that groups are second-choice modalities of help, with individual work viewed as preferable for almost all clients. In spite of clear evidence to refute this stereotype, it persists.

Another myth is that groups are the most economical means of serving people and therefore are used primarily to save money. Though some groups are economical — educational groups, for instance, where information or skills are taught to persons together rather than one at a time — most groups are not time savers. Before and as they are conducted, they require that workers spend time — to plan, to meet as needed with members individually before the group begins and, on occasion, to supplement the experience as the group is taking place, to maintain records that are required about the group itself and about individual group members, and to evaluate each meeting and plan for the next one.

It is important that workers who are doing pregroup planning not succumb when their agencies want them to form groups for the wrong reasons. A group should be formed when it is the modality of choice in a given situation, not as a cheap or second-class type of service. It should be formed when persons share common needs and can help one another to achieve something of importance for all of them.

If administrators or other staff have misconceptions about the use of groups, the result will probably be lack of adequate sanction for groups and lack of referrals to appropriate groups. To overcome such misconceptions, there needs to be recognition of the fears and fantasies that agency staff may have about groups and there needs to be education about the goals of groups and about the dynamic forces that define group processes. The worker planning a group needs to be sure that agency administrators and staff understand what is being offered, for whom it is indicated, what brings about change, and how outcomes are to be assessed.[14]

In planning a new group, the social worker needs to remember that the group is always part of the larger system in which it is imbedded. Its success depends upon cooperation from key staff members. To gain such cooperation, key staff need to understand the group's purpose, the means that will be used to achieve that purpose, and the ways in which the group will contribute to its members and to the mission of the organization. The sanction and support of persons who will influence the development and course of the group and who will be influenced by the group are decisive.

To determine the feasibility of developing a group, the practitioner needs to do an organizational analysis to ascertain the supports that exist in the agency as well as factors in the agency that need to be worked on if agency sanction and support for group formation is to be obtained.[15] In some instances, when groups are well established and positively regarded in the agency, sanction will be easy to secure. But when groups are not well established or positively regarded, it is essential that work within the agency take place to overcome negative attitudes, myths, and misconceptions and gain sanction and cooperation.

As planning proceeds, it is a good idea for workers to involve and confer with other staff members who are knowledgeable about the population to be served and whose work may be affected by the group. Depending on the setting, collaboration needs to occur with such persons as physicians, nurses, houseparents, teachers, psychologists, and other social workers. Such staff can be critical in supporting the group or in sabotaging it if they feel threatened or ignored. Certainly, the feelings that such staff have toward the proposed group need to be considered. In addition, such staff may have information, understanding, experience, and ideas about subjects ranging from client needs to organizational issues that would be helpful to the group formation efforts.

When other staff are doubtful about or resistant to the proposed group, efforts of persuasion may be needed. Such efforts need to take into account and address staff concerns and feelings, regardless of their truthfulness or rationality. Resistance may occur when staff view the proposed group as threatening their self-interest. They might, for instance, think that the group will be competition that will take their clients away from them or they might be fearful that clients, when they come together in a group, will criticize and complain about them. They might see the group as creating additional work and an additional burden for them if they are expected to participate in any way. The need is to address such concerns and feelings rather than ignore them in the hope that once the group gets started they will magically disappear.

In regard to agency context, the practitioner needs to consider a range of questions:

- What are the agency's mission and purpose? In what ways will the group that is being proposed complement that mission and purpose?
- Who are the key staff in the agency whose sanction and support for the proposed group are essential? What is the best way to obtain their sanction and support?
- What are the attitudes toward group services that exist in the agency? Will those attitudes present obstacles or supports for successful group formation? If negative attitudes exist, how can they be overcome?
- What is the history of the agency's experiences in work with groups? How can those experiences be drawn upon, if positive, and be overcome, if negative?
- What resources (e.g., staff time, funds, space, materials) will the agency commit to the group?
- What is the nature of the relationship between the agency and the community it serves? In what ways will the agency's place and reputation in the community impact upon the group that is being formed?
- What agency policies and legislative requirements will have a direct effect on plans for the conduct of the group? If these are not conducive to the welfare of the group members, can exceptions be made?
- What arrangements need to be made for staff cooperation, collaboration, and coordination, both intra- and interagency?

Need

Knowledge of the community, agency, and professional context is essential to identify the needs, problems, and issues of people who may be helped through group experiences. So, too, is knowledge of human development from a broad psychosocial perspective, of the personal and environmental obstacles that prevent optimal development, and of the supports that maximize it. People have needs to master the basic tasks of each developmental stage, to cope effectively with the transitions and crises they face in the process of living, and to have opportunities for meeting their basic needs for health, education, financial security, recreation, and social relationships.

The group process is a powerful force in assisting people to meet their needs in the realm of social relationships and role functioning. Several types of problems appear to be most amenable to the use of groups.[16]

1. **Lack of knowledge, skills, and experience**. Lack of opportunities to secure information, develop social skills, and try out new experiences is a hazard to effective functioning. In many instances, socialization has been neglected or inadequate in one or more important areas of social living. Adequate performance of vital roles is dependent upon such resources. Skills are not limited to specific behaviors, but more important, the need is to master an array of communication, relationship, and problem-solving skills. As persons take on new roles, they are expected to master the attitudes and skills essential for successful performance, and they may be ill prepared for that task.

2. **Coping with life transitions**. Transitions are defined as periods of "moving from one state of certainty to another, with an interval of uncertainty and change in between."[17] They include the passage from one chronological stage in the life cycle to another. They include shifts in roles or significant life events, such as giving up a vital role through retirement, unemployment, divorce, widowhood, or physical and psychological changes. Whether the event is sudden or gradual, some degree of stress accompanies the transition.

In addition to the need for knowledge, skills, and material resources, people need to cope with the threats to their past security and competence through understanding their emotional reactions to the transition and using a problem-solving process to make decisions about the future. People with these needs are not emotionally sick; their difficulties are normal problems in social living. For example, as young children enter school, they separate from their family or other primary caretakers for increasing periods of time and must learn to relate to teachers and other pupils and to meet new social and academic expectations. The new demands that face the children create stress for their parents as well. At another stage in the life cycle, elderly people become anxious or face changes or losses in their vital social roles, social relationships, and economic resources. A person passing through a transition may or may not be in a state of crisis. The crisis occurs if the stress becomes acute, disrupting the steady state to such an extent that usual problem-solving methods fail.

3. **Unresolved crisis.** Groups are often used to alleviate a crisis in the lives of individuals or families. A person is in a state of crisis when

an emotionally hazardous situation, so interpreted by the person(s) involved, creates stress which becomes unbearable at the point when some precipitating event places demands on the person(s) for coping resources not readily available. A severe anxiety state sets in, and is not easily dispelled because of lack of effective problem-solving means . . . habitual coping means do not suffice.[18]

Events that often precipitate a crisis are medical diagnoses or accidents, natural disasters such as fires and earthquakes, unemployment, rape, or other physical and psychological violence. Such situations are especially stressful when they coincide with maturation to a new developmental stage.

4. **Loss of relationships**. Separation from a significant person or group is a source of difficulty for many people. Separation of children from parents due to death, divorce, incarceration, or foster placement is a major problem for both children and parents. Loss of meaningful relationships with relatives and friends usually accompanies placement of elderly persons in retirement or rest homes, particularly when relocation is not voluntary. Loneliness, a sense of loss, and grief accompany separation from others. Death of a loved one is, of course, the most devastating form of separation, at whatever phase in the life cycle it occurs. The survivors must cope with intense feelings of loneliness, isolation, guilt, grief, and depression. They must cope with changes in status and roles and economic and social circumstances. In addition to the emotional reactions to the loss of the deceased person, the survivors experience strains in relationships with other people and difficulties in developing new relationships or deepening existing ones.

5. **Interpersonal and group conflict**. Conflict in central life relationships is frequent, predominantly between marital partners, partners living together, parents and one or more siblings, or other relatives. There may be conflict in other relationships also, such as those between close friends, pupil and teacher, worker and supervisor, or colleagues. Conflict may be overt, as evidenced in arguments or physical violence or spouse and child abuse. Or conflict may be covert and expressed through such means as withdrawal from open communication or displacement of hostility onto other people, as when one member of a group becomes a scapegoat or rejected isolate. Conflicts may stem from lack of complementarity in basic needs, such as degree of intimacy or distance, love and affection, dependency-independency, and authority and control. They often have their source in conscious or unconscious differences in values, goals, expectations, traditions, and customs.

Cultural conflicts are prevalent in many societies. There may be conflict between persons and between groups, based on cultural differences, prejudice, and discrimination. Interpersonal dissatisfactions and conflict are often based, at least in part, on differences in values, norms, and traditions. Ethnic groups have values that may not be understood by others, creating problems for their members in making choices and adapting effectively to their environments. Adaptation to situations is complicated for persons who have been socialized into one culture whose value system conflicts with the value system of one or more other cultures to which the person is expected to adapt. Many people must learn to integrate some aspects of two or more cultures, often made the more difficult because their own culture is devalued by the dominant society.[19]

Members of one culture may become hostile toward the dominant culture when they know their rights are violated through legal and social inequities and discrimination in housing, employment, education, and health care. Feelings of distrust, suspicion, resentment, and hostility may characterize relationships between members of groups who differ in regard to race, ethnicity, or religion. The result may be negative stereotyping, interpersonal and intergroup tensions, even violence. Persons may hold attitudes that restrict their own choices or they may be the victims of the attitudes of others toward them. A person may be torn by internal conflict, stemming from differences in the values and norms of that person's various reference groups. Variations between cultures, then, can result in a variety of intrapersonal, interpersonal, and group conflicts.

6. **Dissatisfactions in social relationships**. People often feel severe dissatisfaction with their relationships. Loneliness is a pervasive social problem: it is among the leading causes of suicide and contributes to physical illnesses and other psychosocial problems. Surveys show that one fourth of the population of the United States suffers from chronic loneliness.[20] Such persons lack affectional support systems. People often perceive deficiencies or excesses in their relationships with others. They may fear entering into intimate relationships or be unable to become intimate when such a relationship is desired. They may feel concern about the adequacy of their sexual adjustment, suffer from extreme shyness or timidity, or feel that they are unable to be assertive in appropriate ways, that they are too abrasive or overly aggressive, or that they are excessively vulnerable to the criticisms of others. Low self-esteem or a distorted sense of identity may prevent them from entering into and maintaining relationships with desired others. A positive and realistic sense of esteem and identity depends, to a considerable extent, upon

the quality of relationships within a person's family and network of relationships in the community.

7. **Illness**. Members of groups may have problems that have been diagnosed as a medical or psychiatric illness or disability. Workers need to understand the problems in psychosocial functioning associated with each client's condition. Physical, social, and psychological well-being are intimately interrelated. Social, emotional, environmental, and economic stresses usually accompany mental and physical illness and handicaps, which, in turn, often threaten interpersonal relationships and role performance.

8. **Lack of resources**. Lack of economic and social resources is the most serious problem facing many clients of health and social agencies. Many people face a frustrating array of social problems occasioned by the lack of adequate income, housing, employment, day care facilities, legal aid, and, medical resources. Many neighborhoods lack adequate health, educational, and recreational opportunities, esthetic qualities, and public transportation. In many such situations, the problem is created primarily by external factors to which the client is responding appropriately. Ben Orcutt has pointed out that "all poor people do not have social, psychological or relationship problems, but being poor greatly increases one's vulnerability."[21]

Assessment of Need

The needs of people are identified through various means. There are times when people apply for a service because they themselves perceive that they have needs that are not being met adequately. At other times, the needs of particular persons for group experiences are first identified by agency personnel who may recognize that a group would be an appropriate form of help.

But people often have needs of which they are not aware or they may not know that services exist that can meet needs that they have. In such instances, outreach by the worker to potential group members is necessary. Knowledge about the characteristics of a community's population and its resources contributes to the identification of such needs and the ability of the worker to do effective outreach. To obtain such knowledge, the practitioner needs to do the work necessary to gain the requisite familiarity. The worker needs to take the time to learn about the characteristics and possible needs of persons in the targeted community, be that community geographic, service, social, or familial.

It is not sufficient for workers to think that clients will teach them about their needs once the group gets under way, though certainly a great deal of teaching by clients will take place then. Instead, it is imperative that the worker learn as much as possible during the planning process about potential needs that persons in the client population may have. Such learning can take place in may ways: by talking with potential clients themselves as well as with relevant others, such as teachers, nurses, and/or parents, and with other social workers who have experience with clients in the target population. In assessing need, it is also pivotal for the worker to become familiar with the professional literature that exists about the targeted client population.

Sometimes when clients have applied or been referred for services, the assessment of need takes place in an intake interview that is rather formal in nature. Often in the group formation process, the assessment of need is done by reaching out to persons and talking with them informally. In either situation, whether in a formal or informal interview, the worker needs to consider the kinds of questions that will elicit from potential group members an indication of what they see themselves as needing and wanting. Asking the question directly (e.g., "What do you believe are your needs?") is likely to bring only a limited response. In fact, people's answers to that difficult question are not apt to be particularly helpful.

In assessing need, what is important is to try to get a real sense of the persons being interviewed: How do they spend their day? What do they usually do on the weekends? What are some of their concerns? Some of their hopes, dreams, aspirations? What are their families like? What do they talk about when they are with their peers? The responses of potential group members to such questions tell the worker a great deal and can be substantial indicators of client need.

Opportunity to observe potential group members, even to "hang out" for a bit with them, if that is possible, can also be instructive for the worker's assessment and understanding of client need during the pregroup planning process. Many opportunities exist for such observation. Depending on the target population, the worker can mix with teens in a lounge, with parents as they drop off or pick up their children for day care or from school, with patients as they sit in a clinic waiting room, with elderly persons as they eat lunch. If mingling with people in informal groups, the worker need not say much during the observation other than to introduce herself. Rather, the intent is to listen to what people are talking about. Such observation provides an indication of the nature of the concerns that persons in the target population have. It also allows potential group members to get a sense of the worker, which can make recruitment for the group easier when it takes place. With a person individually, in a waiting room situation for example, after introducing herself the worker wants to strike up a conversation rather than initiate an "interrogation" about needs. Such a conversation provides the worker with understanding that will ultimately be helpful to the group that is being planned.

The assessment of need cannot be carried out from one's office without getting out into the community and talking with a range of persons in addition to potential group members. Relevant others such as teachers or parents, other staff at the agency, staff at other agencies, all may be knowledgeable about need and have much to contribute to its assessment. As the worker engages such persons in conversation about need, it is not unusual for themes to emerge and for the worker to begin to identify some concerns that are expressed repeatedly. Such themes are clues for the worker about needs that might be addressed by the group that is being planned. Once the worker has developed ideas about what needs the proposed group will aim to address, it is helpful to go back to some persons in the target population as well as to some relevant others and agency staff and talk with them again to test out and invite honest feedback to the ideas about need that have been formulated.

Different persons may perceive needs similarly or differently. The agency's perception of need, for example, may or may not be in harmony with the perception of need held by the worker who is doing the planning. Similarly, the worker's or the agency's perception of need may or may not be the same as the perception of need held by prospective clients. An essential task for the worker in the planning process is to clarify needs and reconcile different perceptions of need that have priority for the group that is being planned. If the perceptions of need that are held by different persons are not complementary, it will be a struggle for the group that is being formed to survive.

In regard to the component of need, the practitioner should consider many questions during the pregroup planning process:

- What are the needs of persons in the population targeted for the group that is being planned as perceived by themselves? the sponsoring agency? other social workers? other relevant persons? the worker who is planning the group?

- What are some of the important commonalities and differences among these perceptions of needs? In what ways are the perceptions complementary? In what ways in disharmony? What are the differences in the perceptions of needs that must be clarified and/ or reconciled?
- What are elements in the social context of potential group members that impact upon the needs (e.g., values, attitudes, economic conditions, community resources)?
- What are the developmental needs of potential group members?
- What needs will the group that is being planned aim to address?

Purpose

The elements of need and purpose are integrally interconnected. A group's purpose flows directly from the identification of the needs that the group is formed to address. Once those needs have been specified, then the purpose of the group is to meet the identified needs.

Purpose refers to the ends toward which the group is formed. Groups in social work have specific purposes that are related to the overall purpose of the social work profession, which can be described generally as to maintain, improve, or move toward effective psychosocial functioning. Though effective functioning is the aim of all groups in social work, what will enable the members of a particular group to achieve that broad purpose needs to be identified and defined if the group's purpose is to have substantial meaning for its members. The group's specific purpose must also be in harmony with the functions of the sponsoring organization.

The purpose of a group encompasses both the ends that the group will pursue collectively and the hopes, expectations, and objectives that each group member hopes to gain individually from participation in the group. When common needs of potential group members are identified and used as a basis for the organization of a group, it is likely that the goals of each member will be related to the purpose of the group. For example, a group's purpose may be to help sixth-grade pupils make a satisfactory adjustment to junior high school. The goals would be related clearly to the needs of particular members of the group. They might include such aims as gaining understanding of the norms of behavior of the new school as these differ from those of the elementary school, developing satisfactory relationships with multiple teachers as contrasted with one classroom teacher, coping with feelings of loneliness due to separation from old friends, reaching out to others and making new friends, and learning about and selecting appropriate extracurricular activities. The achievement of one or more of these goals would contribute to the general purpose of a satisfactory adjustment to the new educational system.

During the pregroup planning process, the worker formulates a tentative idea of the purpose of the group. That tentative idea derives from a number of sources—the social worker's purpose of enhancing the social functioning of people, the agency's particular function and purposes, the assessment of needs, problems, and environmental circumstances, and the prospective members' perceptions of what they want to have happen as a result of membership in the group.[22] At this point, however, the worker's idea about group purpose is tentative. The reactions of potential members to this beginning idea need to be explored. Expressing the idea of purpose, even if it is tentative, can stimulate prospective members to express some of their own ideas regarding the group's purpose and their preliminary thinking about their own goals as they fit with or conflict with the worker's idea of purpose. Openness and flexibility regarding purpose on the part of the worker are essential during the planning process.

Several types of groups predominate in social work. Each conveys a general target within which a more specific purpose needs to be defined. In planning, however, it is helpful for the worker to identify the type of group that is being designed.

Socialization groups. Numerous groups are organized to develop members' competence in areas of common need. They may also be referred to as psychosocial educational groups to distinguish them from formal education and from groups that deal only with cognitive aspects of learning. They go beyond imparting information or teaching specific skills to using the group process to help members better understand and cope with the emotional reactions to the information and apply the learning to their life situation, including taking action to change environmental conditions that hinder their growth.

Therapy and counseling groups. By far the most prevalent in practice are groups that have a therapeutic purpose. The general purpose of such groups is to help people change or improve in some aspects of their psychosocial functioning that interfere with their ability to develop and maintain satisfying social relationships, resolve interpersonal and group conflicts, and meet their own and others' expectations for the performance of vital social roles. They are used to help members cope with and solve problems and issues that threaten self-esteem and identity, including the resolution of crises and successful adaptation to life transitions.

Support and self-help groups. Support and self-help groups have been proliferating at a rapid rate, particularly in the field of health and family services. The primary purposes of these groups are to control what is perceived to be undesirable behavior such as substance use, addiction, overeating, to provide peer support and mutual aid in relieving the stress related to difficult life situations such as separation or a serious illness, or to combat discrimination and enhance self-esteem when persons are stigmatized as a result of other persons' lack of understanding or prejudice concerning their behavior, illness, ethnicity, or situation. Many support groups use the services of social workers, while others are conducted by indigenous leaders who may consult with social workers as needed.[23]

Task groups. Task-oriented groups, organized for the major purpose of accomplishing a particular task, are of many kinds: boards of directors, committees, teams, delegate councils, staffs, and social action groups. Their major purposes may be social planning, coordination of services, policy making, collective problem solving, or social action. They differ from groups whose major purpose is the personal growth of members. But the distinction need not be an absolute one. As Marcia Cohen and Audrey Mullender[24] discuss, growth oriented groups may accomplish many tasks, including activities directed to changing some aspect of the environment that is an impediment to their psychosocial functioning.[25] A growth-oriented group may change its purpose to become a task-centered one. Furthermore, the members of task-oriented groups often develop meaningful relationships with each other, share eventful activities, and certainly gain in self-esteem and social competence as they complete a task successfully.

The area of purpose, as it develops throughout the life of the group, is discussed in chapter 7. In the pregroup planning process, it is important that the worker consider a number of questions regarding purpose:

- What is the purpose of the group and the goals of the potential group members as perceived by themselves? the sponsoring agency? other social workers? other relevant persons?

- What are some of the important commonalities and differences among these perceptions of the group's purpose and the members' goals? In what ways are the perceptions complementary? In what ways in disharmony? What are the differences in the perceptions of purpose and goals that must be clarified and/or reconciled?
- What is the worker's tentative conception of the group's purpose? How will that conception be explained, clearly and succinctly, to potential group members? How will members' reactions and ideas be elicited?
- In what ways is this tentative conception of purpose related to the needs that this group is being formed to meet?

Composition

The particular constellation of persons who interact with each other in a group is an important determinant of whether the participants will be satisfied with the experience and the hoped for outcomes will be achieved. In some groups, such as classroom groups and natural groups, composition is predetermined. With these groups, the worker's focus during the planning process in not on determining membership but rather on learning about the needs of the particular persons who will be the group members. In other groups, composition is not predetermined and the worker's focus in planning is on making decisions about who will comprise the group. The very foundation of group composition, however, are the commonalities of needs shared by the members that the group aims to meet through its purpose.

Several ways of determining the members of a group can be delineated. Some groups, such as therapy and counseling groups, are characterized by selective intake and placement according to specific criteria that seem relevant to the purpose of the group. Other groups, such as support groups, observe a self-selection process in that they are open to anyone who chooses to come. Their members are attracted to such groups by their purpose, perceiving that personal needs will be met there. In such groups, the worker still has a responsibility to help the members consider whether they will benefit from participation and to screen out persons for whom the group might be inappropriate.[26] Still other groups obtain their membership by inclusion of persons who share a particular status or experience. Examples are living groups in institutions or patients facing a particular medical procedure. Persons may or may not have a choice about whether to become members of such groups.

Formed groups for which the social worker makes the decision about whether to recommend membership to a person occasion the most concern about composition. According to Fritz Redl, "The very fact of group mixture in itself may sometimes play a great part in what happens in a group, even when the best conditions and the most skillful professional leadership are taken for granted.[27] If persons are placed in groups that are unsuitable for them, they may disturb, be harmed by, or drop out of the group. If the composition of a group is faulty, it is less likely to become a viable and cohesive social system. Different results flow from different combinations of people. No group can be designated as being homogeneous or heterogeneous; rather, there is homogeneity or commonality along certain characteristics and heterogeneity or difference along others. What is important is that there be a good fit between any one person and the other group members.

The dilemma in pregroup planning, however, is whether it is possible to compose a "perfect" group. Some writers believe that a favorable mix of member characteristics can be created deliberately by paying a great deal of attention to planning the composition of a group.[28] Others believe that predicting member behavior in a group based on pregroup assessment of individuals is impossible and should not be attempted.[29] The position taken here is that the complexity of human beings, both individually and collectively, makes faultless prediction and perfect group composition impossible to achieve. However, based on the knowledge of potential group members that the worker can gain in advance, it is beneficial to think about the mix of members in the group that is being planned.

The most important consideration in group composition is the purpose of the group. Commonality of need among the group members which, in turn, brings about a purpose that they share is paramount in the determination of group composition.

Although there are many opinions about group composition, there has been little systematic study of who fits together in groups. Perhaps the most generally accepted principle is what Redl calls "the law of optimum distance." Groups should be homogeneous in enough ways to ensure their stability and heterogeneous in enough ways to ensure their vitality.[30] This principle is based on the premise that the major dynamics in a group are mutual support and mutual aid between members.

Criteria for Membership Selection

Both the descriptive characteristics of people and their behavioral attributes need to be considered in planning for the group's composition. As their name implies, descriptive characteristics describe people—e.g., their age, gender, race, ethnicity, grade in school, occupation, or other "positions" that individuals can be said to occupy. Behavioral characteristics, on the other hand, depict the way an individual acts or can be expected to act— e.g., conforming, impulsive, shy, aggressive. Considerable agreement exists that homogeneity of goals and of some descriptive characteristics provides for feelings of compatibility and interpersonal attraction, leading to mutual acceptance and support. At the same time, heterogeneity of behavioral characteristics, such as patterns of coping and social skills, provides for the stimulation that ensures the group's vitality. Differences make people aware of options, choices and alternatives.[31]

Similarity in descriptive characteristics can enhance the functioning of a group. People hesitate to join groups in which they feel very different from the other members. Group members who share the experience of being in a similar stage of psychosocial development tend to face common life tasks to be mastered and certain common interests to be pursued. Unless there is some strong sense of common fate or a powerful commonality of situation that can overcome age differences, groups are most productive when members' ages are fairly similar. Age is a more important factor in relatively short-term groups than in long-term ones. It is also more important in childhood than in adulthood.

Sex-linked values and norms of behavior are important to the development of identity and successful role performance, even though these continue to change rapidly. Owing to the fact that gender identity, the subjective sense of being male or female, becomes a major component of personality, expectations and role sets become an integral part of gender identity. Women and men in groups are apt to use power and handle opportunities for intimacy differently. Linda Schiller[32] and Barbara Daley and Geraldine Koppenaal[33] see differences between women's groups and men's or co-gender groups in their increased emphasis on intimacy, empathy, and self-disclosure and decreased emphasis on power and control and conflict. Charles Garvin and Beth Reed suggest that in co-gender groups women often occupy less powerful positions.[34]

Cultural values and practices associated with social class, race, ethnicity, and religion are important factors to consider in thinking about group composition during the pregroup planning process. In our society, differences in such factors tend to separate people from one another in work, play, education, and place of residence. Depending upon the group's purpose, homogeneity or heterogeneity in these areas may be readily apparent. In others, they may seem irrelevant to the purpose of the group. But since cultural values and practices influence attitudes, patterns of behavior, and interests, they cannot be ignored. Even when they do not seem relevant immediately to the group's purpose, cultural factors must be recognized and attention must be paid to them in decision making about the group's composition.

One principle is to try to avoid having only one person with an important characteristic in a group. This principle applies to any descriptive characteristic, be it age or gender or grade in school, but it is especially important in regard to cultural factors such as race and ethnicity. Being the only person with a given characteristic contributes to one's sense of difference and nonbelonging. Being the only person of a particular race or ethnicity contributes to one's feeling of being a "token" representative of one's cultural group, which is a very difficult position in which to place a person.

People with similar medical diagnoses are often placed in the same group. A common diagnosis predisposes members toward the development of empathy. In fact, a strong common condition can be so important that it may override criteria for composition that one might use more generally. One example is of a group for couples in which the husband had epilepsy that could not be controlled through the use of medication. There were five couples in that group, with ages ranging from twenty-four to sixty-nine; the members were from different socioeconomic classes; all were "Anglo" except for one Puerto Rican couple. Ordinarily, such group composition would be seen as contrary to good practice. But the commonality of having uncontrollable epilepsy was so important that the group became very cohesive. In this group, the differences that existed between the members were far less important than they might have been in a different group where so crucial a commonality did not exist.

In considering group composition during the planning process, the social worker is concerned not only with the capacities and problems of people but also with modes of coping with the problems. How individuals express themselves, deal with stress and conflict, and defend themselves from threat and hurt influence the nature and content of group interaction. Diversity of ways of coping with problems facilitates the exchange of ideas and feelings between members, provided there is a potential for a strong bond in relation to the purpose and focus of the group. However, members who are too far from the behavioral level of others in the group may struggle unproductively. Irvin Yalom reports that findings from studies indicate that a person perceived by self and others as deviant derives little satisfaction from membership, is less valued by the group, is more likely to be harmed by the experience, and tends to drop out of the group.[35]

When members live together and their problems are those of communication, relationships, and cooperative living, it is usually desirable to work with the unit as a whole. Examples would be a cottage group in a residential treatment facility, a small group foster home, or a family. It is necessary to add the caution that sometimes people need to get away from their families or living groups in order to look at them more objectively and to consider and practice new patterns of behavior that can be tested out later in the living group itself.

Some social workers have suggested that persons with certain problems should be excluded from groups. Some would exclude persons who are grossly ineffective in communication skills, who lack the capacity to understand their own behavior, who are unable to share and need the complete attention of a worker to themselves, or who have weak motivation. They would exclude persons with certain forms of emotional difficulties, e.g., narcissistic, suicidal, and psychotic patients, or those who have severe problems with intimacy or self-disclosure. While it is true that some persons with such problems may not be suitable for particular groups, numerous examples of the successful use of groups with these very same populations can be found. Persons with such problems in relationships and role performance are the very ones who most need the mutual aid and support to be derived from membership in an appropriate group. The question is not whether persons with such problems can be helped; rather, it is whether there is a good fit between the person and other members of the group, together with a practitioner who has the necessary knowledge and skills to use a group for the members' benefit.

In certain instances, it may be necessary to delay entry into a group until a member's basic needs for survival, from both a physical and social stance, are met. Some persons referred to groups come with great uncertainty about whether it will be possible for them to eat, be sheltered, clothed, or nurtured with any continuity and dependability. Some clients may be so overcome with grief or anxiety that they cannot be expected to participate in a group until they have been given immediate help with their particular critical needs on a one-to-one basis. Or some such persons may benefit from concurrent individual and group service. Some persons may find the idea of participating in a group and speaking in front of one's peers quite scary. They might benefit first from individual help that could ready them for eventual group participation. Others might welcome participation with their peers immediately and find the idea of meeting individually with a worker intimidating. For such persons, group participation might ready them for eventual one-to-one help.

Selection of Workers

The characteristics of the social worker, as a member of the group with a special professional role, are an important facet of planning in regard to group composition. There are times when an agency has no options about which staff member will be assigned to work with a particular group. At other times, a choice of worker among agency staff is possible. In either instance, consideration must be given to the characteristics of the social worker and the characteristics of the group members, especially in regard to ethnicity, race, social class, gender, and age. This is not to say that the worker and the group members must share the same descriptive characteristics. There are advantages and disadvantages to both sameness and difference between worker and members. Alfred Kadushin concludes that, with too great a similarity between worker and clients, there is a risk of overidentification and lack of objectivity; with too great a difference, there is a risk of difficulty in achieving understanding and empathy.[36] Clearly, it is imperative that practitioners approach work with clients who are different from themselves with comfort and sensitivity. The weight of the evidence from research is that competence is a more important consideration than the descriptive characteristics of the worker are as these match or differ from those of the members. Barbara Solomon affirms this and sets forth the skills and the underlying knowledge required for the nonracist practitioner.[37] The nonracist practitioner is able to (1) perceive alternative explanations for behavior, (2) collect those verbal and nonverbal cues that are helpful to choose the most probable alternative in a given situation, (3) feel warmth, genuine concern, and empathy for people regardless of their race, color, or ethnic background, and (4) confront clients when they distort or misinterpret true feelings of warmth, concern, and empathy that have been expressed. The same characteristics would be essential also to practitioners working with clients who differ from them in other important ways.

An important issue in planning composition pertains to the number of practitioners who will work with the group.[38] Differences of opinion exist about the efficacy of co-leadership and of solo leadership. One rationale for the use of co-workers is that it improves the accuracy of assessment and the objectivity of workers. One practitioner may observe something that the other misses. A worker's perceptions of the group may become more realistic when they are tested against those of a colleague. A second major rationale is that the use of co-workers can enrich the experience of group members. Since the members can perceive how the co-leaders communicate with each other and handle their differences, they can learn new ways of communication and problem solving. Workers serve as models for members. If the co-workers are of different genders, they can model gender roles for members as well as appropriate heterosexual relations.[39] A third rationale for the use of co-workers is as an aid in group management and the maintenance of safety, particularly with large groups or with groups composed of members, such as those with Alzheimer's disease, who require a great amount of attention within the group.

One rationale for the use of only one practitioner with a group concerns the influence of additional workers on the group process. With the addition of a second worker, there is greater complexity of relationships and communication with which each participant must cope. Each member must develop and sustain a relationship with at least two professionals, which dilutes the intensity of the worker-individual and the worker-group relationships. Members must fathom the workers' differences in expectations for each of them and for the group.

Working with another person is not easy and the difficulties that co-leaders have in working together are likely to be detrimental to the progress of the group. Frequent difficulties are those of rivalry for the affection and attentions of the members, struggles for power to influence particular members or the group's structure and content, and pressures on the co-workers to "prove" themselves to one another and to the group members. If the workers do not share the same theoretical perspectives on practice, they may disagree about ways to intervene in and with the group. Such disagreement can create confusion and uneasiness for the group members. In addition, group members may make unfavorable comparisons between the co-leaders and even pit one against the other.

If co-leadership efforts are to be effective, the practitioners need to spend a great deal of time together—to debrief after each session, to plan for the next one, and to work through their difficulties in roles and relationships. Open and honest communication between co-leaders is essential and takes time and effort to develop. The practical matter of cost in time and money is a factor to be considered in making decisions concerning the number of workers assigned to a group. Since the co-workers must spend time together outside the group, the use of two workers is more than twice as expensive as is the use of only one worker.

Most frequently, the use of more than one practitioner serves as a vehicle for training practitioners. Opinions vary, however, about the use of co-leadership for training purposes. One belief is that trainees need the security and support of a colleague to reduce their anxiety about leading a group. The thinking is that a less able and less experienced worker can learn from observing another worker and from receiving feedback from a colleague. While co-leadership for training purposes can be of value, the difficulty is that in many training situations role definitions are not clear and the trainee is placed in a one-down position, with resultant feelings of inadequacy, especially when given the misleading label of co-leader. If such a pattern of leadership is used, it is necessary to acknowledge the differences between the two workers to each other and to the group members.

Pairing a trainee with an experienced leader may create rather than alleviate anxiety. Beryce MacLennan sees the problem in this way: "It is, however, a paradox that, while the use of co-therapists may potentially provide a sheltered environment in which to learn, very frequently, because of the complicated relationship between the therapists, the group is harder to lead."[40] Often, after the trainee's initial sense of relief at not having to be solely responsible for the leadership of a group, the trainee begins to wish she were the sole leader, especially as her fears lessen and her confidence and ideas grow.[41] At that point, the trainee may experience the co-leader relationship as a confining one. That relationship can be confounded further when the senior leader contributes to the evaluation of the trainee's performance, either formally or informally.

Size of Group

In planning a new group, the optimum size should be in relation to the nature of the interaction desired. Margaret Hartford reviewed the social science literature on the size of groups and concluded that if individual participation, satisfaction, and engagement of the group members in a process that will bring about changes in themselves is the aim of the group, obviously it must be small enough for each person to be heard and to contribute, and also to feel the impact of the group upon his beliefs and behaviors. However, groups should not be so small as to over-expose members or to provide too little stimulation.[42]

That finding still leaves room for the judgment of the worker in determining exactly what size a group should be. Yalom concludes that there seems to be a preference for groups of seven or eight members, with an acceptable range of five to ten.[43] He is, however, referring to semiclosed adult therapy groups; other groups, such as groups of families, need to be larger.

The smaller the group, the more the demand that each member become fully involved in it and the greater the potential and demand for intimacy of relationships. The less anonymous the actions, feelings, and histories of the participants, the higher the rates of participation and the greater the influence of the group on each member. More time is available for each person to test out his attitudes and ideas with others. The smaller the group, the stronger the group pressures on each individual. The smaller the group, the easier the access of a member to the worker and of the worker to each member. The smaller the group, the greater its flexibility in modifying goals to meet the changing needs of its members. However, too small a group may result in a lack of adequate stimulation so that some of the dynamic forces that promote positive changes in people are compromised.

As the size of the group increases, each member has a larger number of relationships to maintain. Each member not only has more other members to interact with but also responds to the dyadic and triadic relationships that have developed. There is less pressure to speak or perform and more opportunity to withdraw occasionally from active participation for silent reflection. Beyond the number of approximately eight to ten, formality in leadership emerges and so do subgroups within the larger group. As groups increase in size, more communication tends to be directed toward the worker rather than toward other members and to the group rather than to specific members. The larger the group, the greater the anonymity of the members and the greater the difficulty in achieving true consensus in decision making. A larger group tends to have greater tolerance for domination by a leader, and the more active members tend to take over the discussion.[44]

Persons differ in regard to the range of relationships they can encompass, on the basis of prior experiences and factors of personality. According to Robert Bales and his associates, "increasing maturity of the personality associated with age permits effective participation in larger groups."[45] Age does influence size, to some extent. But people may be retarded or advanced in their social development. Young children, for example, become overstimulated and confused in a group that seems large; they need to work out their relationships with a few as they move toward efforts in cooperation. For some prospective members, however, the demand for intimacy and active participation in the small group may be too great. The increased anonymity that is permitted in larger groups may be exactly what some persons need at a given time. It cannot be assumed that the smaller the group the greater the value it will have for its members.

In planning, the worker needs to take into account the likelihood that some dropouts and absences will occur once the group gets underway. Therefore, if possible, it is a good idea to initially compose the group that is being formed with a few more members than is the ultimate goal. Doing that allows the group to absorb the loss of some persons that is to be expected. If absences and drop-outs occur in a group that is small to begin with, that group may seem to its remaining members as being of low prestige and undesirable. The result may be rapid and premature disintegration.

To influence the formation of a group whose composition will further the achievement of goals, the worker needs to consider the following questions during the planning process:

- What persons could benefit most from the projected group and, at the same time, not damage the group experience for others?
- What are the important descriptive characteristics of the prospective members? What will be the degree of homogeneity or heterogeneity in regard to such factors as age, grade in school or occupation, gender, race, ethnicity, religion, socioeconomic status, intellectual ability, health, and previous group experiences?
- What are the important behavioral attributes of prospective members? What will be the degree of homogeneity or heterogeneity in regard to such matters as interactional style, patterns of relationships and communication, motivation, and level of psychosocial functioning?

- What are the important commonalities and differences between the members in regard to their descriptive and behavioral characteristics?
- What should the optimal size of the group be? If new members are to be added later, what will be the process of their selection?
- How many practitioners will work with the group? What characteristics and special competencies are important for the workers who will give service to the group? If there is more than one worker, what arrangements will be made to enable them to be truly collaborative?

Structure

As it is used here, *structure* refers to the arrangements that are made to facilitate the conduct of the group, particularly in regard to time and place. Decisions about time and place may seem relatively insignificant at first, but they can have a major impact on the group that is being formed.

Duration

Anticipation of the duration of the group is a part of planning. It is intended that some groups will continue for several months or more and some for only a single session. Others range in duration between these extremes. The duration of the proposed group needs to be related realistically to the purpose of the group and the needs that the group aims to meet. The group's duration has implications for members' behavior. In a group that they know will be in existence for only a short time, members may move in rapidly and focus on the group's content but not invest a great deal in interpersonal relationships. On the other hand, in groups that they know will be together longer, members tend to invest more in their relationships with each other and with the worker as well as in the group's traditions and norms.

While groups of relatively long duration — several months or more — have predominated in social work practice, today's funding patterns and requirements have led to an increase in the proliferation of short-term groups. Ideally, long-term groups are needed if a group's purpose is to develop or restore effective functioning in social relationships and social competence when there are obstacles to the achievement of these goals. It takes time for many people to develop meaningful relationships with each other and with a social worker and to use such relationships for their own and others' benefit, to work through the problems, and to stabilize positive gains before the group terminates.

Nevertheless, short-term groups, usually identified as those between one and twelve sessions, can be quite effective in meeting numerous needs and purposes that are more circumscribed in nature. Short-term groups can be used to prepare their participants for a new role or situation, for example, becoming a nursing home resident, entering a new school; to provide education, particularly when the focus is on presenting a limited amount of content within an atmosphere that makes possible some expression of feelings and ideas and some modification of attitudes and behavior, for example, becoming a foster parent, understanding the needs of an adolescent child, undergoing a particular medical procedure; to help people cope with personal or family crises, for example, a child's suspension from school, the illness of a parent or sibling. In addition, short-term groups can be used for diagnostic purposes by a worker, especially with children, to clarify through direct observation the ways in which problems of children are manifested in social situations.

Another trend in practice is toward the use of one-session groups. Such groups are used to provide information, reduce anxiety, and lessen a sense of isolation through interacting with others who share a similar stressful situation. Single-session groups are particularly useful in medical settings when patients and/or their families may be available for only a brief period of time. Such groups require that a leader take a fairly directive stance and have a central role in fostering group process while at the same time remaining sensitive to and responding flexibly to individual needs. Even with their short duration, single-session groups provide opportunity to involve their participants in a process of sharing and helping one another.[46]

In short-term groups, including single-session groups, the stages of group development are condensed, but present. The degree of cohesion that develops is dependent upon the attraction of members to the stated purpose of the group, clearly focused content, and relatively strong motivation to participate in the group. Short-term groups do demand a willingness to share thoughts and experiences and enter into open communication with strangers at a fairly rapid pace. This is difficult for some persons for whom familiarity with others needs time to evolve.

Short-term groups have a number of advantages. They attract some people to join a group who would be unwilling to make a commitment to participate in a long-term group. In short-term groups, members are more willing to stay the course and thus there are fewer unplanned terminations. In such groups, there is often an enhanced sense of hopefulness that positive changes are possible and that they will occur.

Some people need continued service beyond the one to twelve sessions usually considered maximum for short-term service. The issue is not whether brief or longer service can be effective, for both can be, but rather under what circumstances and for what purposes each type is preferable. Clearly, the group's duration needs to be thought through by the worker in the pregroup planning process.

Frequency of Meetings

How often a group will meet is another area that needs thought in pregroup planning. Groups can vary from the once a week format that seems to be the most common. For some groups, it is advisable that meetings take place more often. In open-ended groups, for example, that have a rapid turnover of members, frequent meetings may be a means of retaining some continuity of participation. Groups in hospitals, especially on children's wards, may meet every day. Separation from their families and friends, anxiety about medical care, and adaptation to a patient role point to the intensity of the children's needs, requiring frequent meetings. Yalom has made a similar case for frequent meetings with patients in mental hospitals, where the average stay is only one to two weeks and where there is continuous turnover of patients.[47] The same might hold true for in-patient substance treatment programs. Crisis intervention groups also tend to meet more often than once a week, owing to the need for quick attention to the upset in the steady state and the attention that must be given to each member's acute situation.

Other groups may need to meet less often than once a week. When members are inundated with many simultaneous demands, it may be possible for a group to meet only biweekly or even monthly. Parents of a child with a serious illness, for example, may not be able to attend a group more often, particularly if they are also working and caring for other children. Persons who are themselves physically ill may be able to regularly attend a group only if it meets less frequently.

Length of Meetings

The length that group meetings will be is another temporal factor that needs consideration in pregroup planning. With some groups, there may be no option in regard to the length of meetings, for that will be determined by the environment in which the group is located. In schools, for example, groups usually must conform to the length of class periods. Another example is in day treatment programs, where groups must be fitted into a larger schedule of activities.

When there is a choice in regard to length of meetings, however, the worker must consider the group's purpose and content as well as the capacities of members for sustained interaction. The most frequent length of group sessions tends to be an hour and a half, which provides time for an opening, a work segment, and an ending period. Shorter sessions, sometimes only a half-hour long, may be as much as young children or seriously disturbed adults can tolerate. Groups in which work on activities or projects takes place may need longer meetings.

Time of Meetings

In pregroup planning, the worker needs to think about the impact that meeting time will have on group composition and attendance. Some people are able to attend a group in the evening who may not be able or willing to do so during daytime hours and vice versa. The routines and responsibilities of potential group members must be taken into account in scheduling the group and in arranging to provide adjunct services, such as care for young children, refreshments, or escort service, when and if these are needed. Working hours of social workers need to be adapted to the members' situations if services are to meet clients' needs effectively. Accessibility of service should be a primary principle of practice.

Meeting Place

For most groups, a decision about meeting place is obvious—the group will meet at the facility of the sponsoring agency. At other times, however, the meeting place may not be automatic and may require decision making and selection by the worker. When a choice of meeting place needs to be made, member comfort is a crucial consideration. Many possible sites may engender discomfort for some group members and the worker needs to be sensitive to that. For example, some former hospital patients may not want to return to the hospital for group meetings; some persons may not be comfortable attending meetings in a church that is not of their own denomination; some may feel embarrassed or stigmatized to be seen entering a particular site; some persons may feel uncomfortable attending meetings at the home of another group member. The worker also needs to consider the location and ease of access of the meeting place.

Meeting Space

The success of a group is influenced by the physical environment in which it meets.[48] The adequacy and atmosphere of the room in which the group meets has an important impact on the development of relationships and group cohesion. With children, the room itself can invite problematic behavior or it can help to provide needed limits; meeting in a room with many inviting distractions can unnecessarily turn the group leader into a disciplinarian.

Some arrangements of space tend to keep people apart, such as chairs in rows or along walls. Chairs arranged so people face each other tend to draw people together. In one agency in which groups of adults meet, the room is bright and light, chairs are informally arranged around a table, and a pot of coffee is provided from which members may help themselves. A contrast is a room with a long board-type table and stiff chairs where no refreshments are permitted. Another contrast is a room that is dirty or full of supplies and equipment not to be used by the group or that contains broken-down furniture. Such rooms, too often prevalent, do not send messages of welcome or respect for the group members.

To foster participation in discussion and intimate relationships, the ideal is a room that is quiet and large enough only for the necessary activities and for an informal circle of chairs within such distance that each member can readily be seen and heard by others. The circle is a symbol of closeness. The space in the center provides some distance, and the spaces between the chairs indicate varied degrees of closeness and remoteness. In an open circle, however, no hiding is possible. A table can be distancing but it can also support members and reduce self-consciousness. A constant location is desirable to reinforce members' identification with the group and provide a sense of continuity.

Social workers need to think through the impact of the physical setting on the members, do what they can to plan for an adequate setting, and then make the best of what is available. Within even poor physical facilities, it is possible for workers to create and maintain a physical atmosphere that is consistent, supportive, and trustworthy.

In planning for a group's structure, the worker needs to consider a range of factors in regard to time and place:

- What are the temporal arrangements for the group and the rationale for them: duration? frequency of meetings? length of meetings? time of meetings?
- What are the physical arrangements for the group and the rationale for them: meeting place? meeting space? arrangements in the meeting room?

Content

Groups do things. The members talk about certain matters; they convey messages through nonverbal behaviors; they engage in activities. Groups vary in the extent to which their content is preplanned, develops spontaneously out of the interaction between members, or is determined by the members through a decision-making process. Content refers to the means that the group will use to achieve its purpose. It encompasses what is done in the group, how it is done, and why it is done. In pregroup planning, the worker needs to think about the what, how, and why of the group's content and develop some tentative ideas that can be proposed to the group.

For some groups, content may be determined largely by state regulations or agency policies. Examples are parenting education groups that are required for foster parent certification or driver education groups that must be taken by persons who engaged in drunk driving. The content of such groups, largely of an educational nature, may be delimited by preset curriculums over which neither members nor group leader may have much to say.

In most groups, however, content will be decided upon by the members and the worker together. During the planning process, the worker needs to think about content possibilities, especially as they relate to the purpose of the group and the goals of the group members. It is through the group's content that purpose and goals are achieved. The worker also needs to take into account the members' age and stage of development. It would be unrealistic, for instance, to ask a group of seven-year-olds to engage in hour-long, discussion-only groups, while such a demand would be quite realistic for a bereavement group of adults who have recently lost a spouse. Content also needs to take into account the group's situation and surround. It would be unrealistic, for example, to ask fifth-graders to settle down immediately in a group that begins as soon as their school day ends. Such a demand, however, would be quite appropriate for a reminiscence group with elderly persons that meets mid-morning at a senior center.

In thinking about group content, the worker also needs to consider the resources and supplies that will be available to the group. Obviously, the group's content needs to be planned with that availability in mind. Does the agency, for example, have funds to rent space or pay activity specialists for what might be popular activities for adolescents, such as rock climbing or camping trips? Gaining knowledge of the resources that will be feasible, accessible, and obtainable is an important part of pregroup planning.

Planning for the first meeting of a new group is also an important part of the thinking that is needed regarding content. The first meeting of a group helps set a tone for the group and for the nature of the interactions that will follow. Since the emotional tone and quality of relationships tend to determine whether members will return after the first meeting, careful attention needs to be given to the nature and sequence of the content of that meeting. What is important is that the plans that the worker develops for the first group meeting complement and recognize the needs and concerns that group members, at that point in the early life of the group, are likely to have. Those needs are discussed in chapter 12 where the Orientation and Inclusion stage is addressed.

In considering the area of content during the pregroup planning process, the worker needs to ask the following questions:

- What will be the general nature of the content of group sessions, that is, reflective discussion, activities, educational material? What is the rationale for their use in achieving the group's purpose and meeting the members' goals?
- How and by whom will group content be planned? Are there policies and regulations that require particular content? If necessary, can these be changed or adapted to meet the needs of the group?

- What resources and supplies will be available to the group?
- What will be the nature and sequence of the content of the first meeting of the group?

Illustrations of Planning

The final component of planning, pregroup contact, is discussed in chapter 6. Before closing chapter 5, however, two plans for groups are presented. One, for a group in a mental hospital, summarizes plans made in each area of the pregroup planning model. The second, for a group in a settlement house youth program, looks at the process of planning and the interaction between components.[49] Both are included here to illustrate the content and process of planning in order to clarify the framework that has been presented and demonstrate its use in actual practice.

A Group in a Mental Hospital

Social and agency contexts. Within a large mental hospital, a social work intern was assigned to a ward of regressed and withdrawn patients with schizophrenia. Most patients in the hospital are there for very short stays, according to policies that prohibit compulsory hospitalization for more than a few days without a court order. There are, however, several wards for longer-term and severely dysfunctional patients who are there voluntarily or have been committed. The hospital has an unusually good treatment program for these patients. It has a policy of encouraging social workers to work with groups of patients as well as to offer help individually. The ward has a well-functioning team consisting of psychiatrists, nurses, technicians, and social workers. The social work intern participates in team meetings at which the progress of each patient is discussed and decisions are made concerning any changes in treatment, and the intern has access to other staff as deemed advisable. Ongoing collaboration with other professional staff on the ward is necessary to ensure that all staff members will support the patients' attendance and help patients to apply learnings from the group to their daily living.

Need. At a meeting of the ward team, the nurse identified several patients not in groups who needed help in relating more realistically to staff and to one another. The patients' behavior was characterized by apathy, lack of interest in ward and wider hospital activities, and much restless behavior. They sat on benches in a corridor with very little interaction between them. They seldom responded to efforts to engage them in conversation. They were among the newest patients on the ward and had not responded well in therapeutic interviews. They seemed unable to seek and use relationships with other patients: some were even unaware of the presence of other people and unable to respond to comments and questions made by staff in ways that they could be understood. Other members of the team agreed with the nurse's assessment and recommendation that a new group be started for them.

Purpose. The purpose of the group was defined as helping the patients to become aware of and develop supportive relationships with others, at each one's level of capacity to do so, and to begin to develop some sense of self-esteem and competence. Within this purpose, specific goals varied with each patient but were most often to help patients feel comfortable in being with others and learn that it helps to listen and be listened to, to help patients identify problems in getting along on the ward and try to lessen those problems, to help patients learn that they are acceptable to others, and to enhance participation in appropriate aspects of the hospital's program. All these goals are directly related to the use of the group for the enhancement of social relationships and role competence.

Composition. The decision was made to begin the group with seven patients, small enough for the members to be able to interact with each other and large enough for them not to be too frightened by the intensity of too close relationships. Based on an assessment of the psychosocial functioning of each of the new patients on the ward, the decision was made to include the seven men who seemed most unable to participate in ward activities. Among these seven, however, there were two who were more advanced than the others in their ability to talk and respond to other people. The age range was from twenty-eight to forty. Three black and five white men were included. The social worker was a white male. The common needs of the patients were the primary consideration, but there was no one who might feel too different from the others and there seemed to be sufficient heterogeneity to provide as much stimulation as these men could tolerate.

Structure. It was decided that this would be a closed group, with new members added only in the event of a vacancy, making it possible for the members to develop trust and support from each other over a period of time. It was to be an informal, process-oriented discussion-activity group. Patients who have extreme difficulties in social relationships and low self-esteem need a considerable amount of structure and continuity of experience. They also tend to have, like young children, short attention spans. For these reasons, the group was set up to meet three times a week in order to provide continuity of experience, with meetings lasting only one-half hour until members indicated they could tolerate longer meetings. The duration of the group was tentatively scheduled for three months, by which time it was expected the members would be ready for more advanced forms of treatment. The group was to meet before lunch when the meeting would not interfere with other ward activities and schedules. The meetings were to be held in a pleasant small recreation room, and arrangements were made for the group to have exclusive use of the room, with no interruptions during the scheduled time. Later, patients would be taken out of the ward to test their ability to use more freedom and try out new experiences. When this happens, a case aide will be available to assist the worker in helping the members to use the new experiences.

Content. Because these patients are unable to engage in any focused discussion, and requests to talk are very threatening to them, it was planned that the content of the group consist of simple nonthreatening activities and brief discussion periods. Coffee and tea would be offered to reduce anxiety, give the men something to do with their hands, and enhance motivation to come to the group. Beginning meetings would be structured sufficiently for patients to come to know what to expect and develop some sense of security and support. The worker decided to begin the first meeting with a reminder of the purpose of the group and its expectations, emphasizing that the members will benefit from coming. There would then be a short period of doing something that makes few demands in relating to others and in verbalizing—stretching, a name game, follow the leader, tossing balloons, whatever seems appropriate. Then it would be time to talk in a structured way, often taking turns in saying one thing they felt about coming to the group, one thing they would like to try to do in the group sometime, or what their favorite foods are—the possibilities are endless, but they should make a minimum of demands on the patients. In a brief closing, the meeting would be summarized very briefly and a reminder given about the next meeting.

A Group in a Settlement House Youth Program

Agency context   The settlement received a small grant from a consortium of settlements designed to encourage work with girls in its youth program. The consortium's belief was that girls had been traditionally underserved in settlement youth programs. No requirements were attached to this

Composition   grant except that the agency use the funds to work with groups of girls. Funds were used to hire a part-time worker for the project. A person who had considerable experience in work with children and groups was selected.

Agency context   The settlement's program director called a meeting of the new worker, the agency's camp director, youth director and talent search director (all persons in the agency responsible for

Social context   work with youth) to discuss the project. Girls in the community who were in the sixth grade were identified as a target group for service. It was felt that they especially were being under-

Composition   served in settlement activities, since they felt too old for programs for elementary school youngsters and too young for the settlement's teen pro-

Need   grams. Experience at the settlement and at the agency's resident summer camp had demonstrated that sixth graders are entering a difficult transition period as they develop emotionally, physically, and socially and go from elementary school to junior high school and from latency to adolescence. Literature also indicated that

Need   the self-image and self-confidence of girls began to change for the worse at just about this age and stage in their development. In addition, it was known that the junior high schools in the

Social context   community were very unstructured in comparison to the tight structure that existed in the elementary and parochial schools in the community.

With this target group in mind, the worker spoke with a number of public and parochial school teachers and administrators in the community. Both sixth and seventh grade teachers and administrators confirmed that girls of this

Need

age group were largely unserved in any type of after school programs. Public school personnel spoke of the lack of after school services because of massive cutbacks that had just been made in the Board of Education's budget. The principal of the local Catholic school also mentioned the

Social context

lack of supervised after school activities and the large number of very protective parents of chil-

Need

dren in her school who did not let their children play outside after school in a neighborhood they saw as dangerous. These parents, she thought, would allow their children to participate in an after school program at the settlement.

The guidance counselor for seventh graders at one of the two local junior high schools identified the transition from elementary to junior

Need

high school as an especially difficult one for the girls in this neighborhood. Once in seventh grade, she said, truancy, drugs, pregnancy, and alcohol become major problems. Many of the new seventh graders, she added, dealt with the comparative lack of structure of the seventh grade in one of two ways: "They become quiet and terrified and fade into the woodwork or they decide now is the time to break out and go free and they start to act out like mad."

At this point, the worker spoke informally with a number of new seventh graders and neigh-

Need   borhood parents. They confirmed the view expressed by the junior high school guidance
counselor as they spoke of their own difficulties
in entering junior high school or of the predic-
aments faced by their children.

Considering her knowledge of developmental
stages, the comments of the junior high school
Need   guidance counselor, and the lack of structure
she knew to exist in the local junior high
schools, the worker began to think the group
Purpose   might be particularly helpful if it were to concentrate on decision making. She hypothesized
that seventh graders who "faded into the woodwork" or who "acted out and got into trouble"
Content   had difficulty both in making decisions for
themselves and in handling the increased free-
Need   dom of junior high school. Girls who "faded
into the woodwork" in junior high, she hypothesized, were most likely those who in sixth grade
were shy and withdrawn. Girls who "acted out"
in junior high might be those who in sixth grade
Composition   were loud and domineering. Both types of girls,
she felt, probably had difficulty making or keeping friends.

Composition   Thus, the group might be composed of both
types of girls: shy and withdrawn and loud and
domineering. Since both types of girls had difficulty making decisions, the shy girls tending
to be "followers" who "went along with the
crowd" and the domineering girls tending to be
"insensitive leaders" who "told people what to
Purpose   do," a tentative group purpose was arrived at: to
help the group members make decisions sensi-
tively and independently.

Need

Composition

Need

Composition

Pregroup contact

The worker then returned to the sixth grade teachers in the community with whom she had spoken initially. She described to them the characteristics of the girls she had in mind and asked them whether they could identify such youngsters in their classes. Every teacher with whom she spoke was able to easily identify girls in the two categories and readily acknowledged that these were girls who were having special problems in school. The worker then asked each sixth grade teacher to identify the girls he or she had in mind for such a group. The worker decided on an initial group size of ten, considering that it would be likely that some girls would drop out and that there would be absentees. She also felt that such a group would function best if there were more "followers" than "domineering" members (too many leaders and too few followers would have made group management quite difficult, she felt).

The worker then set up individual meetings with each of the girls identified by their teachers as possible group members. The meetings took place at the local schools. The worker described to each girl the kind of group she had in mind and the characteristics of the girls she wanted to serve. Her criteria for considering a girl for the group were three: (1) that the girl indicate that she wanted to be in the group, (2) that she see herself as either a "follower" or an "insensitive leader"--i.e., that she be able to identify with and see herself as the kind of girl the worker described to her, (3) that she indicate that she was unhappy being a "follower" or "insensitive leader"--i.e., that she wished to change this aspect of her behavior.

Pregroup contact

Most of the girls connected easily to the worker's description. For the "followers" there was often a look of relief as the worker described the group. One "insensitive leader" commented immediately, "Bossy! Yeah, that's me." Once a girl had met the three criteria, the worker contacted

Pregroup contact

the girl's parents. She made home visits to the parents of each of the eligible girls, explaining the group, eliciting their concerns, and asking for their permission to allow their daughters to participate. Such visits provided the worker with

Social context

information about each girl's home and family situation. Parents seemed to appreciate the worker's involving them. After meeting the girls, the worker felt that weekly meetings of the group would not be sufficient. She felt that

Structure

meeting twice weekly would be best. She also decided that meetings should be held immediately after school since many parents had indicated that they would not permit their daughters to attend group meetings after dark. The worker was surprised when quite a few parents said that they would not allow their daughters to walk to the settlement by themselves. This meant the girls would need to be picked up at school and

Structure

escorted home after group meetings.

The worker felt that many of the girls had difficulty verbalizing their thoughts and feelings during her interviews with them. Thus, she felt

Content

that lengthy discussions would be difficult in the group, especially at first. She also knew that lengthy discussions would be dominated by some of the members and not participated in by

Content

others. Thus, she decided that group content would need to consist of both activity and discussion. She formulated some program ideas

Purpose

and decided to wait until the group began meeting to decide exactly which activities she would attempt, based on the interests of the members. Content, however, was to be directly related to the purpose of the group, in that time would be allotted for the girls to make decisions about it and then look at the roles they had played in both the activities and the decision making.

Planning, Self-Determination, and the Race for Numbers

Despite recognition of the importance of planning, all too often it is disregarded or done summarily in actual practice. Two factors might possibly explain its continuing neglect. First, planning may seem to some to negate the value that social workers place on client self-determination. Not wanting to tell people what to do and not wishing to manipulate clients, some social workers may avoid planning because they view it as synonymous with manipulation and with the denial of self-determination. Such an explanation for the lack of planning was suggested by John Dewey, a progressive educator and social scientist whose work has greatly influenced social group work practice. Dewey suggested that lack of sufficiently thoughtful planning contributed to a teacher's inability to maintain control in the classroom. Such planning was usually not done, he said, because it was thought to be opposed to the freedom of the individual.

But Dewey rejected such thinking. Because some planning is rigid and leaves little room for individual freedom, he said, it does not follow that all planning must be rejected. Dewey wrote that, on the contrary

> there is incumbent upon the educator the duty of instituting a much more intelligent and more difficult kind of planning. He must survey the capacities and needs of the particular set of individuals with whom he is dealing and must at the same time arrange the conditions which provide the subject matter of content for experiences that satisfy these needs and develop these capacities.

Dewey stressed, "The planning must be flexible enough to permit free play for individuality of experience and yet firm enough to give direction towards continuous development of power.[50]

Pregroup planning does not diminish but instead enhances the opportunities for client self-determination. It results in increased clarity about the
group that is being established. Such clarity, in turn, increases the client's
ability to make a clear and informed decision about whether to participate
in the proposed group. Planning can result in minimizing client manipulation and domination by the worker and in maximizing client self-
determination.

Planning does not mean imposing on people. As planning is carried out
and service is initiated, the worker's tentative conceptions about the group
being formed may change, especially as the worker begins to get to know
better both the clients and their situations. It is important that the worker
be flexible and open to change. But the probability that increased knowledge
will change conceptions does not negate the importance and value of the
worker's immersion in the planning process.

A second reason that little attention is given to planning may be found
in the profession's emphasis on action and direct work with clients. Social
workers may view planning as a rather passive activity that unnecessarily
takes time from such direct work. Perhaps the tendency to rush into action
without having done the needed planning is exacerbated by increased emphasis by reimbursement systems on numbers served. Quantity has become
paramount. But one can certainly argue that thoughtful pregroup planning
results in an increase in the numbers served while simultaneously enhancing
the quality of service.

A group's first meeting may have to be deferred while planning takes
place. But the regular attendance of members that is characteristic of well-
planned groups will soon overtake the numbers of persons served in groups
that start quickly but then fall apart. As in the fabled contest between the
tortoise and the hare, quickest is not necessarily best. The race for quantity
that characterizes today's funding pressures will be won by an approach that
stresses thoughtful preparation.

6   Pregroup Contact: Selection and Preparation of Members

A fundamental part of the planning process, pregroup contact entails the securing of appropriate members for the group being planned and their preparation for participation in that group. Different procedures are used by different organizations to accomplish this, but basically pregroup contact aims to help people know about the availability and nature of the service, determine their eligibility for service, ascertain if their goals are sufficiently similar to those of others to be met through a group, and prepare them for entry into a particular group.

Members are secured for group participation in essentially one of two ways: either agency staff go out to persons in the community and inform them of an available service or persons come to an agency to request a service. The method of selection of members for group participation also ranges. In some groups, a person's desire to participate is in itself sufficient for membership; in others, an intake procedure is required and a person must be accepted for membership.

Recruitment and Outreach

Many groups are formed to accommodate all the persons in a particular target population who wish to attend. For example, a health maintenance organization may start a wellness group for adult members who have been recently diagnosed with diabetes, a senior center may form a safety awareness group for center members who live by themselves, an employee assistance program in a university may offer a group for staff who are members of the sandwich generation, i.e., caring for their parents and their children simultaneously. Such groups can be designated as Come One Come All (COCA) groups in that they are open to all members of the target population. They are geared toward persons who share a common human need for help in some aspect of social living, but who are generally functioning within a normal range of expectations. Such groups are usually of a preventive nature in that they aim to help their members maintain effective social functioning. Workers who are going to recruit for COCA groups must think about how and where to publicize the group to get the attention of persons in the target population in a way that will be inviting of their attendance and participation.

Other groups may be targeted more specifically to particular persons who workers know to have a distinct need or situation in common. For example, the director of a senior center may know that seven center members have lost adult children to cancer in the past two months, social workers at an agency that serves women with AIDS may know that a number of clients want to tell their children that they have AIDS but have not done so because they are fearful and unsure about how to tell them, a school social worker may be aware that at least twelve third- and fourth-graders who are new to the school have moved to permanent housing in the neighborhood after having lived in homeless shelters for more than a year. In each of these instances, the workers believe that commonalities of need based on social situations are likely to be present. Here, the groups that the workers want to form can be designated as By Invitation Only (BIO) groups. BIO groups are similar to COCA groups in that they are geared toward persons who share a common human need, but BIO groups are aimed at particular persons to whom the worker wants to extend a special invitation. Workers who are trying to form BIO groups must think about how to approach and what exactly to say to the persons they speak with so that their response to the invitation that is extended will be positive.

Often, the possible candidates for membership in BIO groups are known directly to workers. Through their own direct work in an agency, they become aware of particular persons with particular needs. Sometimes they know of only a few persons with a particular need, not enough to compose a group. But the need they have identified may be pressing, even if it applies to only a few persons. In such an instance, workers might contact other staff, in their own agency as well as in others, to ascertain whether other persons are known who share the identified need. If so, then a plan to reach out to such persons needs to be made, including decisions about the content of the approach and by whom it should be made.

In still other groups, the COCA and BIO approaches to recruitment might be used in combination. Social workers in the employee assistance program, for example, might publicize the "sandwich generation" group generally, while at the same time they might extend personal invitations to a few particular persons whom they know to be struggling with the simultaneous care of parents and children. Or social workers in the AIDS organization might invite personally those mothers they know to be grappling with telling their children and also publicize the group more widely by putting signs up in the agency's waiting room.

When workers reach out to recruit persons for groups, whether they use COCA and/or BIO approaches, it is important that they be aware of how difficult and scary it can be for persons to get themselves to attend a group that is new and unknown to them, especially when they were not the ones to initiate the request for group membership. Thus, outreach to and recruitment of potential group members need to be done with sensitivity and perceptiveness. There are times when workers are so intent on getting persons to agree to join a group that they address them as if they were customers whom they must convince to buy the item (i.e., the group) that is being sold. If workers approach recruitment as if they must sell a product, no matter whether a client wants or needs it or not, their hard-sell approach is likely to cause the potential "buyer" to feel pressured. Wanting to get rid of the "salesperson," potential group members may adamantly deny their need for the group or they may accede and agree to come when they actually have no intention of doing so.

Sometimes just the opposite occurs. Workers reach out to and approach someone who, based on their knowledge of that person and her situation, they may be quite sure can benefit from the group that is being formed. They tell the person about the group and invite her to attend. But then, if the potential member's first reaction is one of noninterest, they feel they must not violate that person's right to self-determination. Since they do not wish to impose, they, too quickly retreat, accepting the person's negative response at face value and never exploring with the person her needs and the group's possible benefits. Such action on the part of the worker is a misuse of the principle of self-determination and exemplifies ineffective outreach.[1]

When approaching a person to join a BIO group, the worker begins with some information about the potential member's situation, at least to the extent that that person fits the category of need that the group is being formed to address. But it is important that the worker not make assumptions and immediately begin a sales pitch for the group. Instead, a conversation is required with the person to whom outreach is being made, during which the potential member's thoughts and feelings about the situation and about participation in the group can be elicited and explored. The worker needs to be open to the possibility that the person and the group are not a good match and that group membership is not right for this particular person at this particular time. If, on the other hand, group membership for this person does seem to make sense to the worker, but the potential member seems reluctant to join, the worker needs to be prepared to articulate and then discuss the reasons that he believes the group will be of value. Such articulation is not synonymous with imposition. Ultimately, the choice to join a BIO group belongs to the person to whom an invitation is being extended.

Recruitment for COCA groups is of a more impersonal nature. Workers can use a range of methods, either singly or in combination: signs can be posted and flyers can be placed at the agency or on neighborhood bulletin boards in well-trafficked areas, notices can be put in newsletters and in area newspapers that are likely to be read by possible group members, arrangements can be made to speak about the group at a gathering, such as a PTA meeting, where potential group members might be present, letters or brochures can be sent to all those on the agency's mailing list even though it is known that many on that list will not be interested in the group. Because of the fear of the unknown that is usual for people, when notices are posted or mailed out, workers should not expect a large response rate. Such notices usually briefly describe the group, giving an indication of its purpose and content and the population to whom the group is aimed. Included are the name and telephone number of the worker that persons who are interested can contact.

In COCA groups, pregroup screening does not usually take place. Instead, contact with the worker, usually on the telephone, is done more to ascertain whether the person really is interested in the group, to answer questions the person may have, and to help the caller feel more at ease in coming to a meeting of the group. The disadvantage of the COCA approach is that practitioners begin their work with a minimal amount of prior knowledge about the prospective members. Similarly, members begin with a minimal amount of knowledge about the group. An advantage of the COCA approach is that entry into a group can be made without the formal intake procedures that can be distancing for some persons.[2]

Assessment

When a person comes to an agency to request help, a more formal procedure is usually initiated to ascertain what that person's needs are and whether a group service is in order. For counseling and therapy groups, for example, assignment to a group is generally based on a process of exploration and assessment. The worker who does the assessment, however, may not be the worker who will be leading the group. When the two workers are different, it is important that what was learned about the person during the assessment process be conveyed to the worker who will be leading the group. It may be a good idea, as well, for the group worker to then speak with the person directly to explore concerns about group membership and to prepare the person for group participation.

According to Max Siporin, assessment is "a differential, individualized, and accurate identification and evaluation of problems, people, and situations and of their interrelations, to serve as a sound basis for differential helping intervention."[3] The importance of assessment or diagnosis for sound social work practice has been recognized from the profession's beginnings.[4] Assessment, as it is used in social work, goes beyond the identification of a problem or illness to an appraisal of the interrelation between biological, psychological, sociocultural, and environmental factors and to positive motivations and capacities. To achieve an accurate appraisal or the meaning of the facts that have been secured, the worker makes appropriate use of typologies of needs and problems, sources of information, and criteria for judging the adequacy of the functioning of individuals or groups and their environments.

Assessment is an ongoing process, not just a first step in practice. From appropriate fact finding about the members and the group system, the practitioner formulates opinions about the nature of the members' characteristics, problems, and potentials. This leads quite naturally and logically to planning for what should be done to enable the members to improve their functioning or to influence changes in the wider social system. The worker later evaluates the impact of the intervention on the members and the group process, which itself involves further fact finding and opinion forming, and so the cycle of understand, plan, intervene, and evaluate goes on in a dynamic way.

It is neither necessary nor possible to have all the facts about persons to make a preliminary judgment about their suitability for a particular group. Workers begin with what facts are relevant to the decision to accept a person for placement in a particular group. They then continue to add to their storehouse of knowledge as they judge what additional information will be helpful in serving individuals and the group as a whole.

In the process of assessment, the goals of the prospective members should be paramount. A person's positive motivations in seeking help or her aspirations are at least as important as her problems are, or, in the words of Mary Richmond, "Our examinations of the yesterdays and the todays should be with special reference to the client's tomorrows."[5] If workers start with the person's interest in having something be better about self or situation, their subsequent acts are apt to be goal directed. Prospective members may be clear about what they hope for or have only vague feelings of discontent with the current situation. They may be articulate or need much help in expressing themselves. Accompanying the positive motivations toward the opportunity available, resistance to change may be evident. Fear of the unknown and of their own capacities to meet expectations may interfere with their ability to identify some goals related to the group's proposed purpose.

To observe and test for capacities, positive attitudes, areas of successful accomplishment, and supports in the environment are equally as important as knowledge about problems and deficits. For it is such strengths that can be used and built on in the group. Knowledge of normal growth, development, and behavior relevant to particular subcultures and situations, as well as deviations from norms, is used by practitioners to make possible a valid social assessment of the members and their social situations.

Identifying a type of problem is one important part of understanding it. The severity of the problem needs to be ascertained. Some problems may be as minimal as the need for help in anticipating the demands of a particular stage in the life cycle to prevent a problem from developing. Usually transitional or socioeducational groups are the most appropriate forms of help. Most cases that come to the attention of social workers involve life transitions, changes in roles, and relationships. On the other hand, many problems are severe ones that create tremendous stress for the clients and also often have negative effects on those with whom they interact. Some problems are diagnosed as physical illness or mental disorders. Practitioners need to remember that social work treatment is not directed toward a disorder; it must be tailored to the person-situation gestalt, the network of multiple interacting factors that influence how the person reacts to stressors and pathologic processes.[6] They need to differentiate instances when problems are extensive, pervasive, and catastrophic from instances when change is less problematic. The severity and chronicity of the difficulties have an impact on the kind of service to be provided and the kind of group in which it will be provided.

Guidelines for the Content of Assessment

Crucial for success in helping members use group life toward the achievement of individual and group purposes is the worker's acumen in assessment. The tasks of fact finding and evaluation are somewhat different for each group, depending upon its particular purposes, composition, and structure. Nevertheless, certain guidelines provide workers with a frame of reference for viewing each member in relation to the group and to the external situation. A basic assumption underlying the framework for assessment is that human behavior is the product of the interaction between persons and their environments. Every human being has an interdependent relationship with others and is a component of a number of interlocking social systems. Certain dimensions of behavior can be understood only in terms of the structure and function of these networks of interaction and the member's status and role in them. The practitioner's assessment relates, therefore, both to individuals and the persons to whom they are connected and the significant social systems of which they are a part. At both individual and group levels, the worker is concerned with the nature of stresses from internal and external forces and with the capacity and motivation of the system to withstand stress, cope with change, and find new or modified ways of functioning.

Any group experience occurs in association with continued life experiences at home and in the community. William Schwartz captures this idea well when he states that a group does not meet for ten sessions but rather for ten weeks.[7] The social worker's relationships, no matter how close, are tangential to those experienced by the members in everyday life. It is these relationships that need to be changed, supported, or strengthened.[8] Within a developmental perspective, the assessment takes into account the interrelatedness of affect, cognition, values, and behavioral patterns. It seeks to ascertain the capacities and limitations of members in each major area of ego functioning, with special reference to self-esteem, identity, judgment, perceptions of reality, adequacy of communication, balance between freedom of expression and rigid control, the appropriateness of defenses and coping patterns, and, above all, the range and quality of social relationships. Most members have both abilities and difficulties in social relationships when they enter a group, and the group serves as an arena for working on and improving peer relationships.

External circumstances combine with intrapersonal and interpersonal processes in affecting the adequacy of a person's functioning. The major social systems in the community provide resources and opportunities or, too often, barriers to the fulfillment of needs. An adequate assessment takes into account the impact of these systems on individuals, families of members, and the group. A question is the extent to which these systems provide nondiscriminatory access to services for all people and to what extent they create stress and serve as obstacles to effective functioning.

Of great importance in assessment is the impact that race and ethnicity have on a person's functioning. Effectiveness of functioning needs to be measured in culturally sensitive ways with recognition and acknowledgment of the critical influence that race and ethnicity have on a person's worldview, belief system, and extent of opportunity. With some persons, recency of migration or immigration and extent of acculturation need to be considered.[9] Similarly, the importance of worldview, belief system, and extent of opportunity also needs to be considered during the assessment process in relation to a person's gender and sexual orientation and their central impact on a person's social functioning.[10]

Several writers have offered detailed outlines of the content deemed to be essential for making sound assessments.[11] Gertrude Wilson and Gladys Ryland and Ronald Toseland and Robert Rivas have given much attention to the interrelationships between the assessment of individuals, the group as a whole, and the group's environment.[12] Practitioners can become overwhelmed by the vast amount of data it is possible to secure, unless they have clear guidelines to assist them in exploring for pertinent information and selecting appropriate means for obtaining the desired information. The following questions provide guidelines for assessment.

1. Who is the client in terms of demographic characteristics, stage of development in the life cycle, ethnic background and identity, social class, and family structure?
2. What problem or problems are of concern to the client, the worker, and significant persons in the client's social network? Are the problems suitable to be addressed in a group? To what extent are the problems related to changes in roles, developmental tasks, or crises as contrasted with impairments in ego capacities or developmental arrests? To what extent is the problem due to lack of environmental resources or social supports or to lack of fit between the person and subsystems of the environment?
3. How, when, and to whom did the need or problem become evident and what were the precipitating factors?
4. What are the client's attitudes toward self, peers, family members, and persons in positions of authority?
5. What are the range and quality of the person's relationships within the family, with peers, and in the group?
6. What are the capacities and resources within the client and in the network of social systems that can be supported and developed further in behalf of the client?
7. To what extent is the client motivated to become a member of the group? What indicators are there of positive motivation and what is the nature of apparent resistances?
8. What feasible goals, acknowledged by the client, are congruent with the group's purpose?
9. Are the agreed upon goals appropriate to the characteristics of the client and the social situation?
10. What types of intervention are apt to best meet the needs of the particular client?

The amount and nature of the information sought vary with the many facets of the service, particularly its purpose and structure and the practitioner's theoretical orientation. The preliminary assessment cannot encompass all aspects of the person's or group's functioning. In accord with the value of the right to privacy, the information sought should be limited to what is essential for achieving agreed upon goals. If a service is one of primary prevention or enhancement of normal development, the data obtained are often limited initially to the descriptive characteristics of the clients, phase of development, common experience or status, and certain potential risks to healthy development. Later, during the process of service, the worker elicits additional information as it seems particularly relevant. If the service is a therapeutic or rehabilitative one, helpful treatment relies upon the worker's understanding of the nature, causative factors, and course of the problematic situation and the adequacy of the client's current functioning in particular situations.

When pertinent information has been obtained, the actual assessment consists of the analysis of the person-group-environment configuration. The purposes are to identify the most critical factors operating and to define their interrelationships. The assessment is the practitioner's professional opinion about the facts and their meaning. Mary Louise Somers and Helen Perlman have both referred to this process as one of problem solving by the worker, performed through a process of reflective thinking.[13] Harold Lewis states that it is a logical process that also incorporates intuitive insights.[14] Realistic appraisal provides the basis for action that should be guided by facts. What is to be understood are the nature of the need or trouble, the factors that contribute to it, the participants' motivations and capacities, and a judgment about what can be changed, supported, or strengthened in the person-group-situation configuration. Assessment is not completed when a problem or condition has been identified and pertinent data have been obtained from appropriate sources. There remains the need to explain how it has come to be the way it is. The practitioner draws inferences from the data and relates these judgments to the service that must be given. The behavioral science theory used largely determines the inferences made.

Knowledge of the psychosocial development of people throughout the life cycle alerts the worker to what should be observed and checked out if the members are to be well served. Each phase of development incorporates psychosocial tasks to be mastered if the person is to make a successful transition to the next stage. Every culture has norms or expectations used to judge the extent to which a person or a group is functioning adequately. Appraisal of a person's position on a continuum, ranging from very effective to very ineffective functioning, clues the worker in to both capacities and problems. The assessment is made against standards for physical, cognitive, emotional, and social functioning deemed to be within a range of normality for persons within a given stage of the life cycle and within a given culture. These norms need to be differentiated according to such important influences on psychosocial functioning as age, gender, urban or rural community, school grade or occupation, race or nationality, religion, and economic status.

Determining the adequacy of behavior needs to take into account such judgments as whether the behavior is appropriate to the client's stage of development, how long it has persisted, whether it is a reaction to change in circumstances or a devastating crisis, whether the behavior interferes with only one or several roles, what the type, severity, and frequency of symptoms are, and whether there are changes in behavior of a kind not expected in terms of normal maturation and development.

The social worker considers the fact that all phases of human development overlap, that each person has his own rate of maturation and development within what are average expectations, and that there are many variations within a normal pattern of functioning. A person's feelings about her assigned roles, the way she interprets them, and her responses to the expectations of others give clues to the fit between persons and their environments. A person may adapt well in one situation and poorly in another. The worker is, therefore, concerned with variations in effectiveness of role functioning in different social systems—whether ineffective functioning in one system is affecting ability to adapt elsewhere and whether successful functioning in one system can be used as a bridge to more effective functioning in other systems.

Clients come from varied cultural backgrounds. One task for the worker is to ascertain the influence of race and ethnicity on psychosocial functioning. Persons in positions of power, including social workers, may come to expect stereotyped behavior and plan and act accordingly. Awareness of one's own norms and culture is essential to prevent stereotyping, as is accurate knowledge about other cultures and lifestyles. Accurate assessment requires the ability to consider alternative explanations of difficulties. When a causative statement is proposed, the worker has made a choice from among alternatives: accuracy requires that the selection of alternatives be a conscious one. Barbara Solomon gives the example of a girl assessed as being discriminated against in school or, alternatively, as a child having difficulty adapting to a new school in which she feels isolated and lonely.[15] The need is to determine which alternative is more probable through careful exploration of one's own preferences and of the member's situation, including environmental factors. Explanations must be individualized. Lewis points out, for example, that not everyone subjected to social injustice has developed the same responses; the assessment explains how a particular individual was victimized and what the person's responses were to the event.[16] Strengths, as well as difficulties, are located. Such an approach deemphasizes stereotyping, through establishing the unique as well as the common responses to factors that contribute to a particular condition.

The practitioner's decision-making ability is somewhat limited by the need for rapid intervention in many urgent situations. Ultimately, however, skill in rapid assessment is achieved through extensive and thorough knowledge of human behavior. Knowing when and how to alter initial assumptions is also essential to the exercise of professional judgment. The product of an analysis is, according to Siporin, a formulation that integrates the data and draws conclusions about the interrelated factors that contribute to the problematic situation, leading to decisions about interventions to be implemented.[17]

Pregroup Interviews

Pregroup interviews are used for two purposes: to make an assessment of a prospective group member and to prepare that person for entry and participation in the group. The two purposes might be addressed in a single pregroup interview or they might be done in separate meetings. Even if done separately, however, there is likely to be overlap between the two purposes, with some information gathering and some orientation occurring simultaneously. Both purposes, if they are to be achieved, require that the worker be skilled in interviewing in order to set a positive climate, make the applicant as comfortable as possible, engage the prospective member, and explore the person's thinking and feelings. In interviews for assessment purposes, as discussed in the previous section, the worker aims primarily to elicit information about prospective clients and their situations. In interviews for preparation purposes, the worker's focus is primarily on orienting prospective members to the group they will be joining and to the expectations of membership.

Assessment interviews can provide the worker with information about the prospective member's patterns of relationships and about the person's perceptions of self in relation to others. Understanding such patterns and perceptions, as well as the person's goals and expectations of self and others, helps the worker and the prospective member make a mutual decision about the suitability of the group for the person and of the person for the group.

In making such a decision about the fit between person and group, it is helpful for the worker to learn about the person's prior group experiences.

The benefits of pregroup interviews to prepare clients for participation in a group have been well established. In a controlled experiment comparing sixteen groups whose members had pregroup interviews with an equal number without interviews, Diane Meadow concluded that the pregroup interview is useful in facilitating attendance and developing clarity of purpose and expectations.[18] Irvin Yalom concluded that evidence from a compelling body of research demonstrates that systematic preparation of patients for group therapy facilitates the patients' course in that therapy and supports the efficacy of advance preparation of the group.[19] W. E. Piper and E. L. Pennault similarly found that such preparation reduced anxiety, increased participation, improved adjustment to therapy, and created accurate expectations regarding roles, behavior, and process, which in turn led to better attendance and greater interest and satisfaction with treatment.[20]

There are many reasons for the use of pregroup interviews. When prospective members are prepared through such interviews, they enter the group with a feeling of acceptance by the worker and are at least somewhat ready to engage in relationships with others. The leader can then focus not only on relating to each member but also on promoting communication between the members.

In pregroup interviews, a worker-member relationship is initiated that, it is hoped, is accepting, empathic, and supportive. This kind of relationship enhances motivation to participate, eases entry into the group, and serves as a bridge for the member to enter into relationships with other members. It is especially desirable to have the person who will be the group's practitioner conduct the interview.

When an interviewee's initial ideas about the group and its expectations are clarified, that person's initial anxiety and uncertainty are lessened, and thus positive motivation is enhanced and resistance is reduced. Most new group members have apprehensions, fantasies, and fears about membership in groups.[21] The members may fear that the group will make unrealistic demands on them for instant intimacy. They may have a pervasive dread of forced self-disclosure, fearing that they will be forced to confess shameful transgressions and thoughts; they may fear emotional contagion—that they will catch the problems of others or be sicker by association with others, especially when the group is composed of physically or mentally ill clients, or they may believe that groups are second-rate forms of help. They may doubt that they can be helped by anyone other than an expert or that their individual concerns will get attention in a group. They may fear that they will be excluded or rejected by other members or by the practitioner, that their privacy will be invaded and that "the whole world will know how weak they are," and that, in the group atmosphere, they will lose control of their feelings and behavior in the presence of others who will ridicule them. The interviewer needs to explore the prospective member's ideas, accept the feelings, and provide reassurance about the naturalness of these fears.

Understanding the nature of the group and the worker's role in it is necessary for the person to make a realistic decision about group membership. A direct statement about the group and why a person is thought to be a good candidate for membership needs to be made clearly and reactions to the information secured. Even young children and persons with serious mental illness can usually understand a simple, nonthreatening explanation. During pregroup interviews, the workers can instill hope by clearly articulating their beliefs in the value and benefits of group experience. Evidence from research indicates that instillation of hope during initial interviews is a factor in continuance of treatment.[22]

The pregroup preparatory interview provides an opportunity to orient clients to the nature of participation that will be asked of them in the group. Thus, some of a person's fearful fantasies of forced self-disclosure, invasion of privacy, pressures toward conformity, and loss of control can be examined openly and expunged. Patricia Hannah recommends that six expectations be expressed to potential members during the pregroup preparatory interview: (1) commitment to the group and its work, (2) belief in the democratic/collective process, (3) value of the here-and-now experience and honest interaction between members, (4) importance of mutual support and acceptance, (5) clarification of the worker's role, and (6) value of taking risks in order to achieve goals.[23]

Illustration of an Interview

The following illustration presents excerpts from a taped interview with a recently discharged patient from a mental hospital. The patient was referred to a group in a community setting by her psychiatrist, who had talked with the group worker and provided her with information about the patient's schizophrenia and current state of psychosocial functioning. She needed to break out of her social isolation, enhance her self-esteem, and develop skills in relating to other people.

Mrs. M. arrived early for her appointment with the social worker, who greeted her, inviting her to take off her coat and find a comfortable chair. The worker said she understood that Mrs. M. was here to learn about the mental health group and decide whether or not she wanted to become a member. Mrs. M. responded with "Uh-uh-yes." The worker gave information briefly about the purpose, composition, and content of the group, stopping frequently to ask Mrs. M. if she understood. The response was always "Uh-huh." She listened intently, with nonverbal gestures indicating extreme anxiety.

WORKER: Sometimes people feel uncomfortable about being interviewed.

MRS. M.: *(laughing)* That's me.

WORKER: Yes, most people do at first. Could you tell me what you think of your doctor's suggestion about the group?

MRS. M.: Well *(pause)*, I just came here because the doctor arranged the interview, so I'm here . . .

WORKER: Uh-huh.

MRS. M.: And I do want him to think I'm trying.

WORKER: Well, I know that he thinks that the group would help you and that being with other people will improve your health.

MRS. M.: That's what he told me.

WORKER: But, you're not sure you want to try it.

MRS. M.: Well . . . when you tell me about the group, it makes me feel a little dazed . . . *(silence)*

WORKER: A little dazed?

MRS. M.: Yes—that's how I think I feel.

WORKER: Can you tell me more about that feeling?

MRS. M.: I'll try. What will happen to me in the group? It'll be so confusing—so strange—all so new.

WORKER: It will feel that way at first, but I'll be there to help you feel more comfortable.

MRS. M.: Like here today?

WORKER: Yes—you're not as anxious now as when you first came in, are you?

MRS. M.: No. No. Could you tell me again what we'll be doing in the group—what it will be like?

WORKER: Certainly. (W. explains what the purpose of the group is, how it can help, who will be in it, and what the content of the sessions will be.)

MRS. M.: So, we'll hash over each others' problems?

WORKER: Well—yes. But not only that. It's also what's going on in your daily lives—how you can get along living in the community—and learning social skills.

MRS. M.: I guess I need that. There are no lectures, then?

WORKER: No, but what do you think about that?

MRS. M.: Well—if there were, I could just listen—I wouldn't have to talk.

WORKER: You won't be forced to talk until you're ready.

MRS. M.: (*sigh of relief*; Mrs. M. asked questions about when the group would meet, whether there would be a fee, how many members there would be, whether the group would do other things, to which questions the worker gave answers and tried to determine the meaning of the questions to Mrs. M.)

MRS. M.: Well, yes, I just don't know. It seems rather . . . (*inaudible*)—just to be around people who are sick like me—it'll be almost like being back in the hospital again. That's scary.

WORKER: I think I know how scary that feeling can be.

MRS. M.: Yeah, it's really scary.

WORKER: It's true that all members of the group have been in mental hospitals, but that does not mean they do not have many abilities and good qualities. They all want to make it in the community and they're in the group because we think they can make it in the community—and the group can help them with that.

MRS. M.: Well—I want to make it, too.

WORKER: That's something you have in common with the others. The group can help you to enjoy being with other people and getting along well with them. That's what it's for.

MRS. M.: When your whole life has been disrupted like mine has been, I just don't feel any satisfaction with anything or anybody.

WORKER: Would you like to?

MRS. M.: Oh, yes, I would, but it seems so hopeless.

WORKER: Hopeless—that's a scary feeling.

MRS. M.: Yes (*silence*). Could the group help?

WORKER: I feel quite sure that it can, and your doctor feels it can, too.

MRS. M.: That's what he said.

WORKER: But you still feel unsure about it.

MRS. M.: Well—it's so scary to have to meet new people.

WORKER: Yes, it is. But you'll have help with that. You'll be surprised how helpful members can be to each other.

MRS. M.: I've always been shy about meeting people.

WORKER: And that's what the group is for . . .

MRS. M.: Maybe I should try it—all my life—getting out and making friends—I haven't been able to—I haven't been able to.

WORKER: Would you like to learn to do that?

MRS. M.: (*sigh*) You think I could?

WORKER: Yes, I do—in the group.

MRS. M.: Well, I'll give it a try.

WORKER: Good. (Then W. gives information about the importance of not just dropping out after first meetings and of giving the group a real try for at least two months and answers more questions about the conduct of the group and other members.)

MRS. M.: If you think I should come next Tuesday, I'll be here. Both you and my doctor seem to want me in the program.

WORKER: And I hope you'll soon feel that you really want to be in it, too.

MRS. M.: Well, I do want to come, but I know I'll feel like a sore thumb sticking out all over.

WORKER: That's not a pleasant feeling, but you're not like a sore thumb with me.

MRS. M.: It's not so hard to talk with you now (*smiling*).

WORKER: You're not nearly as anxious as when you first came in here, and after you get used to the group, you won't be so anxious there either.

MRS. M.: I will come to the group on Tuesday. (There followed discussion of transportation, a visit to the meeting room, an introduction to the receptionist, an invitation to call the worker if Mrs. M. had any more questions that needed answering.)

MRS. M.: Goodbye and thank you. I'll see you Tuesday.

In this situation, the social worker agreed with the psychiatrist's judgment that Mrs. M. could make appropriate use of the group. There are instances, however, when the social worker decides that any group, or a particular group, is inappropriate for the client at the time. When the interviewer has doubts about the group's suitability, those doubts and the reasons for them need to be shared directly with the person. For example, if the conclusion were that the group would not be appropriate for Mrs. M., then a statement such as "Maybe you are not ready for the group now" or "I think you may need something different from what the group could offer," with an indication of what led to that conclusion, would be in order. The worker would then want to elicit a response to that observation from Mrs. M. Her response would tend to confirm or disconfirm the worker's judgment. When the decision is not to admit a person to the group, the worker needs to explore and respond, with sensitivity and empathy, to the person's feelings about the decision, whether or not it is jointly made. It is important, too, that the worker be prepared to offer an alternative—to search for a more appropriate group, to offer individual or family help or a different type of service through referral within the agency or elsewhere.

Working Agreement

The outcome of pregroup interviews should be a preliminary working agreement or contract, covering the general purpose of the group, the needs or problems to be addressed, the reciprocal role of worker and members, and mutual expectations. Such mutual agreements are fundamental in helping to determine the direction, structure, and nature of service. But they need to be used with flexibility, for aims cannot be formed completely in advance. As John Dewey stated:

> The aim as it first emerges is a mere tentative sketch. The act of striving to realize it tests its worth. If it suffices to direct activity successfully, nothing more is required, and at times a mere hint may suffice. But usually—at least in complicated situations—acting upon it brings to light conditions which had been overlooked. This calls for revision of the original aim; it has to be added to or subtracted from. An aim must, then, be flexible; it must be capable of alteration to meet circumstances.[24]

Flexibility makes it possible to redirect efforts, as appropriate to the needs of clients or according to changing circumstances.

A tentative working agreement is derived from shared experience in exploring the potential members' needs and situations. Its major values are that it provides both workers and clients with involvement and participation and signifies mutual commitment and responsibility. The agreement provides a common frame of reference for the participants so that each is clear about what is expected. Such agreement establishes a foundation for periodic review of progress and next steps.

In the pregroup contact phase of the planning process, decisions must be made concerning a range of questions:

- How will potential members apply for group membership or be recruited for a particular group?
- What guidelines for assessment will be used to ascertain the needs of potential group members?
- What criteria will be used to determine a person's suitability for participation in the group? If an applicant is not suitable, how will that decision be shared with the applicant and what alternative help will be offered?
- What will be the major themes and content of the pregroup interviews with potential group members?
- Who will explain the group to potential members and help them make a decision about whether they wish to participate?
- How and by whom will potential members be oriented and prepared for entry and participation in the group?
- What will be the form and content of the initial worker-member agreement or contract?

An effective plan for the selection and preparation of members for entry into a group requires decision making based on sound use of knowledge within a theoretical perspective.

7   Purpose

Clarity of purpose is indispensable to a group's success. It motivates members to participate wholeheartedly in a group. It guides the group's content. It serves as an important ally for both members and workers alike by providing a framework for what the group does. It provides a standard that can be used to evaluate the group's progress.

A group's purpose is defined as the ends that the group will pursue collectively. Purpose describes the group's aims and destination, what it is anticipated that the group and its members will achieve as a result of their participation together. Within a common group purpose, individual group members may have specific expectations and particular hopes and goals they wish to achieve as a consequence of taking part in the group. Such individual goals are encompassed within the overarching purpose of the group. For example, the purpose of a group for blind elderly persons may be to help its members achieve increased satisfaction in their daily lives. Given that group purpose, the personal goal for one member may be to interact more with her family members, while the individual goal for another member may be to overcome her fears of leaving her apartment by herself. As Dominique Steinberg puts it, "Individual goals reflect those personal needs and desires that group members bring to the group, and group purpose is the common cause that ties those needs and desires together."[1]

Wide agreement exists that clear goals are important. Max Siporin ably summarizes the reasons for clarity of purpose:

Objectives that are clear and explicit evoke investment and commitment. When accepted by the individual, there is also an acceptance of responsibility for action to implement them. They give to the individual a conscious sense of purpose and hope. They stimulate awareness of the interrelationships between purpose, choice, and activity and provide a standard against which to judge performance and progress. When shared with others, objectives provide means for communication, identification, and relationships with others, and when goals become consensual and mutual, they become a basis for joint effort, provide a common frame of reference, and enable communion and community.[2]

Several studies on the use of purpose in social work practice affirm the importance of clarity. On the basis of a study in six family service agencies, Julianna Schmidt found that when workers made a purposeful effort to formulate objectives and communicated these to clients, a high proportion of clients accurately perceived and agreed with the objectives. When workers did not specify objectives, a majority of the clients did not understand how the service was to benefit them, and a lack of congruence occurred between the goals of the worker and clients. Schmidt writes, "A lack of clarity . . . confuses the client's perception of what his worker is trying to do. . . . . The client's attention and concern may be directed more toward deciphering the worker's intent than to ways in which he can involve himself in the planning and utilization of the helping process."[3] Schmidt's conclusion was that workers' sharing their views supported, rather than inhibited, the members in clarifying their own goals.[4] Gerald Raschella found that clients served in outpatient mental health centers were less likely to drop out prematurely when a high degree of congruence existed between worker and client in the specification of the goals for service.[5] In still another study, Charles Garvin found that early knowledge of the goals and expectations of members helped the worker understand group interaction and predict the degree of investment that members would have in the group. He concluded that clarity of purpose contributes to goal achievement.[6]

Purpose Evolves from Need

Client need is the foundation upon which a meaningful group is built. A group's purpose evolves and flows from a need that is perceived by members and worker alike and the mutual wish to meet that need. If need is not recognized and acknowledged by the members of a group, then that group's purpose is apt to have little meaning for its members and the likelihood is that the group will fail. It is essential that a group's purpose be connected integrally to members' perceptions of what they want and need. Clients will stop coming and a group will disintegrate if members view the group as unconnected to their real needs and interests.

Purpose and Content

A group's purpose should not be confused with its content, i.e., with what the group will do. Purpose and content are different. Purpose identifies the group's ends, while content is the means to achieve those ends. A group's means or content are not ends in and of themselves. Confusion between purpose and content is evident in statements such as, "The purpose of this group is to talk about the difficulties in being a single parent" or "The purpose of this group is for members to express and explore their feelings about being caregivers of persons with Huntington's disease" or "The purpose of this group is to help new foster parents learn about regulations and entitlements of the foster care system."

In each of these statements, what is identified as purpose — "to talk about," "to express and explore," "to learn about" — actually is the group's content, i.e., what the group will do. Essential to the identification of a group's purpose is a clear statement of the ends toward which the group will strive. In what ways, for example, is it hoped that talking about difficulties will be helpful to the single parents who are members of the group? Similarly, in what ways will expression and exploration of feelings be helpful to group members who are caregivers of persons with Huntington's disease? What are the reasons that learning about the system's rules and entitlements is important to new foster parents?

Knowing the reasons that they are being asked to talk, to express, to explore, to learn, and the ways in which it is thought that such talking, expression, exploration, and learning might be helpful to them is crucial for the members of a group. Their motivation and the quality of their participation are greatly enhanced when they have such understanding. Knowing what they are going to do is not enough. Members need to understand why they are doing it. Their willingness to engage in the work of the group, especially at times when that work is painful or difficult for them, increases remarkably when members view what the group does and what they are being asked to do as purposeful and designed to accomplish ends they want to achieve.

Defining Broad Purposes

When a group's purpose is stated at a high level of generality, it has little meaning to its members. To merely say that a group's purpose is socialization or education or therapy or support or counseling or self-help is not enough. Such statements do identify a type of group and do give an indication of what a group is about, but they are too global to provide significant direction or focus.

Within such general purposes as socialization, therapy, or support, it is necessary to define the meaning of these terms for a particular group. Practitioners need to ask what socialization, therapy, or support would really look like in a particular group and really mean for the particular group members with whom they are working. Socialization in one group, for example, might mean helping members to be able to listen to and interact with their peers more effectively, while in another group it might mean helping members to express anger and assert themselves in more constructive ways. Defining the meaning of a broad term such as *socialization* for a particular group and its members has important implications for the group's content. It also allows both the worker and the group members to know when the group's purpose is being achieved. In fact, a statement of purpose that has meaning for a group and its members can serve to spur members toward its achievement.

Hidden Purposes and Client Self-Determination

Workers often find it difficult to express clearly, simply, and explicitly their perceptions of the group's purpose. They are often fearful of sharing directly with group members their ideas about the purpose of a group.[7] Two reasons seem to account for their reluctance to do so. First, workers may worry that stating their ideas about the group's purpose will scare away prospective members and dissuade them from coming. In many groups in social work, the issues being addressed are difficult and painful. When that is true, workers seem apprehensive about honestly presenting the group and their view of its purpose to potential members. Stating difficult issues directly is not easy to do. It is far more comfortable, at least in the short run, for workers to draw members into a group by presenting a purpose that they think will be inviting and to use such a statement of purpose as a bribe to get members to come. The thinking seems to be that once the group gets off the ground and the members are hooked, then honesty about the group's purpose will be possible.

In an effort to make the group sound inviting, workers may sidestep stating the purpose altogether. For example, a new mother of a child born with a cleft palate was asked to join a group. The fact that the group was for mothers of children born with cleft palates and aimed to address their special needs went unmentioned in the worker's invitation to participate. Instead the group was presented by the worker as "a nice place to talk with other new mothers where there will be coffee and donuts." Examples abound of children in school or community groups who are never told by their workers that such groups aim to improve their behavior in school or their interaction with peers. Instead, workers often offer recreational activities as a subterfuge and emphasize that such groups will go on trips or participate in special activities. The difficulties the children may be having and the reasons they have been asked to be in the group are evaded and go unmentioned. Another example is of practitioners who form a reminiscence group in a senior center. Rarely do they share directly with the group members the reasons for and benefits of reminiscing at their stage of life. Too frequently, workers do not realize that being explicit about a group's purpose comes as a relief to potential group participants. Talking honestly about purpose inspires hopefulness that this group will address needs and concerns that they see themselves as having.

When disparity exists between the stated and the hidden purpose of a group, trust, respect for members, and honesty are violated. For a worker to state, and for the members of a group to understand, one purpose and then for the worker to pursue and try to "sneak" in another purpose is not congruent with empathy, acceptance, and genuineness. It is unethical and terrible practice. When that is done, group members may feel as if they have been mistreated and their trust in the group and in the worker violated. Often, their response to such feelings of having been used is to drop out of the group. Even worse, when group members object to or refuse to participate in and go along with the worker's hidden purpose, the bad practice often gets compounded as clients are then mislabeled "resistant" or "not ready" or "uncaring." Blaming the client for what is, in fact, the worker's unwillingness or inability to be direct and honest is unfair. There is a principle involved here: if the practitioner cannot say it to clients, then the practitioner has no right to try to do it.

The second reason that workers are reluctant to share directly with members their ideas about group purpose is that they do not wish to impose their ideas onto the group. They want the group to belong to its members and they mistakenly believe that client self-determination requires that the defining of purpose be done solely by the group members.[8] As a result, instead of sharing their thinking about purpose, they ask open-ended questions of the members, such as, "What do you think the purpose of this group should be?" Often, they then sit quietly and say nothing while members struggle to respond. Such lack of help from the worker usually results in long silences between the members, which are particularly uncomfortable when they occur as the group is just beginning. Alternatively, the lack of worker input may evolve into confusion and frustration between the group members, who need some direction and help from the worker at this early stage in the life of the group.

Especially in a group's beginnings, the worker's role needs to be an active and participatory one. It is, in fact, the worker's responsibility to help the group become aware of its reason for being. If workers have done the thinking necessary to plan and form a group, then it is probable that they have a vision for the group and ideas about the group's purpose. To share those ideas with the group, along with the thinking that gave rise to the group's formation, is a way of including the members and, in fact, can help the members to share their own thinking and ideas. Rather than imposing upon the members, such sharing of the vision for the group on the part of the worker can serve to stimulate the thinking and the ideas of the group members. Through choice of words, tone of voice, and physical stance when they express their own thinking and ideas, workers can communicate an invitation to members to participate fully and can let members know that their ideas and views are needed and will be welcomed and appreciated. This is precisely the opposite of an imposition. In fact, for workers not to share their ideas and thinking about the group's purpose is to deprive the group and its members of valuable expertise and input.

Presentation of Purpose

Explanation and clarification of purpose is not a task to be completed in one or two sessions. Rather, it is an evolutionary and continuous process of definition and redefinition that takes place throughout the life of a group. The purpose that is identified when a group begins is not immutable or unchangeable. It deepens and develops and changes as the group matures. Both the group's purpose and the members' goals become clearer as the group meets and members develop relationships with one another and with the worker, explore needs and concerns, open up communication about things that matter, ventilate their feelings about themselves and their situations, discover areas of common concern, and develop hope that things can be better.

But in order for this process to begin, workers need to directly share their ideas about purpose with members from the start. Even though the initial purpose of the group, as perceived by the organization and the worker, may have been explained and discussed with members individually during pregroup interviews, it is nevertheless important that the members have an opportunity together to hear and react to the worker's explanation, to discuss it, and to make it their own.

A good starting point for the worker is to relate to the members how the group came about, to recount the thinking and events that led to its formation and to its composition. An understanding of the group's history gives grounding to the group and reduces the anxiety that members are likely to feel in the beginning. The worker's presentation of this material needs to be clear, honest, direct, and without professional jargon. To present the purpose in positive terms of what members can expect to achieve through the group connects the purpose to the positive motivations of members. To express hope that members will be able to "get along better with others" or "be able to better understand and bring up your children" or "have a greater chance of completing high school" does not deny the need for help but does tend to enhance motivation toward change. However, expressing hope and presenting purpose positively does not mean that the worker sidesteps and sweeps the problems under the rug. Those need to be acknowledged in a way that is neither stigmatizing nor blaming.

An excerpt from a meeting of a group at a community center provides an example of the way in which one worker approached the discussion of purpose at the group's first meeting. The group was for persons who had taken and failed the GED test for the high school equivalency diploma and who wanted to take the test again. The group consisted of eight men between the ages of twenty-two and twenty-eight who were also participants in a basketball league sponsored by the center. It was led by a full-time social worker on the staff of the center.

The group members arrived singly or in pairs. Miguel and Robert came together, Luis was alone, then Frank and Larry, then Joseph, and then Daniel. They seemed surprised to see one another, surprised at who else was in the group. It was obvious that they had not talked about the group beforehand, and some seemed almost embarrassed to be seen in the room. I greeted each person individually, shaking his hand and telling him I was glad he'd come. I had some soda and pretzels laid out on a table near the door and invited them to help themselves. I had set up the chairs in a circle. Luis had moved his chair outside the circle and I asked him to please move in, which he did. I was just about to start when Ralph burst in, "Sorry, I'm late." I told him we were just about to start and he was welcome to have some refreshments. "I just got here and now I need to tell you I may have to leave early to pick up my brother over at the next building," Ralph said. I nodded OK and pointed to the empty seat in the circle. Ralph sat down, shaking hands with Luis who was next to him as he did so.

"I'm very glad to see you guys," I began. "You know this group has been in the planning stage for a couple of weeks now. Raoul [the head of the basketball league] and I were talking and he told me that there were a number of men in the basketball league who had taken the GED exam in January and who had failed it and who were feeling pretty bad about it." Miguel interrupted, "You can say that again." Larry said, "I thought Frank and I were the only ones. I didn't realize there were others." "That exam is a bitch," Ralph said emphatically. I continued, "I began to think that it might make sense to get those who had taken and failed the exam together, that maybe we could help one another to pass the exam." "How the hell can we help each other?" Joseph muttered. "Yeah," Ralph echoed, "we're the ones who flunked it." "Yes," I said, "but I still think you can help one another." The group was clearly skeptical. Mumbling and looks of doubt and disbelief were apparent. I decided I needed to address their skepticism. "Well," I said, "for one thing, the test has different parts and some of you are better at some parts than others. We could figure out who's good at what and pair up." "Like tutoring, you mean," Frank asked. I nodded. "Well, I'm good at the history stuff, but I hate writing," Frank said. "The writing's OK, but forget the math," Joseph said. "Ah, see, you got the idea," I said. "We can figure out what each person's strengths and weaknesses are and who can help whom." The skepticism seemed to diminish some.

"There's also something else," I said, "and that's attitude. The GED is an important test. It means a lot to your futures. And when a test is that important, it's not unusual to be nervous and scared when you take it, to freeze up, to not be able to concentrate." "You got that right," Luis said. "Not me," Ralph disputed, "I don't get nervous for no one." "Bull," Miguel retorted. "I've seen you blow big shots in basketball." Ralph shrugged, but became silent. I went on, "I think this group could help you be less nervous the next time you take the test." "I don't know how it's going to do that," Daniel said, "but it would be good if it could." "That's something we can look at more in future meetings," I said.

"Before this meeting, I met with each of you individually," I told the group, "and in those meetings I got a sense of the reasons that passing the GED is important to each of you. I think it would be good to spend the rest of this meeting talking about some of that. It would be important for everyone to know the meaning the test has for everyone in this room. I know some of you know each other from playing basketball, but I think you have a lot of other things in common as well. A lot of times we walk around thinking, 'I'm the only one in the world who's had a certain experience or felt a certain way' and then when we find out we're not the only one and there are others, it comes as a great relief. Based on my individual meetings with you, I think that's going to be true here. So I'm asking each of you to talk about the reasons that passing the GED is important to you and also, perhaps, how you felt last month as you were taking the test. Miguel, will you start us off?" Miguel began to speak.

————

This group seems to have gotten off to a good beginning. The initial statement of purpose articulated by the worker—to help the members pass the GED exam, to help them be less nervous when they take the test—is one that the members want to achieve. The worker is direct in acknowledging that all the group members have failed the exam, yet his statement of that fact is not belittling to them. In fact, he clearly lets the members know that he believes they have the strengths and the ability to help one another. He also lessens unfair self-blame on the part of the members when he tells them that it is not unusual to become anxious when taking such an exam. Overall, the worker's tone is a hopeful and confident one.

As this group develops further, the meaning of its purpose will likewise continue to evolve. Its meaning will deepen and expand, especially as the group members further identify, clarify, and articulate the personal goals they hope to achieve and the ways in which those goals can be advanced within the group's overall purpose.

Purpose in Involuntary Groups

In groups where members are required to attend, agreement about purpose is imperative if the group is to be viable. In such groups, members may start out feeling resentful about the compulsory nature of their attendance. This may be true, for example, in parenting groups whose members are required to attend if they wish to regain custody of their children or probation groups where group attendance is a condition of the members' release from prison. The members of such groups may be present physically, but their willingness to actually participate may be absent. They may go through the motions of mandatory participation without really getting involved.

The nature of the participation and involvement of members of such compulsory groups begins to change and turn around, however, when they begin to sense that there may be something they can gain, something that in fact they want to gain, from the group. Purpose is the key here. For instance, the group becomes important to them when parents realize that they want and need to better understand their children and interact with them in more positive ways, or when probationers begin to admit, perhaps first to themselves and then to other members and the worker, that they do not know how to say "no" to friends who influence them negatively and that they want to reject the invitations of such friends.

In involuntary groups, the views of purpose and goals that are held by workers and members may be far apart initially. Workers need to strive to bring them closer together, to reach a mutual agreement about purpose. To achieve this, workers need to be prepared to articulate clearly their points of view about the needs that they see group members as having. They need to state the reasons that they believe participation in the group can be valuable for group members even though they may have little choice but to attend. They also need to listen attentively to what the members themselves see as their needs and goals. If mutual agreement about purpose can be reached, if the commonalities shared by members and workers about what both hope that the group will achieve can be identified, then the nature of member participation will be transformed. An involuntary group will, in effect, become voluntary for the group members as they become motivated to realize the purpose.

Purpose as Ally

Purpose needs to be attended to and revisited throughout the life of the group. Even if the worker has explained the purpose and discussion of that purpose has taken place during the group's early meetings, members may have taken in only part of that explanation and discussion because they were apprehensive and preoccupied with fitting in. Thus, discussion of purpose may need to take place often during the group's orientation stage as it begins to have more meaning for the members.

As the group progresses, members may gain a fuller sense of the group, of the other group members, of the possibilities that participation might offer them, and of what they might be able to achieve. Similarly, the worker's sense of the group's possibilities may also grow. Thus, the discussions of purpose that take place during the group's middle stages can be expected to have more breadth and depth because they will reflect the enhanced understanding of both the group members and the worker. Such discussions can also be expected to be more meaningful to the group members.

Clarity of purpose is an important ally of the group and its members as well as of the worker. It encourages meaningful work and seriousness of effort. It is a decisive reference point that can be used by both members and worker. When the group gets offtrack, reference to purpose can bring the group back to its work and to the reasons for its existence.

When a group member, in seeming frustration, asks, "What good is all this discussion?" or says, "I don't understand what the point of all this is," it is important that the worker not regard such comments as threats and interruptions to the "real" work of the group. Instead, they need to view such questions and comments as the opportunities they genuinely are to encourage the group members to enter into valuable discussion of purpose. It is precisely such discussion of purpose that enables group members to continuously clarify their needs as well as their ongoing participation in the group. It is, in fact, such discussion of purpose that assures that membership in the group will have significance for the participants.

Evolution of Purpose: An Example

The story of a group in a day treatment program for persons with chronic mental illness illustrates well a number of the areas that have been discussed in this chapter, particularly the connection between client need and group purpose and the way in which purpose evolves and grows in meaning over the life of a group, not only for the group members but for the worker as well.[9]

The group began as a socialization group. The worker, a second-year MSW student, was instructed by her supervisor to focus on the clients' "lack of motivation and abundant free time." This was an open group that met weekly, composed of six to twelve members identified as "seriously and persistently mentally ill." Though composition varied from week to week, the group had a core membership of eight clients whose attendance was fairly consistent. Prior to starting the group, the worker spoke with clients informally as they ate breakfast, played pool, and participated in games of bingo. During her conversations with the program participants, they described themselves as lonely, bored, and lacking things to do on the weekend. As a result of her contact with the clients, four themes regarding client need were identified by the worker:

1. need for increased and validating social contact,
2. need to practice interaction in social situations,
3. need for encouragement and support in the exploration of new activities,
4. need for practical suggestions about what to do with free time and ways to initiate involvement in free-time activities.

Given her observations of need, the worker tentatively formulated the group's purpose as she saw it prior to the first meeting of the group:

To motivate and encourage members to partake in constructive social activities outside of the day program, to support members as they venture forth, and to provide and generate concrete suggestions of activities and involvements that are available to them.

The first meeting of the group, however, demonstrated to the worker that her initial formulation of purpose failed to address the more basic and pervasive needs of the group members. In that meeting, it became apparent that the group members were unable to engage in successful interpersonal interaction. Some of the group members blurted out statements that had little connection to what was being discussed. Some laughed aloud at other members, while others said nothing. Some members continued insensitively to urge one clearly embarrassed member to talk about whether she was going to have sex with her boyfriend. The participation of the members in this first meeting was chaotic and confused. The members did not really talk to or hear one another. After this meeting, the worker noted,

The purpose statement that I had formulated reflected *my* needs and goals for the clients more so than it addressed *their* developmental and social needs and goals. I came away not knowing what would make sense in regard to purpose, but with the strong sense that the statement of purpose I had formulated was way ahead of where the clients were, for they really seemed not to know how to interact with one another and were not ready to venture far beyond the day treatment program into other social situations, despite their saying they were bored and lonely.

The worker's experience with the group stimulated her continued thinking about the needs of the members and what the group's purpose might be. Thus, she reformulated her conception of the group's purpose:

To help members talk about their difficulties in making friends and feeling comfortable in social situations. To gain practice and experience in new social situations and to learn to cope better with loneliness and weekends.

Though more closely related to the group members' needs, this statement confused purpose and content and also remained overly ambitious. In the group meetings, members were unable to articulate or discuss their situations. A trip to Rockefeller Center clearly demonstrated that the members were not yet ready or able to participate in activities outside the program. Following the trip, the worker noted:

> The trip revealed that I am pushing too fast. The clients followed me like sheep and showed little interest in anything around them. They seemed scared and relieved to return "home" to the program. My aims and goals are too high or at least too early. The clients are telling me a lot about their needs, not in their words but through their behavior.

Continued experience in and with the group led the worker to a third and much more direct and succinct formulation of purpose:

To improve members' abilities to interact socially.

This statement of purpose had clear implications for what the content of the group might be. The group itself would become a place where members could learn, practice, and experience satisfying social interaction. The members' endorsement of this group purpose was evident in the enthusiastic nature of their participation in the group as illustrated in the following process recording.

> I wrote my new idea about purpose on the board and read it slowly and distinctly aloud. The group members were attentive and looked as if they were trying to take in every word. Several members were nodding. Elaine proceeded to copy the statement on a blank piece of paper. . . . We spent a little while talking about the purpose statement. Unlike the other times when I had tried to engage the group in discussion of purpose, they now participated actively. This purpose seemed real to them . . .
>
> I explained that I'd prepared a short demonstration of the kind of thing we might do in the group, but would need a volunteer. Alice volunteered gladly. Group members were laughing because they didn't know what to expect. I described a scenario that Alice and I were going to role-play for the group. I asked group members to imagine that Alice was a client at the clinic who was very depressed. I would be playing another client who walks by her in the reception area and

tries to comfort her. I emphasized to Alice and the rest of the group that Alice's character was not feeling like talking to anyone. She was simply sitting in the reception area, waiting to see her therapist. She was depressed and wanted to be left alone.

The skit unfolded as follows. I approached Alice and tried to get her to tell me what was wrong. I appeared to be very concerned, but frenzied in my attempt to elicit a response from her. When she kept her head down, I grabbed her and gave her a big hug. I then went on to tell her how I could understand how she felt and that I was having a hard time too. I began to speak louder and faster, going on and on about my boyfriend and how he hurt me and how bad I felt. I then stopped, calling, "Time-out."

Group members jumped in right away with observations about my behavior and Alice's response. Most of the group members realized that my behavior was inappropriate, particularly in light of Alice's body language. Sylvia picked up on the fact that I turned the attention from Alice's problems to my own. Several group members pointed out that I never found out from Alice what was wrong, and yet I kept talking and shared a problem I was having that might have nothing to do with her. The most interesting part of the discussion centered around the hug. Alice and Gena thought that it was a nice gesture on my part. Several other group members pointed out that it was not appropriate. I picked up on this and pointed out that it is important to respect people's personal space. I pointed out that, in situations like this, when we don't know people well, we should never be afraid to ask them what they need or how they feel about receiving a hug or wanting to talk. I emphasized that asking someone what they feel comfortable with is always a good idea, no matter what the situation.

I was quite impressed with Alice's response to all this. She said that she liked my hug and that she was the type of person who would do just the same to someone who looked upset. She reflected for a moment: "Maybe other people are not comfortable with that, though." She said that she had never thought about that before. I pointed out to the group that Alice has a lot of warmth and affection to offer, but that she is right: she (and others) must be careful about in what situations and to whom this affection is offered.

That the group's purpose was now meaningful and real to the members was demonstrated by the nature of their participation in the group meetings that followed. In groups such as this, whose members may have difficulty articulating their ideas about purpose in words, the quality of their participation is, indeed, a barometer of the degree to which the group's purpose is on target in addressing members' needs.

A process excerpt from the group's eighth meeting well illustrates their involvement and interest, with one member even taking a risk to raise a highly personal concern.

> I then introduced the role-play exercise that Ms. D. (co-leader) and I had prepared. I told the group that we would need a volunteer. Several people raised their hands. Ms. D. picked Elaine. Prior to enacting the role-play, Ms. D. explained the scenario to the group. The hypothetical situation we constructed was to feature Ms. D. as the "friend" who could not stop talking, Elaine as the demure, polite, and timid friend, and me as Elaine's conscience (or, the comic booklike "bubble" above her head verbalizing her true thoughts).
>
> Ms. D.'s character talked and talked nonstop. She asked Elaine about her weekend but interrupted her almost immediately, telling her how she spent her weekend shopping. She again interrupted Elaine and informed her that she "must" try meditation. I would interject every two minutes or so with something like, "God, why doesn't she just stop talking. I wish she would just shut up! I don't want to hear about meditation. Can't she see that I'm not listening to her anymore?" The group seemed to enjoy the role-play. They laughed, looked attentive, and clapped when it was over.
>
> When the role-play was over, a lively discussion ensued. Group members picked up on the dynamic between Elaine and Ms. D. They commented on how Ms. D. was clueless about Elaine's needs and did not listen to her. All group members nodded yes and smiled when Ms. D. asked if they ever had experiences in which their unverbalized thoughts looked something like what I had been saying throughout the role play.
>
> The most interesting part of the group came toward the end. Lydia made a statement to the group. She said: "I feel like people roll their eyes when I talk and care nothing about what I have to say. That's why I don't talk very much in this group. I often don't want to come."

The deepening of the meaning and implications for group content that purpose can have is evident in this group. Well illustrated here, in addition, is the worker's growing understanding of the group members' needs and of the implications that these have for the group's purpose. The worker's flexibility and willingness to adjust and redefine the purpose to meet the client's needs helped this group become one of relevance for the members where their participation and motivation became strong.

In too many groups, clarity of purpose does not exist. All too often, when group participants are asked, "What is the purpose of your group?" they are unable to reply or their answer is fuzzy and vague. Or they respond with mere words that have little real meaning for them, for example, "The purpose of this group is to make friends and get along better with others," recited in singsong fashion by a nine year old. All too often, when workers are asked the same question, they too are unable to offer a clear and succinct response. Such lack of clarity of purpose is a major contribution to the premature demise of many social work groups. For a group to be helpful, clarity and consensus about a purpose that is capable of mobilizing the energies of its members are imperative.

8   The Problem-Solving Process

Problem solving is a process that is central to social work practice with groups. It is used to address questions and difficulties, both group and individual, that arise at any time during the life of a group. Although the word *problem* tends to have a negative connotation, the problem-solving process in not meant for use solely in negative situations. Rather, the word *issue*, synonymous with *problem*, might better describe the target of the process. The problem-solving process can be used to address any issue that arises for the group or for an individual member. In fact, use of the problem-solving process is an opportunity for the group to become stronger as members work together to address issues of concern to all.

Problem solving can be used to examine and resolve issues around how the group will be conducted, how group content will be determined, for example, or whether eating will be allowed during group meetings, and how problematic behavior and roles of members will be addressed, such as inconsistent attendance on the part of members or the monopolization of group meetings by one member. The problem-solving process can also be used when the group focuses on a difficulty with which *one* of its members may be struggling individually, what to do about a teacher whom the member sees as being unfair to him, for example, or fear on the part of a member about applying for a job. If practice with groups is to be effective, it is essential that workers appreciate the importance of the problem-solving process and understand how to help groups engage in that process.

As it is used in social work practice, the problem-solving process is based upon the work of John Dewey, a progressive educator and social scientist, who was particularly interested in reflective thinking and decision-making that was rooted in the examination of one's actual experiences.[1] Problem-solving emphasizes a process of reflective thinking. It integrates feelings with rational thought processes and takes into account both conscious and unconscious elements. Emotions influence cognitive processes.

The problem-solving process provides a progression of steps that guides a group in systematically tackling an issue of concern and reaching some decision and action to address it. The problem-solving process that Dewey articulated consists of seven steps:

1. Recognition that a problem (i.e., a difficulty or an issue) seems to exist,
2. identification of the problem,
3. exploration of the problem,
4. consideration of possible solutions to the problem,
5. selection of what seems to be the best solution to the problem,
6. implementation of the solution,
7. evaluation of the results of the solution's implementation.[2]

Steps in the Process

Recognition That a Problem Seems to Exist

The problem-solving process begins when one or more persons in the group, worker and/or member, has a sense that an issue or difficulty is present. At this stage in the process, though, that sense is vague, perplexing, and not well defined. The worker, for instance, may leave a meeting with a feeling of dissatisfaction about something that occurred. Or the worker may observe that members seem particularly silent in response to questions or that there seem to be contradictions between what members are saying and how they are behaving. The sense that there is a problem can also originate with a member. A member, for example, may feel unhappy about something that took place in the meeting or may realize that he or she is having difficulty expressing a point of view in the group. Thus, a vague sense of uneasiness on the part of worker and/or member that an issue exists, without a clear definition of what exactly that problem is, characterizes this stage of the problem-solving process.

Identification of the Problem

In this step of the process, the problem is defined by the group. The vague sense of uneasiness that characterizes step 1 is brought to the group, by the worker or by a member, and identification of what is really going on is sought. The worker, for instance, may make an observation directly to the group that although they say they feel at ease in the group they seem uncomfortable and discussion does not seem to flow with ease. Discussion of the worker's observation may lead the group to identify that many of the members feel a sense of shame about having to come to a group of "strangers" to talk about issues that they believe they ought to be able to handle within their own families and without the help of "outsiders." Or a member may tell the group that it is difficult for her to express her honest opinion in the group. Discussion of her uneasiness may reveal that there are other members who feel similarly and that a few members are dominating group discussions and greeting viewpoints with which they disagree with scorn and derision.

Crucial to this step in the problem-solving process is the worker's and/or a member's willingness to share directly with the group their sense that a problem may exist even when they are not sure exactly what the issue is. Such observations are a jumping-off point for group discussion that can be productive in defining issues that the group needs to explore. Before such exploration can take place, however, members need to arrive at a clear and common understanding of what the issue is that needs to be addressed.[3] Interestingly, the common understanding of the issue that is arrived at by the group may be quite different from the observation that launched the group's discussion, for as conversation proceeds it may become evident that a core difficulty underlies the problem as it is initially expressed.

Exploration of the Problem

In this step of the process, the group needs to engage in discussion of the problem. The members' perceptions of what contributes to causing the problem, the reasons that they think it is an issue, and their feelings about the problem are all important areas for discussion. During such problem exploration, disagreements between members may arise. Members may have different perceptions about the nature of the problem, stemming from differences in their life experiences, personal and cultural values, and norms. Such differences need to be examined by the group. The different perceptions that members have need to be expressed, understood, and appreciated.

Because real exploration of an issue may be time consuming and because the expression of difference may make some members, and workers as well, uncomfortable, there is a tendency to rush this step in the problem-solving process, to move too quickly and prematurely to consideration of solutions before the problem has been fully explored. Such a rush to solutions is a mistake that frequently results in solutions that are ineffective because they are not rooted in sound understanding of the problem. Effective solutions are those that evolve from the knowledge of the problem that members gain during the exploration stage of the problem-solving process.

Consideration of Possible Solutions to the Problem

When a problem is explored thoroughly and thoughtfully, possible solutions to that problem begin to become apparent. Often, the problem or issue with which the group is grappling can be addressed in different ways. Thus, more than one solution or way of addressing the issue usually is possible. In this step of the problem-solving process, possible solutions need to be considered by the group. Such possible solutions are elicited from the members and also may be offered by the worker. They are based on the past personal experiences, social and cultural characteristics, and the social and physical environment of the group members.

In this step of the process, it is important that the group consider a range of alternative solutions and not seize too quickly and prematurely on one solution that may seem immediately apparent. The technique of brainstorming, in which members list every possible solution they can think of, is helpful here. In brainstorming, such listing is done without censoring—members are asked to add to the list whatever solutions come to their minds even if they think that solution might be silly or impractical.

The group then needs to reflect upon the possible solutions that have been listed. Based on the values, norms of behavior, attitudes, emotions, resources, and community and family support systems of the members, the group identifies those alternatives members think might be possible and effective. As alternatives are considered, some will be recognized quickly as not feasible or not worth further consideration; others will be seen as having the potential for sound decision.

Selection of the Best Solution

Once alternative solutions are identified and discussed, the group needs to decide which solution seems best. Such a decision will be based not on rational thinking only; unconscious factors, values, experiences, and external factors are powerful forces in the selection. At times, there will be spontaneous recognition by the members that a particular decision seems right and the selection of a solution will come quickly. At other times, the choice may be less obvious and the selection of a solution will be time consuming. The group will need to weigh the advantages and disadvantages of each alternative solution that has been identified. Conflict may develop between members about which solution should be adopted. Depending upon the way the group has learned to address conflict in the past, the group may develop a solution that is reasonably acceptable to all. If the group is unable to do that, it may resolve the conflict by means of elimination of dissenting members, subjugation of some to the power of others, compromise, or majority rule.

In this step of the problem-solving process, it is important that the group try to think ahead and appraise the probable consequences of the alternative solutions that are under consideration. Role-play can be particularly useful in helping the group play out for itself such probable consequences. The rehearsal that role-play provides can be a valuable aid to the group in determining the solution that it wishes to adopt.

Implementation of the Solution

Once a solution has been decided upon, it needs to be implemented. A course of action for putting the solution into operation needs to be determined. The group needs to clarify the roles of worker and members in carrying out the decision. The actual steps to be taken and the persons to be involved in the process need to be identified.

Evaluation of the Results

The final step in the problem-solving process is evaluation. The group needs to look at whether implementation of the solution is bringing about the desired consequences. There may be a sense that the solution is achieving the intended results with success. Or the group may find that the solution is not working as it had hoped in addressing the identified problem/issue. If the solution is effective, no new action is necessary. If it is ineffective, then the group will need to revisit the issue. The group may decide to try another of the possible solutions that it had identified earlier. Or it may decide that the early steps in the problem-solving process—identification and/or exploration of the problem/issue—were flawed and that the entire process needs to be repeated.

In evaluating the effectiveness of the solution, it is important that the group be realistic in regard to its expectations of success. If the group expects positive results to occur "instantly" or "magically" or with immediate consistency, then disappointment will probably be the result. It is not unusual for success to take time and work on the part of the members and for there to be lapses and backslides as a new solution is implemented. Thus, it is important that the group not expect results too quickly and that it not give up on a solution prematurely. It is also important, however, that the group not become discouraged if a solution is ineffective. There needs to be a willingness on the part of the group to persist in its efforts to address a problem that is of concern.

Initiation of the Problem-Solving Process by the Worker

The problem-solving process can be initiated by workers when they let the group know that they think there is an issue that needs to be addressed by the group. The willingness of workers to make observations to the group about problems that they detect, even when those observations are somewhat tentative, is key. Often, such observations lead to substantial discussion and work by the group. Thus, it is important that workers not shy away from making such observations because they are not fully formed or because they fear that they may be incorrect. Workers do need to have *reasons* for bringing to the group the issues that they see and need to be willing to share those reasons with the group directly. But that does not mean that observations can be made only when workers are absolutely certain of their veracity.

It is possible that the group may reject an observation made by the worker as erroneous or unimportant. If that happens, there is still value in the group's consideration of what the worker has said. It is also possible for the worker to repeat an observation that may have been spurned by the group when it was first raised if the worker believes it still has validity. Ultimately, though, it is up to the group to decide whether the worker's observation is accurate. Workers' observations certainly cannot be imposed upon a group.

Initiation of the problem-solving process by a worker is illustrated in a group of parents of developmentally disabled adults, many of whom, as children, were placed in large, poorly run state institutions where they had some highly negative experiences. Their parents are bitter about this. All the group members are currently the primary caretakers for their adult children. Early in the life of this group, the worker had the sense that members felt she did not and could not understand their experiences and feelings because she was not a parent of a developmentally disabled child herself. After a couple of meetings, during which she sensed an underlying attitude of distrust toward her on the part of the group members, she decided to bring this issue to the group. Clarissa, the worker, began the group's fifth meeting by sharing her observation.

CLARISSA: This is our fifth meeting and I'd like to share with you something that I've been sensing. As you all know, I am not a parent of a disabled child. And I sometimes get a feeling that you don't think I can be very helpful to you, that I can't possibly understand all that you've been through.
ANNE: (*interrupting*) That's not true at all, Clarissa. We all like you.
GRADY: That's right. We all think you're very nice.
WORKER: Well, I'm not really talking about your liking me, though I'm glad you do. I'm talking about your feeling that I can't possibly understand. Sometimes, when I've made a comment, I'll notice some of you looking at one another with doubtful expressions. Other times, I've noticed you moving around in your chairs and I get the sense you're thinking I'm being insensitive or too hard on you.
DENISE: No, Clarissa. You don't have to worry. We like you and we think you're doing a good job.

At that point, the worker decided to not pursue discussion of the subject further. Her belief was that her comments had opened the door for the group's thought about this subject and had demonstrated her willingness and receptivity to look at the issue. Her thinking was that she could bring up the issue with the group again if her sense that it was a problem persisted.

Three weeks later, when she did continue to sense that this was an issue, she decided to raise it again with the group, this time being more specific in sharing with the group what contributed to her belief that an issue existed.

CLARISSA: A few weeks ago, I told you all that I had the feeling sometimes that you didn't think I could be very helpful because, not being a parent of a disabled child myself, I couldn't possibly understand your experiences. You reassured me then that you thought I was doing a good job and shouldn't worry. But I want to raise this again with you because I still have a sense that it is an issue and that you have some doubts about my ability to understand your experiences. Let me give you a more specific example of what I mean. Remember, last week, Lenny was talking about how he had to fight against prejudice to get the best possible education for his daughter and that having a child with Down's syndrome makes him stronger? I pointed out that he should feel proud. When I said that, Lenny (*looking at Lenny directly*), you kind of rolled your eyes and said, under your breath, "Yeah, proud," and I felt as if you were humoring me and feeling that I couldn't know the least of it.

LENNY: Well, Clarissa, I guess that's true. You don't know how sick and tired of fighting we get. Now that I'm old, I try to let things roll off my shoulders. I have little energy left to fight with.

RAY: I used to fight with anyone and everyone who would stare at John or say stupid things about him. I always knew it was just ignorance speaking, but it still always hurt. I don't think parents of "normal" children can ever understand what we go through, never mind so-called professionals.

DENISE: I think only we know the sadness that we feel. Sometimes I think (*visibly upset*) . . . we're all alone.

LENNY: Of course, we're alone. Other parents may feel sorry for us, as do some professionals. But they can never understand what we go through on a day-to-day basis.

DENISE: No one understands our situation. I think that so-called professionals understand least of all. We are frequently left to figure out what is right and wrong for our children by ourselves. Social workers and psychologists remain clueless!

WORKER: It must be painful—to feel so isolated.

DENISE: It hurts like hell. Just last week I took Robin to the clinic for a psychological update. Now you know Robin is very high functioning and verbal, right? Well, this idiot psychologist only spoke to me and looked afraid of Robin. He asked *me* all of the questions and made my daughter feel terrible.

ANNE: Sometimes at the end of the day you're so frustrated you're ready to just give up. Frustrations with professionals are constant, especially the ones who think they have all the answers. It's one thing to work with our kids and it's a completely different thing to be their caretakers.

LENNY: Sometimes you feel stupid as a parent because you did something wrong and then you feel immense guilt. It angers me—we can't win (*bangs his fist on the table*).

DENISE: But then every once in a while you meet a professional who really cares. That's what keeps us going.

———

As this excerpt demonstrates, distrust of and negative attitudes toward professionals *was* an issue for the members of this group. Even though they denied there was a problem the first time the worker raised the issue, the members' response when she brought it up a second time was quite strong. Obviously, this was an issue around which members had much feeling, one that was important to them. By raising the problem and being open and nondefensive in listening to the members' experiences, the worker gave the members permission to talk about an issue that, out of a sense of politeness, they might otherwise have seen as taboo. She let the group know that this important issue could be talked about.

Over the weeks that followed, the group engaged in the problem-solving process. Particularly during the exploration phase, having an opportunity to recount to the worker, as well as to one another, their negative experiences with persons in professional positions, and feeling that others understood, greatly enhanced the trust that developed and the members' willingness to be honest in the group. Ultimately, the solution adopted by the group was a simple one: when they felt the worker was not understanding, they would be direct in letting her know that.

Initiation of the Process by a Member

The problem-solving process can also be initiated by a member who may feel uncomfortable or unhappy with something that occurs in the group. When an observation is initiated by a member, other members of the group may greet that person's statement with disdain. Especially if the member's observation is vague and not fully formed, as it is likely to be when it is being voiced for the first time, other members may want to quickly discount its validity. They may feel blamed or that they are going to be put on the spot and therefore try to evade discussion of the issue that is being identified.

When an observation is made by a member, workers need to intervene in two ways. First, workers need to ask the group to give the observation attention and not discount it. Second, workers need to support the group member so that he can express and clarify his thinking. The worker's role is thus to help the group enter into rather than avoid the problem-solving process by taking the first step toward problem identification.

Exploration and Solutions

Particularly important in the effective use of the problem-solving process is thorough exploration of a problem/issue. All too often, the group's exploration of an issue is skimpy and insufficient. Workers and members alike tend to rush to find solutions quickly, often to problems that have been inadequately defined and incompletely explored. The focus is on action ("What should we *do*?") rather than on the means to achieve the best possible action ("How can we make a good decision?" "What is really going on here?" "What seems to be contributing to the difficulty?") as perceived by all of the members.

Some practitioners may be uncomfortable with the ambivalence, differences, and uncertainties that exploration often accelerates. So, in a rush to bring certainty to an issue, or to decrease anxiety, or to avoid conflict, or to get busy with a task, or to feel a sense of accomplishment, workers may avoid or shortcut exploration by the group. Exploring an issue involves asking members to remain engaged with that issue—what it looks like, what contributes to its occurrence, the reasons it takes place—and to resist the tendency to move too quickly to solutions. Such premature solutions are almost always ineffective because they are not rooted in an understanding of the issue and do not address its underlying causes. Effective solutions are those which evolve from the understanding that group members gain through in-depth exploration.

The experience of a current events discussion group in a senior center illustrates well the link between thorough exploration and effective solutions. In this group, the worker noticed that members were not listening to one another, were interrupting one another, and were talking over one another.

As a result, the noise level in the meeting room would heighten. Some members would begin to yell in order to be heard, while others seemed to give up and were not expressing their thoughts at all. By the time a meeting ended, members seemed frustrated and annoyed as they left the room. The worker resolved to bring this issue to the group.

I waited until everyone was seated and, before discussion of a current events issue could begin, I said to the group, "I have an issue I want to raise with you. I've been noticing that in this group people often talk all at once. Sometimes you interrupt one another. Often, I think you don't really listen to one another . . . " Before I was even finished, Joseph interrupted, "You're right, people in this group are very rude." Louise agreed. Sophia shook her head and said, "People *are* very rude in this group, and I think we should do something about it." I asked Sophia what she had in mind. "Well, why don't we ask people to leave the meeting if they interrupt," she said. "That's kind of strict," Sam stated. "It sounds like we're school children." "I don't think we need to punish people," Louise said, "We can be good, we won't interrupt," she added. "Yeah, we'll be good," Lenore echoed. "OK," I said, "I hope everyone will re- member." Group members assured me that they would.

The discussion then started off well. People seemed more polite and did not interrupt one another. But as the meeting progressed, the mem- bers seemed to fall back into their former patterns—talking over one another, not listening, interrupting. I would try to remind them of their agreement to not interrupt, but I found myself having to yell over the din. At times they would hear me and one of the group members would yell, "C'mon everybody. We said we'd be good." It would quiet down for a few seconds, but then, especially when the topic was heated, it would quickly become loud and the members would again interrupt and talk over one another.

The worker reported that she felt very frustrated, herself, as she left the meeting that day. With help from her supervisor, she realized that she had allowed the group to jump to solutions by encouraging Sophia to say what she thought the group should do without ever asking the group to explore what they thought contributed to their interruptive behavior. She resolved to bring up the issue with the group at the next meeting and this time to stay with the exploration of the issue.

I began the meeting by once again raising the issue. "Remember last week, I made the observation to you that people were talking all at once, interrupting, not listening to one another." Joseph rolled his eyes and said, "Yes, we remember." Others nodded. Clearly, the group knew what I was talking about. "Well, last week you all said you'd try to be 'good' and not interrupt," I said. "But then, especially when the topic got heated, there you were again talking over one another." I paused. "We do that a lot," Sophia responded. "It's like we can't control ourselves." Lou said. "Before we get to what we should do about it," I said, "I think it would help if we look at that, at the reasons we can't seem to control ourselves as Lou just said, at the reasons it's hard to listen and not interrupt. Why do you think that happens?" Through my tone of voice and body posture, by not "yelling" at them or "blaming" them for being "bad," I tried to invite an honest and nondefensive response.

In the exploration of the issue that followed, members were quite reflective. Some of them talked about having become increasingly opinionated and less open to others' differing views as they had grown older. Others said that now they lived alone and often would go through a day without talking to another person. They admitted that they wanted to be sure to be heard in the group even if it meant cutting off another person. Still other members acknowledged that they did not like to be assertive and that when everyone else was talking loudly and all at once they resigned themselves to not being heard even if they had ideas they wanted to express.

After a lengthy and full exploration of the issue, the solution that the group arrived at was not different from that which it had adopted previously: members would try to listen to one another and not interrupt. This time, however, members were much better able to follow through. Their understanding of the reasons for their behavior increased their sensitivity to the needs of other members and ultimately to their ability to be responsive. When members reverted to their earlier behavior, the worker could now call their attention to it with ease.

The antithesis of jumping to solutions too quickly and shortcutting exploration in the problem-solving process comes when a worker focuses on exploring an issue without ever helping the group to look at possible solutions. Such an error in the use of the process occurs with much less frequency than does the premature move to solutions. But it, too, is an ineffective use of problem-solving.

Perhaps the practitioner who focuses on problem exploration and neglects problem solution believes that if members see and understand a problem, then they will automatically know what to do and be able to solve it. Such an assumption is erroneous, however. The worker needs to help the group consider possible solutions and then select, implement, and evaluate the one that seems best. Those steps are crucial. Just as cursory attention to problem exploration is ineffective, so, too, is perfunctory consideration or absence of solutions.

Throughout its life, in each of its developmental stages, a social work group engages repeatedly in use of the problem-solving process to address the broad range of issues that arise. The group's ability to engage in problem-solving with depth of reflection and participation grows as it gains practice in its use. In fact, use of the problem-solving process in the group can enhance members' ability to employ it with understanding and reflection in their lives outside the group.

As with most processes that are described as a series of linear steps, the actual use of the process involves back-and-forth movement between the steps. As Helen Perlman emphasizes, there is overlap and the process proceeds not linearly but in a kind of spiral.[4] The group may work simultaneously on more than one step of the problem-solving process.[5] Exploration, for example, does not always wait until problem identification is totally concluded. In actuality, exploration may result in fuller identification of an issue.

Addressing an Individual's Problem in the Group

When individual members bring personal problems or issues with which they are grappling to the group for help, the problem-solving process is once again important to the group's work. If skillfully applied in addressing one group member's problem, the process provides an opportunity for *all* members to examine their own situations, concerns, and experiences and thus to benefit, themselves, as they attempt to help one of their members. When this occurs, mutual aid between members is activated.

Mutual aid is essential and central to group work practice.[6] A straightforward definition of mutual aid is provided by Dominique Steinberg: "Mutual aid simply refers to people helping one another as they think things through."[7] Mutual aid takes place when group members help one another by drawing upon their own experiences, knowledge, and thinking. But mutual aid is very different from mere advice giving. It is also different from the "aggregational therapy of individuals," a term coined by Margaret Hartford, who notes that when a worker responds to one group member and then another in sequence, what takes place is not work with the group because it is not maximizing the full potential of the group.[8] It is different, too, from the "group casework" described by Ruth Middleman as a "hot-seat pattern" in which the worker engages in extended back-and-forth discussion with one member while the other members watch.[9] Even if it is other members and not the worker who put an individual member with a problem on a hot seat, what takes place is still individual work within the group rather than group work.

What characterizes mutual aid in the problem-solving process when it is used to address an individual issue raised by one member is the application of that issue by all members to their own experiences and situations. Thus, the questions they ask of that member and the suggestions and advice they ultimately offer to that person come as a result of their own active examination of the issue being raised as it has been relevant in their own lives. Such thinking benefits both the receiver and the giver of help and is key to the reciprocity that constitutes mutual aid.

Perhaps it is easy to recognize that aggregational therapy and a hot seat approach do not utilize the potential of the small group. Perhaps it is apparent that allotting time sequentially to group members to talk about issues of concern one by one is individual work within a group rather than group work. But sometimes members can seem to be participating actively and group work can appear to be taking place when actually it is not.

When one member raises an issue and other members rush to offer advice to that person, individual work rather than group work is what is occurring. The advice of the other members, when it comes without adequate exploration of the issue and without the other members applying that issue to themselves and their own experiences, is shallow. Such advice, even when it is offered out of a desire to be helpful, benefits neither the giver nor the receiver. Suggestions that are offered off the top of the head are superficial and do not really involve the givers. Furthermore, the rush to solutions and the "instant" advice results in the receiver feeling that the other group members do not really understand.

An illustration of individual work in a group is demonstrated by the following excerpt from a prevocational skills group in a day treatment program.[10] All group members were young adults who had been hospitalized with mental illness and who were now contemplating a return to work or to school.

Sara told the group that she was very nervous about going back to work. She told the group that she's gained weight and that her clothes do not fit, that she's worried she won't be able to get a job because of the bad economy, and that she doesn't know what to say about the gap in her employment history. "What am I going to say I did for two years—that I was hospitalized and under psychiatric care and doing nothing?" she exclaimed. On the other hand, she also said she'd like to have some money and that she felt useless staying home, especially when her sister was pressuring her to go to work.

Group members quickly jumped in with a series of suggestions. "Maybe you're not ready to go back to work, especially if you're feeling so nervous about it," Doris said. Robert advised Sara to go on a diet. John told her not to listen to her sister. Chris said, "Go for it, Sara. Just grit your teeth and go on a job interview, it will get easier when you do." Frank urged her to lie on her job application, "Just say you were working in your sister's office."

Sara rejected these suggestions. "I couldn't lie on my application, I just couldn't do that," she said. "And if I went on an interview and didn't get the job, I couldn't handle it. I'd be sick for weeks." Finally, Sara said in frustration, "I don't want to talk about this anymore. Let's talk about something else." The group went on to another subject.

In this excerpt, the issues that Sara raises—readiness to work, pressure from relatives, feelings of anxiety and inadequacy, fear of failure, how to explain having been hospitalized—are directly applicable and relevant to other members of the group. Those issues are ones with which many other members have had experience. Yet the focus is maintained solely on Sara. The group seems active. In fact, six members explicitly offered advice to Sara. But the solutions they suggest come without depth of thought. They come without their being touched, themselves, by the issues that Sara is raising, without their really looking at Sara's thinking and feelings nor examining their own related thoughts, feelings, experiences, situations. In this excerpt, even though the group appears to be actively involved, what is taking place does not exemplify mutual aid nor work with the group process. Instead, it is individual work within the group.

To become group work, it is necessary for the members of this group to apply the issues that Sara is raising to themselves and their own experiences and situations. To do so necessitates that they review and think about those experiences. In trying to apply them to another person, they gain greater understanding and mastery themselves. Have they encountered similar doubts, questions, concerns? Have they sustained similar pressures? Have they found themselves feeling similarly to the way that Sara is describing? Members need to recount to one another, and to Sara, their own related experiences and their thoughts and feelings about them. Ultimately the group does want to offer advice to Sara. But that advice will have significance and impact, for them and for Sara, if it is rooted in their own personal situations.

Applying the Problem-Solving Process to an Individual's Issue

When one member brings up an issue in the group, the problem-solving process needs to be utilized. That process, when applied to a personal problem or issue raised by *one* group member, is very similar to the problem-solving process used with a *group* issue or problem. This time, the process consists of an eight-step progression in which the exploration of the issue is divided into two phases. First, the issue being raised by the individual member is explored. Then, the experiences of the other group members are explored as they relate to the individual's issue. Overall, the progression of the problem-solving process applied to an individual's issue is as follows:

1. One member raises a problem, issue, or situation of concern.
2. The problem is identified by the individual and the group.
3. The individual's problem is explored. As it is explored, additional information may be gathered from the individual about the situ-

ation. Group members need to really listen to what the individual is saying. They may ask questions about the problem and about the feelings of the individual. As they listen and question, they come to understand the problem through the eyes of the individual who has raised it. They develop empathy.

4. The experiences of the other members related to the individual's issue are explored. Members recount situations they have experienced and dilemmas they have faced that are relevant to the problem raised by the individual.

5. Possible solutions to the individual's problem are identified, drawing upon the experiences of the other members that have been recounted in the group.

6. With the help of the other members and the worker, the individual decides on a course of action to try. The group helps the individual to plan how actually to implement that solution.

7. The individual implements the solution.

8. The group, at future meetings, follows up with the individual to evaluate the results of the solution's implementation.

The two aspects of the exploration phases of this process, steps 3 and 4, are particularly important. In step 3, when the focus is on exploration of the issue that the individual is raising, a fine line must be maintained between spending too little or too much time in discussion of the individual's issue. If too little exploration takes place, then the other members will not develop understanding of the individual's situation and feelings. As a result, compassion and empathy for the individual and the situation on the part of the other members of the group will not evolve. If, on the other hand, too much exploration takes place, the individual will have the sense of being on a "hot seat" and of being "grilled" unsympathetically by the other members. The sense of being assaulted by the others may cause the person to become unexpressive and uncommunicative rather than forthcoming.

Only if they truly understand and develop empathy for the individual, for that person's experience and feelings, will other members then be able to recount relevant experiences and dilemmas of their own, the fourth step in the problem-solving process. Empathy is the essential quality in gauging the timing of the third and fourth steps of the process. The worker needs to help the members maintain their focus on the individual until a sense of comprehension and empathy on their part is evident. Such understanding and empathy may be conveyed to the individual by the other members both verbally and nonverbally. What is important is that the group continue its exploration of the individual's issue until empathy develops between the members.

Once they do understand and become empathic toward the individual, other members may begin quite naturally to talk of their own relevant experiences. Thus, they begin the fourth step of the problem-solving process. They may begin recounting their own related experiences and/or feelings with such phrases as "That reminds me of a time when . . . " or "I had a similar experience once when . . . " or "I felt the same way when . . . " At other times, once the worker senses the members' understanding and empathy, members may need to be encouraged to think about and recount experiences and feelings that they believe are related to those being expressed by the individual.

As they recount events and feelings in their own lives, the members are compelled to reflect upon those experiences and their solutions. Speaking about solutions that worked for them results in their consolidating their own understanding and learning. Ultimately, the aim is for the group to identify possible solutions that might be helpful to the individual, step 5 in the problem-solving process. When the advice and possible solutions are offered thoughtfully from the actual experience of the other members, all in the group are able to benefit from the issue raised by one member. The potential of mutual aid, which is unique to the small group, is then actualized.

It is important to note here that the ability of other group members to be helpful to an individual does not require that they have had the exact experience as that member. One member, for example, may bring to the group a problem that she is having with her teenage daughter. Another member, even if she is not a parent herself, can still remember and reflect upon times when she felt similar to the way this member is describing—frustrated, perhaps, or exasperated and irritable. Other nonparent members can also consider their experiences with their own parents when they were teenagers or experiences they might have had in parentlike positions, such as teachers or counselors or supervisors.

What is critical here is that members apply the issue of one member to themselves. Even when that issue seems at first glance to have no relevance to others in the group, the fact is that the commonalities of human feelings and experiences are powerful and can be drawn upon.

Individual Problem-Solving in the Group: An Illustration

The difference between ineffective and effective problem solving around an individual's issue within a group is well portrayed in the following example from a group in a day program for adults with mental illness. The group's purpose was to enhance the abilities of its members to cope with issues in their daily lives. The group had been meeting twice a week for six weeks when Jim raised an individual issue.

Jim was a lonely and reclusive twenty-nine year old who had been diagnosed as paranoid schizophrenic. He lived in his own apartment in a residence for the formerly homeless. Jim had difficulty making friends—at the residence, in the day program generally, and in this group as well. He frequently annoyed the other members by talking of masturbation and walking around with his pants unzipped, by making inane comments that interrupted the group, and by pretending to fall asleep and lying across three chairs during group meetings. Jim started the group's twelfth meeting by directing a question to Debbie, the worker.

"I want to know what you think, Debbie. Hypothetically speaking, suppose you had a friend and you don't have any other friends, but this friend, every time he comes over he smokes pot or does a couple of lines of coke in your living room. I mean he is a good listener and is your only friend and you don't do drugs or anything, what would you do?"

Before Debbie could even respond, Jerry immediately jumped in with a tinge of anger in his voice, "Just tell the guy to get out of your house with the drugs." Allen followed, "Yeah, drugs are dangerous and it sounds like this guy's no good." "I sure wouldn't want anyone doing drugs in my house," Pam said. "That guy must not be a very good friend," Ron added. "Right," Will said, "a friend wouldn't take advantage of you or get you in trouble."

Jim seemed dissatisfied with the response of the others. "I don't really care if he does drugs in my house," he exclaimed with a hint of defensiveness. "If you don't care, then why'd you waste our time?" Pam asked with annoyance. "Yeah, if there's no problem, why'd you bring it up?" Allen added. Jim shrugged his shoulders. The group moved on to another subject. The mood was one of aggravation.

This example is strikingly similar to the earlier illustration of Sara. As in that instance, the issue that Jim raised has relevance for all group members. But other members offer instant advice without taking the time to explore Jim's situation and without reflecting upon their own related experiences. Outwardly, the group seemed active. But, in reality, the members were uninvolved. And their advice came with a hint of hostility and belligerence. Problem solving, mutual aid, and involvement of the group did not take place.

After the group meeting, as she thought about what had taken place, Debbie, the worker, was displeased with what had occurred and realized that Jim and the other members had also been dissatisfied. She resolved to raise the issue with the group again. Jim was not present at the next meeting, so Debbie had to wait for a week to bring up the issue.

"Do you remember the meeting before last where Jim spoke of his friend who did drugs at his house?" Debbie asked the group. Some group members nodded; others said "yes" with an annoyed tone. It was clear that the members did remember. "Well, I think the discussion that took place at that meeting was frustrating for us all," Debbie said. The group agreed. "I'd like us to try the discussion again," Debbie said. "I think we could do a better job of it and engage in conversation that would be more satisfying and helpful for everyone. Is that OK with everyone?" The group agreed. "OK, Jim could you describe the issue again?"

Jim recounted the situation, telling the group that he had a friend who smoked pot or did coke whenever he came over to his house to visit. He said he was not sure what to do about it. This time, though, the worker asked questions and made comments that helped Jim to be more specific. "How often does your friend visit?" Debbie asked. "Once or twice a week," Jim responded. "And you don't like him doing drugs at your house," Debbie commented. "No, I don't," Jim said, "especially when I'm trying to stay clean." "This issue seems important to you," Debbie observed. "Yes, it is," Jim said. With a quivering voice, he added, "I don't have any other friends and having this one friend is very important to me. This guy I've known all my life. We went to high school together. This guy is a college graduate with a good job. He has his own apartment. This guy is somebody."

The emotion and feelings that Jim voiced about his situation caused members to get more involved. They began to empathize with Jim and to ask him questions to help them better understand. The tone of their questions and comments changed from a belligerent to a supportive one. Jim's responses, in turn, became less defensive and more honest. He was now better able to hear the group. Even his physical posture changed, as he sat upright and faced the group. The content and tone of this meeting were very different from the first in which the issue had been raised.

Allen asked Jim if he was worried about the police. "Yes, I am," Jim responded. "But I don't want to end the friendship. I don't want to get caught, either, with my friend doing drugs." Pam asked, "Jim, have you ever talked to your friend about being caught when he does drugs at your house?" "I told him it bothered me," Jim responded. "He stopped for a while, but then he started doing it again." "Why do you think he does drugs at your house?" Jerry asked. "I don't know," Jim said. "When he come to my house, it's usually right from work. He hates his boss, so maybe it's his way of loosening up."

The conversation continued. When it became clear that group members both understood and empathized with Jim and his situation, Debbie asked, "I'm wondering if some of you can remember situations you've experienced that are related to the one with which Jim is struggling now." Ron's response came quickly. "Yes. Last year I had a friend who kept pushing me to use coke. I kept telling him no, I didn't want to do it. He kept pressuring. Finally, I told him that if our friendship was going to continue he had to respect me and what I wanted. After that, he backed off." Others recounted other situations: times they'd tried to convince friends or relatives to do something, times others tried to convince them to do something, friends they'd valued and lost, people who'd gotten them into trouble. Group members, including Jim, listened attentively to one another until the time for the group was up.

The group continued to work on this issue. At the next meeting, other members helped Jim develop a plan to talk with his friend about his concerns. Drawing on their own experiences, some gave Jim suggestions of what he might say and actual words he might use. The group engaged in role-play, with Jim playing his friend and letting the group know how he thought his friend would respond as they took turns playing Jim. The group's interest emboldened Jim to actually speak with his friend, for he knew that the group was a place where he could discuss what had happened once he did talk with him.

___

In this example, the distinct difference between the disastrous first group meeting in which Jim posed the problem and the subsequent fruitful meetings where in-depth exploration took place resulted from a problem-solving process that made use of mutual aid in such a way that both givers and receivers of help could benefit. Speaking about their own experiences helped members put them into perspective and learn from them. It also enabled Jim to draw upon those experiences and apply them to his own situation. Thus, all members of the group were touched, as problem solving, mutual aid, and use of group process were in evidence.

Strengths and Mutual Aid

The expectation that the members of a group can help one another is fundamental to work with groups. Such an expectation makes group work a method of working with people that is affirming of their strengths. In fact, the very act of forming a group is a statement that embodies the belief that people have strengths and the ability to contribute to their peers. To invite a person to join a group is to express confidence that the person has something to give to the group, not just to get from it.[11] Such an expression of confidence enhances the self-esteem of the invitee. For many, it precipitates their viewing themselves in a different, more positive way.

It is the quality of mutual aid that occurs during the group's problem-solving process that is at the heart of effective group work. Margot Breton emphasizes that such mutual aid is powerful, healing, liberating.[12] Leonard Brown captures the importance of mutual aid in the problem-solving process for both individuals and the total group:

> For members to be able to share their ideas and feelings with others is a means of strengthening the giver *and* the receiver. The collaborative problem-solving that goes on during this mutual aid can nurture group members, enhance decision making, and build more cohesiveness within the group.[13]

The ability of members to gain from each other, to consider, to understand, to appreciate, and to build upon each other's experiences, situations, problems, dilemmas, points of view, strengths, and weaknesses is crucial to social work with groups. Such ability, put into motion, nurtured, and enhanced by the worker, is the unique power of group work.

9 Conflict

Conflict is a natural, necessary, and important component of group process. It provides group members with the stimulation they need to examine their own values, beliefs, and feelings as these impact upon their experiences and situations. As a group develops and as members grow surer of themselves and comfortable in that group, they also become more willing to express their true feelings and beliefs and to risk exposure of their opinions and ideas, something they were much less willing to do in the group's beginnings when they were concerned with fitting in. Thus, there is apt to be disagreement in the group, especially in its middle stages, and the differences between members, in ideas, opinions, values, beliefs, feelings, experiences, approaches, and behaviors, are increasingly likely to be voiced by them. Such expression of differences is enriching for the group and for group members individually, as it is an important ingredient in development and change. In addition, if members are helped to address conflict successfully as it occurs within the group, then their ability to do so in their relationships outside the group is also likely to be enhanced. Since conflict is an inevitable and continuing process in human relationships, the ability to manage and grow from it will enrich the lives of group members outside the group as well.

As presented in chapter 2, conflict is behavior in which there is disagreement between two or more persons. At the group level, conflict may lead to enhanced understanding and consequent strengthening of relationships between members because differences are aired and not allowed to remain irritatingly below the surface. Conflict provides stimulation and a basis for interaction. Only through the expression of differences is it possible for a group to delineate its common values and interests.[1]

As areas of disagreement are explored, the areas of agreement become clarified. This clarity, in turn, contributes directly to the cohesiveness of the group. Social conflict may have consequences that increase rather than decrease the group's ability to engage in successful problem-solving activities. To focus on the useful aspects of conflict is not to deny that conflict can be destructive and may lead to the disintegration of the group. Thus, the way in which members of groups recognize, resolve, and manage conflict is crucial to the very survival of the group.

Workers' Fears of Conflict

Group work practitioners often fear the expression of conflict and difference in the group. They worry that conflict will get out of control and destroy the group. They fear that they will be seen as inadequate if they are unable to handle conflict when it arises. In research that examined the contrasts in the group work practice of social workers who had received substantial education and training in work with groups and those who had received little education and training in work with groups, Dominique Steinberg found that a major distinction was in the worker's attitudes toward conflict. Those with little education in work with groups tended to view conflict as a hurdle to get over as quickly as possible so that the group could move on. They tended to quash conflict and the expression of difference in the group or deal with it with members individually outside the group. Those with substantial education in work with groups, on the other hand, tended to see addressing conflict as an important part of the group's work. They tended to help the group take time to identify and explore conflict and difference as they arose in the group.[2]

Instead of seeing conflict as natural and important, many workers with groups view it as negative, threatening, an interruption, something to be disposed of and handled with dispatch so that the group can return to its work. Many workers attempt to avoid conflict, suppress it, or take responsibility on their shoulders alone to resolve conflict without involving the group in a problem-solving process. By doing so, they deprive the group of the opportunity that dealing with conflict can be.

Conflict and Stages of Group Development

Conflict occurs throughout the life of any group, but there are differences in its nature and intensity at various stages of the group's development. The changing individual needs of members and shifting collective needs of the total group during the group's developmental stages form the basis for the nature of the conflict that is likely to occur. Interpersonal conflict in the group's beginnings is likely to be around issues of inclusion and power. Overt expression of conflict and differences around substantive issues is not likely to take place in the inclusion-orientation stage because at this time members are striving to be accepted and liked by the others in the group. The expression of a different point of view by a member at this time in the group's life is unlikely unless it is meant to purposely provoke. In the group's beginning stage, the worker aims to help the members see the commonalities and consensus that they share and that form the group's foundation. If differences are emphasized before a foundation based on commonalities and consensus has been constructed, recognized, and appreciated, then conflict can tear the group apart. Without such a foundation, there is little to hold the group together.

In the later stages of the group, interpersonal conflict is likely to be around issues of intimacy, interdependency, and separation. Substantive conflicts based on differences of point of view are likely to be expressed overtly now as members feel more comfortable and more able to be themselves and to be honest in the group. When the social climate of the group is marked by mutual acceptance and support, members are more willing to risk exposure of themselves and their ideas than in the earlier stages when they were more uncertain of their acceptance and the consequences of self-expression. They recognize that expression of difference need not mark the end of their relationships with others in the group. The expression of interpersonal and substantive differences and disagreements will not tear apart a group that has a firm and solid foundation rooted in substantial and significant commonalities between its members. In fact, during its later stages, conflict and the expression of difference are essential to prevent the group from demanding conformity and becoming stagnant and suffocating.

The Resolution of Conflict

The resolution of major conflicts cannot occur until a group has developed to the point that the basic consensus within the group is solidly built. An episode of conflict can end in several ways: the group abandons the issue through a shift of topic or activity, the group agrees that resolution is not attainable or undesirable, or the conflict is resolved. Research by Leslie Baxter indicates that avoidance of conflict is the prevalent means of coping with it.[3] The result is often an accumulation of unresolved issues. Although avoidance of conflict may relieve tension in the short run, the long-term consequence is dysfunctional.

It is through methods of decision making that conflict is controlled or resolved. Groups often control conflict through a process of elimination, that is, forcing the withdrawal of the opposing individual or subgroup, often in subtle ways. In subjugation or domination, the strongest members force others to accept their points of view. In spite of the popularity of its use as a democratic procedure, majority rule is an example of subjugation because it does not result in agreement or mutual satisfaction. Through the means of compromise, the relatively equal strength of opposing forces leads each of the factions to give up something in order to safeguard the common area of interest or the continuation of the group itself. Each side loses something in order to meet a common need. An individual or a subgroup may form an alliance with other factions; thus, each side maintains its independence but combines to achieve a common goal. Finally, through integration, a group may arrive at a solution that is new and different from any of the contending alternatives, so no one loses and no one wins. The new solution is both satisfying to each member and more productive and creative than any contending suggestion. It is the latter process that, according to Gertrude Wilson and Gladys Ryland, "represents the height of achievement in group life. It has the potentiality of being personally satisfying and socially useful: such action is the basis of democratic government."[4]

In which of these ways a particular group will attempt to resolve a conflict will depend upon a number of interrelated individual and group characteristics. Among these are the nature of the conflict; such attributes of the members as emotional maturity, values, knowledge of the subject matter, and skills in interpersonal relations, the group's prior experience in working with conflict, and the norms that have developed about the way in which differences are dealt with and problems solved.

Morton Deutsch says that the less intense the conflict the easier it is to resolve through cooperative means. When conflict is instigated by fears or unconscious processes, when it threatens self-esteem, or when it concerns major issues of principle, it will be more difficult to resolve than when the opposite is true. As conflict accelerates, the degree of commitment to it increases, as does holding on to one's position. Pathogenic processes inherent in competitive conflict, such as distortions in perception and self-deception, tend to magnify and perpetuate conflict. According to Deutsch,

> The tendency to escalate conflict results from the conjunction of three interrelated processes: (1) competitive processes involved in the attempt to win the conflict; (2) processes of misperception and biased perception; and (3) processes of commitment arising out of pressures for cognitive and social consistency. These processes give rise to a mutually reinforcing cycle of relations that generate actions and reactions that intensify conflict.[5]

The concept of conflict is associated with a number of other concepts: uncertainty, crisis, change, and dynamic equilibrium in a cyclical process. James Herrick suggests a model for viewing conflict, with special reference to group situations (figure 9.1).[6] Some uncertainty exists whenever people come together. There is, for example, uncertainty about goals and means toward their achievement, status, adequacy of resources, roles, and norms.

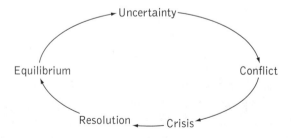

FIGURE 9.1

Such uncertainty leads quite naturally to conflict. The system is under stress. Its members are involved in attempting to resolve the conflict through the group's usual means. Apprehension increases if the conflict becomes intensified and if efforts to control it and to resolve it fail. The conflict may accelerate.

A crisis may occur when the conflict reaches its apex, at which time members become aware that they are incapable of resolving the problems basic to the conflict through their customary problem-solving devices. Emotions reach a peak and the group becomes disorganized. A point of maximum disruption and considerable disorganization, accompanied by unusual susceptibility to influence, exists. The group's resources are mobilized for the necessary change, since there is awareness that some change must occur if the group is to continue. The crisis is resolved through more effective means of problem solving.

Most groups need a period, following the resolution of a conflict with its accompanying changes in the group, to consolidate the changes. The newly achieved consensus reestablishes a steady state. During this period, the members are incorporating these changes into themselves and into the group system in such a way that a certain unity and accommodation exist within the individuals and in the group, if positive growth and change are to result. Within the group unity, there are seeds for further conflict: the existing stability is usually only a temporary balancing of conflicting forces as changes are being worked through.

In day-to-day practice, a crisis need not occur before appropriate changes are made. Most conflicts can be faced and resolved before they reach a point of crisis. A group in a constant state of crisis usually disintegrates: entropy takes over. The successful resolution of conflicts strengthens the consensus within the group and enables the members to move toward the accomplishment of their goals. As Mary Parker Follett said, "We can often measure our progress by watching the nature of our conflicts . . . not how many conflicts you have, for conflict is the essence of life, but what are your conflicts and how do you deal with them."[7] Efforts to deny differences and to suppress conflicts are unsuccessful over the long run. Such devices lead to stagnation, dysfunction, poor morale, or disintegration of the system. Unity in diversity is a value that recognizes differences, uses them to strengthen the group, and makes it possible for conflicts to be resolved through cooperative processes.

The social worker's concern goes beyond the resolution of single conflict situations to an ability to manage conflict. Since conflict is an inevitable and continuing process in human relationships, one of the worker's tasks is to help members to develop more effective means for dealing with the process of conflict. The elements that are crucial to integration as a form of conflict resolution are also the factors that contribute to the effective management of conflict. Mutual acceptance, open communication, and respect for differences make it possible for members to become competent to deal with the conflicts so characteristic of the human condition.

Confrontation

The tendency that many workers have to sweep conflict in the group under the rug or to cut it off prematurely is frequently borne of their fear that confrontation of a member will occur when conflict surfaces in the group. Their belief that confrontation may take place when conflict is honestly addressed in the group is valid. Many workers view confrontation of a person as being synonymous with demolishing that person. As a result of that view, they are wary of confrontation. But such a view of confrontation is not valid. Confrontation need not be aggressive or destructive. Its intent is not to attack or demolish. Rather, it aims to have an individual member or an entire group stop and look at what is taking place, particularly at inconsistencies in behavior and at behavior that is destructive toward self or others. Confrontation need not be harsh. A worker's confrontation of the group or an individual member can be done directly but with gentleness, empathy, civility, and support. Alice Overton and Katherine Tinker capture this sense of direct but gentle challenge when they say that confrontation can take place "with an arm around the shoulder."[8]

It is not the worker alone who uses confrontation. Especially when conflict is taking place in the group, members confront each other. If their confrontation of one another is of a destructive nature, the worker can act to limit it. Even though direct confrontation can be difficult at times, its thought-provoking nature and intent can be of great value in helping the members of a group to examine and explore areas of conflict and difference between them.

Addressing Differences That Are the Source of Conflict

Differences between members or between the members and the worker in a group are frequently the source of conflicts that arise. The kinds of differences that are particularly prevalent and that generate conflictual situations in a group can be divided into four categories: differences of opinion between the group members, differences of opinion between the group members and the worker, descriptive differences between the group members, and descriptive differences between the group members and the worker. Such a categorization recognizes two major types of differences: (1) those that involve substantive disagreement or difference of viewpoint and opinion and (2) those that are rooted in diversity of descriptive characteristics, such as race or culture or age. This categorization also recognizes that differences, both substantive and descriptive, can exist between the worker and the members of a group. Such differences between worker and members are important and need to be recognized, acknowledged, appreciated, and addressed.

Respect for difference on the part of both the members and the worker of a group is key in dealing with conflict. The importance of such respect seems almost self-evident, but it is not easy to achieve. Often, the participants as well as the worker in a group believe that their point of view is the correct one and they, therefore, are not truly open to honest consideration of the different beliefs, opinions, and ways of looking at things that others in the group may possess. Such openness is identified by Barbara Solomon as crucial to a nonracist practitioner.[9] It is also crucial that the members and the worker possess such openness if conflict is to be addressed effectively.

In general, the worker can help a group gain respect for differences and willingness and ability to address the conflicts that arise by conveying a positive attitude toward difference and four essential beliefs to the members. First, the members of the group need to come to believe that the differences between them can contribute to the richness of the group by stimulating and expanding the diversity of thinking and feelings of the members. Second, they need to come to accept that looking at those differences, rather than ignoring them and sweeping them under the rug, benefits both the group as a whole and themselves as individuals. Third, they need to realize that disagreeing with another person is not synonymous with disliking that person. They need to come to understand that they simultaneously can like a person and disagree with a point of view or behavior of that person. Finally, they need to become confident that the expression of difference will not tear apart the group and that the group will be able successfully to address and resolve the conflicts that arise.

Differences of Opinion Between Members

Differences of opinion are likely to be expressed by the members of a group, particularly when the group reaches its middle stages. At that time in the group's life, when they are feeling more comfortable and less worried about their inclusion in the group, members are better able than they were in the group's beginnings to express their points of view honestly, even when they know their view may differ from those held by others in the group. During the group's middle stages, its members are more willing to disagree with one another. Conflict is more likely to occur. When differences of opinion are expressed by the group members, the worker's aim is to help the members explore the range of viewpoints among them.

The worker wants to be sure that the members feel that the expression of their points of view will be welcomed and respected in the group. It is likely that at least some of the members have experienced the expression of difference in other situations in their lives as resulting in heated arguments, insults and put-downs, and a lack of respect. Members may also have encountered situations where the expression of difference was not welcomed and where they felt they needed to be silent and not voice their honest opinions. The worker's efforts, in the face of conflict between the group members, need to be directed toward enhancing the communication that takes place in the group. The worker's aim is to help the members of the group to listen and really hear one another.

Conflict that resulted from difference of opinion is illustrated in a mothers' group at a community mental health clinic. All members were referred to the group because they had at least one child whose behavior was seen as problematic by personnel at the school they attended. The group had been meeting weekly and attendance had been quite regular, even though the group was a voluntary one. The following excerpt is from the group's eighth meeting. Up until this meeting, Mrs. M. had been very vocal and a monopolizer in the group. She tended to tell the other members what they

should do when their children misbehaved and she was critical and judg-
mental of other members' actions as parents. Mrs. P. had said little in the
group, but seemed to be actively listening to the others.

"I'd like to tell you about something that happened yesterday with my
son," Mrs. P. said at the beginning of the meeting. Pleased that Mrs. P.'s
participation was becoming more active, I nodded to her encouragingly.
She began, "Well, I'd been thinking that I was short of money in my
purse, but I wasn't sure 'cause I'm not the most organized person and
don't keep an exact count of what's in my wallet. Anyway, I kept thinking
I was missing money, so I kind of kept my eyes open. Sure enough, there
was Ralph taking money from my wallet when he thought I was in the
kitchen. I caught him red-handed. I was shocked. And I could see he was
scared. So I sat him down and started to talk with him about what he'd
done . . . " At that point, Mrs. M. interrupted and spoke quite loudly to
Mrs. P., "You sat him down? You talked? That's stupid. What on earth
good is that going to do? Why be so namby-pamby? You needed to let
him have it. If that were me I would . . . " Mrs. P. stood up. Visibly upset,
and with her voice quivering, she said to Mrs. M., "I don't care what you
would have done. I've had it with you. You think you know everything."
Then, looking directly at me, Mrs. P. said, "I'm sick of her. She shouldn't
be in this group. She doesn't think she needs it, she thinks she knows it
all, so why is she here? If she stays in this group, I'm leaving." Before I
could respond, Mrs. R. said directly to Mrs. P., "Oh no, please don't leave.
We need you in this group." Mrs. G. added, "Sit down, please. You
shouldn't let her (motioning toward Mrs. M.) drive you away." "Well,
OK," Mrs. P. said, as she sat down, "but something's got to be done about
her (she, too, motioned to Mrs. M.). Mrs. M. seemed surprised and was
silent. The group members were all looking at me.

The seeming dilemma in this group is not as difficult as it may at first
glance seem to be. It is unlikely that Mrs. P. will carry out her threat to leave
the group. Given the length of time that the group has been meeting and
the regularity of attendance, it is probable that Mrs. P. has become invested
in the group. With just a little encouragement from other group members,
she does in fact sit down. Similarly, the length and regularity of the group's
meeting and attendance make it unlikely that conflict between the members

will bring about the group's demise. Certainly, regularity of attendance is an indication that members value the group and that they therefore do not want it to fall apart as a result of the conflict.

At the end of this process excerpt, the members are looking at the worker expectantly. But that does not mean that she needs to solve the problem for the group. Instead, the worker needs to ask the group to explore the issue. At this point in the life of the group, it is a valid expectation that the members will be able to look at the conflict that exists between them. It is also fair to expect at this time in the group's development that members will be able to discuss their differences respectfully and with directness and openness. The worker needs to convey to the group her faith in their ability to handle conflict as well as a positive attitude toward difference.

In this example, there are two areas of conflict that the group needs to address. One is Mrs. M.'s role as monopolizer in the group and the reciprocal part that other members have played in permitting and even contributing to her domination. Discussion of ways to address that issue are contained in chapter 10 of this volume, "Roles of Members."

The second area of conflict is that of the differences of opinion between the group members about ways to handle their children's misbehavior. In regard to the substantive points of view about parenting practices, the worker can help the group members to view exploration of their different viewpoints as the opportunity that it actually is to expand their thinking, understanding, and beliefs as they look at the range of approaches that different group members seem to prefer.

Differences of Opinion Between Members and Worker

There can be times in a group when members express and seem to agree upon a point of view with which the worker disagrees. Workers are often perplexed about how to handle such differences of opinion between themselves and the members. They do not want to impose their opinions upon the group. Some workers believe that to challenge the clients' viewpoints violates the principle of client self-determination, which is central to the practice of social work.[10] Yet if workers say nothing when members express opinions with which they disagree, then their acceptance of those opinions is implied. If, on the other hand, workers quickly express their disagreement and challenge the members' statements, then the members' reaction may be to withdraw into silence or to express superficial conformity. However, the real feeling of the members may be that the worker does not understand. In addition, members may come away with the sense that in this group one's beliefs cannot be expressed honestly.

Such withdrawal and sense that one's beliefs cannot be expressed are illustrated in the following excerpt from a group in a single-room occupancy hotel (SRO) for adults who had been homeless. After the building had been open for some eight months, social work staff decided to hold meetings of the tenants on each floor, with the aim of creating a greater sense of community between them. Each floor included the tenants' bedrooms, several bathrooms, and a large central kitchen. This excerpt is from the first meeting of the tenants on the second floor.

After the introductions and an explanation of the purpose of our meetings, I asked the tenants how things were going. They responded with a chorus of "fines" and "goods." I asked what they liked most about living in the building, and there was a range of responses. Ms. James said she was relieved to finally have a place of her own. Her sentiment seemed unanimous. "You can sure say that again," Ms. O'Neill agreed. Many of the tenants said they thought their health had improved since moving in and that they were feeling less stressed and exhausted.

I asked if there were any complaints. "No, none," many quickly said. They reiterated how nice the building was and how much they liked it. Finally Mr. Levitt acknowledged, "There's just one thing I don't like. Sometimes I see someone I don't know who I know doesn't live here coming out of the bathroom." "Yeah, that's happened to me," Ms. Brand agreed. "And sometimes there are strangers using the kitchen, dirtying up the place and making a lot of noise," Ms. James added. "Have you said anything to management?" I asked. "Oh, no," many in the group responded immediately. "We don't want to complain," Mr. Lewis said. "But you need to let management know," I said. "No, no, compared to what we've been through, this is nothing," Ms. Lydell said. Many in the group nodded. "Well, when you see someone you don't know, do you ever ask them who they are?" I inquired. "No way," Mr. Lee responded. "How about reporting them to the guard downstairs?" I asked. "No," the members replied emphatically. "Who knows who they are?" said Ms. Brand. "You could really get in trouble by challenging them or reporting them. Who knows what they might do to you then?" "I think there's a lot you can do about this," I said. "Maybe you could do something as a group," I added. "You could all go talk to management together." "Perhaps," Ms. James said, "but I think the best thing to do is to just keep quiet and put up with it." "Could we move on, now?" Ms. Brand suggested.

After this meeting, the worker expressed a sense of great dissatisfaction. "The tenants seemed so passive," she said, "and they seemed to feel so powerless." However, she felt that the more she tried to convince them that they could and should do something about the strangers on their floor, the more the tenants seemed to dig in their heels around their view that they needed to simply accept the situation and not make waves, especially since their housing now was so much better than the situations in which they had been living. In this example, the views of the worker and of the group members differed. The difference of opinion was not well handled and the result was a feeling of frustration and annoyance for both worker and members.

In situations such as this one, where difference of opinion exists between worker and group members, workers need not to jump in immediately to express their viewpoint and thereby attempt to change the view of the members. Nor do workers need to say nothing and, through their silence, seem to be indicating agreement with the members. Instead, it is important that workers encourage group members to say more about their thinking, about what has contributed to it, and about where they are coming from. In short, workers need to realize the importance of taking the time to understand the clients' points of view.

If the members feel that the worker has listened to and heard them, that the worker understands their thinking and the situations out of which that thinking arose, then the worker is in a better position to challenge their views, if that is what the worker believes is necessary. Such a challenge is a confrontation that aims to help the group members stop and think about the views they are expressing. Knowing that the worker understands and has taken the time to learn about their views leaves the members of the group more open to the worker's challenge of them. In the above example, for instance, the worker needed to take the time to learn what contributed to the members' view that it was best to accept having strangers on their floor and not to question or complain about that.

Greater understanding of the clients' point of view may bring greater acceptance of that viewpoint on the part of the worker, who needs to be open to that possibility. In the SRO example, for instance, the worker needed to appreciate how relieved many of the tenants were to have permanent housing and how such relief contributed to their fear of voicing complaints about anything that took place at the residence, lest they jeopardize their resident status. Furthermore, the worker needed to realize that the fears the residents expressed about retaliation from the strangers they encountered on their floor should they report them were realistic. Such understanding might or might not change the worker's resolve to challenge the members' viewpoints, but it is essential nevertheless.

After exploring the thinking and beliefs of clients, it is possible that workers may continue to disagree with the view that group members are expressing. If so, then workers can express their disagreement directly. It is important, however, that their expression does not close off discussion, that it is nonjudgmental, and that it invites even more in-depth exploration of the issue. The actual words, tone of voice, and body posture of the worker can be used to invite such exploration. Phrases such as "It seems to me that . . . " or "You may disagree, but I think that . . . " or "Let me present a different point of view . . . " help to free members to express their own views, even if they differ from those expressed by the worker. The worker's aim is not to impose a particular view upon the clients. Rather, the art of practice involves workers' ability to express their own viewpoints in ways that do not impose but instead encourage group members to examine their thoughts and feelings. The worker's expression of a point of view can help group members, in turn, to explore their own points of view. To thoughtfully and sensitively challenge clients to explore their views is central to group work practice. To do so does not intrude on the clients' right to self-determination.

Another example of difference of opinion between the worker and the members of a group is illustrated in the following vignette, taken from a group of single mothers.

The members were discussing the difficulties of setting limits and disciplining their children. Ms. Joseph said that when her son was bad she made him kneel down with his knees on a hardwood floor and stay there for an hour. If he was especially bad, she made him kneel with a potato grater under his knees. "That's what my mother did with me when I was a child, and it worked," she said. "Nowadays you really have to show your kids who is the boss." The other group members nodded in seeming agreement. "You've got to be firm," Ms. Grant added. "Yeah, show that you're in control," said Ms. Rudolph.

In this instance, the worker disagreed with Ms. Joseph's method of discipline. At the same time, as a result of her work with this group, she had come to know Ms. Joseph and she believed that Ms. Joseph was not an abusive mother who needed to be reported to child welfare authorities.[11]

Instead of immediately disagreeing with and challenging Ms. Joseph's method of discipline, the worker asked her and the other members of the group to tell her more about how their parents disciplined them when they were children.

"Well, my mother didn't use a potato grater, but what she did was almost the same," Ms. Grant said. "When my brother and I had done something really bad, she made us kneel down on uncooked rice." Simultaneously, Ms. Lumet and Ms. Brown said, "Yeah, me too." "Is that a widely used punishment in your countries?" the worker asked. "Yes, very much so," Ms. Grant said. "It's used throughout the West Indies." "Do you think it is effective?" the worker asked.

What followed was an in-depth discussion of methods of discipline in which all in the group, including the worker, were able to express their points of view. The worker's openness to learn about and understand the experiences and thinking of the group members, as well as her willingness to express her own point of view, helped the differences of opinion that existed become an opportunity for the group to engage in a full and thought-provoking exploration of the subject.

Descriptive Differences Between Members

Differences in the descriptive characteristics that exist between group members can be the basis for conflict between them. Descriptive character-

istics are those traits such as race, age, gender, sexual orientation, socioeconomic status, and grade in school, among others, that can be used to describe
a person. Particularly prevalent in the occurrence of conflict between group
members are differences in the values, norms, traditions, and worldviews
that different racial, cultural, and ethnic groups may hold. Diversity in race,
culture, and ethnicity is often unique to social work groups. By virtue of
their residential neighborhood, friendship, and work groups, many persons
participate in a world of relative racial, cultural, and ethnic uniformity. If it
is discussed and explored, the diversity that exists between the members of
a social work group can provide a unique and rich opportunity for members
to be exposed to a range of beliefs and attitudes.

But differences that are rooted in race and culture often seem to be feared
by group members and therefore not talked about openly. Too often, discussion of such differences seems to be a taboo. Perhaps this is because of
the historical legacy of slavery and oppression based on race and the existence of societal prejudice, bigotry, and stereotyping, all of which can combine to make race a difficult area for discussion. Andrew Malekoff articulates
principles for addressing diversity in a group. He recommends that diversity
be talked about as a normative issue and not only in reaction to emergent
conflicts or crises. Furthermore, he urges workers to directly and caringly
confront racial issues, such as stereotypes or put-downs, as they are expressed.
Malekoff also emphasizes the importance of promoting understanding and
respect for the worldviews and values of group members who are culturally
different.[12]

Allan Brown and Tara Mistry believe that social work groups are a social
microcosm of the wider society in which group members' frames of reference may be different because they are socially determined. They state,

> Part of the black person's frame of reference is that they experience
> living each day in a racist society controlled by white people, and the
> white person's frame of reference takes for granted their superior status
> and power as a white person in relation to black people and all those
> from minority ethnic groups.[13]

Brown and Mistry view race as having a powerful effect on group process
and on the feelings of the group members and workers.[14]

Discussion of conflict that is rooted in racial, cultural, and ethnic difference needs to not be taboo. Just as it is important to discuss conflict based

on differences of opinion between group members, so too it is crucial to discuss conflict based on descriptive differences between the members. Though they may be more difficult to talk about with ease than other areas, differences that are rooted in race, culture, and ethnicity should not be set apart and placed in a different category from other differences. The practice principles that apply to their discussion are not unique from those that have been set forth in this chapter.

The following example illustrates a worker's bringing up cultural difference with a group. The group was composed of ten tenth-grade girls, five of whom were African American and five of whom were Latina and recent immigrants from Puerto Rico, the Dominican Republic, and Ecuador. The worker was white and of Eastern European background. The group met weekly in the high school the girls attended. It was part of a teen pregnancy prevention program and aimed to help the girls be able to make proactive choices about their sexual activity rather than simply respond to peer pressure. The group was time limited and was to meet for eight sessions. Much of the content of the group involved discussion of sex, some educational in nature and some attitudinal. In assessing how the group was going, the worker realized after the third meeting that the verbal participation of some members was quite active while some other members said very little, although they appeared interested in what took place in the group. She then realized that those who were verbally active in the group were African American while those who were not verbally active were Latina. She resolved to raise this with the group at the next meeting.

When the girls were seated, the worker began. "I'd like to share something with the group that I realized after our last meeting," she said. "It seems to me that some people in this group have been participating a lot during our meetings. Others, though they seem interested, don't say very much." Roberta interrupted, "Yeah, they (she motioned to the Latina girls, who were all sitting on the right side of the circle) never say anything." Roberta's tone was not antagonistic, but more matter-of-fact. "Yes, I agree," the worker said. "In fact, I've noticed that the more talkative girls in our group are African American and the quieter girls are Latina. Have you noticed that, too?" she asked. A chorus of "yeses" and nods greeted her observation. "I wonder why that is," the worker said. "What are some of your ideas?"

The girls then got involved in lengthy exploration of the worker's observation and question. "Can you understand us?" Vanessa asked the Latina members. "Sometimes we use slang words. Do you know what we mean?" Louisa admitted that she did sometimes have trouble with English. "But I understand most of it," she added. Rosa, Yvonne, and Maria all said they could understand. "But sometimes you talk very fast," Rosa said, "and then I have trouble following." "We can try to slow down," Patricia responded. "OK, I think that will help," the worker said. "But I think there may be something more going on here," she continued. "A lot of what we talk about is sex. And I think there are differences among you in the ease with which you're able to do that." "What do you mean?" Janet asked. "Well, I think maybe Rosa, Louisa, Yvonne, Anna, and Maria may not be used to talking about sex, and so it might be hard for them to do so." (Rosa and Louisa nodded their heads as the worker said this.) The worker continued, "And I think maybe Janet, Roberta, Patricia, Vannessa, and Keesha are more used to talking about sex and doing so is easier for them." Rosa was the first to respond, and this was the first time she had spoken up since the initial meeting when members were asked to introduce themselves. "What you say is true," she said. "In my country, one does not talk about sex. One doesn't talk about it with strangers. Even in my family we don't talk about it. My mother doesn't know much about this group. But if she knew we talked about sex here, I don't think she'd let me come."

The worker's awareness of the possibility that cultural differences were having an impact on the participation of the group members and her willingness to raise that possibility with the group, in a way that was nonjudgmental, nonblaming, and at the same time direct and honest, was crucial here. Her doing so resulted in full and nondefensive exploration among the members of differences in cultural norms and attitudes. Furthermore, when the group members seemed to want to come to a solution prematurely, the worker helped them continue to explore the issue. As a result, the understanding of the members was increased. Had the members responded to one another and treated their differences with antagonism and insults when the worker made her observations, the worker could have pointed that out to the group and thereby limited such behavior. But the tone of nonblame and nonanger the worker used when she brought up the issue contributed to the

willingness and ability of the group members to respond similarly and to look at their differences with honesty and respect.

Descriptive Differences Between Members and Worker

Social workers often work with group members whose descriptive characteristics are different from their own. It is not uncommon for differences to exist between worker and clients in relation to race, culture, and ethnicity, and also in regard to other descriptive characteristics such as age, religion, gender, sexual orientation, socioeconomic status, or health condition, to name but a few. Workers are often fearful of acknowledging and discussing such differences publicly in the group, perhaps because they fear that to do so would be to admit to the group members that the descriptive differences that are present make it impossible for them to understand, empathize with, and help the members of the group. But just as discussion of descriptive differences between the members can be enriching and needs to not be taboo, so too is it important that descriptive differences between the worker and the members be acknowledged, recognized and explored.

To be able to talk about descriptive differences between themselves and the group members, workers must be persons who are comfortable with themselves and who do not feel defensive about their descriptive characteristics and the experiences and situations that have flowed from them. Elaine Pinderhughes emphasizes the importance of the practitioner's understanding and appreciating the different perspectives, needs, and values of persons of different cultures. To do so, she says, requires that practitioners have awareness and understanding of their own cultural backgrounds and of the ways in which their backgrounds influence their interactions with others.[15]

In addition to gaining self-awareness, workers also have a responsibility to learn as much as possible about the experiences and situations of the group members with whom they are working and to try to understand those experiences and situations even if they themselves have not lived them. Workers must, in a sense, do their homework, taking the time they need outside the group to gain the knowledge that it is important for them to have about the members. Not all that knowledge will come from the members, for they are not there primarily to teach the worker. It is unfair for workers to take on a role of an innocent ingenue who pleadingly entreats the group members to teach them. Nor is it helpful for workers to take on a role of a

hip know-it-all who shows off to group members how much like them they are. Instead, workers need to be honest and open about the descriptive differences that exist.

Descriptive difference between worker and group members can be raised by the members, as the following example from a literature discussion group in a senior center illustrates. Here, age difference was the point of conflict, with the worker aged twenty-nine and the average age of the members more than eighty. The following is taken from the tenth and eleventh meetings of the group.

RALPH: There's no way a young person like yourself could really understand or help somebody my age. Not that there's anything wrong with that. I mean, how could you?   •

HILDE: Oh no, I don't think that's true at all. Richard (worker) is very helpful. (*Others voice agreement.*)

WORKER: Hold on a second. This is actually something I've often thought about. How do you think I'm unable to help you, Ralph?

RALPH: Well, it's like this. It's not that I don't think you're doing a great job here, because you really run the group very well. It's just that I'm eighty-six years old. I have physical problems that I never dreamed of when I was your age, and there's no reason I should have thought about that kind of thing. And why should you? I'm the sum of fifty-six years more life than you are. Now that certainly doesn't mean I know more or I'm any better. It just means I've had that many more experiences.

ELLA: But I don't see it that way. I think that anyone who wants to can understand another person. You don't have to walk through fire to talk to someone who has.

HILDE: I have so many dear friends who are younger people. They keep me young with their ideas and their energy.

WORKER: But do you feel like they can relate to you? Can they understand you as an older person?

HILDE: Why should they be able to? Why should they want to?

RALPH: That's just it. There's no reason they should want to. It's not that we are uninteresting people, but when you're young the world is your oyster. You're ready to tackle the world, and that's how it should be. But when you are our age, you're not so sure about things anymore. You realize you don't have all the answers you thought you did.

WORKER: But you see, I do want to understand you, and I believe I can. Not everything about you—maybe not even that much—but something. I think there's a common ground where we can talk to each other—have a give and take. You're eighty-six, I'm twenty-nine. But we are both men trying to find something meaningful and satisfying in life.

RALPH: That may be true to some extent, but it's like this. When I'm sitting in the doctor's office or even just walking along the street and I see someone my own age or in somewhat similar dismal health, we exchange a knowing glance, and in that look there is an understanding that you just can't talk about.

WORKER: (silence)

GRETTA: I think what Ralph is saying is true . . . but you can go too far with it.

WORKER: What do you mean, too far?

GRETTA: I believe there are valuable things you can get out of a relationship with any intelligent person.

MOLLIE: Intelligence isn't the only criterion. There's also sensitivity and the ability to empathize.

GRETTA: I include that as part of intelligence.

WORKER: Wait a minute! Let's stick with this issue of whether or not a younger person can be helpful to an older person, other than helping them to cross the street . . . Ralph, I definitely relate to what you're saying about a certain connection to people who you're in the same boat with. But what kind of connection do you think you and I can make?

RALPH: Well, that's a good question. Let me think about that one.

HILDE: I would rather be with a younger person and forget about my age than sit around and sigh with someone my own age.

WORKER: But can anybody ever really forget about their age?

MOLLIE: I think not.

HILDE: But you needn't dwell on it!

ELLA: Well, look, it's there whether you think about it or not.

WORKER: I want to ask the group the question I just asked of Ralph—what kind of connection can you as an older person have with me, a young man? In what way do you think the age difference between you and I comes into play in our relationship?

ADA: Everyone is a different person with different experiences. I don't think anyone here is the same, and we can all learn from one another (*silence*).

RALPH: Hmm . . . I can't quite put my finger on it. Maybe I'm just resentful of your youth.

WORKER: Hmm!

RALPH: I was once a good-looking young man myself, you know.

GRETTA: Now you're a good-looking old man (*laughter*).

RALPH: Youth is so sure of itself. So unteetering in its attitudes.

WORKER: You know, Ralph—you have some of the same myths about youth that I had about aging. I certainly don't feel that sure of myself or unteetering.

RALPH: Well, you should!

WORKER: Why?

RALPH: That's one of the joys of being young!

(One week later.)

HILDE: You know, Ralph, last week I was thinking about what you said about young people and I had an experience I want to tell you about. (She spoke of how she went to see her ophthalmologist, a thirty-three-year-old woman. Hilde has often said how much she likes this person. At this appointment Hilde was talking about how her failing vision was so depressing to her. The doctor than chastised her for such talk and gave an annoyingly superficial pep talk. Hilde was dismayed by the doctor's lack of understanding and said that Ralph was right, younger people can't really understand the aged.)

WORKER: Wait a second! I'm guilty without a trial! I would say your doctor showed a real lack of empathy, but she is just one person.

RALPH: No, that's really the way it is. There's certain things a younger person just can't understand. He hasn't had to deal with them, and rightfully so.

WORKER: I believe that's true to a certain extent, but couldn't your eye doctor have waited a minute, thought about what you said and not just fed you aphorisms about when the going gets tough, the tough get going?

ELLA: Yes, she could have. I've known some young people who were very understanding.

MOLLIE: Charles Dickens was certainly a young man who wrote quite perceptively about older people.

RALPH: Yes, he wrote about them. But it was all conjecture. You see, it just had to be.

WORKER: Of course, that's true, but I don't believe you have to have cancer to help someone who does or be a thief to work with criminals. If I can help you be more comfortable with yourself or to see something about yourself that you're not aware of, or to stimulate discussions that have some meaning or interest for you, then I think I'm helping.

RALPH: Well, yes, I would agree with that. I just think that there are limits to how far you can empathize.

WORKER: Um-hmm.

The worker with this group handles the members' questions about whether he could understand them, given that he was so much younger than they, with aplomb. In the presence of a well-articulated challenge from Ralph, and then Hilde, the worker at times becomes somewhat defensive. But then he seems to catch himself in the tendency and back off from that inclination. He invites exploration of the issue even when some of the group members want to sweep it under the rug. Most important, he does not shy away from examining descriptive differences and, instead, facilitates their exploration.

Descriptive difference between workers and group members can also be raised by workers when their sense is that they are having an impact on what is taking place in the group. Such a situation is illustrated in the following vignette from the fourth meeting of a group of single mothers in a community-based youth service agency. All the members and one of the co-leaders of this group were black. One co-leader was white. The vignette comes from that worker's recording.

———

The women were talking about incidents that their children encountered at school. Many of them talked about situations in which they believed their children were treated unfairly by school personnel—blamed for something they didn't do, not listened to, made to sit in the back of the room, etc. In all their stories, race was never mentioned. But my sense was that they were talking about white teachers at the school and that they were leaving race out of their descriptions because of my presence.

I kept thinking that and wondering what to do. Finally, I just said it. "Let me ask you a question," I began. "As the only white person in this room . . . " Before I could finish, Joan said, with good-natured irony, "Oh, we hadn't noticed." At that, everyone, including me, had a good laugh. I continued, "Well, I'm wondering whether race is a factor in the incidents you've been recounting, whether you're talking about white teachers who you think have been unfair to your kids, at least in part because they are black." The response to my question varied. Some members did think race was a factor, others did not. Their actual response was not so important here. What was important, I think, was that I had broken the ice by specifically mentioning race. Now it was out on the table, and we all knew that race could be talked about in this group. We didn't need to walk on eggshells. Now we all knew that.

The worker's assessment was accurate. Demonstrated here is the fact that descriptive differences, including race, can be talked about openly; they are not taboo. The timing of such discussion, however, needs to be considered. In this vignette, the worker's question about whether race was a factor in the incidents the group members were describing was a real one. It arose quite naturally from the content of what members were saying. The worker did not bring up racial difference in a way that was artificial or that came from a sense that she was obliged to do so. Rather, in this situation the question of racial difference was real and avoidance of the need to raise it would have undermined and limited the work of the group.

Direct discussion of conflict and difference is essential and core to the practice of group work, whether that conflict be rooted in difference of opinion or description, whether that conflict be between members or between the worker and the members of the group. Such discussion improves understanding, expands perspectives, and enriches group life. It results in the strengthening of relationships between group members and between the worker and the members of the group. It also enhances each member's ability to deal with conflict in their lives outside the group. Avoidance of such discussion interferes with the group's work and makes it doubtful that the group will be able to achieve its purpose.

10   Roles of Members

Throughout the life of a group, members occupy different roles. Some are task roles, and they may contribute positively to the accomplishment of the group's purpose. Others are socioemotional roles, and they may aid in the development of positive relationships between the members. Other roles, both task and socioemotional, may do exactly the opposite. Some task roles may hinder the group's accomplishment of purpose and some socioemotional roles may detract from the development of positive relationships between members. Workers need to maintain continuous awareness of the roles that exist in the groups with which they work and intervene differentially to address the roles of members, especially those that contribute negatively to the group and to individuals. In the inclusion-orientation stage of group development, the worker needs to intervene actively and directly to try to prevent members from establishing destructive roles for themselves or for others in the group. As the group progresses to its middle stages, however, the worker's intervention now needs to focus more on helping the members themselves to look at a negative role that has developed and to apply the problem-solving process to address the issue.

The Concept of Role

The concept of role is central in the small group where members often assume or are placed into particular roles by the other members. At the same time, groups can be places where members have opportunities to test out a range of different roles.

When persons enact or perform a role, they are responding to a set of expectations that others have for their behavior, but they are also acting in accordance with their own expectations and motives. No two persons enact a role identically. When persons meet the expectations, they usually receive positive feedback; when they fail to meet expectations, negative sanctions are likely to be applied. There may or may not be consensus among significant others concerning the expectations for role performance. The expectations for behavior both influence and are influenced by the individual in the role, by the social system and its component parts, and by the expectations and demands of the wider social milieu. The roles of a person are not static but undergo constant definition and redefinition as the person acts and as other persons respond to the actions.

Roles become differentiated as definitions develop about what is to be done in what way by whom. When a division of labor becomes stabilized over a period of time, expectations for performance of the responsibilities become institutionalized. Thus the family has conventional roles of husband-wife, wife-mother, son, and daughter. These roles are examples of those that are assigned automatically to a person by society on the basis of age, gender, and marital status. In a peer group, there is the basic role of member, associated with the position of being in a particular kind of group. In each member's role set are his or her relationships with the social worker, other members of the group, and various people in the external system who have expectations concerning the member's attributes and behavior. Such diverse expectations need to be articulated sufficiently for effective operation of the status and role structure. Marvin Shaw cites evidence from research that role conflicts will ordinarily be resolved in favor of the person or group that is most important to the occupant of the role.[1] The extent to which conflict concerning expectations is reduced determines the effectiveness of the group's role system.

For social work purposes, an influential group is one in which the member's role is defined as a collaborative one in relation both to other members and to the social worker. Persons are not only in help-using or client roles but also in help-giving roles to others. There is a mutual aid system to be built on and used. The word *member* implies that one belongs to the group and participates in interdependence with others. The members are participants in all aspects of the social work process: the selection of goals, the determination of means, and the processes of assessment and evaluation. To put it another way, the group operates as a democratic system. This emphasis does not deny the special authority of the worker to influence individuals and the group's structure and processes; it does, however, indicate the way the worker's influence is to be used. Nor does emphasis on mutuality deny the development of leadership functions between the members of the group. It means that members are given freedom of choice within the definition of the group's purpose, their abilities, and the rights of others. Members are encouraged to do as much for themselves and for each other as they are able. Each is expected to contribute according to ability and each is assured that that contribution is valued. The roles of both worker and member are clear to all concerned, and so are the expectations for officially differentiated roles as these are developed in the group. This conception of roles implements professional values.

As a group becomes organized, certain members may acquire a position related officially to the purpose and structure of the group, for example, officer, coordinator, or committee member, each with its particular expectations. These positions are acquired as a result of certain choices that persons have made or that the group has made for them — usually a combination of both. Authority to influence others in certain ways is inherent in these institutionalized roles. These roles are part of the formal organized structure of the group.

Task Roles

Many task roles have been identified by Robert Bales and Philip Slater, Kenneth Benne and Paul Sheats, and Grace Coyle.[2] These task roles may exist whether the task be personal problem solving or decision making for corporate action. One example of a task role is that of information or opinion seeker, a person who asks for information pertinent to the situation and for clarification of suggestions and opinions. An opposing role is that of information or opinion giver who offers facts, generalizations, experiences, or opinions pertinent to the experience in which the group is engaged. A particular group member may be able to express feelings that stimulate others to do likewise or seek out the feelings of others in the group. Another member may typically initiate or suggest a new activity, issue, or means of working on a problem. An elaborator is one who develops further the feelings expressed or the suggestions of others, in terms of examples, meanings, or consequences of a proposal. A coordinator reconciles the various points of view or coordinates the activities of subgroups. A critic forms and expresses judgments of other members, things, or the group's functioning. A critic may also question or evaluate the logic or feasibility of a proposal. Other task roles include the teacher or demonstrator of activities, the spokesperson for the group, the procedures technician, and the recorder.

Socioemotional Roles

In addition to the institutional or task toles, every group develops a set of personal or, more accurately, as Norma Radin and Sheila Feld call them, contextual roles.[3] These roles are oriented, be it positively or negatively, toward the socioemotional needs and characteristics of the group and its members. Such roles are often illustrated by such labels as the shy one, the scholar, the clown, the scapegoat, and the monopolizer. There may also be an encourager who praises, gives support, reassurance, or acceptance of the contributions of others. A harmonizer senses the differences between members, attempts to reconcile disagreements, and relieves tension in difficult situations. The ego-ideal embodies the group's values and becomes an object for identification. The bully intimidates the group members and makes the group feel unsafe for its members. The help-rejecting complainer asks group members for assistance and then typically rejects the suggestions that they offer, causing group members to feel annoyed and frustrated.

Promoting Role Flexibility

The roles that emerge in a group may be constructive for both the individual in the role and for the group, or they may be mutually destructive. Margaret Hartford notes that the establishment of roles leads to stereotypes: "A person may be so typed within the group that he cannot move out of the set of expected behaviors. Thus he may be caught in a type of behavior he cannot change and his participation and contribution may be limited."[4] To understand these roles, the social worker needs to consider what there is about particular persons that accounts for their role in the group and what there is about the other members and the group situation that accounts for the fact that the group expects one of its members to behave in this way. A complex combination of individual and group influence is at work.

When members become stereotyped into a role, they tend to become known by the label given them. Other contributions they might make to the group are ignored. Regardless of their desires, such persons become typed and stuck in a particular role. The role into which they are cast, or into which they cast themselves, affects their perceptions of what they can and cannot do, and, thus, their self-esteem. Hartford suggests that the role of the worker may be "to reinforce those roles which are consistent with group organization and the pursuit of group goals, and to discourage those which are hindering individual and group development for the benefit of each."[5]

It is important that the worker attempt to promote flexibility of roles between group members and try to keep members from becoming locked permanently into particular roles. Often in groups, patterns of behavior will become stabilized in such a way that the group will expect a member to behave regularly in a particular manner. To lock someone into a role means that the group members will not allow that person to behave in different ways than they have come to expect, even when that member may wish to do so. A good example is the person who is in the role of clown. In the group's beginning stage, the clown brings laughter and relieves tension at a time of anxiety and is therefore welcomed and rewarded by the group members. But what happens as the group moves along and the clown wishes to be serious? Often the clown's attempts at seriousness are greeted with disappointment by the other members, who have come to expect that the clown will always be funny. For the clown, however, attempts to behave seriously may represent a positive change in behavior and may be an indication that the clown is beginning to take himself more seriously and respectfully. One of the opportunities that group membership presents is that it gives members a chance to test out different ways of behaving. To lock a member into a particular role is to eliminate that opportunity of membership. In addition, rigid role expectations deprive the group of the new contributions that individual members may be able to make.

Familiar Roles

The number and range of possible roles that can exist in a group are great and varied. Perhaps most fascinating and most perplexing are the role behaviors members assume or are forced to adopt that are related to the satisfaction of the participant's or the group's particular, and often unconscious, needs. Such roles may be assumed by persons, predominantly as an expression of their own emotional needs. It is important to keep in mind, however, that there is always some interaction between individual and group needs in the creation and persistence of such role behaviors. Primary among such roles are the monopolizer, the isolate, and the scapegoat.

The Monopolizer

The monopolizer is a dysfunctional role common in group situations. The person in the role of monopolizer feels compelled to hold the center of the stage. That person may become anxious in the group's beginning stage if other members are silent; thus, the monopolizer may talk on and on to fill the void of others' silence. Alternatively, the monopolizer may become anxious whenever another member is at the center of attention and may try to maintain a central position for himself by talking on and on.

The way in which the monopolizer is regarded by other group members usually undergoes a change as the group progresses. In the very beginning of the group, when members are feeling uneasy and unsure of themselves, the monopolizer may be welcomed. Other members may be relieved that someone in the group is talking and thereby relieving the pressure that would be present for them if there were awkward silences to fill. As the group progresses, however, and members begin to have and to want more to say, the monopolizer now engenders the annoyance of others in the group. At this point, when the monopolizer talks on and on, other members may shift in their chairs, roll their eyes, sigh out loud, or demonstrate other signs of disapproval. Instead of sensing the positive regard of others that was present in beginnings, the monopolizer now feels their irritation. This can make the monopolizer talk all the more, being afraid to stop for fear of attack by other members. Perhaps unconsciously, the monopolizer hopes that by continuing to talk the group can be appeased or diverted and the rewards for talking a lot that were present when the group began will return.

The Isolate

An isolate is a person who lacks bonds with others; isolation is a relative concept, for it is impossible to be completely separate from other human beings. All isolates are not the same or in similar positions in a group. Isolation may be temporary or lasting, forced or voluntary. When one is a stranger in a new group, temporary isolation is normal and to be expected, for there is always some ambivalence about joining a group and some toward newcomers on the part of older members. Some people can develop bonds with others in new situations much more easily and rapidly than others can. Another type of isolation is psychological withdrawal from the group. Instead of finding a place in the group, some members withdraw, perhaps because of lack of interest but often because of fear of the group.

Some persons are isolates because the group makes them so by rejecting them. One reason may be that isolates deviate so far from the values of the group that other members cannot understand them. Another reason may be that isolates may attempt to break through the usual initial isolation in ways that are inappropriate. Isolates may, for example, assume a pose of not caring and a bravado that tries to tell the other members that it does not matter what they think. With rejected isolates, a vicious circle is set up. Such isolates usually want and need affection, but when they fail to receive it they become troubled and increasingly hostile; then they feel guilty because of their hostility and experience a great sense of insecurity about their position in the group. Other members do not give rejected isolates the positive responses they hope for; in a psychological sense, rejected isolates do not become members of the group.

Though few members of a group are in as difficult a situation as the rejected isolate, there can be other members who also may not truly belong to the group. Some members are near isolates on the fringe of the group. They desire to belong, and may feel some minimum acceptance, and yet they are not quite of the group. Such persons often need the group so badly, however, that they do not seek to withdraw from it.

The Scapegoat

The genesis of the term *scapegoat* is a biblical one, going back to an ancient Hebrew ritual of atonement in which the chief priest of a village would symbolically lay the sins of the people on the back of a goat and then cast the goat into the wilderness, thereby cleansing and ridding the people of their sins. In the small group, the scapegoat is the person upon whom group members project their hostility and the negative feelings they may have about themselves. In doing so, group members attack the scapegoat, verbally or even physically.[6] The person who is a scapegoat thus represents the qualities and becomes a symbol of tendencies or characteristics that other group members do not like in themselves. The scapegoat performs a valuable function in channeling group tensions and in providing a basis for group solidarity.

But, as with other roles in the group, the role of scapegoat is a reciprocal and interactive one. The scapegoat is not merely the innocent victim of others' attacks, though those attacks can be quite cruel. Rather, the scapegoat behaves in such a way as to elicit the behavior of the other members. The behavior of the person who is the scapegoat may be quite obviously provocative or it may be more passive, subtle, and difficult to identify. In a group where there is a scapegoat, it is important that the worker identify the behavior of the person in the scapegoat role that elicits the actions of the other members.

One example of a scapegoat is Gladys, a thirteen-year-old member of an after school group in a community center. Glady's passivity and seeming helplessness, which set her up to become a scapegoat in the group, can be seen in the following process excerpt involving Gladys and another member, Yolanda, during the group's second meeting.

After giving up on playing pool, Gladys took notice of the ping-pong table, as Yolanda continued to play pool by herself. I (worker) asked Gladys if she knew how to play ping-pong. She said she didn't. I explained the game to her and suggested that we could help her learn to play by practicing hitting the ball back and forth. Gladys started, saying, "I'm not going to be any good at this." When she missed the ball, Gladys would say sarcastically, "Boy, that was a great shot! Did you see that fantastic shot I just made? Bet you can't play as bad as me. "To be good at anything usually takes practice, Gladys. Give it a chance," I said. But Gladys seemed to delight in failure. She didn't really try to successfully hit the ball. I found myself getting somewhat angry at her self-defeating attitude. After a while I got tired trying to convince Gladys that she could learn to play.

Yolanda came over and joined in the ping-pong game. She started to make fun of Gladys every time she missed the ball. Gladys responded by making fun of herself. "I'm so stupid, I can't even hit this little ball," said

Gladys. "You *are* stupid," Yolanda responded. "If you don't hit it better, we're not going to let you play," she added. I pointed out to them that not everyone is good at doing everything and that sometimes new things take a little time to master. We continued to play for a few minutes more. "She makes me sick," Yolanda said. "What's the sense of playing with her if she doesn't even try? She can't even hit the ball with her big stupid self." Gladys responded calmly, seeming to bait Yolanda, who was obviously annoyed, "But I told you I didn't know how to play." Yolanda sucked her teeth and rolled her eyes at Gladys. "Do you know what you did that made Yolanda angry?" I asked Gladys. "Yeah, she's mad because I don't know how to play, that's why, but that's too bad . . . " Gladys looked intently at Yolanda, trying to evoke a response. There was complete silence, as the tension grew. "Gladys, I think it's more what you don't do that makes Yolanda mad," I said. "You seemed to give up and to not really try to hit the ball." After a pause, Gladys calmly said, "I'm just not very good at sports. I told you that." Yolanda waved her hand and said, "Forget her!"

Scapegoats occur not only in children's groups. The following excerpt from a group of elderly women with mental illness who live in an adult residential facility illustrates that. The group is a "word group" in which members play a game called Ghost. Similar to Hangman, the game asks each member, in succession, to choose a letter until a word is completed. Each person's aim is to avoid completing a word, but members must have a word in mind each time they add a letter. The group's purpose is to enhance communication skills and, as one group member put it, "to keep our minds agile." Ruth is a scapegoat in the group, which is composed of seven members who have been in the group and have lived in the residence for years. The worker is new to this group, but has been working at the residence for a few months.

I approached the round table in the day room at 9:15 to find six women sitting together, engaged in casual and comfortable conversation. I sat down and greeted everyone. The group members told me they predated me by "years." Just then I noticed Ruth notice me from a seat by the window about ten feet away. She folded her newspaper and lethargically and, it seemed, unhappily made her way to the table. She sat down in the only remaining empty seat, quietly, downright fearfully, looking out from under her brow and the long black hair hanging in her eyes without a word, nod, or gesture to anyone. Doris, unsmiling, sat on Ruth's immediate left, "Oh, no, don't tell me I have to sit next to *her*." Lois, to Ruth's right, commiserated, "Well, I got her on this side. Oh, great. I can tell you already, this game's gonna be over for me in a real hurry." Ruth sat slumped over, looking down. She reacted in no way that I could see. "What do you mean?" I asked Lois. "She just always wins. Oh, c'mon, let's just play." The game began.

Later on in the meeting a word was being made that began "P-U-L." Ruth added a "C." "Doris, it's your turn," I said, "P-U-L-C." Doris looked at Ruth with confusion. "C? P-U-L-C?" she said. She seemed annoyed, paused, and finally said to Ruth, "I challenge you." With a smirk on her face, Ruth shot back to Doris, "Pulchritude." A chorus of "oh brothers" came from the other group members. "Pulchritude," Doris exclaimed. "I never heard of it. What is it?" Lois whispered to me, "She's got those big words." Ruth, with annoyance, pursing her lips and rolling her eyes, grabbed the dictionary from the middle of the table, opened it, and turned the pages frantically. When she found the word in question, she shoved the book in front of Doris, who looked almost scared. Elaine asked Doris what it said. "Physical comeliness," Doris replied, reading from the dictionary. "I never heard of that. What does it mean?" Elaine asked. When no one responded, I told the group it meant "beauty." At that point, Ruth said "Q" in a short, curt voice. The members shrugged their shoulders, Elaine said "U," and the game resumed.

Still later in the meeting, Lois started a word with the letter "M." Ruth quickly said "N." Thinking that Ruth had misunderstood Lois, Doris explained to Ruth that Lois had said "M." Curtly and without looking at Doris, Ruth impatiently said, "I know." Looking confused, Doris repeated the letters, "N? M-N?" She shook her head. "I challenge you, "she said to Ruth. With seeming triumph, Ruth responded, "Mnemonic." Bertha and Elaine both spoke at once, "Mnemonic? What the hell is that?" Ruth ignored them. When I asked Ruth to explain the word, she quickly said, "Memory device," looking down and with no affect. "I don't even understand her definitions," Marjorie said in exasperation.

In both the after school and the residential groups, the dynamics that give rise to the role of scapegoat are apparent. The interactive nature of the roles is evident. In each group, members behave with meanness toward the scapegoat. Yolanda's annoyance with Gladys is expressed quite clearly, as is the group's noninclusion and rejection of Ruth. In fact, in the Word Game group, members talk about Ruth as if she were not present, referring to her not by name but as "she."

But, in each group, the problematic behavior of the scapegoat is also evident. Gladys approaches games with passivity and never really tries. When members express their annoyance at her behavior, she responds by saying, "I told you I wasn't very good." That response only serves to increase the frustration of the other group members. Ruth seems to flaunt the extensiveness of her vocabulary and to laud it over the other members, enjoying their puzzlement over the words she has in mind. In her quiet, curt way, Ruth seems to look down on the other members of the group and they, in turn, are resentful of what they sense to be her attitude toward them.

Differential Intervention by the Worker

The worker's understanding of the group's stage of development is key in making a decision about how to intervene to address the dysfunctional role of a group member. The worker intervenes differentially, depending upon the group's developmental stage. In the early life of the group, when the member's role is not yet firmly established and when the ability and willingness of members to enter into discussion about the dysfunctional role are limited, the worker uses indirect means to help the member not get stuck in the role and to help the other members not trap that person into a negative role. At this point in the life of the group, techniques of support, encouragement, and limit setting are particularly helpful.

But, as the group progresses, indirect means will not be effective. Now, when a member's dysfunctional role has become established, that negative role needs to be addressed directly by involving the group in a problem-solving process. Now, the members are more willing and better able to actively engage in direct discussion of the issue. During the group's middle stages, the worker needs directly to confront the group and the individual in the negative role with the situation, help them explore the process that has led to the establishment and maintenance of the dysfunctional role, and then assist all in the group to determine how they can address this issue.

Intervention in the Beginning Stage of the Group

In the beginning of a group, during the inclusion-orientation stage, the worker's interventions are aimed at preventing a member from assuming a dysfunctional role and at stopping the group from placing any of its members in such a role. At this stage in the life of the group, the worker needs to be active in providing the group and its members with direction, structure, and limits that are aimed at fostering norms of respect and acceptance. At this early time in the group's life, when the members are feeling uncomfortable, unsure of themselves, and worried about how they will get along with the other members and how they will fit in the group, it is unrealistic for the worker to expect the members to engage in direct discussion of the roles of group members. Instead, it is the worker who must intervene actively when it seems that a negative role is emerging for a particular member. The worker attempts to promote flexibility in role structure so that members may experience varied ways of contributing to the group and testing out their capacities. The worker's supportive comments and actions are directed toward encouraging members to try out new ways of communicating more effectively with others or toward recognizing and modifying inappropriate patterns of behavior. Such interventions on the part of the worker are directed both to the person in the role and to the group.

With emerging monopolizers, for example, the worker attempts to encourage spread of participation between all the members. The worker does this by stating it as an expectation, requesting that members take turns, encouraging others to enter the discussion or activity, and using comments that summarize so as to invite others to join the conversation. The worker also gives monopolizers nonverbal cues, such as looking away from them and calling upon others to speak, all in the hope that monopolizers and the other members will realize that such a pattern of participation is not desirable. At the same time, the worker conveys acceptance of the monopolizer. Since talking is often an attempt to deal with anxiety, the anxiety rises if the person is attacked by others, which sets in motion a cycle of increased talking. If the worker can convey interest in the monopolizer, and suggest ways to participate effectively, the cycle might be broken. Often, limits need to be set in a supportive way, through requests to give others a chance to participate or to wait until others have expressed themselves.

With isolates, the worker needs to encourage their participation in the group while simultaneously inviting the other members to involve and include them as well. Recognizing the feelings of the isolate, acknowledging that participation in something new may be difficult but that it is important, trying to assure that the isolate can succeed in the group's discussion and activity, pairing the isolate with another group member for a particular activity, and avoiding questions that tend to elicit defensiveness are some of the techniques that the worker can use to try to encourage the isolate in the group's early life.

In the group's beginnings, the worker's intervention with a scapegoat also is focused on trying to prevent a person from getting trapped into such a role. To do so, the worker's attention again needs to go toward the person in the role and the total group simultaneously. An important first step is that the worker become aware of what the behavior is on the part of the person who is being scapegoated that is eliciting the response of the other members. The worker then needs to try to encourage that person to modify that problematic behavior. If, for instance, a person's behavior is marked by passivity and putting oneself down, as is true in the example of Gladys that was described earlier, then the worker would attempt to encourage the person to be more active in her efforts to participate and less negative toward herself. At the same time, the worker would encourage the other members to behave positively toward and with more acceptance of the person who is becoming a scapegoat.

With any problematic role in the group, be it a monopolizer, an isolate, a scapegoat, or another dysfunctional role such as a clown or a bully, in the beginning stage the worker's interventions aim to alert the person moving into the role that changes in behavior are needed. Simultaneously, the worker strives to let the group know that negative behavior toward another member is not a preferred group norm. By actively intervening to provide the individual and the group with direction, guidance, and limits, the worker hopes that all in the group will get the message that is being conveyed— that the member who is in danger of coming to occupy a dysfunctional role needs to change the behavior that is troublesome and that the members who are acting to place that person in such a role need to change their behavior toward that person as well.

Intervention in the Middle Stages of the Group

In addressing a dysfunctional role in the group's uncertainty-exploration and mutuality and goal achievement stages, the worker needs to intervene differently than in the group's beginnings. If a negative role has persisted and become established in the group despite the worker's efforts to prevent that, then it is clear that neither the person in the dysfunctional role nor the members who were putting the person in the role acted upon the worker's messages that they needed to change their problematic behaviors. For the worker to continue to convey such messages is highly unlikely to be effective. The focus of workers' efforts at these later stages in the life of the group needs to change. Now workers need to involve the entire group in addressing the problem rather than continue to attempt to bring about change through their own interventions alone. To request the entire group to engage in problem solving around the issue is an appropriate and even crucial demand to make at this point in the group's life. Now, the members are more able to explore the problem and engage in direct and honest discussion about what is taking place. Workers' roles during the group's middle stages is to help the members to do just that.

To engage the group in problem solving, workers need continuously to bear in mind that roles are reciprocal, that both the person in the role and the other members of the group play a part in creating and maintaining the dysfunctional role. The group, therefore, needs to examine both sides in the situation, the behavior of the person in the role and that of the members who are placing the person there. Workers first need to help the group identify the problem of dysfunctional role behavior in the group. The next step for workers is to encourage the group to explore the problem by examining how the situation came about and what part all in the group are playing to perpetuate the problematic role behavior. Finally, workers aim to help the members decide how they want to try to resolve the situation.

Throughout the group's problem-solving process, it is crucial that the worker be fair to both sides, to the person in the role and to the members of the group who may be playing a part in placing the person in the role. The worker needs to be seen by all in the group as someone who can be understanding of the different perspectives of all members of the group rather than as someone who is partial to one side or the other. To have such impartial understanding, the worker needs to be self-aware and to recognize that countertransference reactions may be operating, resulting in the worker's taking sides. To be effective in helping the group to address the situation, it is essential that the worker be able to accept and empathize with all members of the group. Ultimately, the worker's aim is to help each side talk with the other, honestly and openly, so that each can begin to accept and empathize with the other. If members believe that the worker has taken a side, if they suspect that one side or the other is being blamed for the situation, then it is unlikely that members will be willing to engage in the honest exploration of the problem.

Worker intervention in a problematic role situation when the group has matured is illustrated by the example of Gladys, the thirteen-year-old described earlier who was being scapegoated by the other members of an after school group in a community center. The worker's efforts during the beginning stage of the group to encourage Gladys to try harder during group activities and not put herself down, and her attempts to urge the other group members to include Gladys and not taunt her, were ineffective. In fact, the situation worsened. Gladys became even more passive and provocative and the group members became even more outspoken and insulting toward her. The worker realized that she then needed to bring the issue to the group directly and ask them to address the problem.

When everyone had gotten their juice and cookies and were in their seats, I told the group that there was a problem that I'd been observing in the group that I wanted to bring to everyone's attention so they could address it. The group members seemed curious. "I've noticed that Gladys is having a hard time in the group," I said. Yolanda groaned out loud and then muttered, "She deserves it." I held up my hand toward her and asked her to hold it. "On the one hand," I said, "I've noticed that Gladys does some things that get you mad." "You can say that again," Yolanda said emphatically. Again, I asked her to stop. Gladys was looking uncomfortable. Because I knew this was going to be a difficult meeting for Gladys, I had purposefully positioned myself in the seat right next to her. I patted her knee as I continued, "I've also noticed that some of you are treating Gladys pretty badly," "Don't blame us, " Denise said, "she asks for it." "That's what I think we need to talk about," I said. "One of the reasons for this group is to improve our relationships with others. Well, here's an opportunity for that to happen. I think a good way to begin this discussion is for you all to tell Gladys what she does that bothers you and how it makes you feel. And then I think Gladys needs to do the same—to tell the group what you do that she doesn't like and how it makes her feel. This discussion may be hard, but I hope you are all willing to participate in it, because I think it's important." The girls seemed to take what I said seriously. Everyone, including Gladys, nodded, indicating their willingness to get involved. I even heard Roberta tell Yolanda she should get serious.

In this excerpt, the worker presents her observations in a way that lets the group know that she is able to be impartial, understanding, and fair to both sides. Had she simply admonished the group members for being unkind toward Gladys, the chances are that they would have been unwilling to engage in discussion of the issue, for they would have felt misunderstood and unjustly blamed by the worker. Moreover, they would probably have felt that the worker was unable to appreciate how difficult Gladys's behavior could be and how it made them feel. On the other hand, the worker also helps Gladys feel supported. By sitting next to her, by acknowledging that the discussion is difficult, by limiting Yolanda's outbursts, the worker lets Gladys know that she will help her express her point of view in the discussion that is to follow. It is important to note that such indications of support for Gladys do not mean that the worker is not being fair to both sides. The worker's support of Gladys, in a situation that she knows is not easy for her, is different from being on Gladys's side of things. At the same time that the worker supports Gladys, she is not overprotective of her.[7] In presenting the issue to the group, the worker does not employ phrases such as "one of our members" or "someone in this group" to avoid mentioning Gladys by name. Instead, she is quite direct and, in being so, sets the tone for the discussion that is to follow.

"Let's begin by telling Gladys what she does that you don't like," I said. Speaking directly to Gladys, I added, "Gladys, it may not be easy for you to hear what people say, it may even seem as if you're being ganged up on. But I hope you'll really try to listen, because this is important." Again, I squeezed Gladys's knee. "OK, I'll start," Roberta said. "Gladys never really tries to do anything well. And when we get mad at her, she just shrugs it off as if it doesn't matter." "What do you mean when you say that Gladys doesn't try to do anything well," I asked, trying to draw Roberta out more. "Well, the other day when we were playing kickball, she didn't really try to kick the ball, she had her eyes practically shut, and then when she made an out she just laughed." "Yeah," Lois declared. "and because of that we lost the game and Gladys just laughed some more." I asked Roberta, "How did it make you feel when Gladys did that?" "I got mad," Roberta said. "It's frustrating. She doesn't try, and then when you get mad at her for not trying she acts like she doesn't care. And that just gets you madder." "But I told you I wasn't any good at sports. I don't like sports," Gladys said defensively. "Wait a minute, Gladys," I said. "For now, just listen to what the girls are telling you. You'll have a chance to respond, I promise." Gladys didn't look pleased, but she sat back in her seat and did seem to be listening as others in the group spoke.

Lois was the next to speak. She echoed what Roberta had said, also stating that Gladys' halfhearted efforts were frustrating and made her angry. Many other members nodded in agreement, and there were many "yeahs" and "that's rights" from them. "Gladys is a klutz." Yolanda said loudly. "She shouldn't be allowed in this group. She acts like a baby. She shouldn't be allowed in any group. She's an asshole." "Stop it, Yolanda," I said firmly. "I want the group to tell Gladys how they feel, but calling her names is hurtful and that's not what we're looking for here." "Yeah, Yolanda, cut it out," Roberta said. Yolanda seemed chastened and quieted down.

Once again, in this excerpt, the worker does not act overprotectively toward Gladys. She invites and encourages the members to be direct in letting Gladys know the impact that her behavior has on them. In fact, she draws them out and helps them to express their ideas and feelings more fully. But when Yolanda's input aims to hurt Gladys, the worker intervenes. She limits Yolanda and lets her know that her name-calling is unacceptable. When Gladys starts to respond to what Roberta has said, the worker stops her temporarily. Getting into a kind of tit-for-tat discussion of the I-do-not-you-do-so variety, in which each side becomes intent on maintaining its position, will not be helpful here. Instead, as difficult as it may be for Gladys, the worker needs to help her to listen to what the group members have to say. Once Gladys has heard them, the worker can then help her to express her point of view.

When everyone in the group had spoken, I turned to Gladys. "Gladys, I know this must not have been easy to hear. Tell me what you understand the group to be telling you." Gladys looked down at the floor and was silent. I let the silence sit there. "Well, they don't like it when I don't try," Gladys began. She stopped. "Yes," I said, "I think that's part of it. What else?" "And then they don't like it when I act like I don't care," Gladys continued. "Yeah," Maria said, "that part's as bad as not trying, maybe even worse." "But you don't understand," Gladys said. "I really am no good at sports, so I pretend like I don't care. And if I put myself down before you do, then you can't yell at me." "You don't have to be good at sports," Roberta said, "as long as you try and as long as you care when you're on a team. If we knew you were trying, we wouldn't get so annoyed with you." "OK, I'll try harder, I promise," Gladys said. "Whoa," I said. "Wait a minute. I'm glad you're going to try harder, Gladys. But people in this group have been pretty mean to you and we need to also look at that. Just as everyone told you what they don't like about what you were doing, can you tell the group what they've been doing that you haven't liked?" "Well," Gladys paused, then quickly said, "I hate it whenever we choose teams. Nobody ever wants me on their side and they make it very clear that they don't want to take me. I'm always the last . . . " "Cause you're the worst player," Jeanette interrupted. "Wait, Jeanette, let Gladys speak now," I said. "I'm always the last one chosen," Gladys continued. "And how does that make you feel?" I asked. "Terrible," Gladys said, "so I pretend that I don't care."

In this excerpt, the worker acts to assure that the group does not shortcut the exploration phase of the problem-solving process and arrive at a solution prematurely. She intervenes to be certain that Gladys has a chance to express to the group what has been taking place from her vantage point. If this group is ultimately to arrive at an effective solution, it is essential that each side has the information it needs to understand and empathize with the viewpoint of the other. The worker's interventions must be designed to help each side to tell its story fully enough so that such understanding and empathy can develop. Only then is the group ready to look at possible solutions that it might adopt. As in addressing any problem, if a solution is arrived at prematurely, it will not be effective. In fact, even if a solution is reached after thorough and thoughtful exploration of the issue, the worker and the group should not expect that solution to work instantly and magically. Even with everyone's understanding, empathy, and best efforts, there will be lapses and backsliding. But when these occur, the worker can help the group to draw upon its history with the issue and can ask the members to look periodically at how things are going in regard to the scapegoating.

The discussion that took place in this group continued over more than this single meeting and was highly significant for Gladys, for the other members individually, and for the group as an entity. Gladys shared with the group information about the position she occupied in her family, especially in regard to an older sister, that contributed to her behavior in this group. Such information enabled members to understand, empathize and put into perspective the behavior they witnessed in the group. Group members also talked philosophically about the need that people have to put others down and thereby feel superior and powerful themselves at the expense of others. After much discussion, the group decided that Gladys would try to participate energetically in group activities and not put herself down when she did not do well at something, that the group would try to encourage Gladys and not put her down, and that the group would engage, as well, in activities other than sports, such as art, cooking, and drama, that called upon different strengths and abilities of members.

The problem-solving process in which this group engaged to address the scapegoating of Gladys exemplifies the process in which any group in its middle stages needs to participate when a negative role has developed, one that is painful to a member and troublesome for the group. Whatever the dysfunctional role, be it that of clown, help-rejecting complainer, monopolizer, or any other, the worker's interventions, as in the example of Gladys, must be direct and impartial in asking all in the group to clarify what the problem is, what its meaning is to the person in the role and to the other members of the group, what the members do to perpetuate the situation, and how the group might work to address the issue. In any dysfunctional role, the problem is a result of the interaction between the person in the role and the needs of the group and its members. The group's thorough exploration of the problem and of the part that each member is playing in its occurrence is crucial to the problem-solving process that takes place and to the ability of the group ultimately to arrive at an effective solution.

As painful as a negative role may be for a member of a group, addressing the issues related to such a role with simultaneous supportiveness and directness provides a pivotal opportunity for the person in the role and for the group. The chances are great that members who have difficulty relating to others in the group also have similar struggles in their lives outside the group. It is likely that persons who occupy roles as clowns or scapegoats or monopolizers are in similar positions in, and have difficulty relating with the members of, the other groups, both formal and informal, to which they belong. To address such roles in the group can make a huge and highly significant difference for such persons as they are able to generalize and to apply the learning and heightened awareness they gain to the ways in which they participate with others outside the group. All members of the group can, in turn, gain from such discussion as they are helped to examine their own behavior, how they treat others, and how they want others to regard and relate to them.

11 The Use of Activity

The purposeful use of activity has been a prominent part of social work with groups from the method's beginnings. Group work's use of activity encompasses the doing of something, engagement by the members in playing a game or in cooking or in making something or in acting or in singing or in sewing or in hiking or—the possible activities are endless!—supplemented or complemented by discussion that the activity stimulates and inspires. Participation in the informal conversations that occur during the activity, as well as in the discussion that surrounds its planning, performance, and evaluation, are integral. The doing of the activity and the talking about it are not separate components; instead, they go hand in hand. In social work with groups, when its use is based on the needs of a group and of its members, activity can make a significant contribution to the achievement of the group's purpose and to the realization of the goals of individual members.

Development of the Use of Activity in Group Work

The use of activity in work with groups has not been without controversy, despite the prominent part that activity has played in social group work practice. Interestingly, the debates that took place historically about the place of activity in group work practice were reflective of the method's early ambivalence about whether it saw itself as a method within the social work profession or whether it was a part of the recreation and progressive education movements.[1] From its early development in settlement houses, youth-serving organizations, and religious institutions, group work used activity to educate immigrants, provide opportunities for recreation and the use of leisure time, and foster democracy, Christian values, and Jewish identity.

In the early use of activity in group work, the content of a group, that is, what a group actually did, received emphasis rather than the group's process and the relationships between the members. The emphasis on content had an adverse effect historically on group work's acceptance as a method in social work. Group work and recreation or informal education were seen, erroneously, by many as synonymous. During the 1930s, activity and its emphasis on *doing* had less status than the *talking* that was the domain of work with individuals, the dominant social work methodology of the time. The desire of many group work practitioners to become part of social work and their fear that the use of activity would place them outside the profession led them to deemphasize the use of activity.

However, as group work moved toward a closer identification with social work in the 1940s, the connection between activity and the interaction between group members that it could enable became more appreciated and accented. In a 1946 address at the National Conference of Social Work, Grace Coyle recognized the connection between group content and process:

> Social group work arose out of an increasing awareness that in the recreation-education activities which went on in groups there were obviously two dimensions—activity, including games, discussions, hikes, or artistic enterprise, on the one hand, and, on the other, the interplay of personalities that creates the group process. To concentrate on one without recognizing and dealing with the other is like playing the piano with one hand only. Program and relationships are inextricably intertwined. Social group work method developed as we began to see that the understanding and the use of the human relations involved were as important as the understanding and use of various types of program.[2]

Coyle followed up her interest in recreational-educational activities in a chapter, "The Art of Program Making," in her 1948 book, *Group Work with American Youth*. There, she described and illustrated activities appropriate for members of clubs, interest groups, and programs of national youth agencies.[3]

A milestone in the exposition of program content was the publication in 1949 of *Social Group Work Practice* by Gertrude Wilson and Gladys Ryland. This volume included an extensive "Analysis of Program Media" and emphasized the values inherent in play, games, dance, music, dramatics, arts and crafts, trips, and camping. The book was the first to explicate the importance of activity, used purposefully, for persons of all ages and for various purposes and problems. It looked at activity in relation to values, purpose and function of the agency, developmental needs and interests of group members, and characteristics of the group.

By 1960, the intrinsic connection between the use of activity and the purpose of social work became increasingly recognized and appreciated, at least "officially," by social work's national organizations and by group work practitioners. Although some social work practitioners regarded the use of activity with disdain, national social work organizations viewed as unique group work's knowledge about the skillful and purposeful use of activity to meet human needs. In 1959 the Council on Social Work Education published a major study of curriculum that included a separate volume on the social group work method in social work education that was written by Marjorie Murphy. It gave considerable attention to the use of activity. In it Murphy wrote:

> The group worker is concerned simultaneously with program content, and with the ways in which persons relate to each other. Achievement, however, cannot be measured in content and process themselves, but in relation to the social work goal, enhancement of members' social functioning, as far as this can be observed in changes in thinking and behavior.[4]

A major book that contributed to understanding and appreciating the use of activity in group work was *The Non-Verbal Method in Working with Groups* by Ruth Middleman. Written in 1968, it is still the only book that deals exclusively with the subject.

Because of the value that activity can have, social workers who work with groups continue to discover its importance. Evidence of this can be found in the substantial number of articles in group work journals and publications and presentations at group work conferences over the past decade on the use of activity in work with groups.

Values of Activity

The use of activity supplements or complements verbal exchange. Activity can make a variety of contributions to the members of a group and to the group as a whole. Activity may be used to (1) reduce stress and satisfy needs for pleasure and creativity, which are essential to mental health, (2) enrich the social worker's assessment of particular members' needs and of group interaction through direct observation of the behavior of members as they interact around an activity, (3) facilitate verbal communication of feelings, ideas, and experiences, (4) stimulate reflective and problem-solving discussions, leading to understanding of selves, others, and situations, (5) enhance the development of relationships between the members and the cohesiveness of the group, (6) provide opportunities for giving to other members or persons in the environment, (7) develop competence in basic skills appropriate to phases of psychosocial development and thereby enhance self-esteem, (8) enhance competence in making and implementing decisions, and (9) make better use of or change some aspect of the environment.[5]

Pleasure and Creativity

The promise of pleasure inherent in many activities should not be underestimated as a therapeutic force in the life of individuals and the group. Play and laughter are indispensable to the maintenance of good health and a sense of well-being. Pleasurable activity reduces stress and enables people to gain new perspectives on themselves and their situations. Social workers perhaps give more attention to the expression of negative emotions of anger, hate, and sadness than to the positive ones of love, affection, and joy that are essential to effective social functioning. Many children have not learned how to have fun with others and many adults find it difficult to engage in pleasurable activities. The work ethic and emphasis on success in work or education may lead to feelings of guilt for enjoying oneself.

All persons have a need to be creative, to have the power and ability to create something with imagination, expressiveness, and originality. Creativity may bring deep satisfaction by tapping in on people's strengths and past successful and pleasurable experiences.

A social work student whose internship was at an in-patient psychiatric hospital expressed interest in forming a singing group. Asked why she wished to form such a group, she stated, "I never see the patients having any fun. A singing group would be fun." She also noted, "The patients here are never given any choices. In a singing group, if nothing else at least they could have some choices about what they wanted to sing." The student went on to form a singing group, a voluntary group that turned out to be a huge success. Patients on the unit had to be reminded about other groups, but would often approach the student intern and ask, hopefully, "Is today the singing group?" Though they had to be coaxed to attend other groups, they came to the singing group early and were waiting for her when she arrived, for the members truly enjoyed singing together. Many of the members of the group had had long histories of multiple hospitalizations and few successes in their lives. Yet it turned out that every member of the singing group, when they were younger, had had a successful and positive experience in a high school chorus or glee club.

Assessment of Members' Needs and Group Interaction

The value of activity for purposes of assessment has long been recognized. When group members are engaged in working alone or together on some task, the social worker can directly observe the capacities and difficulties of the members. Members' behavior as they interact with others in varied situations can be observed firsthand. The advantage of seeing what members actually *do*, as opposed to what they report, is invaluable. Perceiving their performance in varied situations helps both the members and the worker to recognize the members' responses to situations, the things that give satisfaction as contrasted with those that frustrate, the conditions under which individuals approach new relationships and materials and those in which they avoid them, the situations in which they cannot share, and the tendencies toward hostile aggression or withdrawal from people or activities. The worker can then apply such observations either immediately in the group or at a later point with individuals or with the total group.

A social worker in a community center decided to form a men's cooking group when she realized that there were a number of single or widowed men at the center who were spending a large proportion of their fixed incomes on restaurant meals because they did not know how to cook or how to do even simple tasks in the kitchen. The group developed both a cooking and a social focus. Over the course of a late-afternoon/early-evening meeting, the men would shop, prepare a meal, eat together, clean up, and plan the meal for the following week.

Mr. Broglio was a member of the group whom the worker also saw individually because he was an isolated person who had no friends in the community. Mr. Broglio reported to the worker that he wanted and tried to make friends, but that others were not nice to him. He tried to reach out to others, he said, but was always rebuffed and did not understand why this was so.

The worker could understand Mr. Broglio's situation only after she had the chance to observe the way he interacted with the other members of the cooking group. In his interactions, he would become almost tyrannical, putting other people down as he "dictated" to them what to do and how to do it. "Don't stir it that way, you're doing it all wrong," he would say loudly to another group member, as he literally tore the mixing bowl out of his hands. At other times, he would talk over and seem oblivious to the other members as he tried to get his way in planning the exact menu he wanted. His behavior in the group surprised the worker. Such actions were not apparent to her when he would discuss his situation with her one on one. Observing Mr. Broglio's behavior in the group allowed her to raise issues with him that she thought were problematic in his efforts to make friends and to illustrate the issues she raised with specific examples.

Communication of Feelings, Ideas, and Experiences

Many people find it difficult to articulate their thoughts and feelings in words. Such persons are able to express their ideas directly in an activity or to use an activity as a concrete aid to help them subsequently express in words ideas that may be abstract. Activity can also be used to help members express themselves about issues that may be emotional and difficult for them to talk about. With many members, insistence that they express themselves verbally can exacerbate feelings of inadequacy and inarticulateness. Engaging in activity permits members to enter into conversation as they are ready to do so, without the sense of pressure that is often present when discussion is the only activity. Thus, activity can aid discussion and enhance the quality and content of communication between members.

In an elementary school, a social worker was working with a group of fifth-grade girls who were having behavioral and academic difficulties. She found that the girls had trouble sustaining discussions in the group. Often, they responded to her questions with shrugs and one-word answers. To help them express their ideas and feelings, she thought it would be a good idea to engage them in an activity that would aid them in doing so. She divided the group into two subgroups and, using magazines that she brought, she asked each subgroup to create a collage, one on what's good about being in the fifth grade and the other on what's bad about being in the fifth grade. The group members set to work and seemed to enjoy the task. Much discussion took place between members about what pictures to include. The group spent the entire meeting working on the collages.

At the next meeting, the worker asked each subgroup to explain to the other what pictures they had included in their collage and their reasons for doing so. The group members were quite able to talk about this. The pictures aided them in expressing their ideas verbally and served as a jumping-off point that enabled them to do so. Had the worker simply asked the girls to discuss what is good and bad about being in the fifth grade, they would have had great difficulty doing so. It was interesting that many of the same pictures ended up appearing in both the "good" and "bad" collages. The group members thus expressed their ambivalent feelings around the increasing independence that was starting to occur for them. The collages helped them to express that ambivalence.

Speech is but one means of communication, but it is a basic tool for all human beings. Nonverbal communication must usually be understood in verbal terms before it can be integrated and used by a person. Verbal skills are essential to success in education and to the successful fulfillment of almost any social role. Numerous simple devices may be used with a group to open or extend verbalization. The display of a thing that is a symbol of an unexpressed interest or concern may open up discussion. Examples are books or magazine articles on the discipline of children for use in a parent education group or on boy-girl relationships, sex, or drugs for use with adolescents. A family of dolls or a doll house is often used with young children; a movie, a painting, or a drawing that portrays people in situations somewhat similar to those of the members is useful with clients of all ages. Some persons find it much easier to talk into microphones, toy telephones, or through puppets and games than directly to the worker and other members of the group. The "I'm only pretending" quality to such devices makes them useful when members are not yet ready to face their feelings, thoughts, and situations directly. Such experimentation with props often leads to direct verbal expression.

The quality of pretending is also present in role-playing, an activity in which a group observes some of its members enacting roles in a skit for the purposes of analyzing some real-life situation in which a group is interested. The spontaneity in role-playing makes it possible for members to more freely communicate their feelings and thoughts to others. The taking of roles often reveals underlying ambivalence and resistance that a person feels but has not been able to express verbally. The activity reveals to the participants and other members the feelings that need to be dealt with for goals to be achieved. It makes it possible for participants to recreate the experience of a personal situation and then be directed toward understanding of it.[6]

In groups of children, play tends to predominate. In play, for example, children express feelings and ideas about the world they cannot verbalize. As they relive experiences in play, they express anger, hate, love, joy, and other emotions. The unpleasant character of their experiences does not prevent children from using them as a game; they often choose to play out the unpleasant experiences as well. In work with young children, play materials should be simple: dolls and toys that do not break easily, materials that have high projective values such as finger paints, crayons, puppets, darts, toy telephones, and tape recorders. In hospitals, for example, dolls and medical or nursing kits enable youngsters to experience their feelings and then correct their misperceptions about diagnosis and treatment.[7] In one military setting, coloring books that depicted the deployment of the father were used with children. These pictures encouraged the expression of a range of ambivalent feelings about the absence of the father from the home.[8] In another instance, young children who had been sexually abused learned to express their feelings through puppets who told the long-held secrets. The puppets provided just enough distance—a safety factor. Children who have been molested have often been warned to keep it a secret or face dire consequences. One child, talking through a puppet, poured out details of his abuse. Suddenly, he tossed the puppet out of his hand. The worker asked, "What happened to pac-man?" The child replied, "He is dead. He got killed because he told the secret."[9] It is important for children to express their secrets so they can release anxiety and begin to deal with the traumatic events.

Activity, though, is not limited to use with children; rather, it is valuable in work with all age groups. Its use is consonant with the action-prone temperament of adolescents, serving to aid teenagers in examining feelings and problems they might have difficulty addressing in discussion alone.[10] For adults, there is also great benefit to the use of activity as a stimulant to discussion of feelings and difficulties. Examples of this are seen in the work of Erica Schnekenburger, Miriam Potocky, and Maxine Lynn and Danielle Nisivoccia, who write about the use of activity with persons with mental illness, of David Pollio, who writes of the use of basketball in a group of young men who are homeless, and of Lesley Waite, who describes the use of drama in a group of adults who are developmentally disabled.[11]

Understanding of Selves and Situations

Self-disclosure is essential before feelings and experiences can be understood and their negative impact on the quality of daily living mitigated. Reflective and problem-solving activities and discussion may lead to understanding of self, other people, and traumatic experiences. That this is possible, even with children, is indicated in the record of a group composed of severely neglected and abused eight- to ten-year-old children.[12] The children had been released for adoption but had serious developmental lags in their ability to form and sustain relationships, characterized by distrust of adults, inability to have fun and relate to other children, and deep feelings of rejection and insecurity. Telling a story about the birth of a child and the development and experiences of the child and family, combined with the use of pictures of people cut from magazines, were the major activities in the early meetings.

In one session, after a story was told by the worker, the members of the group were asked to tell about the new baby in the family. Jennifer looked at a picture of a baby and said, "This baby's got a black eye." (There was no sign of a black eye in the picture.) When the worker asked how the black eye could have occurred, Thomas said, "Someone punched her." The members became agitated and could not continue the discussion. A little later, however, Beverly talked about her broken bones and trips to the hospital. Thomas talked about being scared he would be beaten. Others started to talk, too. Often, only partial ideas were offered, but agitation and frustration were expressed through body movements and fights between the members. As the members came to recognize they all shared having been abused in the past, they began to be more able to relate to each other.

Later, after having developed some trust in the worker, the children involved themselves further in storytelling. They wove the story together with some of their life experiences. They came to distinguish their birth mothers and rejecting foster mothers from their present accepting foster parents by calling them "old mommas" and "new mommas." Ben told the members that they needed to pray for "old mommas" and "old poppas, too." The children began to express the idea that the "old" parents could no longer hurt them and that not all parents abused their children. They moved to talking about their current "good" homes and what their pro-posed adoptive homes would be like. Although these talks were often disconnected and intertwined with other activities, these children were capable of some understanding of their feelings and past events and sepa-rating that out from the current reality, preparing them for being able to belong in an adoptive family.

Development of Relationships and Cohesiveness

Properly selected experiences facilitate the development of relatedness and serve as an aid in sustaining and deepening relationships. Ken Heap notes that group membership, by definition, "provides a context for meeting others and thereby breaks into the spiral of isolation, rejection, and social failure."[13] Activity may stimulate the members' interest in and involvement with each other and the opportunity to develop satisfying relationships and to repair dysfunctional ones. Having something to do, even such a simple thing as doodling, sharing a cup of tea, or playing a name game, reduces anxiety about one's acceptance by others and encourages interaction with others. As people interact together, they become aware of their feelings toward each other—their shared interests, ways of expressing selves, difficulties, and capacities. Shared experiences provide an opportunity for the members to cooperate or to compete: the group becomes a testing ground for assessing themselves and learning to handle cooperation and competition. Since a major therapeutic force is interpersonal learning, every possible medium should be used to help members to learn from each other.

Activity is often used to enhance the relationship between the members and thereby also the cohesion of the group. Members develop meaningful relationships with each other through shared experiences. Each experience provides a somewhat different kind of opportunity and challenge in relating to other members of the group. By providing fresh experiences common to the members that differentiate this group from other groups, identification with the group is enhanced. Some people share more fully of themselves when they engage in activity that is more varied than "just talk"; hence their identification with each other is apt to be enhanced. Experiences in which each member participates enhance mutual understanding and tend to equalize status. They make for group centeredness by stimulating interaction around a current shared experience.

The use of activity to enhance interpersonal learning and relationships between group members is described by Lainey Collins in her work with groups in an after school tutoring program where reading and writing were important activities.

Although spelling was de-emphasized during the initial writing activity, many group members found it difficult not to spell words correctly before putting them on the paper. During writing time, the room was full of voices asking for the spelling of this or the spelling of that. It was overwhelming for group leaders who attempted to answer all of the questions, and began to take away from the time spent on the activity. This problem was brought to the group and it was decided that when the group was working on a large project, the group would be split into four smaller groups who would work together. It was then agreed that spelling questions could be asked of other group members in the small group before asking the group leader. Members were then able to bring spelling questions that they could not answer in their small group to the larger group and the leader.[14]

As a result of this decision, group members shared the spelling process. Such sharing encouraged members to also begin to share their own writing with their peers and to feel a sense of accomplishment as they presented their work and as they listened to and heard other members' writing and reading. As the group continued, members even collaborated on stories they wrote together, sometimes using the different languages that were spoken by the group members in a single multilingual story.

Giving to Others

Activity allows the members of a group to give to others. Children, for example, may express their positive feelings toward each other through exchanging valentines, making gifts, and sharing their talents with others. As important as the giving of concrete gifts and tokens is the giving of support and encouragement to other members that activity may invite. Such support, beneficial to both the receiver and the giver, is illustrated in a brief exchange that took place in a ceramics group composed of adolescents at a community-based mental health clinic.

In the first session of the group, each member was making a simple pinch bowl. In this, their first contact with the clay, they were having a difficult time maintaining an ideal wetness and thickness of their pots and controlling the pressure of their fingers on the clay. Lucy pushed too hard and broke through the edge of her bowl. "Oh, I ruined it," she cried out. "I broke the side of my bowl. I hate this. I can't do this." Trying to be helpful and encouraging to Lucy, the worker stated, "It looks like something other than a bowl now." Jason, picking up on the worker's cue, quickly said to Lucy, "Yeah, now it looks like a pitcher." "Do you really think so?" Lucy responded, looking somewhat relieved. Jason nodded emphatically and smiled at Lucy. "Well, OK." Lucy's face lit up. As a result of Jason's encouragement, she went back to work to turn her bowl into a pitcher.[15]

Competence and Self-Esteem

Psychosocial functioning is enhanced as people learn to communicate effectively and have reasonably accurate perceptions of self, other persons, and situations. Clarification of attitudes and behavior in relation to varied social situations may, however, be beneficial only if it helps a person to master problematic situations. Apparent changes in feeling and thinking need to be tested in the crucible of experience. It is especially important to have opportunities to master tasks in areas in which members of the group have previously found themselves lacking. Thus, experiences in doing need to complement experiences in talking. According to Quentin RaeGrant, Thomas Gladwin, and Eli Bower, social competence—the ability of people to interact effectively with their environments—"leads to increased ego strength and this stronger ego is in turn inherently better able to cope with conflict and anxiety."[16] This may, in turn, lead to increased group competence: a spiral of success is set in motion.

The following excerpt from a creative writing group in a residence for adults with chronic mental illness demonstrates the power of activity to bring people together and raise self-esteem.[17]

I plugged in a wave-sound machine and passed around rocks, seashells, and beach pictures. For our first poem, I explained, we would go to the beach. "What is this?" Miriam looked nervous and unhappy. "I can't write poetry! I can't do it!" she screamed. "I mean, poetry is for people who went to college, and I never went to college. I did other things. I worked as a secretary. I wasn't—I didn't learn poetry! I have my Bible, that's all I need. I don't need this garbage! This is terrible! I'm not staying!" She stormed away. "She'll be back," Henry offered, quiet and confident.

Miriam couldn't be persuaded to give it a try at that time, though, with the encouragement of the worker and other members, she did return to the group at a later date. The truth was, all of us, like Miriam, felt nervous, as if the very word *poetry* evoked all that was intimidating and incomprehensible to us. We had to be convinced that if we could feel, then we could write poetry. Henry persuaded us, "Try it. Just say what you're feeling. You hear waves crashing against the shore . . . " Taking the cue, I wrote, "Waves crashing against the shore" on the paper taped to the wall. "Keep going. What are they like? How do they make you feel?" I said. "Tremendous waves," said Lorraine, who was sitting by the wall near the table. "They bring themselves to the shore, one after the other after the other . . . Oh, I hope you don't mind my joining in. I grew up by the beach on Long Island, and so this is bringing back a lot of memories." "Right!" said Lois, "It does for me, too, of the seashells in the sand." "Close your eyes," I said, writing feverishly. "What are you doing?" "I pick them up and hold them to my ear . . . "

We continued, eliciting such strong and immediate reactions, which easily led to the expression of memories and feelings. When we decided to end, I read the lines I had taken down on the paper taped to the wall. Memories were evoked:

I pick the shells up and hold them to my ear
and I can hear the ocean.

Senses were activated:

Cool breeze coming from the ocean
Open my shirt and feel the sunshine.

Feelings unfolded:

Looking out into the horizon,
I want to go on an adventure.

And they understood themselves better by sharing genuine, honest reaction. As I finished reading, the group erupted in spontaneous applause. We could not believe what we had built together. We had done something we never thought we could do. "This has brought me back to my childhood, growing up on the beach," Lorraine said, "I did all those things—collected seashells, listened to the waves, took long walks. I haven't done that in a long time. I miss those days. This afternoon, I won't be hearing the noise here at the residence . . . I'll be hearing the sound of the waves."

———

Psychosocial functioning is strengthened also as people acquire confidence in their abilities to perform roles in ways that are personally satisfying and that meet reasonable expectations of others. Mastery of tasks enhances self-esteem. Especially relevant to issues of self-esteem are groups that engage in the completion of a project.

After having met for six months, a photography group composed of members of a senior center decided they would like to create an exhibit at the center that captured the work they had done over the year. The social worker who worked with the group agreed, thinking that the creation of such an exhibit could provide an excellent ending for the group that could involve group members in a range of individual and collective efforts.

Creation of the exhibit involved a variety of tasks and activities. As a group, the members reviewed all the pictures they had taken since the group's beginning. Such a review provided wonderful opportunities for group members to reminisce about all that had taken place in the group over time. Members decided which pictures to include in the exhibit and how to group them according to themes. Next, the group took two trips to see different exhibits of photographs on display in the city. Specifically, they looked at how the photographs in these exhibits were arranged and captioned. Returning to the center, they worked in pairs to develop captions for the photographs chosen for their own exhibit. Pairing the members to work on captions allowed some members who did not write particularly well to contribute ideas for the content of the captions and allowed others who did write well to create the final captions. Other members went to a local lumber store to purchase material for the flats which they then built for the display. The entire group got involved in creating the arrangement of the titles, pictures, and captions. Finally, the group selected one of its members to emcee the opening of the exhibit at the center. All in the group made suggestions about things they wanted to be sure she included in her remarks about the group and the exhibit. All in the group helped her to rehearse her remarks.

The quality of the exhibit resulted in group members receiving a great deal of positive feedback and recognition from others for their work. Perhaps even more important, the members themselves took pride in their creation and derived from it a sense of mastery and accomplishment for their complex efforts.

When groups engage in planning and completing a project, both process and product need to be considered simultaneously by the worker. The process of participation is important, but so, too, is the end result. When the worker demands that the members do the best they can, self-esteem is enhanced. When the members recognize that the efforts of all of them are needed to accomplish the task, they develop a sense of empowerment through group effort and participation.

Self-esteem is a necessary ingredient of social competence. Many members of groups are burdened by a sense of low self-esteem. Often, they have been the victims of the negative valuations of others, have been discriminated against because of their race, sexual orientation, or gender, or have been labeled as deviant. They have had innumerable experiences with failure in family, educational, work, or friendship roles. Heap writes that "such low self-esteem is self-nourishing, since it conditions the expectations and behavior with which new situations are met and thereby maintains the likelihood of new failure. It also frequently inhibits clients from risking new encounters at all and causes their withdrawal into a stultifying but protective passivity."[18] In working toward the aim of self-esteem, it is particularly important that the members achieve a sense of success in whatever they are doing, through group support and mutual achievement. The shift from an attitude of "I can't" to "I'll try" to "I can" is a powerful motivator for success in social functioning.

Varied experiences contribute to strengthening the ego's capacity to cope with the give and take of social relationships and expectations for performance. As Henry Maier says, the group can be used as an "arena for trying out and living out new experiences."[19] Through selected experiences, members come to discover the consequences of their behavior and the means for coping more effectively with difficult tasks. They may demonstrate to each other their actual competence and be faced with questions about success and failure. The culture of the group is crucial in the appropriate selection and use of experiences. There needs to be a norm that accredits trying and learning and one that helps members to face a realistic appraisal of their efforts, without blame or negative criticism for failures. The group becomes a safe place to risk new ways of practicing what members find hard to do.

In using activity to enhance social competence, the worker needs to assess the extent to which persons have mastered the tasks associated with each phase of human development relative to their age, gender, ethnicity, health, and environment. In helping clients to achieve competence in the performance of particular tasks or roles, the worker primarily uses an educational process. Howard Goldstein differentiates the educational role of the social worker from that of the school teacher. In social work, "the learning process is primarily directed toward the acquisition of knowledge that will aid in the completion of certain tasks or in the resolution of problems related to social living."[20] To adapt more effectively, people need the necessary knowledge and skills.

Some groups are composed of members, be they children or adults, who have encountered serious obstacles to their development. The use of activity in such groups can provide members with opportunities and a supportive environment for learning. The use of didactic and experiential techniques, such as role-play, rehearsal, and problem solving around hypothetical situations, accompanied by verbal discussion, can be particularly helpful in teaching. For example, activity can help parents gain skills and knowledge about child-rearing practices and can help children develop basic social skills that will enable them to get along better with peers and adults. Mastery of such skills enhances self-image and increases the likelihood that more and more difficult challenges will be attempted. These skills can be carried over from the group to daily living in the community.

Competence in Decision Making

Members of groups often need to enhance their competence to make and implement decisions, the outcome of problem solving. The decision may be that of an individual group member or of the total group. The decision may be a minor one or one of major concern either to the individual concerned or to the life of the group. All the steps in the problem-solving process come into play: identifying the issue, exploring it, securing possible solutions, analyzing them, and making a decision. Whitney Wright's description of a ceramics group composed of adolescents at a community-based mental health clinic illustrates how activity can help members explore personal issues.[21]

Kevin, one of the group members, was frustrated at his limited ability to form the clay. The rest of the group was moving to more advanced pieces, but Kevin was still stuck. He began to smash his clay with the rolling pin.

KEVIN: I'm never going to be left back in school. I'm too smart for that. That's for stupid people.

ERIKA: You don't have to be stupid to be left back.

KEVIN: Yes, you do, and I'm not stupid.

WORKER: I think Kevin may be voicing something that others of you could be feeling. Everyone works at a different pace and is comfortable with different skills. Each of you is moving along at a different pace with your clay projects. Seeing other people's projects could make someone feel left behind by the group.

LUCY: Raneir is going really fast.

RANEIR: (*shrugs his shoulders*) I think it's fun.

WORKER: So what if everyone had to go as fast as Raneir?

ERIKA: We wouldn't do a very good job.

KEVIN: It wouldn't look like that (*he points to a dog that Raneir was working on*).

WORKER: So it can sometimes be a good thing to go at a slower pace, even to stay back a year in school.

ERIKA: I stayed behind last year.

WORKER: What was it like for you?

ERIKA: It was a lot better. I felt like I could do things better.

In addition to exploration of an issue, activity can be used to help group members identify possible solutions to an issue and then to prepare them to implement their decision. In one group, for example, parents used role-play to examine different approaches to asking the school principal to provide privacy for their children in taking showers in the gym. Playing out each alternative led to consensus on their part about what to do and how to do it. In a group of twelve-year-old boys, a decision was make to invite a girls' group to share an event with them. But the boys seemed reluctant to tell the girls what they would be doing together. Engaging in rehearsal prepared the boys and enabled them to extend to the girls their invitation to join them.

Better Use or Change of the Environment

Groups may be directed toward constructive attempts to make better use of or to change some aspect of the environment that affects the group itself or the well-being of some of the members. Activity in the group should be related to the lives of the members in their families and communities. When people are unable to influence the forces that affect their lives, they develop a sense of powerlessness.[22] Social work help should not only focus on strengthening the ego's coping capacities and the functioning of groups but also reduce obstacles in the environment when that is possible to achieve by the members of the group. Effective social action promotes both social growth and improvement of environments.

Derryl Lubell provides an example of patients' successful efforts to improve their hospital ward.[23] A group of patients treated by peritoneal dialysis completed an eight-session group whose focus was on the impact of medical, family, and social factors on their lives. At the end of that group, they requested and secured an extension of time to focus on problems in the ward. To combat the boredom felt by many on dialysis, the younger patients organized a film program, improved the television rental service, and conferred with the dietitian on menu changes. The older patients spearheaded a move to become more involved in planning and taking responsibility for their own treatment. They complained about negative experiences with a new dialysis machine and the nurses' refusal to disconnect it when the pain became unbearable. The record reads:

> I suggested that the patients invite the head nurse and physician to a meeting so that they could discuss the issues directly with them. With hesitation, group members supported this idea and asked me to extend the invitation to the staff. I then described this invitation to the doctor and nurse as an opportunity both to enlist the patients' support for the planned changes and to encourage them to move toward responsible self-care. I also warned staff that they should expect some anger and demands and discussed briefly with them ways of handling the situation. The staff seemed pleased with the opportunity to present some of their thinking to the patients, and the meeting went well. Together, staff and patients decided that as soon as the patients complained of pain the nurse would disconnect them from their machines without waiting for the physician's permission. In turn, the patients agreed to tolerate the discomfort as long as possible while the staff made various technical adjustments.

In a group of residents in a long-term care facility, Toby Berman-Rossi reports that one common theme, as is true in many institutions, was dissatisfaction with the food.[24] With the social worker as mediator, the group met with staff from the dietary department several times, resulting in better understanding between patients and staff and some important changes in the menus. As they achieved some success, they felt more in control of their lives: they felt empowered. Similar benefits are reported by Harold Lipton and Sidney Malter in their work with a group of patients with spinal cord injuries who were dissatisfied with nursing routines and inadequate sharing of information by physicians.[25] Still another example is that of Judith Lee's work with homeless women in a shelter that combined work toward preparing the members for successful living outside the shelter with efforts to make the shelter more responsive to the needs of the residents.[26]

Examples of social action activities demonstrate their use in community settings as well. For example, when a threat was made to close a clinic for disabled children, parents' groups were eager to act to prevent closure. They mobilized a mail and telephone campaign and interested a local radio station and newspaper in the cause. The staff developed viable proposals for funding. As a result of these efforts, the administrator agreed to withdraw the plan to close the clinic. Carel Germain and Alex Gitterman report that "services to this needy group of children and their parents were safeguarded. In addition, the parents' self esteem, competence, and sense of identity and autonomy were enhanced by their having taken action on their own behalf in a matter of deep concern to them."[27]

A typical theme in groups of adolescents is conflict with parents concerning rules, discipline, and privileges. In one group, following an outpouring of complaints, the worker asked the members what could be done about it. The first responses were that nothing could be done; then there was a shift to asking the workers to talk to their parents; then a decision was made to plan for and follow through on a joint meeting with parents.[28]

Decisions to take action in relation to some obstacle in the environment are made through the use of a group problem-solving process and the carrying out of activities necessary to implement the decision. Voluntary participation in social action is growth producing for the members when action is taken *with* rather than *for* the members. Empowerment, as both Ruby Pernell and Barbara Solomon demonstrate, is both a process and a goal.[29] As people learn how to solve problems, they gain some power over their lives, enhance their self-esteem, and reduce feelings of hopelessness and helplessness. In small or large ways, they also make environments more responsive to the needs of people beyond the group.

The Use of Activity in Group Work Practice

To use activity effectively in group work practice requires skill and understanding on the part of workers with groups. Knowledge of human development and skill in assessment, understanding of the stages of group development and of the needs of the group and of group members in the stages, and skill in relating activity to the group's purpose are all essential to the meaningful utilization of activity.

Human Development and Assessment

The use of activity as a medium for growth and change necessitates its appropriateness to a given situation, based on individual and group assessment. Members respond in different ways to the same activity. Members who are very shy and fearful, for example, should not be pushed to try things that create anxiety beyond their capacity to cope with it. They need help to move from parallel participation to group interaction. Members who are very rivalrous can work on this problem through engaging in such activities as role-playing and, when ready, competitive games; they will need help to learn to handle wins and losses. Where self-esteem is low, the activity needs to be one in which successful completion is assured. Members of any age who have had few satisfying social experiences will need a great deal of support from the worker in daring to try new experiences, whereas those who have had numerous satisfactory social experiences are more able to translate the skills learned elsewhere into the group.

Creative use of activities designed to contribute to the resolution of particular members' problems in relationships is illustrated in an article by Ruth Bittner on work with a group for mothers and their young children whose purpose was to alleviate dysfunctional mother-child relationships.[30]

The S. family was referred to a child development center by its pediatrician who was concerned about Lisa, age two and a half. She was extremely shy and unable to relate to people; the relationship between mother and child was pathological. Mrs. S. was unable to give up extensive early symbiosis with Lisa. Treatment of the marital couple had resulted in some progress, but the relationship between mother and child remained unchanged. So Mrs. S. and Lisa were referred to a group composed of four mother-child pairs. The goal was to help Mrs. S. and Lisa to differentiate from each other.

The content of the group was designed to further its purpose. Coffee was available for adults and fruit juice for children; name tags were different colors for mothers and children to differentiate mother from child and one person from another. The meetings began with a song which addressed everyone by name and encouraged eye contact, and there was a similar closing song. These rituals were used to ease the transition in and out of the group and to enable mothers to connect with each other. Toys for children were selected for the specific purpose of helping them to move away from and back toward their mothers.

In the early meetings, Mrs. S. would clutch Lisa tightly in her lap and insist that Lisa was too frightened to move off. A wooden rocking boat served as a vehicle for moving Lisa away from and back toward her mother. The boat was placed close to the mother's chair so that mother and child faced one another. The mother sat the child in the boat and rocked it while the worker pointed out how the child was moving away from and then coming back toward the mother, providing a safe way for trying out separating from each other. Other play materials included a slide and a barn and small animals with which Lisa gradually grew able to play. Mrs. S., who was extremely shy in relating to other members of the group, gradually became able to participate in discussions about her relationship with Lisa and how to help Lisa to progress in her social development.

Such examples demonstrate the in-depth knowledge of human development and psychosocial assessment that underlie the therapeutic use of activity. They also demonstrate creativity and flexibility in the use of materials and equipment.

The content of a group experience needs to be sensitive to the values and norms of the culture of the members. Melvin Delgado, for example, points out that activity-oriented approaches are especially beneficial to members of Hispanic backgrounds.[31] The activities used need to be related to the interpersonal and environmental issues with which the members are currently dealing. They need to be supportive, stress cooperation rather than competition, and be consistent with a typical present-time orientation. He cautions that the emphasis on action does not mean that the members do not benefit from discussions pertaining to psychosocial difficulties; rather, it is the interweaving of doing and talking that is important.

E. Daniel Edwards and associates make similar points concerning successful work with American Indians.[32] They used an activity-discussion group for enhancing the self-concept and identification with being Indian of girls, aged seven to eleven. The content consisted of a variety of activities typical of the Indian culture. Talking supplemented doing. For example, when there was conflict in playing games, the game was terminated, and the members were asked to talk about how they were feeling, how important it is to listen to others and speak for oneself, and how conflicts are resolved. They discussed ways of handling negative remarks about American Indians. They were encouraged to share what they learned in the group at home. In the final meeting, which took place in the home of the leader and was attended by the members' families, the girls reviewed and demonstrated what they had learned in the group. A research evaluation showed positive changes in self-concept and a high correlation between the positive responses of the girls to an activity and the emphasis placed on that activity in the group.

Flavio Marsiglia, Suzanne Cross, and Violet Mitchell-Enos recommend that group work with American Indians should include culturally specific activities, especially some kind of art/craft component. Based on their experience with adolescent American Indian students, they note that it is easier for group members to express themselves through art and then explain their feelings and experience to the group. In addition, they found that members' art work provided a way to track changes in the way group members were identifying culturally.[33]

Stages of Group Development

Assessment of the group's stage of development and the needs of individual group members and of the total group in each stage is important in the worker's consideration of appropriate activity.[34] In the inclusion-orientation stage, for example, suitable activities are those that help members to become acquainted, release tension, emphasize commonalities between members, and provide for a sense of quick accomplishment. In that stage, activities should not require intimacy and closeness or stimulate aggressive behavior. They should have some clear structure but also allow for some flexibility in order to provide a safe environment for interaction between the members.

Inappropriate activity in a group's beginnings is illustrated by Wright, who describes a painting group at a clinic for adolescents with HIV whose workers sought a break from the discussion groups they were used to leading. At the first group meeting, they asked members to trace the outlines of their bodies on long rolls of paper and then decorate their images. The group members seemed ill at ease but went along with the activity. When it was time to fill in the bodies, one member left it blank and said she had nothing inside. Another put X's over his eyes and said he was already dead. Still another drew a skull and crossbones for a face. Another took the back of the paint brush and ripped up his outline. The members made fun of each other's paintings and even ruined a few of them. The improper demands for intimacy made by this activity contributed to only two members returning for the group's second meeting. After that, the group did not meet again.[35]

When the group moves into the stage of uncertainty-exploration, activity needs to provide opportunities for the members to work through conflicts, help them learn to share and handle competition, and require them to make decisions. In the mutuality and goal achievement stage, activity may require a higher level of interaction between members, more self-disclosure, greater individuation, higher demands for competence and facing failure, and opportunities for generalization to the world outside the group. In the separation-termination stage, the content often repeats earlier experiences so that members become aware of their progress. Activity at this stage becomes directed more to the situations of individuals and emphasizes movement away from the group and toward the community. Some groups will use rituals or good-bye parties as a means of handling powerful feelings of loss that are expressed symbolically through food, picture taking, and gift giving. Activity in the ending stage needs to provide opportunities for reminiscence, review, and evaluation. The use of activity in termination is illustrated by process from the ceramics group that was described earlier in this chapter.[36] The group's final project was a collage. Such a project allowed members to contribute at their own level of skill while, at the same time, it was something that all in the group could produce together.

WORKER: Everyone can add what they want to the collage.
RANEIR: I want to make a house to put on it.

WORKER: What does a house mean to you?
RANEIR: Safety.
WORKER: So this group has been a safe place?
ERIKA: Yes.
WORKER: Has it always been?
LUCY: No, not always. Sometimes it wasn't safe.
WORKER: When wasn't it safe?

The group discussed times when they did not trust each other and what happened in the group to help them gain each other's trust.

LUCY: I'm gonna write *trust* on the collage because it was important here. Maybe we can write *trust* and *safety* in the house you're making.
JASON: I'm just doing this dot. That's it.
WORKER: You don't want to add anything else?
JASON: I don't feel like it.
WORKER: This needs to be completed today so we can glaze it next week. So what we've put together at 5:30 is what the collage will look like.
JASON: What's the point? The group's ending anyway.

The group discussed how people felt about not meeting anymore—both the advantages and the disadvantages. Members expressed how they became close with each other, how they liked helping each other and being helped, and how much they will miss the group.

Activity and the Group's Purpose

A hallmark of the use of activity in social work with groups is its purposefulness. Activity is not just busy work for a group, not used merely as a way to keep group members occupied. Rather, when thinking about activity, social workers need to assess the usefulness of a particular activity in furthering the group's purpose. Activity is the means by which a group moves toward the achievement of its specific goals for individual members and for the group as a unit, within the context of the agency and the wider sociocultural milieu. Thus, clarity of goals for the use of a particular activity is essential. In considering activity, the worker needs to think about the nature of the hoped for outcome and the potential carryover to other experiences both within and outside the group that a particular activity might have.

In some social work groups a range of activities may be used to help in the achievement of purpose. A single group, for example, may employ games, role play, drawing, and writing during different group meetings. Other groups may use one activity throughout, and they may even be described by that activity. Thus, a worker may form a ceramics group or a singing group or a drama group or a cooking group or a writing group. Valid questions that can be asked of such groups is how are they distinguished from classes and why should they be led by social workers rather than by artists or actors or chefs or journalists. One reason is the attention to individual and group development, to the group's process and the interrelationships between group members that a knowledgeable and skillful social worker brings to such groups. Another is the attention to the group's purpose that characterizes the leadership of such groups by a social worker. In such groups, the social worker sees the activity not as an end in itself but rather as a means to achieve personal and social goals of the members.

Members of groups that use one activity throughout may be attracted at first to attend the group because of the activity. In other words, they may come initially because they want to participate in ceramics or singing or writing. In such groups, it is important that the individual and social purposes of the group be discussed and not hidden. Notwithstanding such discussion, however, primary attention in such groups during their beginnings may go toward participation in the activity. But, according to Wright, as such groups progress to their middle stages of development the individual and social purposes of the members assume increasing importance and the centrality of the activity recedes.[37]

In groups that use activity, it is easy for inexperienced social workers to overemphasize the activity and give inadequate attention to the members' feelings, interpersonal relationships, and group development. The result may be resistance to the activity of the group, lack of commitment to the project, and the deterioration of the group. In a group that uses activity, the focus is not on the activity in and of itself but rather on ways to use the activity, along with verbal content, to achieve particular goals and the group's purpose in the realm of psychosocial functioning.

Selecting Activity

Some social workers avoid the use of activity because of the faulty notion that its use requires that they have special abilities in a host of cultural, recreational, and social skills. More important are knowledge of person-environment interactions and skills in assessment. Essential to the use of any form of content is an assessment of each member's needs and problems, capacities, and interests, of the tasks that are typical of each phase of psychosocial development, of the stage of group development, and of the particular issues being dealt with in the group at a given time. It can be assumed that any social worker has had varied experiences in group living and in social and cultural activities. It is out of these life experiences, with special efforts to recall the many things one has done in the past, that ideas for activities come. Workers can capitalize on their own interests and skills, provided that their use will meet the needs of the group. In some groups, outside resources can be used. The most simple everyday tasks, too, may be the most valuable for the group, and these are readily learned by workers. Furthermore, there are excellent resources available in the form of books on games, crafts, simulations, role-playing, dramatics, dance, arts, and experiential exercises that can be used by social workers.[38]

A simple activity may be used to accomplish more than one purpose, if it is adapted to the changing needs and capacities of the members. An illustration is of a group of adults with mental illness in a day treatment center.

      The goals of the group are to assist these regressed patients to learn to relate to each other, to express their feelings and thoughts appropriately, and to develop the social skills necessary for living in the community, with the hoped-for result of lessened social isolation. In the first meetings, the group played very simple name games in order to become acquainted and feel comfortable with each other. The game was played with tennis balls, an acceptable adult form, each with a member's name written on it. The activity has been modified, almost on a weekly basis. One week the members tossed the balls around and had to name the member they were throwing to. Another time, they shot baskets in teams, with more agile members demonstrating the activity to others. At a more recent meeting, the members wrote down some of their favorite things on the balls, mixed them up, and then tried to identify whose favorite thing was on the ball they picked. The leader made adaptations of the activity to move the group toward more complex interaction and verbal communication as part of the activity. Almost nonverbal and afraid to risk trying in the first meeting, members now choose and talk about what they dislike as well as what they like, address each other directly, and express pleasure in helping each other. When problems in relationships have occurred within the activity, the members have become able to participate in simple discussions that recognize the difficulty, express negative as well as positive feelings, work out the difficulty within the group discussion period, and then see how successful the solution is the next time. Thus, the activities have been a means for reducing social isolation.

In this group, playing with tennis balls took on great symbolic significance, creating a bond between the members. The deliberate progression made it possible for the members to identify how their self-esteem and ability to relate to others had changed over time as they tried adaptations of the familiar and as they discussed the meaning of the activity to them and the difficulties and pleasures they encountered in engaging in progressively more complex demands for doing and talking.

Social workers need to learn to understand the meaning of play, gestures, and other actions, just as they need to understand the verbal language of the persons with whom they work. Words and actions are seldom separable. The two tools of conversing and doing are closely interrelated. The essential question for the worker is when and under what conditions can reflective discussion, decision making, or activity contribute to the achievement of the goals of the individuals who compose the group and to the development of the group as a system.

In using activity, social workers assess the usefulness of a particular activity in furthering the group's purpose.[39] It is essential that the following questions be considered:

1. **Purpose.** What purposes can be achieved through the use of a particular activity?
2. **Relationship demands.** Can the activity be done alone, in subgroups, by the entire group? What intensity of relationship is required? How much closeness and intimacy are required? Does the

activity foster withdrawal from relationships or movement toward others at an appropriate pace? Does the activity suggest cooperation, competition, sharing, blocking, demanding, or attacking behaviors? Is the activity individual or group oriented?

3. **Required skills.** What does the activity require in terms of physical movement, coordination, cognitive ability, language skills, and obedience to rules?

4. **Impact on behavioral expression.** Does the nature of the activity itself tend to free, inhibit, or control impulses? What are the extent and forms of control by the worker and by participants—those that are personalized as contrasted with those that are depersonalized, in that they come from rules or the nature of the material being worked with? What are the freedoms and limits imposed by the activity? What are the implicit and explicit rewards for participating successfully in the activity and how abundant or scarce are they? How are they distributed?

5. **Decision making.** Who makes the choices and how widespread are opportunities for individual choice and group decision making?

6. **Appropriateness to life situations.** How suitable is the form of content to the life situation of members? What opportunity is there for carryover to situations outside the group?

7. **Cultural sensitivity.** What cultural attitudes and values are perceived as being connected to the activity? What are the anticipated attitudes related to cultural backgrounds toward participation in a given activity? How can the activity be adapted to the ethnic, racial, or social class backgrounds of members and the surrounding culture?

8. **Timing.** How ready are the members to make positive use of an activity at a given time, both within a session and at different times in the group's development? Is the time it takes to do it appropriate to the members' interests and attention spans?

9. **Availability of resources.** What supplies, equipment, space, or knowledgeable persons are essential to the use of the activity?

Social workers take responsibility for helping the group to select and use activity. Their contribution may be one of introducing, supporting, modifying, or enriching the experience that a group is engaged in at a given time.

Competence can be achieved by people only to the extent that there are opportunities available to develop it. Many opportunities can be provided within the group, but a given group cannot do it all. The social worker, therefore, refers members to other resources in the community and, when desirable opportunities are not available, brings attention to the gaps in services and cooperates with others to secure more adequate services.

12   Stage I: Inclusion-Orientation

Before a viable group develops as a means through which its members achieve their goals, a complex process of group formation begins at the time of planning for a new group and continues until a group emerges. For, according to Grace Coyle, "collective behavior is something more than and different from the sum of the individuals who produce it."[1] As members interact, a new entity is created: a group is born. The primary task of the social worker during the initial stage is to help a group to form—a group that will be beneficial to its members. If a group is to form, the major task for the members is to become oriented to the group and to decide to be included in the group's membership. Initial working relationships with each other and with the worker are established around these tasks.

Characteristics of the Group

Considerable consensus exists among writers that this stage is characterized by initial anxiety on the part of the members toward the unknown situation. Members enter into the group with feelings and behavior characterized by uncertainty, anxiety, and tension and by self-conscious and non-committal behavior. The relationship of the members with the worker is often one of dependency. As members become acquainted with each other and oriented to the situation, there emerges a pattern of interpersonal relations, values and norms, and communication. Relationships of members with each other evolve out of the efforts to adapt to the expectations for the role of members in the particular group.

When a collection of persons comes together for the first time, a group does not yet exist. The aggregate tends to be a collection of individuals with the center of attention on selves rather than on others. There is a lack of congruence between members and with the worker about the purpose and more specific goals. Membership is not yet determined; there is often lack of knowledge about the criteria for inclusion in the group. In formed groups, the structure is the one established initially by the social worker. In groups in which members have known each other prior to the group experience, there is lack of clarity about how the existing structure will be modified to include the worker. In either instance, there is lack of understanding about the interacting roles of members and worker. Members of formed groups may have developed a tentative relationship with the worker but not with each other. In varied types of groups, relationships between the members will become modified in unknown ways as the members engage together in a new enterprise. As the group develops and changes, the members will need to feel they are accepted and included in the group.

The members bring their own social and emotional needs into the group. The activation of these needs depends upon the group structure, initial feelings about the worker and other members, and the motivation of the members to join the group. If a group is to survive, it has to meet the needs of each member, even though these needs are initially incongruent with those of other members. The members bring their own norms of behavior, based on their values and cultural traditions, to the group. Workers have their own norms as persons, as representatives of an organization, and as members of the social work profession. There is lack of knowledge about each other's values and norms, with lack of mutuality around this aspect of group process. Established patterns of verbal communication have not yet emerged, so discussion is apt to be self-centered, scattered, diffuse, and lacking in continuity. Similarly, attention to any activity may be short-lived. There is lack of clarity about and acceptance of the boundaries to the group's power to make decisions. There is often a fear of self-disclosure and a tendency to deny problems or project them onto others. Cohesiveness is indeed weak, for there is little common basis for members' attraction to the group.

Preparing for First Meetings

In preparing for the first meeting, the practitioner reviews the plan for the group and makes a preliminary assessment of the members. But something more is needed. It is what William Schwartz refers to as "tuning in," which involves reflecting about the group, moving into the meeting with confidence and competence, and engaging in anticipatory empathy.[2]

Self-awareness is essential to the task of helping a group to form. Even experienced workers continue to have some fearful fantasies about entering a new group.[3] They share anxieties similar to those of the members about how they will be received by the members. Since each group is like all others in some ways but unique in other ways, the workers often anticipate what might go wrong. The questions they ask of themselves and worry about are varied: what if the members are very resistant, what if I lose control of the group, what if hostility breaks out, what if no one talks, what if they make overwhelming dependency demands on me, what if they don't like me, or, perhaps the most anxiety-provoking of all, what if nobody comes? Awareness of these doubts and fears may free workers to move from preoccupation with self to reflective consideration of the needs, capacities, and initial anxieties of the members. As they try to feel what it would be like to be in the members' situations, their capacity for empathy is enhanced.

Self-awareness is also crucial in relation to accepting professional authority for the conduct of the group. The members rightly look to the worker for guidance and direction. The worker's role is not as a client-member but as a member with the role of responsible professional practitioner with special knowledge and expertise. The active role does not violate the principle of client self-determination or autonomy, because people cannot make wise choices without the necessary orientation to and knowledge of the new and often strange situation of being in a group developed for social work purposes. Within the role, of course, the worker's responsibility is to enable members to participate actively in the tasks essential at the time of a group's beginning.

Workers engage in other forms of preparation as well. Knowing who the members will be, they review their knowledge about the particular characteristics, needs, and situations of members and use literature and other resources to increase their knowledge. For example, Mrs. K. was to work for the first time with a group of patients who had been diagnosed as borderline. She reviewed, therefore, the most up-to-date knowledge about that syndrome and clarified its implications for her work with the group. Workers also set the stage for the first meeting, on the basis of knowledge of the meaning of space to people, and make sure that necessary supplies are available.

Development of Relationships

The social worker uses understanding of the meaning of the new experience to the members of the group to develop an initial working relationship that will sustain the members through the period of initial uncertainty and anxiety and serve as a catalyst for promoting the development of relationships between members.

At the point of entry into a new group, there is co-presence between the members, but psychological bonds are not present unless members have known each other previously. Coming together psychologically is accomplished through social exchange between members. Someone makes an overture and, according to Erving Goffman, the "adaptive line of action attempted by one will be insightfully facilitated by the other or insightfully countered, or both."[4] Thus, a pattern of affective ties and communication emerges. It cannot be known in advance what the configuration will be, for that depends upon the interaction between many individual, group, and environmental factors.

The predominant socioemotional issue for the members is inclusion. The members decided earlier that they wished to give the group a try, but they also have many doubts about the appropriateness of the group for meeting their needs. The first tie is to the worker, who usually has had one or more interviews with the members before the first meeting. The members still have concerns, however: will the worker like me, be interested in me, compare me favorably against others, and accept me as a member of the group? The members' inner, if not avowed, questions tend to be: what am I here for, what is expected of me, who are the other members, how will I measure up to them, do I really want to get acquainted with them, and will I find a place for myself in the group?

This ambivalence is referred to by James Garland, Hubert Jones, and Ralph Kolodny as approach-avoidance.[5] In approaching the group, for example, the members desire to have a good relationship with the worker and other members, want to be accepted, and want to be able to participate appropriately in the group. At the same time, they have many fears: of the unknown, of being rejected, of getting involved, of losing a sense of privacy, or of being criticized. They, therefore, behave cautiously to avoid being hurt.

When people enter a new group, they scan the situation for signals that indicate to what extent they are welcome. They may be especially sensitive to those signals that indicate aloofness, arrogance, indifference, or mild hostility, as these are communicated through tone of voice, facial expression, or gesture. Such messages are often more potent than verbalized ones are. They may communicate warnings to be wary, retreat, wait and see, avoid others, or reach out to others. People may perceive the signals fairly accurately or may distort and misinterpret them. People tend to have highly selective awareness of others, predominantly unconscious, so that they see and hear only certain things. Such distortions interfere with effective entry into new groups. In their efforts to cope with the new situation, certain members may have positive feelings of interest, hope, trust, pleasure, curiosity, friendliness, or satisfaction. Negative feelings may run a gamut of insecurity, anxiety, distrust, rejection, doubt, confusion, discomfort, disinterest, self-consciousness, resentment, or disappointment. Combinations of positive and negative feelings seem to be quite universal. They seem to be as prevalent with members of groups in youth service agencies in which membership is thought of as desirable and voluntary as with members in hospitals or correctional institutions.

Trust

In each new situation, an individual faces, to some extent, a renewal of the basic conflict of a sense of trust versus distrust and needs to synthesize these polarities. Achievement of trust is relatively easy or hard, depending upon the extent to which members have previously developed a basic sense of trust. If members have not worked through, in a fairly satisfactory way, the basic issue of trust versus distrust, they repeat feelings of being unloved or rejected, they are often suspicious of other people, and they lack confidence in themselves and others. Each new experience offers some occasion for mistrust, until the unknown becomes familiar. Until members can come to trust the people involved and the situation, they cannot participate in truly interdependent relationships with others. But trust is also related to the extent to which workers are able to accept and respect all members, with their similarities and differences from the worker and from each other.

Social workers convey trust by modeling, through their own attitudes and behavior, the qualities of acceptance, empathy, and genuineness, which are components of a professional relationship. They help members relate to each other through the small courtesies that indicate interest in one's comfort and that acquaint members with each other. They help members express their feelings of doubt about whether or not they can trust the worker and the group. In one example:

In a first meeting of a group of fifth-grade boys, the worker recognized that they were suspicious about the group. The worker said, therefore, that maybe he should explain to them what the group was about and how they had gotten into it. He shared with them the information that he had met with the vice principal, who had thought these boys could do better in school if they were in a group. The boys looked skeptical, and, when they did not respond to his request for responses, he went on to say that he and the principal thought that the group would be a safe place in which they could talk about some of the troubles kids often have and do things that might help them get along better. Then he added, "Some of you seem to feel the group is some kind of punishment." The boys were verbally silent, but a couple started to giggle. The worker added, "Perhaps you don't think you can trust me." The comment identified the boys' feelings accurately. First one, then others asked such questions as Are you connected with the police? Will you squeal to the vice principal on us? Will you squeal to my mother? and, If I mess up here, will you kick me out of the group? Facing these doubts, finding acceptance from the worker, and being assured of confidentiality began a gradual change from active resistance to positive motivation to be in the group.

Recognizing with the members that the experience is a new one, that it is natural to feel uncertain, and that the group experience will be a valuable one for the members is a specific means of developing an atmosphere of mutual trust. Providing accurate information about the purpose and content of the group, along with a caring relationship, provides support.

With the necessary amount of support, members of groups who have a basic sense of trust will move rather quickly into fuller exploration of the potentials and demands in the group experience. In groups composed of such members, an initial working relationship with the worker and one another develops fairly quickly. An example is a group of parents who voluntarily joined a parent education group to learn how to understand and be helpful to their teenage children. With a minimum of anxiety and basically positive motivations toward the service, the period of inclusion-orientation was achieved within the first session.

Many persons lack a basic sense of trust in others and in their own ability to cope with situations. For some, the symptoms will be withdrawal and fearful responses to efforts to engage their participation. With severely disturbed patients with mental illness, for example, this is usually a prolonged period in which the worker nurtures and develops the capacity for trust. This may be done through providing opportunity for members to be somewhat dependent on the worker and engaging them in a variety of simple activities that are clearly within their capacities and that focus on individual or parallel participation but that also can be done cooperatively. The members may be encouraged, but with a minimum of pressure, to discuss everyday events and common experiences and may be provided with some gratification in the form of food or concrete achievements. Within a protective and permissive environment, members gradually become able to express their feelings, ideas, and goals. It may take a period of many weeks before a relationship of trust in the worker and each other is established. The process is somewhat similar to that used with very shy and fearful young children.

Self-Awareness

Through their own attitudes and behavior, social workers try to convey acceptance, accurate empathy, and genuineness. They face numerous challenges to their skills in facilitating the development of relationships that will further the members' goals. To develop an effective working relationship, they need to be sensitive to their own interpersonal needs. They learn to recognize that each member has a particular psychological meaning for them. They may react with fear, hostility, affection, or overprotection: some members trigger these reactions. A clinging, dependent person, for example, may reactivate a worker's unresolved dependency need. An elderly client may stir up feelings of inadequacy or fear of aging or death. A person who complains continuously about other people may stir up feelings of impatience. It is hard for some workers to accept conflicts as constructive and useful in problem-solving, so they tend to deny the conflict, which only erupts later in less constructive ways.

If they lack faith in the group process, some social workers have difficulty in relating to the connections between members as distinct from relating to each member as an individual. They need to be able to express empathy with all members of a group and with the group as a whole. But they may identify with children against their parents or with shy, conforming members more than with outwardly aggressive ones. Fearing the relinquishment of some of their authority, they may take over parental roles rather than help parents learn to be more effective. They may have difficulty in feeling comfortable with rambling discussions, provocative questions or comments, or disruptive activities. Fearing chaos, they may be controlling, holding the reins too tightly. They may try to keep the discussion light and nonthreatening for self as well as for the group.[6] They may find it challenging to help members to bridge the differences between them, when groups are composed of members from more than one ethnic category, social class, or religion.

An important step in becoming able to develop effective relationships with members is to recognize one's own difficulties but then to move from self-awareness to self-control; that is, as Barbara Solomon said, "the ability to control heretofore unconscious aspects of one's personality which have served as an obstacle to establishing warm, genuine, and empathic relationships with certain kinds of people."[7] As practitioners become more able to recognize and then control their difficulties, they become able to enhance the development of a sense of cohesion or group bond, which is the result of the degree to which members have achieved psychosocial closeness to each other. This bond, in turn, provides a strong motivation for members to continue in the group.

Stereotyping is a major deterrent to developing and sustaining effective relationships. Some practitioners are not able to respond to a member of a different ethnic group as a unique person instead of as a symbol of a particular category of people. It is imperative that cultural differences be recognized and respected and that ethnic identity be fostered. Attention to culture should not, however, be at the cost of individualization, a major principle of practice. Shirley Cooper indicates that if ethnicity is overemphasized, clients tend to "lose their individual richness and complexity: there is the danger of no longer treating people—only culture carriers."[8] Workers may emphasize ethnic factors to such an extent that individual needs and solutions to problems become obscured. The point is important, but lack of emphasis on culture may also oversimplify the member's situation. Cultural factors need to be viewed as they interact with psychological and environmental ones in a particular situation.

People from minority groups have valid reasons for initial distrust of white practitioners because many white people are prejudiced and discriminate against nonwhite people in many subtle and overt ways. Barriers between workers and clients of different races and between members need to be recognized and dealt with early in a relationship. If workers are able to communicate their awareness of racial and ethnic differences in a sensitive manner, the potential for developing a helping relationship is enhanced. Workers begin to bring such differences into the group discussion by introducing the subject naturally and at an appropriate time rather than imposing discussion of race and ethnicity out of a feeling that such differences must be talked about instantly. When differences of race and ethnicity are discussed, it is important that workers are sensitive to the members' responses.

People who have experienced discrimination are often particularly sensitive to the social workers' attitudes in the initial contact. They value being treated with respect, but often they have not been so treated. Effective work with groups requires that practitioners observe those formalities that are overt indications of respect, such as proper introductions, use of titles and surnames, and shaking hands. Such formalities are important to black clients who have been denied these symbols of courtesy. They are important to people of other cultures also. An example is given by Joan Velasquez and associates, who point out that the Spanish language includes two terms for use in addressing another person, depending upon that person's status in terms of both age and social role. Addressing persons who are older or in a position of authority by their first names is perceived not as a friendly gesture, but as lack of respect; social workers are in positions of authority and should, therefore, be addressed by their surnames and titles. It is a sign of disrespect for a Hispanic client to disagree with a person in a position of authority. If unaware of this cultural norm, workers may misinterpret silence or acquiescence as resistance, which mitigates against developing a relationship characterized by mutual trust.[9]

Along with the need for symbols of courtesy and respect, Ignacio Aguilar notes that in the Mexican-American culture it is the custom to have an informal and personalized conversation before entering into a business transaction.[10] An example is of a group of women in a community mental health center that serves a multiethnic population.

An elementary school principal became aware of the need for some of the Spanish-speaking mothers to understand how they might become supportive of their children's education. Accordingly, a group was formed through referrals from the school, composed of seven women between the ages of twenty-four and thirty, who spoke little English but recently enrolled in an English-as-a-second-language class. All were born in Mexico and received their education there. A Spanish-speaking social worker was assigned to the group. The stated purpose of the group was to help the members to be able to support their children's education in this country, where the expectations are quite different from those in Mexico. Since education is highly valued, the mothers shared a desire to help their children to succeed in school.

In the first meeting of the group, the bilingual worker expressed pleasure that these women had desired to be in the group. She invited them to have coffee and get acquainted with each other. They chose to tell each other about their children. They addressed each other and the worker by the *usted* form, which persisted for several sessions, after which they moved to the informal "tu." Although given consent to use the informal form of address and first name by the worker, the formal term continued to be used. During the first meeting, the formality extended into topics of group discussion and a tendency to agree with the worker. The orientation and goal-setting process could not, therefore, be completed in the first meeting. The members were reserved about sharing feelings and difficulties. During the meeting, it became evident that they lacked self-esteem and felt devalued. The worker decided to introduce some of the arts of Mexico as a tool for bridging the two cultures.

After preliminary greetings and sharing of refreshments, the second session began with the worker informally showing the members a small porcelain mouse from Tonola in Mexico, which was admired by all. Mrs. R. said she had seen one of these in a friend's house. She said she has something just as cute from Oaxaca and offered to bring it next time. The worker asked if the others might have something of beauty to share with the group. Mrs. M. asked if it could be a lace shawl instead of an art object. She was assured about this, and slowly, then, other members said they could find something of which they were proud. From there, Mrs. R. said that maybe they could teach their children to take pride in their heritage. Through such a seemingly simple act by the worker, a bridge was built between the two cultures, which contributed in a small way to the group's purpose and to the development of shared relationships between the members so that they were then ready to share some of the problems they were having with the children and engage in setting goals.

The importance of informality and personalized contacts is not unique to Hispanic cultures. D. Corydon Hammond emphasizes its importance in establishing relationships with Native Americans.[11] Within some Asian cultures, there is a similar expectation that time will be taken for social amenities and for getting to know a person. The offering and accepting of a cup of tea aids in setting a climate that will be comfortable for the discussion of problems. In some Asian cultures, as well as Hispanic ones, respect for authority is important. For example, for persons reared in traditional Japanese families, it may be exceedingly difficult to disagree with someone in a position of authority. In such situations, the worker does not press the members for agreement or a decision before the members become somewhat comfortable about expressing difference. It is important that the worker pose options rather than assume that the first "yes" signifies agreement or support of an idea.[12] Etiquette may dictate agreement when an expert makes a suggestion. In many Chinese families, saving face or preserving the dignity of the family takes precedence over open communication, and signs of affection may not be demonstrated directly. The social worker's task is to develop a supportive climate in which it is safe to allow for expression of feelings rather than the enactment of expected role behavior.

When a worker and members share a similar ethnic background, it is often easier for the worker to accept and empathize with the members. Similarity may provide the member with a positive model of ethnicity. It is, however, easy to overemphasize the similarities within a category and to fail to take into account the many individual and family differences. It has been noted, for example, that in black client-black practitioner relationships, problems often develop. The practitioner may either deny the common tie to the members or overidentify with them. In spite of sharing a common racial experience, unless workers can recognize their own countertransference reactions and learn to control them it is unlikely that an effective working relationship will develop.

Working across ethnic lines has both positive and negative implications. It is possible to capitalize on the values that come from learning about and facing differences as well as from learning about and facing similarities. Social distance between people can be reduced. In Alfred Kadushin's words:

> If the worker's professional training enhances the ability to empathize with and understand different groups and provides the knowledge base for such understanding, the social and psychological distance between worker and client can be reduced. If the gap is sufficiently reduced, clients perceive workers as being capable of understanding them, even though they are the product of a different life experience.[13]

Solomon emphasizes that an important skill is the ability to confront members when they distort or misinterpret the positive feelings that the worker has for them. When workers are too threatened to open up the issue, "the client is denied an opportunity to learn something about himself and how he relates to others."[14] The worker's failure to explore the issue with the members interferes with the development of relationships.

Social Class

Ethnicity interacts with social class, contributing to potential barriers to effective worker-group relationships. Social class largely determines the people with whom one associates and with whom one feels comfortable.

That social class is one of the more important influences of clients' expectations about help has been suggested by a number of studies.[15] Clients from middle-class orientations tend to expect that value will be placed on introspective and reflective discussion and on verbal sophistication, that the helper's role will be a relatively inactive one, that other family members may be involved in treatment, and that treatment will be prolonged. Clients from less advantaged socioeconomic backgrounds, on the other hand, tend to expect that the practitioner will be direct, supportive, and active, that "cure" will occur more rapidly, and that the practitioner will do something in an immediate, tangible way to relieve discomfort. They may be confused by the demand for verbalization as contrasted with action. Too often, it has been assumed that the reluctance of some clients to question the expectations and their passive compliance with the worker's definition of roles are due to lack of motivation. Rather, such behaviors may be a sign of confusion and uncertainty. Unless workers appreciate the importance of money and other material resources in relating to people, they are apt to interpret certain problems as internal to the person when the problem is a societal one. Stereotypes about a culture of poverty or about the limited potentials of poor people interfere with developing truly helping relationships that build on strengths and hopes for a better future.

Gender

Concerns are raised about the influence of the gender of the worker on the development of relationships. Many women are concerned that counselors and therapists tend to perpetuate sex-role stereotypes and that this "may harm rather than help their patients by training them to conform to narrowly defined roles and adjust to unhealthy life situations."[16] From their review of research on psychotherapy and behavior change, Morris Parloff, Irene Waskow, and Barry Wolfe concluded that the effect of the practitioner's gender on outcome has not been confirmed.[17] Charles Garvin and Beth Reed have said, too, that little is known about the "effects of female leadership on member perceptions, behaviors, or on group development, structure, and so forth."[18] Nevertheless, as with ethnic and social class differences, social workers need self-awareness and sensitivity to issues of gender. It is probable that the attitudes and values of the practitioner, rather than gender per se, are of primary importance in the development of a worker-group relationship.

Hope and Motivation

Initial motivation is influenced by the personal and social characteristics of members, the adequacy of members' psychosocial functioning, the social agency and its place in the community, the extent of support from significant persons in the environment, and cultural factors that influence attitudes toward and the use of institutional resources. These are, in turn, often related to the initial application or referral, whether initiated by the group member or someone else, and the extent to which membership in the group is voluntary. But even voluntary attendance does not imply eagerness and motivation to become a part of a group. Most people come to a new experience both wanting it and fearing it. As Hazel Osborn has said vividly, "Just as we must remind ourselves that there are many shades of grey between black and white, so we must recognize that all voluntary affiliations are not equally fervid. Joining is more like a five to three vote than the miniature landslide we might prefer."[19]

Whatever the initial motivation, it is modified as a person has experiences in the group. The fact that most people want the goals of improved personal adequacy and social functioning for themselves is an ally to social workers in their efforts to support the initial motivation of members. Another ally is the powerful fact that all people have potential for growth and development. Yet most people also have some resistance to involving themselves in a group.

Resistance is a trend of forces against using the help that is offered. It consists of those attitudes and behaviors that interfere with making progress. Resistance is not necessarily negative. Indeed, it is often a sign of good ego strength to be able to resist the advice and suggestions of others, including the worker, when such ideas go against one's own realistic understanding of one's situation and the consequences of following the advice. Change means discomfort or disequilibrium, for it means giving up the comfort of the familiar present for an unknown future. There may be a sense of hopelessness about oneself and one's situation. Some persons may be reluctant to admit they need help. If they value independence more than interdependence, they believe they should be able to "pull themselves up by their own bootstraps." Some associate the present experience with similar past experiences that were unpleasant.

The worker's own value systems, in part, determine their skill in this important area. A belief in the potential for change in each human being tends to be communicated nonverbally to the group. If this feeling is picked up by one or more group members, they may, in turn, influence others toward hoping for something better for themselves. What the social worker strives for is to motivate the members to select one or more specific goals toward which they may work.

Within some of the common reactions to becoming involved in a group, there are striking differences in initial motivation. Sometimes, there is eager anticipation of belonging. In a children's hospital, for example, a group was initiated for five- and six-year old girls and boys. Its purpose was to help the children to understand the varied treatment procedures and develop relationships with other children that might sustain them through the difficult period of hospitalization. When the social worker entered the ward to invite the children to come to the group, she found poignant desire combined with apprehension about exclusion. One little boy in a wheelchair asked, "Do you want me?" in a tone that expressed both wonder and fear. A girl tugged at the worker's skirt and, in a high pitched voice, asked, "Me, too— me, too?" The oldest boy asked, "Is there room for one more—is there room for me?" How different this initial behavior is from the hostile reactions of adolescent boys who were referred by a judge with the admonition to "be in this man's group or go to Juvenile Hall," hardly a positive motivation toward the service. Such differences in motivation are reflected in the members' feelings about and reactions to the social worker.

An example of strong initial resistance that changed into positive motivation is of a group of five boys, aged eleven to thirteen, sponsored by a child welfare agency. In late September, reports had come to the social worker that the boys were engaged in early delinquent behavior. As a small gang, they had raided neighborhood fruit trees, stolen from the variety store, stayed out after curfew, and were often truant from school.

The social worker approached the mothers of the boys to secure their permission for the boys to be in a small group. The mothers agreed to have their sons come to a meeting at the school on Friday afternoon. They were advised to tell the boys that the worker would sponsor them as a club whose purpose would be to provide interesting social experiences for them and to help them with their personal and school problems.

First Meeting. I looked up to see George, age thirteen, standing in the doorway of the meeting room. He was dressed in clean but worn clothing. He was a short and stocky youngster, had a deep voice, and his whiskers were starting to grow. He had the manner of an old man, with deep concerns. I invited him into the meeting room and asked if he knew whether the other boys would be coming. He evaded answering and asked me, "What is this all about?" I said that I had offered to sponsor the boys as a club. He asked why. I told him that the school, the juvenile police officer, and the mothers had told me that he and his four friends had been in some trouble and that I could help them do better—so I wanted to help them out. He then asked me a number of direct questions: What did I mean they had been in trouble? Who was it that snitched on them? What made me think they needed an adult sponsor for a club? I responded to these questions directly and honestly. I listened as George blasted the school for sticking its nose into their business and expressed many complaints about the school. I said I certainly couldn't promise to solve the problems about school, but I could make things better for them outside of school. George wanted to know exactly how.

I talked about the idea of forming a club and suggested a number of possible things they might do. George listened with interest but was skeptical. He told me that they already had a leader—he was the leader of the gang. I sensed that I was threatening his role and explained that he could continue to be the leader—that a sponsor was something different. He wanted me to spell out the difference. He then asked me if the school had "planted" me to do this job. I again told him that I was a child welfare social worker, but both the school and the police had informed me that he and his gang were getting into trouble and thought they needed help with things that might be "bugging" them. George then admitted they were all "bugged about a lot of things."

I suggested that George take my offer back to the gang so that the boys might decide whether or not they wanted me to work with them. He jumped out of his chair, ran to the window, lifted the shade, and signaled with his hand. Almost immediately, four faces appeared at the window and George directed them to come into the room. I was somewhat surprised that George formally introduced me as each one entered the room. When all were seated, I offered to serve them some cookies and coke. Their faces lighted up. I noticed that four of them gobbled down their food.

When we finished eating, I asked George to tell the other boys about our discussion. This he did in a businesslike manner and was completely accurate in describing my proposal, even emphasizing that I'd help them with what they were "all bugged up about." Steve and Bill immediately said they liked the idea. Wendell and Bruce waited for George to say he thought they should do it. I suggested that they did not need to decide today: they could tell me whenever they were ready. They began to talk about what they could do if they became a club.

As the boys left, George told me that they had all decided to take me up on my offer. I said I was pleased and they could come to the same place on Friday. He said they'd all be there.

In this first session, the social worker demonstrated the skills essential to reducing resistance to an offer of help. Observation of appearance and behavior gave clues about how to approach the leader of the natural group. He displayed acceptance through welcoming first the indigenous leader and then the other boys, making them feel comfortable and lessening anxiety and hostility. He made it clear that he would not usurp the indigenous leader's power. He conveyed an attitude of genuineness by answering questions honestly and without becoming defensive. He listened in a nonjudgmental way to complaints.

The social worker provided support through the relationship, offering reassurance about roles, and securing the support of parents for the boys belonging to the group. He encouraged the exploration of feelings and the possibilities for the group's content. He gave essential information to both the group and the parents and gave advice to the parents concerning the boys' membership in the group. He made appropriate suggestions concerning possible activities and discussion. He confronted George, in a gentle way, with the fact that the boys were in trouble with the school and the police. He explained the purpose of the group, the reasons for referral to the group, the roles of social worker and indigenous leader, and the group's right to make the decision about whether or not to accept the offer.

Clients need support from significant people to be motivated to use a service. The group is a major source of support, but it may not be sufficient. The social worker needs to take into account the extent to which the environment provides support for the members. Studies show that both continuance in treatment and outcome are related to the availability of environmental supports.[20] Thus, a frequent task for a group's worker is to seek support from significant others in enhancing the motivation of clients in the use of service. When a child is the member, the minimal involvement of the parents or guardian is that of granting informed consent for the child to have help for a particular purpose. That also is an ethical act.

Orientation

Orientation to the worker, other members, and the plans for the use of the group is necessary to reduce some of the uncertainty and anxiety, to enhance the potential value of the group for its members, and to motivate the members to use the group for meeting their needs.

Purpose

The purpose of the group needs to become explicit if the group is to be of optimum benefit to its members. The members of the group are most receptive to change when their goals and aspirations are similar and are meshed with the social worker's purpose. The process by which this occurs is presented in chapter 7.

Structure and Membership

Social workers provide direction for the initial organizational structure of the group. Although the degree of their activity may vary somewhat according to the group, it is usually more apparent during this stage than at any other point in the group's development. Workers have responsibility to orient the group to the agency's rationale for the particular form of organization and for the decisions concerning time, place, frequency, and content of meetings. The members' reactions to these plans are sought and modifications made when appropriate to the members' needs and within the governing policies of the agency. The members have a right to know the source of authority for establishing and changing procedures, including the part they have in this process.

Uncertainty and anxiety about the basis of membership in a group are usually present in formed groups. In natural groups, the concern tends to be one of ambivalence about the inclusion of a social worker in the group. Questions from members about the reason they were referred to or selected for the group need to be responded to with brevity and honesty. Later, there can be clarification of the members' questions and concerns about this. Even in groups in which the members have sought a place, the provision of information about the major criteria for group composition may enable members to feel some sense of commonality, a necessary first step toward identification with the group. Similarly, giving them information about anticipated changes in membership helps to provide a sense of security. Members need to know if there are expectations that they be prompt and attend regularly. They need to know under what circumstances others will be added or terminated from the group.

Development of Norms

If the potentially dynamic forces in the group are to operate, a system of norms needs to emerge that is appropriate to the particular purpose of the group and the characteristics of the members. In this respect, Irvin Yalom refers to the practitioner's role as that of culture builder.[21] A commonly accepted set of norms provides support and security for the members and contributes to the development of cohesion.

Persons often come to social work situations ignorant of what particular behaviors will be expected of them. They bring their own norms with them into the group, but if this is a first experience with a social worker they have no experiential base for knowing what to expect of the worker and what is expected of them. An illustration is of a group composed of eleven- and twelve-year-old boys who were making a poor adjustment in school and had been referred to a group for help with their problems.

The worker sensed the members' discomfort about the silence that followed his suggestions that the members talk about what they might discuss or do in the group. He then repeated an earlier explanation that the purpose of the group was to help them get along better in school and added that he knew it could be very hard to do well in school. One member then told a story about a new boy in school who was "teased by the kids and given a rough time by the teacher." A silence followed. The leader interrupted the silence, saying that he knew it would be hard for the new boy in school, that they were in a somewhat similar situation, coming to a new group and not knowing what to expect from the worker and maybe from each other, too. "Yeah, that's exactly it," was the boy's response.

The worker, after getting a similar response from other members, then told them about the plan for the group, how this group was different from classes, what his role would be, and how they could participate in the group. He stopped often to get their responses to the information. Members of groups, such as this one, should not be expected to discuss the content of the group until they have some understanding of what the group is for and what is expected of them. The worker's understanding of the latent content of the reference to the new boy's troubles and sensitivity to what it might mean to have a first experience in a social work group facilitated the members' readiness to learn more about the group's potential for meeting their needs.

Facilitative Norms

The norms that facilitate the progress of the members and the development of the group include, but are not limited to, the following:

1. mutual aid and mutual support,
2. flexibility and experimentation, which promotes the idea that it is good to try out new things and new ways,
3. the ideas that differences are normal and acceptable, that members can learn from them, and that conflict can be constructive,
4. the assumption that participation is expected according to readiness and capacity,
5. the view that self-disclosure is not dangerous and privacy is respected,
6. the expectation that members should assume increasing responsibility for their own functioning as time goes on, participating in decision making and evaluative processes,
7. a communication network that emphasizes interchange between the members,
8. a commitment to the group as an important event in the lives of the members, and
9. procedural norms about attendance, fees, confidentiality, space, seating, and so forth that are appropriate to a particular group.

These are not rules that the worker enforces: indeed, they cannot be enforced. They represent desirable conditions, based on values, through which the group can facilitate the growth and development of its members.

The worker strives to develop compatibility about norms. Similarities of expectations tend to create both stability and progress in therapeutic social systems. When asymmetry of expectations occurs, strain in communication is likely to follow. Periodic stress is bound to occur and is essential to progress. But when it is too severe in initial meetings, it is more likely to be disruptive to what is still a tenuous connection between the members. To resolve the problem of what members may expect and what may be expected of them appears to be an indispensable requisite for initiating the mutual aid system. Without some resolution of the problem of discrepancy in expectations, continuation in the group becomes doubtful.

Mutual Expectations

In the first one or two meetings, much of the content concerns mutual expectations. Leonard Brown found that exploration of expectations leads to congruence between worker and members on their attitudes toward the group.[22] They share similar perceptions concerning the experience. Workers of groups in which agreement was highest initiated the discussion of norms in the first meeting. These workers helped the members stay with the topic. They were able to pick up and respond to nonverbal cues indicating that a member might be ready to react to something said earlier. They were able to recognize and encourage expressions of feelings about the experience. In contrast, in those groups in which agreement was low, the workers were less likely to initiate the topic and to deal with it in early sessions. In one group of parents, for example, it was never clarified whether the group would focus on personal or family problems of members or engage in social action. The major conclusion of Brown's study was that developing mutual expectations as early as possible is significantly related to the effectiveness of group functioning and member satisfaction.

Clarity and compatibility about expectations not only prevent discontinuance but also have a positive effect on progress in problem solving. In a study, Charles Garvin found that when workers accurately perceived the expectations of members, their responses tended to be more appropriate and there was significantly greater movement in problem solving than in instances in which workers did not perceive the members' expectations correctly.[23] From a survey of research in the field of family service, Scott Briar concluded that "there is strong evidence, both from casework and psychotherapy research, that clients are more apt to continue in treatment when they and their therapists share similar expectations."[24]

Clarifying Expectations

Clarifying expectations occurs through a process of verbal interchange between the members. Even relatively nonverbal clients can participate if the worker uses activities through which members may express themselves and through which their capacities for verbally expressing their feelings and attitudes may be increased. The skills of the worker include the appropriate use of all of the interventions: supporting the members in their discussions, structuring the situation in ways that facilitate the expression of norms, providing information, clarifying norms, gently confronting members when they violate the accepted norms, and selecting appropriate content. But, as Edgar Schein points out, there are also special mechanisms for the creation and enforcement of norms.[25] The members are likely to develop and act in accordance with the norms if the worker systematically pays attention to certain messages that are communicated and ignores others, for example, by verbally supporting appropriate self-disclosure and efforts to try out new experiences, commenting on the extent to which there has been a spread of participation in discussion, or noting the absence of a member. Casual remarks or questions consistently geared to a certain area convey clear messages to members about the behavior expected of them.

Another way in which norms are transmitted is through education. By teaching the members how to listen and respond to each other, workers support the expectation that members will become able to communicate with each other. Still another mechanism for developing a group with therapeutic norms is the allocation of status and rewards. By the kind of activities proposed, for example, workers have an opportunity to stress cooperation rather than competition and success for all rather than success for some and failure for others.

Children want to set rules for their groups, sometimes more rigid ones than they are able to follow and sometimes quite realistic ones. In a group of six fifth-grade girls in a school, the worker explained the purpose of the group and engaged the members in playing a name game to get acquainted. After all of the girls had been introduced by a partner, the worker said:

> My name is Mrs. C. The important thing about me that I think you would want to know is that I'm not a teacher. I'm a social worker and I'm going to be your group leader, as I told you before.

MICHELLE: May I ask, If you're a social worker, why are you here? A social worker gives mothers a check.

KATHY: No, stupid. That's not what a social worker does.

MICHELLE: You're wrong.

KATHY: No, I'm not.

WORKER: Well, sometimes social workers do help a family to get a check, but they do many other things, too. Did you have another idea, Kathy?

KATHY: Yeah, you can call a social worker if your check doesn't come, and it has something to do with the county. But, another thing—if my brother was in trouble, my mother could ask the social worker to come and help her with the problem.

JEANINE: Does your mother have a social worker?

KATHY: (loudly and facing the worker) Last Christmas my mother fell in the garage and was knocked out all day. She's never been out that long before and the social worker came to help.

KIM: How long can we stay here?

WORKER: Until ten minutes after 1:00.

KATHY: I wish we could stay here all day.

KIM: Me, too.

WORKER: Do you want to continue to talk about social workers or . . .

BETTY: A social worker . . .

KATHY: My brother-in-law . . .

JEANINE: My mother had a social worker . . .

KATHY: I want to tell you about my brother-in-law.

WORKER: Kathy, could you please let Betty or Jeanine finish what they want to say? Could we listen to each other and let each one have a chance to talk?

JEANINE: Walking to the chalkboard, she wrote: Our Rules: (1) Listen to each other. (2) Give everyone a turn. (3) Say please, like Mrs. C. did. Kim went to the board and added: (4) Say please and be quiet instead of shut up.

JEANINE: (to Kim at the board) Please add, Be friendly to each other.

BETTY: (to Kim) And add, We can have fun talking here.

Through exploring the members' ideas, limiting Kathy's monopolizing behavior, and suggesting a norm, the worker stimulated the group to respond to the worker's intervention and, in a sense, made the worker's suggestions about shared communication their own. Although the members called them rules, they obviously are not regulations that can be enforced but rather statements about desired ways of behaving. Members of children's groups often set rules that are rigid and enforced through punitive means. Such rules have little place in social work. When they are proposed by members, the worker needs to comment on their inappropriateness to the group's purpose, explore with the members what they hope to accomplish through such rules, identify the underlying problems masked by rules, and work toward alternative solutions to the revealed problems.

In another group of depressed adolescent girls in foster homes, a norm of self-disclosure was established in the initial session.[26] Judith Lee and Danielle Park describe the following:

Pat asked, "What do we do here anyway?" I said the group was offered so they could discuss things that bother them as teenagers and as foster children. . . . I asked how that sounded to them. Pat said angrily, "I don't like that foster children part—neither the foster nor the children." I said, "Good—tell us more." She did, and the girls went into their reactions to the word *foster*—it means being on welfare and being unwanted—we're not on welfare and we're wanted. . . . Glenda said thoughtfully, "Being foster is like being some kind of new and strange race—nobody knows what to do with it." Serious nods. "Except to hide it," I said. "Yeah," and relieved laughter. I said, "Here you don't have to hide it and you can share what makes you mad about it." "Right on," Kenya said.

In response, the girls shared more about their experiences with foster and natural parents and learned it was safe to disclose their feelings, established commonality, and related the content of the group to its purpose.

Ethical Considerations

There may be wide disparity between the expectations that the worker has for the members and those of the members themselves, or there may be wide disparities between the members of the group. If they are to make good use of the group, the members need to know what rights and responsibilities they have in relation to each other and to the worker and what the basic rules are that govern their relationships with each other. An unequal power distribution is inherent in the differences between roles of members and workers, and practitioners are figures of authority. Roselle Kurland and Robert Salmon make it clear that to not provide the direction and limits that a group needs is to abdicate responsibility to serve the group effectively.[27] The members' perceptions may, however, exaggerate the extent or the facets of the worker's power. Clarification of expectations helps members to understand and assume the rights and responsibilities that are theirs. Workers likewise need to be sure that their expectations are relevant to the capacities and sociocultural milieu of the members.

Members often come to groups with some fear of the worker. One common fear is that the worker will violate the members' right to privacy by revealing to others what is known about them and that these revelations will be to the detriment of the members. Hence, dealing with these fears in the initial interviews is essential but needs to be repeated now so that all member have a common understanding. A direct statement that this group is one in which the members have the right to express what they feel and think, without fear that the worker will talk about them outside the group unless they are told about it first, usually suffices for a first meeting. The worker's sensitivity to the reactions of the members is a clue whether this theme needs to be pursued further. Confidentiality, though, is not limited to the worker, for members acquire information about each other. The worker serves as a model for the members in this respect, and in addition, expresses the hope that they will not share information about each other outside the group.

Children are often reluctant to discuss difficulties at home or at school because they are dependent upon their parents, guardians, or school personnel. They fear that what the worker shares with other adults will be used against them: they fear collusion between the worker and other adults. Work with children almost always involves work with the significant adults in their lives. Full confidentiality cannot be promised, but it is reassuring to the child to be told that the worker will be talking with certain adults, what the reasons are for doing so, and what kind of information will be shared and what will not be shared.

Members of groups have a right to expect that, when it is desirable, the worker will use information constructively in their behalf. Pertinent information may be given to appropriate persons in order that the best possible service may be provided. The agency is responsible to the client and also to the community that supports it and makes its services possible. This dual responsibility may create problems in applying the principle of confidentiality to specific situations. Mutual trust will be developed between the worker and the group as varied situations occur that are of concern to the members and as the worker deals with these in the person's best interests without violating the community's interest.

Content

The selection of content is a process that relates what is done to the purpose of the group. The major content of the initial stage concerns orientation to the worker, each other, and the group's purpose, structure, and norms. At the very beginning, topics introduced by members tend to be superficial and restricted. The members share demographic information, symptoms, or prior experiences with groups as a means of getting acquainted and learning what they have in common. Such a process reduces the sense of uniqueness and stigma associated with some problems and creates one of the first bonds between the members. When problems are mentioned, the members are often quick to give advice, which is the way they interpret the meaning of mutual aid or helping each other. They try to provide practical solutions to identified problems.

Exploration with members about what they prefer to discuss or to do provides a natural base for understanding their primary concerns and their readiness to deal with particular issues. Aaron Rosen and Dina Lieberman studied the relevance of content to the experiences of clients.[28] Their major finding was that a clear mutual orientation to the purpose of the session between worker and client assists the worker in keeping the focus on relevant content. Thus, content becomes directly related to purpose.

In a study of two groups of adoptive parents by Martha Gentry, discussion of preferences for content led to a consensus that the members wanted to deal with legal procedures in adoption, knowledge about parent-child relationships, the process of informing a child that he was adopted, and the reasons for placing a particular child with particular parents. The findings supported the importance of the worker's initiation and maintenance of an appropriate focus on themes that members felt to be important. According to Gentry, attrition is often related to the extent to which the member's expectations about content are met.[29] Sufficient commonalities between members are a requisite for continuing interaction over a period of time. Exploration is the primary set of interventions used to discover the common ground for discussion or the use of activity. The worker carries responsibility for assuring that the content selected will be such that the goals can be achieved.

Facilitating Group Interaction

Facilitating interaction between the members is one of the most important tasks of practitioners. In their participation in the group, social workers select and use specific skills within the major categories of structuring, support, exploration, information-education, and guidance-advice. Clarification tends to be limited to concerns about the purpose and properties of the group, the members' roles and expectations, and common concerns and interests. Confrontation may be used in the form of gentle requests but rarely in ways that seriously upset one or more members. Within the general categories of intervention, some specific acts are more appropriate during the early stage and some are less appropriate. Although there are common elements in all groups, workers' particular focus and activity are different with every group.

Examples from Practice

Two examples from practice may illustrate similarities and differences in the worker's role in facilitating group interaction during first meetings.

Young Girls   Ten seven- and eight-year-old girls came into a first meeting, excited about the invitation to be in a group, whose purpose was to help the members to succeed in school. The girls had been referred to the group because they were naughty in school, their academic work was unsatisfactory, and they were economically and socially disadvantaged.

Initially, the children were exceedingly quiet and conforming. I introduced myself, explaining in simple words what the group was for. I said,

"Your teachers told me that you wanted to be in this group so you could learn to do better in school. Do you think this is what you heard?" There was no response but positive nodding of heads. I continued, "Your parents gave permission for you to come. Here, we'll do things and talk about things that will help you get along better in school. How does that sound to you?" The girls looked intently at me but were silent, until one girl raised her hand and asked, "Do we all get to come, Teacher—is it for sure?" I reassured the girls about this, told them that I was not a teacher but a school social worker, and reviewed my name for them and wrote it on the board. Since there were no other comments or questions, I suggested that they get acquainted by playing a game. All enjoyed this game, so another one was introduced to help the girls to learn each other's and my name. The girls had difficulty following directions, so I simplified both the directions and the game itself. Some members enjoyed this and succeeded in it, but others gave up quickly when they could not remember a name. Two girls became restless and roamed around the room, investigating the equipment, but came back to the group when I announced that it was time for refreshments. In closing this short meeting, the girls were told about the schedule of twice weekly meetings. But it was apparent that they had no idea when Thursday would be. I said they need not worry about the day, for I would make plans with their teachers to remind them of the next meeting.

In such a group, it will take many sessions before the members become a working group, able to engage in a process of mutual aid.

Mothers of Preschool Children A second example is of a group of six mothers of preschool children that was organized in a child development center for the purpose of helping the mothers to become more effective in dealing with their young children. Through an application and study process, the women had become well acquainted with the clinic's purpose and procedures and had had several interviews with staff concerning the treatment plan for their children and the nature of their expected participation in the plan. Basic orientation to the group had been done through interviews. Furthermore, the women had all seen each other before as they waited for their children, who were in the same therapy group. These facts did not, however, mean that orientation in the group was not necessary.

In the first meeting, the worker was able rather quickly to review the purpose and plan for the group with the mothers and to engage them in some discussion of the group. She said, "You agreed to come to this group because each of you brought children to the clinic who are having emotional problems. The group can help you to relate better to your children and to learn how to help them get over their difficulties." With agreement to this statement, she asked the members to share with each other the reasons for coming and what they hoped to get from attendance here. Although each member differed in her pattern of participation, there was a general tendency to direct statements to the worker rather than to each other, to take turns in reporting, in a restrained manner with little expression of affect, on the symptoms of their children that brought them to the clinic, to look to the worker for approval of their comments, and to express their goals in terms of knowledge about children rather than of changes in their own attitudes and behavior. There was little spontaneous interaction. From here on, the major tasks for the worker were to elicit the expression of feelings about the situations that brought them to the clinic, to search for common ground underlying seemingly different problems and goals, to establish a network of spontaneous communication between the members themselves rather than perpetuate the individual-to-worker-and-back interactions, and to discover some preliminary focus for their work together.

During the first meeting, workers need to be supportive. They do not withhold information or support when the group needs it. They provide whatever information is relevant to the situation. Turning questions back to a group when the members simply do not have the necessary information is not helpful. Knowing when to give information directly to members and when to help them to use resources to find out the facts for themselves is an essential skill.

One of the most crucial skills is exploring, and responding sensitively to, the feelings of members. As workers observe the members and listen to them, they become able to recognize the members' feelings. They do this through observation of nonverbal cues such as facial expression, body posture, and gestures, as well as through the verbalized content. They understand the members' uncertainty and ambivalence and the meaning of some of their defensive maneuvers. As feelings are expressed, they meet them with a feeling response rather than an intellectual one. The principle is to respond to a feeling with a feeling response. Certain types of activity facilitate the expression of feelings; others inhibit such expression. Some forms of communication seem to be more effective than others. One effective skill is to show genuine interest in individuals through giving special attention or recognition. Through attending, workers communicate that they are taking in the uniqueness of a person and paying attention to the member. Another type of comment conveys acceptance of a member's feelings, particularly those that express doubt, hostility, or distrust. Whether or not the members can yet trust the workers' responses, they come to feel accepted and understood and begin to grasp what is expected of them.

The free but protected atmosphere of the group may be a new experience for many members. Particularly during a first session, workers avoid asking questions concerning the members' reasons for feeling or behaving in certain ways. Asking why tends to elicit defensive responses instead of releasing feelings and setting a problem-solving process to work. Such questions may be perceived as reprimands or be confusing to members who do not know what kind of answer is expected. A restatement of the feelings expressed by members can be effective, if workers put into words the feelings they sense the members are trying to express or restate them in a way that they are named and hence recognized. Often, the simplest responses are the most effective. To bring a feeling into the common ground of group experience, workers may ask whether the acknowledged feeling is shared by others. To be able to respond to the underlying meaning of the members's requests, challenges, or comments—interpretation—is an important skill. Within a climate that supports the expression of feelings, workers try not to stir up feelings that cannot be dealt with during the session. Urania Glassman and Len Kates advise that workers may need to modulate the expression of feeling.[30] Premature self-disclosure and exposure of members' vulnerabilities in early sessions may result in anxiety or embarrassment. Workers may make mental note of sensitive areas but hold them for discussion until the person or the group is ready to focus on them. If workers really desire to be helpful to the members and are sensitive to their feelings, their responses are likely to be appropriate.

Facilitating Communication

In some groups, members need help in learning how to communicate effectively within the group and in the community. In an example six recently discharged patients from a state hospital were living in a board and care facility in a large urban city. In the first meeting there had been considerable mistrust of the social worker and his role, several members expressing the fear that the worker would send them back to the hospital. There was, at the same time, a genuine reaching out or wanting to be included in the group. The worker records:

I began the second meeting by asking the members what they thought we might do to make our group a useful one for them. After several minutes of discussion, it seemed that learning to communicate better was a dominant theme. I said, "Well, it seems that we would like to try to understand better what each of us is trying to say—it can be very difficult sometimes to get across a simple message." The members picked up on this comment and talked about how hard it is for them to say what they want to say.

One member, who thus far had given the impression of taking the group as a joke, became very serious and said, "I been in lots of groups. Who knows which way the wind blows? There's too much hate in this room. It might kill us like it did the beautiful people. I feel the edge of pain and the what of sane." There was absolute silence. After waiting for some response, I said "Mark, I'm confused about what you want to tell us. I gather you have fears about being in this group." Mark did not reply, but Bob said, "That's the way Mark always talks—he says a lot of poetic bullshit that always turns me off." Shirley said, "That's what he's trying to do—get you to leave him alone." I asked, "Mark do you want us to leave you alone or were you trying to tell us something else?" He replied, "I just dig weird language."

I asked, "Could you tell us more about what digging weird language is like?" He said, "I just don't know . . . " Then, "I try to say what I mean—what I feel inside—but most of the time I can't do that, so I talk in images." I would have supported Mark at this point, but several members started grumbling, telling me all at the same time about Mark's refusal to talk to people directly. I wondered, "Can you talk to Mark directly instead of talking about him to me?" There was surprised silence. Minnie said, "Mark, I think you're playing games with us." Bob said, "I don't know about that—are you scared to say what you mean?" Mark responded, "I guess it's true. Talking to people scares me, so I guess I try to throw them off balance by making myself hard to understand." The members responded to this statement with considerable approval, culminating in the statement by one withdrawn girl, Cindy, who said, "I know how it feels to be scared, but it feels even worse to be lonely." I said that I understood it could be very painful to feel scared or lonely or both scared and lonely. Mark said, "Yeah, I'm both." I said that other members might have fears, too. There was strong nodding of heads as Bob said, "You've said it directly to us all." I said the group could help them with these feelings as we learn to talk more clearly to each other about things that matter to us.

In making a contribution to the group interaction, workers need to follow the manifest content of the conversation at the same time that they seek to understand the latent content, as was true of the worker in this example. The manifest content consists of the literal and obvious meanings of the verbal messages; the latent content is what is below the threshold of superficial observation.[31] It may be just below the level of awareness, subject to ready recall, or it may be at the unconscious level. Every comment can have more than one meaning. Discovering latent content involves the capacity to ascertain the meaning behind the words. Nonverbal communication may offer clues to latent content, as evidenced in body language, tension, or affect that seems inappropriate to the content. The latent content may extend and add meaning to the manifest content or may contradict it. If the former, the process of communication is enhanced; if the latter, mutual understanding is hampered.

To make sense out of the often apparent unrelated contributions of the members, workers search for the underlying common threads of feelings and meaning and responses to these. They try to discover how a succession of comments and questions by members is linked together around an underlying concern common to a number of members. For example, a common concern in first meetings is often that of inclusion—whether the members really want to belong and feel others want to include them. This concern is seldom expressed directly, but sensitive workers make the inference from their observations of the verbal and nonverbal cues provided in subtle ways during the meeting.

Social workers need to follow the interaction process itself. There is a reciprocal influence of people on each other as they participate in the conversation. Practitioners are concerned with the nature and spread of feelings, opinions, and ideas, who interacts with whom, who initiates behaviors, and who follows the initiator. They are interested in discovering the factors that create a beginning sense of mutuality between the members and, on the other hand, with the sources of tension and conflict in the group.

To open up communication between members, workers seek out the blocks to communication in the group that may be due to physical limitations, interpersonal hostilities, or to differences in culture, knowledge, or values. They assess each member's ability to listen, to observe, and to respond to the message of others with or without distortion of those messages.

Young children need to learn to communicate with the worker, often in new ways. Many children are expected to listen and to obey adults and to respond only to specific questions asked them. Often, they are not expected to enter into discussion with adults present—to give, as well as take, in reciprocal verbal communication. The worker needs to develop interest in the children's viewpoints and to be able to enter into the world of childhood so that they can talk with each other. To talk with children in language suitable to the children's level of understanding without talking down to them is a precious attribute in a worker. Children are not as nonverbal as is often assumed. The clue, to a large extent, is in the adult who is able to listen, to enter into the child's world, and to talk simply and concretely with the appropriate amount of seriousness or playfulness as indicated by the child's mood. Adults, too, have their troubles in listening and talking. Observations of the capacities for communication of the members are used by the worker in making a professional judgment about when to enter the conversation, when to intervene in an activity for a particular reason, and when to support silently the interacting processes within the group.

Motivation to Continue in the Group

Hope is a powerful motivating force. Therefore, it is important that members leave the first group meeting with a sense that the group has the potential to help them meet needs they see themselves as having. Before the closing of the first session, social workers often give a brief summary of what has happened in the group thus far. They make sure the members understand the arrangements for meetings, in terms of time and place, and explore any concerns or problems about such matters. They engage the members in a decision to try out the group a little longer. They elicit from members, or suggest, some immediate goals to be worked on in the next session. They create a bridge to the next meeting. It is hoped that, during the meeting, they have provided a fair test of what it will be like to be in the group through the provision of some immediate satisfactions in doing something together, identifying interests and concerns, and making some satisfying personal or corporate decisions.

In the early period of group life, it is desirable to focus on shared experiences as a basis for the development of motivation. Members usually behave in compliant ways in order to protect themselves from feeling different and from being rejected by others. Initially, discussion or activity should provide for some immediate sense of learning something that is valued or that brings gratification. Early discussion, though scattered, tends to promote a feeling of belonging and reduces the members' anxious feelings. At any one time, there are diverse topics available for consideration by the group, from which a selection is made, either by formal decision or through the influence of a central theme that underlies free-flowing discussion. When clients are in a group, satisfying relationships between the members are at least as important as is the worker-individual relationship. Such relationships develop as the members discover the needs and interests they have in common that outweigh the perceived differences between them. Especially in this stage of the group's development, the worker needs to help the members focus on their commonalities and not on their differences.

Social workers hope that the experience members have had in the first meetings will be such that they will want to continue. Far too often, persons drop out before they have had experience sufficient to be able to make wise decisions for themselves. A number of studies have reported that difficulties in communication and lack of understanding between the worker and client are factors related to unplanned discontinuance after the first session.[32] In a study of adult clients' reactions to initial interviews, it was learned that clients' willingness to commit themselves to a relationship with a helping person was related to two goals: the achievement of some progress in the solution of a problem and a degree of social satisfaction from the relationship with the helping person.[33] In another study, the willingness of adolescents to see a helping person again was positively associated with a perception of the practitioner's desire to help and his ability to understand.[34]

In still another study, lack of information was found to be an important factor in dropouts. So, too, were expectations about treatment. Reporting on research with college students, Yolanda Slocum concluded that "the more favorable the pre-treatment expectations, the greater the likelihood of remaining in treatment and the better the outcome.[35] Factors in the social environment also influence continuation. When there are readily available alternative resources for service, or relevant other persons who do not support the person's quest for professional help, the client is more likely to discontinue.[36]

A Tentative Contract

The members are ready to move into the next stage of group development when a tentative agreement or contract has been reached between the worker and the members concerning (1) the purpose of the group and the ways that individual goals can be met within it, (2) the expectations for the roles of worker and member and the major norms, and (3) the major means of determining content. It is generally agreed that compatibility is fundamental in ascertaining the direction, quality, and content of the group experience. The values of such a contract, according to Anthony Maluccio and Wilma Marlow, are as follows: (1) it is derived from the shared experience in exploring all aspects of the service, (2) it gives both the worker and members a sense of involvement and signifies mutual commitment, and (3) it provides a baseline for periodic review of progress toward the achievement of goals and the conditions of the contract.[37]

A. K. T. Tsang and Marilyn Bogo emphasize compatibility rather than agreement. They state that engagement of members in cross-cultural practice involves trust and compatibility, meaning that differences are recognized and accepted. Complete agreement is not necessary.[38] The preliminary contract is flexible, to be reviewed and modified as the group develops. Garvin reminds us that "from an ethical point of view, the idea of contract has roots in social work's commitments to the self-determination of the client so that the client is not manipulated toward ends he does not seek through means he does not accept."[39]

Guidelines for Practice

When people enter a group for the first time, they tend to feel uncertainty and anxiety about the unknown experience, their relationships with the worker and other members, and whether they will want to be included as a member. Thus, the major tasks for the worker are to develop initial relationships and to orient members to the group. To accomplish these tasks, social workers do the following:

1. Become aware of their own emotional reactions to the members and reflect on what they need to do to be able to relate to each member with acceptance, empathy, and genuineness.
2. Initiate beginning relationships between the members by modeling acceptance, empathy, and genuineness, providing emotional support for efforts to participate in the group, expressing confidence in the potential of the group for meeting their needs, searching for the common ground between members and explaining it to them, and acknowledging the typical feelings that people have in entering a group.
3. Orient the members to the initial plan for the group by presenting essential information and encouraging feedback and suggestions for modifying the plan, discussing ways that goals of individuals can be met within the group's purpose, clarifying expectations concerning the roles of worker and members, and explaining such simple matters as time, place, frequency, and content of sessions.
4. Facilitate group interaction in discussions and activities by suggesting that members question and respond to each other, searching for compatibility between members and with the worker concerning goals, capacities for relationships, and interests.
5. Reach a tentative agreement on what the group is for, its purpose, and how it will work by reviewing the group's use of the first meetings and seeking responses, ascertaining the degree of agreement concerning the preliminary plan for the group, and expressing hope that members will want to be included in the group and return for the next meeting.

It is clear that social workers use their knowledge of human behavior and social systems to help a collection of individuals become a group. The major interventions used are strong doses of support, education-information, clarification of feelings and the plan for the group, and facilitation of the group process. It is likely that members of a group will continue beyond the first meeting if they feel that something happened in the group that was useful to them in the way of a relationship, an attitude of hopefulness, a concrete experience, or a meaningful idea and if they have some sense of knowing what to expect next time. If other significant persons in the environment support their decision to join the group, their own positive attitudes toward it will be reinforced. They will be ready to engage in an active process of further exploring and testing out the potential in the group for meeting their needs.

13 Stage II: Uncertainty-Exploration

Involvement of members in a group does not occur during a brief period of orientation. Following the initial stage, there is a period of exploration of relationships and uncertainty about power. Through engaging in a process of testing the relationship to the worker and each other, members become committed to the group. As uncertainty is resolved, the satisfaction of the members is enhanced and the members are freed to work together on issues, which furthers the group's transition into the next stage.

The first core concern of the members was inclusion, directly related to feelings of ambivalence about their suitability for membership in the group. In this stage, there is further development of the relationship between the worker and members and between the members themselves. The relationship to the worker is sorely tested as some members rebel against the power they perceive the worker to have over them. Members are concerned about how the worker will use that power: will the worker permit them to gain autonomy over their own affairs within appropriate limits? As they test the worker's use of power, the members are learning more about each other, too.

During this time, workers are examining their own feelings and opinions in relation to whatever objections the members have to their use of authority. They realize that the rebellion is not against them personally, which makes it more likely that they will be able to help the members to understand the worker's role. They also become increasingly sensitive to each member's developing relationships with other members.

James Garland, Hubert Jones, and Ralph Kolodny view the major task of the social worker in this stage as dealing with the emotional issues of power and control.[1] Linda Schiller views it as the development of supportive relationships between the members.[2] Indeed, instead of one or the other, work on these two issues seems to go on simultaneously: actually, power and control are components of relationships. The development of supportive relationships through testing the process of acceptance-rejection and reducing uncertainty over power leads to opportunities for the members to find mutual support and intimacy in the group.

Uncertainty over power and control is to be regarded not as an obstacle to be overcome but as behavior consistent with the democratic values of social work in enabling people to participate effectively in the group, with the accompanying power inherent in it. Power may indeed be a force used against other people. But, according to Barbara Solomon, power is the ability to mobilize internal and external resources to achieve some desired goal.[3] It need not reside in one, or a few, but can be broadly distributed. The worker strives to give the members as much power as they are capable of using and helps them to develop that capacity.[4]

Feelings of uncertainty are inevitable, often taking the form of hostility toward the worker. The hostility may be overt or subtle and suppressed, expressed indirectly through complaints about other people, the group, or the organization. Members tend to imbue the worker with unrealistic attributes: if expectations are too high, disappointment is inevitable. The members have their own needs, which they seek to satisfy. The worker cannot meet all the members' dependency needs, their desires to be the one and only, to be loved by everyone, or to succeed in all things. Neither does the worker fulfill the traditional authority roles of teachers, parents, and employers. The members, instead, are expected to share with others and seek their own solutions to problems. The needs and dissatisfactions are varied, but they are concerned with relationships between people.

Members have varied behavioral responses to the tension and uncertainty. They form alliances with other members in pairs or larger subgroups, they maintain aloofness, suppress hostility, or they leave the group. Through the shift of some power from the worker to the members, the members gain a sense of power to cope with their own personal and environmental problems. Authority issues will recur throughout the life of the group, but if the first one is satisfactorily resolved, power no longer tends to be the major issue. Working through the power struggle is essential, leading to mutual acceptance between members and mutual attraction of the members to the group.

The Tasks of Social Workers

During this stage of group development, the members interact with the worker and each other to test out the meaning of the group experience for them and to determine their roles and status in the group. The members begin to examine themselves in relation to the group. They explore the views of each other in relation to the group; as they do so, their awareness of similarities and differences between them becomes acute, resulting in considerable ambiguity and tension. Through dynamic decision-making processes, the members modify their original perceptions of the group and try to change it so that it will feel like their own group, one with which they identify and that, for them, becomes an important reference group. For this to happen, the major tasks of the leader are to

1. further develop understanding of the members and of the group as a social system,
2. strengthen relationships between the worker and between the members through working out authority conflicts,
3. enhance positive motivation and reduce resistance,
4. support the members in their exploration of the group's purpose and their goals,
5. stabilize membership,
6. develop a flexible structure of status and roles,
7. work toward resolution of uncertainty and tension, and
8. engage in activities beyond the group in behalf of members.

These tasks are essential to the development of a viable working agreement and a cohesive group.

These tasks make heavy demands on the social worker's knowledge and skills as well. Unfortunately, giving inadequate attention to this stage of group development occurs too frequently. For example, in a qualitative study of records of a parent education group, Nancy Sullivan found that the group did not move beyond this stage. The worker maintained strict control, driven by an agenda. She was so adamantly focused on the achievement of tasks that the interpersonal forces between the members were overlooked. Dealing with differences between new and old members was viewed as an impediment to progress in learning the educational content. The worker seemed not to notice scapegoating, lack of participation, and misunderstandings between members. The members' needs and desires for emotional connectedness were regularly evident, "rising to the surface and popping through the structure into the active life of the group." Members who deviated from the topics were labeled as sidetrackers. Sullivan describes this group as "worker-driven" and "worker-owned."[5]

Assessment of the Group

Assessment of groups goes hand in hand with continuing efforts to evaluate the problems and strengths of the members. In assessing the group at any given time, workers reflect on the following questions:

1. To what extent are members clear about the purpose of the group and their own related goals?
2. Is the group in a state of dynamic balance, in crisis, or in a state so static that it is unable to cope with change?
3. What is the nature and quality of interpersonal relations between the members and with the worker, with special attention to the conflicts between the worker and members, between the members, and in the group's interactions with other systems?
4. How much congruence or difference is there between the members concerning values and expectations?
5. What is the meaning to individual and group development of the structure and composition of the group and of the pattern of statuses and roles that emerge out of group interaction?
6. How open or closed are the channels of communication and what are the blocks to effective communication?
7. How effective is the group in using problem solving to cope with difference and conflict?
8. What are the personal and impersonal controls within the group and how effective are they?
9. What is the relationship of the group to other social systems in the environment in terms of conformity to or deviance from the norms of the community?

Through such an assessment, social workers discover problems in the group. But, more important, they discover the common ground among the members that can be built on to resolve conflicts and work toward achievement of the group's purpose.

Strengthening Relationships

Relationship to social worker. The social worker is an authority figure with professional power. Most people come to a group with some attitudes toward and problems with authority. The members need to resolve their ambivalence about their relationship with the worker and begin to view each other as sources of support and help.[6]

Often members have had little prior experience with social workers and hence have to learn what to expect from them. Their expectations tend to be colored by experiences with persons in other authority roles. They may become bewildered and confused when workers do not live up to their expectations concerning power and control, may use certain devices to learn about the worker's role and expectations, and may test the worker in subtle or obvious ways. The testing may last for only a brief period. It may be prolonged, if workers have difficulty in understanding and accepting the members, are inconsistent in their responses to them, or ambiguous about expectations, the purpose of the group, its operating procedures, and the roles of worker and member. Or it may be prolonged, if workers are authoritarian in the use of power or make unrealistic promises to the members. If workers have a need to avoid or deny conflict, it will be enacted in more subtle ways or displaced elsewhere. It will be prolonged also in groups composed of persons who have had prior unsatisfactory or disturbed relationships, particularly with persons in positions of authority. The tension and ambivalence about the members' relationships with the worker have their roots in both reality and transferred reactions.

Members of groups commonly test the use workers will make of their power to limit and control them. They may provoke them to use that power; compare them unfavorably with other leaders of groups they have known to learn whether they will become defensive or retaliate; make comments about the worker's race, age, status, or physical appearance; and often test how far the worker will permit them to break rules, behave in unacceptable ways, or hurt themselves before intervening. In such ways, they seek proof that the worker will protect them against their own and each other's hostile impulses.

Such maneuvers also serve as a means of discovering the boundaries to the right to self-determination of individuals and autonomy of the group.

In natural groups particularly, some of the behavior of the members may be with the intent of testing out whether the worker will usurp the role of the group's elected officials or of its indigenous leaders. The worker makes explicit the safeguards that will be provided so that the group can take responsibility for itself as soon as possible. The safeguard for self-responsibility is usually the democratic process itself. The right of the group to make its own decisions whenever possible is based on the principles that it is important for people in this society to learn to govern their own lives and that growth is more likely to occur when changes are felt to be self-initiated rather than authoritatively imposed. Therefore, the active and central role of the social worker, essential in the initial stage, must not continue indefinitely. The worker must release responsibility to the members as they become able to assume it: some power must shift from the worker to the members.

Being in a position of power is often an issue for social workers.[7] They may deny that they do have authority and its concomitant responsibility for the welfare of the group. The worker's feelings about power and about sharing it are tested. Workers may have had negative experiences with figures of authority themselves and may therefore be uncomfortable with the role. They may want to be liked by the members, to be thought of as a friend, and to be democratic. They may confuse democracy with laissez-faire leadership. They may deal with their feelings by abdicating the role or by becoming authoritarian. Such behaviors tend to provoke severe testing by the members, who expect the worker to give professional opinions and take appropriate action in the group, while always respecting the members' right to question those opinions and actions.

Clearly tied to the conflict over the worker's power and the way it is exerted are the members' continual concerns about their status and power in the group, combined with ongoing concerns about trust and acceptance. Members of groups often need to determine whether they can trust the worker and each other with feelings of hurt and anger and whether they accept each other. They gradually become more able to express their feelings and concerns. Sheila Thompson and J. H. Kahn point out that the process that operates is based on the use of two types of information.[8] Each member hears about the feelings and ideas of others and also perceives the reactions to the messages sent by the worker. Each disclosure stimulates the members, leading to another comment, until more and more information is disclosed.

The members learn that the feared consequences of self-exposure do not happen.

Underlying the conflicts over power and control, according to Baruch Levine, is a quest for acceptance as full-fledged members of the group, with some degree of influence or power in it.[9] It is natural to be uncertain and ambivalent until trust is established. In most groups, the members seek proof that the worker accepts and cares about them. Being absent may be a test of whether the worker missed a member. A request for a special favor from the worker or an offer of gifts to the worker may serve the purpose. Learning how the worker reacts to a range of behavioral patterns may be a means of testing acceptance. The members may behave in ways they feel might be disapproved of by workers because they want to see the workers' limits and the ways in which they will use their power.

A group of adolescent girls, for example, asked permission to comb their hair. When told they could do this, the girls tried out every bizarre hairstyle to test the worker's reactions to styles that were forbidden by school authorities. They also tested the worker by using foul language. When the worker commented that these words did not shock her or make her angry, the behavior stopped. Such nonjudgmental behavior can be more effective than trying to impose rules. A similar maneuver by members is to confess to feelings or behavior that might bring disapproval. When workers are able to clarify with members the fact that they are not interested in placing blame and that their acceptance is not dependent upon conforming behavior, the testing is reduced or stopped. This example from a third meeting of a group of depressed adolescent girls in foster care, presented in the previous chapter, illustrates the challenges to social workers in this stage of development.[10]

After some talk about boyfriends, there was a silence. I waited. Pat then wanted to know why social workers care and why they come around, anyway. I sat silently; then said, "It is rough when you don't live with your natural parents; you have to go through a lot of change." Cherise said sadly that she doesn't think that anyone loves you like your natural mother who "birthed" you. Some of the others agreed and each shared her fantasy around how easy and beautiful life would be with her natural mother. Cherise added, "Social workers are all alike; they say, oh how sad, how can I help you? But they can't do anything unless they can bring my mother back." Silence. Then Pat said to me, "Well, what do you think of that?" I had trouble answering, so I asked what they thought, but Cherise asked me again. I then said, "No one can bring a mother or father back and I can hear you are angry about that. You are also wondering what life would have been like with your parents. You hope it would be better than you have now." There were nods and comments of agreement. I said that it is rough, but maybe this group can help to make things better for them by helping them to deal with the things on their minds and the way things are for them now. We shared a thoughtful silence and they began to clean the room.

———

In this situation, the worker responded to Pat's question by ignoring the hostility and responding instead empathically, based on understanding the members' situations. This brought out Cherise's anger and sense of hopelessness and Pat's subsequent challenge to the worker. She then shared her recognition of what the members were feeling, provided strong support and gently offered some hope for change. It is important that the girls deal directly with issues of foster care and express their feelings freely; acceptance of the feelings is a step toward help. In such a situation, assessment of individuals, as well as of the group process, is crucial; for example, knowing that Cherise is the only member whose birth mother is dead helps the worker to understand the depth of Cherise's depression.

There are groups in which one or more members are extremely dependent upon the worker. Such members expect their workers to fulfill the role of a parent figure; they show their feelings by making exaggerated efforts to please them or seek their exclusive attention, being rivalrous with other members for the worker's love and attention, seeking praise or reproof for their actions, or commenting unrealistically, "You never think I can do anything right." They may seek a close relationship with the worker but become frightened by the feelings of closeness, may fear they will be hurt, may try to withdraw from the group or provoke rejection, or may make unreasonable demands on the worker and then feel rejected when these cannot be met.

Distrust of a practitioner may be tied to stereotyped perceptions of differences between the worker and members. Differences between a worker and a group on any characteristic that tends to create or maintain social distance are initially bars to mutual acceptance. The distrust is often aggravated when there are efforts to avoid facing or denying the difference. Some examples are a group of aged clients with a young worker, a black worker with a group of white adults, or vice versa, or a nonhandicapped worker with a group of orthopedically handicapped patients. One example is of a socialization group of black girls between the ages of eleven and thirteen. The worker is black also, but of a lighter complexion and with a different texture of hair than the girls.

Marcia was a new member and was with us for the first time. I asked the group to clue her in on some of the things that we had been doing. Frances and Susan responded, telling her about the group's activities. Marcia seemed preoccupied, however. When the girls finished telling her about the group, she looked at me directly and asked, "Why do you have to have all the good hair—why couldn't I have it?" Before I could respond, the other members chimed in with such statements as: "Yeah, you make us sick. All light-skinned people think they're cute. Yeah, just like this girl in school." This led to talking about the girl in school. After a while, I interrupted by saying, "I can see that you have certain ideas about me. Maybe we should take the time to talk about them." Frances said that so far as she was concerned there was nothing to talk about—this is how they felt. The others expressed strong agreement. Attempts to engage them further were fruitless: they became absorbed in the project they were working on. The crucial issues were lack of self-esteem and the impact of color on people. My own discomfort with the issue of color led me to go along with the members' avoidance of it rather than help the girls to understand and face the differences.

Open recognition of such differences may not only break down barriers to communication but also lead to enhancement of a positive sense of identity. One example is a group of seven adolescent black girls whose members had been adjudicated as delinquents and assigned to a white worker for help with improving their socially unacceptable behavior. For the fourth meeting of the group, the leader had invited the members to a neighborhood center for a swim. She knew that the girls loved to swim, but she also knew that the obvious differences in physical characteristics would be accentuated in this situation. As one girl groaned over the problems of straightening her hair, the worker used this opportunity to acknowledge the outward differences between the races and to comment on how this might make it hard for them to trust her and work with her in the group. This comment led to discussion of the girls' feelings about their race and their troubles with white people. This activity, designed with a particular purpose, marked the turning point in the group's relationship with the worker.

Simple acknowledgment of differences, whether they be of race or age or ethnicity or other descriptive characteristic, often leads to further exploration of them. The worker facilitates the exploration of the meaning of differences and the members' expression of feeling about such differences. That contributes to a reduction in distortions of perception of others occasioned by feelings about such differences. The need to accept difference is accompanied by a need to identify and express whatever will tend to further a sense of unity between the worker and members.

Recognition of the group's various forms of dissatisfaction is important in establishing and continuing a purposeful working relationship with the group. To pass these tests, workers need to assess accurately the meaning of the words or actions of individuals and the level of the group's development at a given time. They need to be sufficiently secure to be able to accept expressions of indifference or hostility without retaliation. This is not always easy. They need to support the ventilation of feelings and concerns, unless contraindicated. Communication of feelings may be indirect. An example is of a natural group of children in which members talked to the worker through each other. In complaining about each other, the real target of communication was the worker. The members of the group also asked questions such as "Why does teacher always meddle with us?" when feelings were those toward the worker. Workers can often assess the real target of the communication through the tone of voice used, the direction of eye movements, or the accompanying gestures. Likewise, members may talk with each other indirectly.

Awareness and acceptance of their feelings toward the testing maneuvers on the part of workers are an important prelude to an ability to understand the members' use of the testing process and to respond in appropriate ways. Owing to preoccupation with problems in relationships, workers might well remember the need for expression and acceptance of positive feelings. Indeed, they welcome and encourage instances of affection. They assure the members of their interest in them and of their desire to support them in their efforts.

Relationships between members. A major task for social workers is to strengthen relationships between the members. They do not just establish a relationship with individuals and then focus on group relationships, but rather simultaneously work on both. The members not only test the worker; they also test each other, using essentially similar devices as in testing the worker. The worker helps the group identify positive ties as they develop as well as recognize difficulties and conflicts.

Rivalries and tensions between members may occur in tiny ways. Sylvia Zamudio, for example, reported that in the second session of a bereavement group composed of nine- to eleven-year-old boys and girls, Mat was seated near the worker. When Mike, a new member, stared at him with a tough demeanor, Mat quickly got up and moved to another chair. Mike took Mat's seat.[11] Such seemingly minor events may escape the worker's attention but escalate into group conflict. Recognition of differences brings them into the problem-solving processes of the group.

Social distance between members is a crucial issue in heterogeneous groups composed of members who differ on such factors as race, ethnicity, religion, age, or sexual orientation. Subgroups tend to develop between members with similar characteristics. To help members accept each other, social workers first need to be in touch with their own feelings and perceptions and recognize those of the members. They need to recognize that members of minority ethnic groups are apt to perceive themselves as having less power than members of the dominant white population.

Struggles for power or acceptance often deal with misperceptions and negative valuations of the differences. Workers often want to ignore the differences, but they will not go away. They need to open up the issue for discussion with the intent of having the group become a safe place for self-disclosure and learning to accept diversity. David Bilides gives an example.[12] A member said, "Get your black ass away from me." Using gentle confrontation, the worker asked, "What does her being black have to do with your anger?" After some preliminary bantering, the worker could help the group to discuss tendencies to stereotype, recognizing how people use ethnic and racial slurs to insult others and achieve power over them.

Recognition of differences brings them into the arena of the problem-solving processes of the group. Through exploration of differences, the members may come to understand that negative feelings exist side by side with more comfortable ones. Workers need to reach out and give to members in appropriate ways. They identify and express their awareness of common interests, concerns, and feelings as these develop in the group. They suggest ways in which members can be helpful to each other. What needs to get worked through in this stage is not only ambivalence toward the worker as a person, and the power of the professional role, but also feelings of competitiveness and rivalry between the members for status and acceptance. The effective practitioner recognizes that working on problems of relationships to each other often precedes working on other problems. With each experience in trying to work it out, the members become increasingly able to recognize and handle conflict. It is how the worker helps them to handle these conflicts that determines whether the group bond will become sufficiently strong so that the members can use the group more intensively for help with other problems.

Enhance Positive Motivation — Reduce Resistance

An integral part of the work in this stage is to enhance positive motivation and reduce resistance. The purposes of resistance are several. Resistance preserves the steady state or existing equilibrium. Any major change disturbs the existing balance of forces, and fear of change may be greater than is the discomfort felt from the problem. Resistance is a means of warding off anxiety, protecting the personality from hurt, and preserving the immature satisfactions and secondary gains that accompany a particular kind of relationship or problem.

The members provide clues that resistance is operating. Being resistant is seldom a conscious process. A person does not say, "I'm going to resist the efforts to help me"; rather, the resistant behaviors are at the preconscious or unconscious levels of experience. The clues are numerous. One clue is the way time is used: coming late, leaving early, or being absent. Another indication consists of maneuvers to control the situation so as to avoid facing issues. Examples are complaining, verbosity or monopolization, arguing to prove that others are wrong rather than to find answers, or prolonged joking or laughing. Other behaviors to avoid facing issues are changing the subject, minimizing issues, denying, forgetting, withholding facts, talking about the past in order to avoid dealing with the present, quickly confessing or admitting guilt to ward off the need to explore the situation, or being unwilling to consider suggestions made by the worker or other members. Many interpersonal responses are largely colored by transference reactions such as dependency, flattery, seduction, berating others, questioning the competence of others, subtle insults, anger that is not realistic to the situation, and open or overt hostility. Such barriers to the effective use of the group experience are built out of the multiple stresses in the lives of members.

Explore and Clarify Purpose

As discussed in chapter 7, exploration and clarification of purpose is not a task to be completed in one or two sessions. It is a continuous process of definition and redefinition of both the long-range and immediate purposes as these become more specific and as they undergo gradual changes. In this stage, as members interact around the primary issues of authority and control, their capacities and needs become known to themselves and the worker, making possible the development of realistic goals. This can be a tremendous relief to the members. The worker's verbal recognition of the commonality of their situations tends to strengthen motivation to use the group for goal achievement. People hear selectively so that, being preoccupied with other concerns in the orientation stage, they take in only part of the explanation and discussion of purpose. Later, they are eager to explore and clarify the purpose for the group and its meaning to them.

In one group of thirteen- and fourteen-year-old boys, for example, this event did not occur until the fourth meeting.

One member commented that here he was again, but he didn't even know how he happened to be in the group. The worker commented that perhaps others wondered about this, too. When he got confirmation of this concern from others, the worker explained that they had been referred by the vice principal of the school. Another boy said he guessed that meant they were the worst kids in the whole school. Following a spontaneous period of complaining about the vice principal, the worker explained that all of them were in trouble in school and that, through the group, it was hoped that they could talk about some of these troubles and do things together that would make it possible for them to get along better. He added that he remembered that one of them had said that being sent to the group meant they were the worst boys in the school; this was not so, and he did not feel that way about them. Feeling accepted by the worker, the members were ready to listen to an explanation and to discuss the purpose for the group and their reactions to the group.

To be noted in this example is the social worker's use of many categories of skills. Within an accepting relationship, the worker offered support in the form of sensitive listening, reassurance, and hope, he structured the situation by focusing the flow of communication, he explored for feelings and opinions, he encouraged the ventilation of complaints and concerns, he provided information, and he clarified the purpose of the group and reasons for referral. He facilitated the group process by seeking responses from the members and by identifying commonalities.

Adults, too, often have doubts about what the worker sees as the real purpose of the group. The following excerpt is taken from a meeting of a group of mothers in a mental health clinic.

———

Mrs. D. asked if the clinic had planned this group because the staff felt the mothers had the problems or was it planned so that the child would be given help. Mrs. B. thought we are here because the clinic thinks that we are to blame for the kids' problems. "Well, I certainly don't agree with that," said Mrs. P. Mrs. J. asked if the group might be set up for both purposes. The worker asked if she could explain what she meant by that. She said she thought that we do have some problems and by meeting together we would be helped and, in turn, the child would be helped. Mrs. O. turned directly to me and said, "I guess you're the only one who knows why we are here." I said I would review with them the original purpose for the group, but I wondered if first they would make some comments about how they see the reasons for meeting. Each of the members responded, some of them mentioning that they had already seen improvement in their children; some saying they wanted to get ideas from others; two saying they found they were not all alone; and one commenting that this was different somehow from just talking to her neighbor about the child. They shared some of their feelings of being different from other members because of the age of the child, their marital status, and their work. Mrs. K. said that she thought all the mothers were learning how to relieve their own irritation at the child, which makes it easier for them and is also helpful to the child. All of them said they agreed with Mrs. K. and gave examples of what they had learned in the preceding meeting.

I pulled together some of the comments the members had made about the reasons for these meetings. I noted that it was true that they would not all benefit in the same way and that I was pleased they could express how they felt. I restated the purpose of the group as explained in the first meeting: it was to help them to become better able to help their children. We are not blaming them for their children's difficulties. That means that, as one of them said earlier, it is to help both mothers and children. The help given to the children here is important, but more important is the parents' understanding and ability to help the child. Mrs. K. said that she liked that idea: if we could learn to be better parents our children would benefit. All the members seemed relieved to have clarified the group's purpose in relation to their own goals.

Motivation for change is related to the extent to which there are shared perceptions by members of the need for change. As the members recognize that the group's purpose is related to the shared needs of the members, a sense of some pressure toward change develops. Individuals' recognition that their own goals can be met within the group, when these are not in conflict with the general purpose of the group, provides strong motivation toward more involvement in and effective use of the group. Not only do workers encourage questions and reactions to the purpose of the group, they also work toward the recognition and elaboration of the objectives of individuals and toward discussion of how one member's goals are similar to those of others or how different goals can be accommodated within the group. They recognize the varied ways by which members make requests for help. A comment by a member, "I'll drop by your office," "I want to go home last" or a nonverbal request in the form of lingering after other members leave often signifies readiness to share concerns and goals with the worker. These requests are usually met with clarification of how the group may be used for help and how the individual's concern, even if unique, can be related in some way to the concerns of others.

Mutuality of goals is not necessarily achieved through talk alone. Activities may be used to identify problems and hoped for outcomes. An illustration is of a group of young boys and girls on a pediatrics ward in which the worker engaged them in playing doctor and patient to identify for them some of their feelings and concerns about being in a hospital and to relate the problems of one child to those of others and to the purposeful use of the group.

When social work service is expected to continue beyond several sessions, it tends to be focused on a constellation of goals, as contrasted with the single purpose typical of brief service. Clarity about goals on the worker's part and the members' part and, more important, congruence between the two perceptions is not achieved in one or two meetings. One outcome of the second stage of group development is that members come to perceive with greater clarity what they want to achieve for themselves through the use of group experience.

A group of young adult patients with mental illness had been unable to participate verbally in formal discussion of the group's purpose until the ninth session of the group. An excerpt from this meeting follows:

VICTOR: What did you say this group is for?

ELAINE: To help with what's troubling us and to help us stay out of the hospital.

VICTOR: Sounds like group therapy to me.

ELAINE: Well that's what it is.

VICTOR: Not to me—group therapy is so boring.

ELAINE: Well, it would make me happy if we could agree that this is group therapy. OK. Tell us what this group is, Victor.

VICTOR: It is a semisocial self-help group.

JONATHON: Why do you call it that?

ELAINE: You said social?

VICTOR: Sure. I don't know what I'd do with my Thursday nights if I didn't come here.

JONATHON: I don't get that and I don't get the self-help idea.

ELAINE: Yeah, you said self-help?

VICTOR: Uh, huh . . . by talking we might help ourselves to learn about our problems and . . . uh, uh, well, and to overcome them.

ELAINE: Well, that is almost like what I said the group is—and that's therapy.

VICTOR: (laughing) Well, all right, but we don't have to call it that.

WORKER: Maybe we ought to hear what the rest of you think, because no matter how it was explained when you first came here, the group has a different meaning to you after you've been here awhile.

VICTOR: To me, it's a step to help you.

JONATHON: Oh, ahh . . .

VICTOR: To help you get out and socialize.

JONATHON: You mean to help you mingle with other people until you get enough confidence to be with other people—other than those of us who were in hospitals.

VICTOR: You said it—that's it.

JONATHON: Ah . . . ah . . . the idea is to be able to have good relations with other people—at home and even with a girlfriend.

VICTOR: Yeah, I used to get in a lot of fights. I used to mess up with people even if I wanted them for friends.

DONALD: It's not comfortable any place but here . . . I mean it.

WORKER: Well, how is that?

DONALD: Oh, ah, oh . . . I can't say it.

VICTOR: 'Cause here is no pretense. We don't have to be on our guard. Everybody knows you've been nuts, you know (*starts to laugh in a nervous manner*).

JEROME: Yeah, we trust each other here.

WORKER: Donald, can you try now to tell us what you wanted to say earlier?

DONALD: Ah . . . no (*silence*). I'm not scared here anymore.

ELAINE: And we are getting better—we're not nuts now.

JEROME: I'd like to have some real friends—I think the group is helping me.

ELAINE: Yeah, that's group therapy.

JONATHON: This group is to help us be more comfortable with others—but that means working on our problems.

ELAINE: Yes, Yes.

Here the worker summarized what the members had been saying about the purpose of the group and then led them into talking about her role with them. The skill of the worker is demonstrated through her ability to support the group by remaining silent when the members were interacting productively, by encouraging the participation of all members, and by requesting clarification of feelings.

Through research, both Florence Clemenger and Marjorie Main learned that the worker's ability to perceive accurately the members' own goals and to formulate treatment goals and plans varied for different members of the group. Clemenger found that a tendency on the part of a worker to stereotype, in a negative way, certain members of a group was related to lack of skill in assessing the members' perceptions of their roles and the group's structure and functioning.[13] Main found that treatment goals and plans for individuals tended to be more fully developed when the worker had made a complete diagnosis of the individual, an assessment of the individual's own goals, and a diagnostic statement of the group's functioning, and used himself appropriately with the group. She found that workers tended to develop goals and treatment plans during the first five meetings for those members who had roles that were regarded as important to the group and that they tended to overlook isolates and other less active members of the group.[14]

In a group, workers' purposes for individuals and the group are reformulated on the basis of their perceptions of needs, capacities, goals, and environmental circumstances of individuals and those of the group as a unit. The focus of the group experience revolves around a purpose recognized and at least partially accepted by all participants in the process. Members of groups are able to perceive clearly the way in which the worker communicates the purpose of the group to them. Workers can develop a high degree of skill in assessing the members' perceptions of the purpose of the group as it has evolved through group discussion.

Stabilize Membership

From an aggregate of individuals who lack clarity about who does and who does not belong to the group and who may or may not be admitted to membership, stabilization of membership gradually occurs. Promptness of arrival and regular attendance are important, yet it may take some time to stabilize these patterns. When there is irregularity of attendance, the composition of the group is different each time, and therefore the group itself is different. The worker's task is to recognize with the members the difference that these factors make. Their individual and group decisions about these matters are important.

The consequences of changes in membership are that the group's progression is decelerated. Robert Paradise asserts that a new member is likely to add to the existing frustrations of the members that are typical of this stage.[15] When possible, it is desirable to delay changes in membership until the struggles for power and control have been addressed. When there are new members, time is taken to orient them to the members and to the group. In addition, they bring their own sets of needs and values into the group, which may be in harmony or conflict with those of the other members.

Time must be taken to attempt to integrate them into the group's purpose and culture.

Stabilization of membership is partly the product of the resolution of problems of ambivalence and resistance on the part of members. Partly, it is the result of greater clarity about the purpose of the group and the organization's policies and procedures concerning membership. Partly, it is sensitivity to cultural values on the part of the worker or some members. In a parent education group, for example, Mrs. G. mentioned that her sons had collected some old aluminum cans. They were using the money to buy shoes for school. Last week they made several dollars, which Mrs. G. divided equally between the boys and herself. The worker commented that Mrs. G. might be expecting too much of the boys by having them give her half of their earnings—since they were saving for shoes for school, particularly. Mrs. G. did not respond, and she did not come to the next meeting.

Tonia Lasater and Frank Montalvo report that Mrs. G.'s dropping out was occasioned by a clash of cultural values unrecognized by the worker. The comments made by the worker reflected his—not the members'—value orientation. Mrs. G. was trying to teach her sons a basic cultural value: in the Mexican-American community, children are taught that sharing, mutual aid, and reciprocity strengthen family relationships and contribute to respect for and dedication to the family. The worker saw the behavior as discouraging the children's independence and exploiting their achievement. Mrs. G. did not make the worker aware of her feelings, choosing instead to withdraw from the group. In her culture, it is as important to respect an individual's feelings as it is to express deference to the worker's opinions.[16]

Joan Velasquez, Marilyn Vigil, and Eustolio Benavides reported that there are greater rates of discontinuance among persons of minority ethnic populations than among white people. They tend to drop out because they do not perceive what they are offered as helpful and because "the partnership which ideally evolves from engaging a client in a positive, purposeful relationship does not develop.[17]

A distinction needs to be made between members' initial attraction to the group and their continuation after the first one or two meetings. Uncertainty about inclusion, if not worked through, often leads to withdrawal from the group. Members are more likely to remain in a group if they have some understanding of their desire to leave, especially if they want to avoid difficult feelings of which they may not be fully aware. When articulated and understood, the decision may be to remain in the group. "Sometimes," according to Cecil Rice, "feeling understood is all that is required."[18]

In all forms of group work, there is considerable discontinuance against the judgment of the practitioner. If a group is to benefit its members, they must remain in it long enough to be influenced by it. Some of the reasons for discontinuance are lack of clarity about the purpose and means to be used in working toward it, problems of inclusion and acceptance, deviation from the group in some important way, cultural dissonance, complications arising out of subgroup formation, early provocateurs, inability to share the practitioner, and inadequate orientation to the situation.[19] Other reasons for discontinuance are environmental obstacles, such as lack of transportation or child care, work schedules that interfere with the time of the sessions, and lack of material resources. Thus, it is crucial that the worker take sufficient time to explore the meaning of membership through discussions within the group or, in some instances, through interviews with individuals outside the group.

Social workers do many small things to stabilize membership. They help members to know who belongs, follow up on absences, work separately with some members around their ambivalence toward continuation at times when such help does not seem appropriate in the group, and discuss openly some of the members' attitudes toward each other and their effect on group belongingness. Elaine Lonergan has elaborated on many techniques that can be used to encourage attendance.[20] These include emphasizing the special ways the group can help, taking the person's reluctance seriously and discussing it, reaching out to members who are absent, expressing pleasure when members tell the worker something positive, encouraging them to bring problems into the group, and expecting people to attend, emphasizing that attendance will help them.

In natural groups, workers engage the members in a problem-solving process concerning the inclusion and exclusion of members, making clear the organization's values and procedures about this matter. In all groups, they continue to get facts about and evaluate the impact of individuals on each other and on the development of the group. There may be instances in which, in spite of every effort, the composition of the group is faulty and some decision about changing the membership should be made, through the addition of new members or the withdrawal of old members. In some groups, there is a difficult combination of people with personality patterns who cannot be helped to fit together or in which membership is too heterogeneous for compatibility. In other instances, there are competing subgroups that cannot develop a working relationship and become part of the group. Decisions to add or drop members in order to correct faulty composition need to be based on accurate assessment and thoughtful planning rather than on the operation of the acceptance-rejection process in an unacknowledged way. Professional ethics make it necessary to find another group or equally useful resource for anyone who is eliminated from the group.

Influence Status and Roles

During this stage of group development, the structure of interpersonal relationships emerges. Out of the process of ranking, leadership emerges in the group. Certain members exert more than average influence upon the purpose and activities of the group. Indigenous leadership changes dynamically with the changing needs and conditions of the group. All members can be ranked in terms of the degree of influence they exert upon the activities of the group. All things being equal, leadership tends to be situational; that is, it tends to alter according to changing individual and group needs. Leadership is usually a shared phenomenon rather than a constant role of a particular member. Even so, some members will have more influence than others. Influence is power; that conflict and competition for power will exist between the members is to be expected, just as conflict will exist about the worker's power. There is some correlation between individual factors that enable a person to exert influence and group factors that acknowledge, recognize, or tolerate that influence. Some members may do little but follow others. Certain indigenous leadership roles may become relatively stable in certain members or they may be performed by different members of the group at different times, as the members expect certain attitudes and behaviors from them.

Two major types of roles emerge in groups—task roles and socioemotional roles. Task roles contribute to the achievement of the group's agreed upon goals. Some socioemotional roles contribute to the development of positive relationships between the members; others place certain members in precarious positions in the group and detract from the group's effectiveness in moving toward its goals. These roles can develop and change throughout the group's life, as discussed in chapter 10.

Develop a Group Culture: Norms

In the initial stage, the norms of the group are primarily those initiated by workers and reinforced by their interventions. Now, a primary task is to develop a group culture that will transform a collectivity into a growth-promoting social system. As the members interact over the issues of power and relationships, a code of norms develops. As this happens, the members move toward self-control and sharing responsibility for their group: they acquire power. The desired norms are those that make it possible for the dynamic positive forces to operate. Those norms include freedom of expression, ethical behaviors, an open structure of communication, mutual acceptance and mutual aid, and motivation for goal achievement.

Social workers influence the development of norms primarily as model-setting participants who demonstrate acceptance, empathy, and genuineness, search for understanding of what is going on, and have confidence in the group process. They also influence norms by approving of certain behaviors and withholding approval for other behaviors, making suggestions, pointing out that a norm has been developed, and engaging the group in problem-solving processes concerning how certain conflicts should be resolved.

Interventions of the worker may be directed toward helping the group itself to recognize norms as these become evident. Workers may do this in a variety of ways: by calling the members' attention to the fact that they are doing things in a certain way or that they now seem to have agreed upon a norm, for example, about confidentiality. They may raise questions that help the members to decide upon norms for the group. Such simple questions as "Do we want to cut off discussion like that?" and "Did you intend to suggest that we do it this way?" or "Is there a better way to work on this?" help to clarify norms of behavior. Gradual clarification of differences in expectations for the group, as divergent from those of other groups to which members belong, is often crucial. Adaptation requires that a person be able to distinguish the norms suitable in one situation from those suitable elsewhere. Members may often be confused about conflicting expectations. A common example is that of a norm that encourages the expression of angry feelings in a social work group and the expectation that these be suppressed at school or at work. Difficulties occur when the members fail to distinguish between what is appropriate in the group and what is appropriate in other situations.

Interventions of the worker may focus on teaching the members how to find better ways of relating to each other through setting limits and giving information. An example is of a group of girls who lack tolerance for frustration. Limits were necessary because the girls often got into situations in which they could injure themselves or other people. In one early session, the members fought over scissors that needed to be shared. They kicked each other, spat, cursed, and behaved in almost ungovernable fashion. The worker did not lecture about breaking a rule—almost universally ineffective. Rather she stopped the group's activity, said she recognized their angry feelings, and, when the members had quieted down, said she would like to tell them what some children do when they want to use the same scissors. She described such alternatives as drawing straws, working in pairs, taking turns, or talking about the problem and making a decision they could all live with. The girls said they would draw straws now. The worker used this approach repeatedly until the girls learned to plan ahead to make decisions.

Development of norms about the distribution of power and control is essential to the group's further development. When desirable, the worker tries to influence the modification of agency rules that affect the group adversely. Margaret Hartford found that overly restrictive regulations often contributed to the failure of a group to form.[21] The worker permits the testing of rules and policies, recognizing that as a right of the members, but also maintains appropriate limits on behavior. Members learn to take control as the worker turns issues back to the group and clarifies their right to determine certain matters.

An illustration of this occurred at the sixth meeting of a group of adults coping with the demands of community living following hospitalization for mental disorders. All the members came early, with the exception of Mrs. J.

I opened the meeting by saying, "I made a mistake last week." The response was "What mistake?" "What do you mean?" I explained, "Last week I told you that the group could decide whether you wanted to meet at 6:30 or at 7:00 o'clock. All of you wanted to begin at 6:30, except for Mrs. J., who wanted to begin at 7:00. I said that we would then begin at 6:45. I took the decision away from you, didn't I?" Mr. G. gave me a knowing smile and said, "Oh, that's all right." Miss L. said, "That's just how it happened. I don't mind." I said, "But you have a right to mind." Mrs. J. said that the extra fifteen minutes made so much difference to her in getting here on time. Mr. P. said, with a grin, "I kind of thought that's how it was." In the guise of good humor and tolerance, the members continued to talk about their annoyance. They wanted to hear me say

over and over again that they could be angry with me and that I had
made a mistake in not really letting them decide when the group would
meet.

In this example, the worker wanted to make her statement very positively
because most of the members were afraid to express feelings and differences,
yet they had covert anger directed at Mrs. J. because she had maneuvered
decisions and monopolized the discussion. Some of the subtle anger was
directed at the worker for falling in with Mrs. J.'s maneuvers to get the time
changed. Through bringing this matter into the group, the worker supported
the norm that the members have power to make certain decisions, to be
open with each other, and to be free to express feelings and concerns.

Groups need to establish norms that deal with differences in values concerning what proper behavior is. At the beginning, the tendency is to seek
commonality and avoid facing differences. True acceptance from others
comes, however, from recognition of both similarities and differences. For
example, in a group of older adults,

Mrs. P. vividly described her visit to a nursing home. She said that the
conditions were disgusting, that patients were lying in their own feces,
and that she would never place her husband in a nursing home no matter
what. Mrs. S., who had been checking nursing homes for her husband,
looked panicked. The worker pointed out that social workers are available
to help with placements and that, while we are all aware of some horror
stories, there are some good nursing homes. Mrs. N. said that she was
determined to take her husband home, virtually at any cost. The members
seemed to be trying to establish the norm that virtuous people took their
relatives home and that people who did not do so were bad.[22]

In such instances, workers need to engage the members in further work to
accept the norm that what is a good decision for one member may not be
for another, that different situations require different solutions. They do this
through supporting differences, providing information, problem solving, and
using such environmental resources as visits to convalescent centers and
nursing homes.

Conflicts about norms often deal with whether expression is preferable to inhibition of feelings and experiences and whether only positive expression is allowable instead of free expression of hostilities and differences. Members test and come to trust the norm that they can express their feelings and bring problems into the group without suffering rejection, punishment, or other severe consequences. An example is of a group of adolescent girls in a residential setting who confessed that they had violated a strict rule. The worker listened to the full story and then responded in a nonpunitive manner, which led to discussion of the rule and consensus that the particular rule was necessary for the protection of the girls themselves. The organization's rule became a group norm.

Through the interaction of members, influenced by certain actions by the worker, norms develop in the group. Through a process of negotiation, a unique normative system develops. Norms, initially specified and supported by the worker, have become internalized. A culture has been created that is unique to the particular group.

Fun and Spontaneity

All is not seriousness in a group: moments of fun and spontaneity contribute to the development of relationships and cohesion. A simple example is of an outpatient therapy group in the psychiatric unit of a medical center.

The members were coming into the room and beginning to sit down. As usual, I waited a little before taking my seat so that members could have some choice of seating. The last member to enter, Mr. G., said, "Here we are sitting in the same chairs." I suddenly said, "Yes. The same chairs. Why don't we just all change chairs?" Everybody smiled and started crossing back and forth between the chairs—it was like children playing Upset the Fruit Basket. There was a lighthearted feeling, the members all looked around the circle and smiled, and it was as though they had laid down their troubles and felt their burden lightened.

This brief activity, directed to the entire group, produced a multiplicity of little changes. All of a sudden, people seemed more relaxed; there was more interaction in that meeting than ever before. Toward the end of the meeting, several members commented on how much we had accomplished after changing chairs. The incident certainly facilitated interaction between the members, but it also demonstrated to these adults that they can learn to enjoy other people. As Henry Maier has pointed out, "In moments of playfulness, clients find an added capacity to deal with heretofore unmanageable events."[23]

A Cohesive Group Emerges

While recognizing with the members some of their interpersonal conflicts, workers guide discussion and other activity toward some strong common interests or concerns. They emphasize similarities and positives as well as differences and negatives. They have a responsibility to provide new opportunities for participating in experiences that have the potential for testing and strengthening relationships, identifying common concerns and capacities, or affirming preferences and making decisions. The use of activity, as well as discussion, will have much merit with some groups. For members to explore capacities and relationships, test out the authority of the worker, and identify common and divergent norms, there must be a real situation in which the persons can be truly ego involved and act out the meaning of these objectives. The action is upon a stage where the chips are not down, where a mistake can be retrieved, where amends can be made.

If all has gone well, the group is a cohesive one with the characteristics that make it a potent force in the lives of its members. The members have delineated goals for themselves that are in harmony with the group purposes. They have come to accept each other sufficiently to want to continue together. They have given up some of their earlier self-centered attitudes and behavior, or overdependency on the worker, and moved into a relationship of interdependence. They have developed some understanding and acceptance of the worker's role in relationship to their roles in the group. They have accepted a norm of experimentation and flexibility and of responsibility for both supporting each other and stimulating each other toward the achievement of individual and group goals. They have come to some acceptance of a set of norms through which necessary control is effectuated within a general climate of acceptance of difference.

Essentially, the earlier tentative agreement has been strengthened or changed so that members accept the contract. Considerable evidence from research exists to demonstrate the importance of such agreement. Charles Garvin has reported that "the existence of the 'contract' is an important correlate of worker activity and group movement."[24] Leonard Brown found that early attention by the worker to the problem of mutual expectations seems to produce reductions in the amount of time spent in testing, allowing the groups to move to their work more rapidly.[25] And, from a review of research, Irvin Yalom and his associates concluded that anxiety stemming from unclarity of the group task, process, and role expectations in the early meetings of the group may, in fact, be a deterrent to effective therapy.[26]

Guidelines for Practice

Exploration of relationships and conflicts between the members and with the worker predominate in this stage of the group's development. Members continue to search for acceptance in the group, compare themselves to others, and compete for status, roles, and power. They test the worker's caring for them, the way the worker uses power, and their right to self-determination. They form alliances with other members in pairs and subgroups. They seek clarity about the group's purpose, process, and culture.

To help the members explore the group's meaning for them and cope with power and uncertainty, workers do the following:

1. engage in ongoing self-examination of their use of authority and reactions to expressions of difference and hostility toward them and between the members;
2. assess each member's participation in the group, based on sensitive listening and observation of nonverbal behavior, assess changes in the group's structure, process, content, and stresses within the group and the group's interaction with other systems; the intent is to identify individual and group strengths and problems, discover the common ground between the members, and make the group the primary agent of change;
3. strengthen supportive relationships between the members by offering emotional support, identify common interests, feelings, and concerns, encourage the group's autonomy according to the capacity of members, and use the problem-solving process to reduce conflicts over the distribution and use of power;

4. engage the members in exploration of their positive and negative feelings, allowing for ventilation of anger, hostility, anxiety, complaints, and concerns, and then moving ahead to understand and deal with them;
5. influence the development of the group, with particular attention to uncertainty and power, patterns of communication that foster mutual aid, and the group's culture of values and norms;
6. stabilize membership by enhancing motivation through demonstrating how individuals' interests and needs can be met within the group's purpose, provide emotional support, prepare the group for the entry of new members, and follow up on absences;
7. regulate conflict through the use of the problem-solving process, making selective use of interventions of support, exploration, information giving, advice, clarification, and confrontation accompanied with empathy;
8. review and clarify, with the participation of members, the essential elements of a contract that will govern the group's operation and content in relation to a clearly defined purpose.

A major outcome of the process of exploration during this stage is that considerable congruence is achieved between each member's perception of the group and the worker's perception of it. Members of groups usually have come to perceive quite clearly the activities of the worker in contributing to the members and the group as a whole. The analytic skills of the worker have been translated into accurate judgments about the perceptions that members have of the functioning of the group and the worker's role in it. Group cohesiveness has developed, defined most simply as attraction to the group, referring to the forces binding members of a group to each other and to the group.[27] The group has become, to some extent at least, a system of mutual support and mutual aid.[28] In a cohesive group, the dynamic therapeutic forces are free to operate so that the members use the group for more intensive work on their needs and problems in psychosocial functioning.

14 Stage III: Mutuality and Goal Achievement

In the third stage of development, the group is a cohesive one in which the members engage in a process of mutual aid and use that process as a vehicle for work on personal, interpersonal, group, and environmental problems. Groups, as described in chapter 1, are ideal social environments for acquiring knowledge and skills, reducing difficulties in social relationships, coping with stress, enhancing social competence, accessing social resources, and removing environmental obstacles.

A group in which members basically accept and help each other has emerged. The members are now fairly clear about their personal goals as these relate to the general purpose of the group. Most members have found an acceptable niche in the group. Membership has stabilized. Motivation is generally strong, but with episodes of ambivalence and resistance, as the group moves more deeply into facing and working on problems. The group now has a set of guiding norms, roles tend to be flexible and functional, communication is generally open and participation is widespread, and interpersonal, group, and environmental conflicts are acknowledged and worked on. Differences between members are recognized and used for collaborative work toward the achievement of agreed upon individual and group goals. Actually, no group moves along in an orderly sequence, but progress is made unevenly with steps forward and back and then ahead to a new level of accomplishment. Most groups are in transition somewhere between identifiable stages of development.

In this stage of the group's development, the major responsibility of workers is to maintain and further enhance the group as a growth-promoting modality so that, increasingly, the members learn to help each other. Workers supplement what the members themselves are able to do.

Maintaining and Strengthening the Group

Relationships

The predominant qualities of relationships in this stage are trust, acceptance, and a search for intimacy and differentiation.[1] There is a noticeable decrease in the ambivalence of members toward the worker and each other and an increase in ability to empathize with each other. Within the positive climate of trust and acceptance, the members display both realistic and unrealistic and both positive and negative attitudes and behaviors. Their perceptions may be distorted. There may be multiple transferences, often below the conscious level of awareness, as evidenced by such comments as "You're just like my father," "She's your favorite," "Johnny never did like me," or "I want to stay here forever."

The members' relationship with their workers is predominantly positive, characterized by less dependence, less struggle against their authority, and more reliance on each other, combined with a realistic dependence at times when help is necessary. Members often develop strong positive feelings expressed in a desire to have the worker to oneself, difficulty in sharing, strong overidentification, or unrealistic dependence. In a group of young women with mental illness who were preparing to leave the hospital, for example, the worker took the members on a shopping trip. In a coffee shop, where they went for lunch, the members were necessarily dependent upon her for guidance and concrete help. Later, as she helped the members to select and buy small articles in a nearby store, one member said, "Come on, Mommy, we want to show you what we want to buy."

During this stage of group development, members tend to identify with their workers. They may begin to dress like the worker or imitate some aspect of her appearance or mannerisms. They may comment that they try to think about how the worker would handle a particular situation. They may comment that they did something to please the worker. Through such means, they incorporate some part of the worker into themselves. Such identifications occur also between members of the group. They enhance the sense of relatedness and, in addition, lead to changes in attitudes and behaviors. The worker, while fostering positive identifications, also helps the members to move to an enhanced sense of their own identities.

Within the general atmosphere of acceptance and trust, negative feelings may occur. Workers analyze whether the feelings about them are limited to one or two members or are widely shared and, if the latter, the extent to which contagion has occurred. Some hostile reactions toward workers are very natural reactions to realistic situations, in which instances the involved members have every right to be angry with their workers, as, for example, when a worker does not follow through on a promise or does not notify the members about an absence. In other instances, hostility toward a worker may be a defense against involvement, or feelings may be displaced or projected onto the worker from other life experiences. Hostility may be expressed against the worker, who represents a parent or other person. Even though such transference reactions stem from feelings that were realistic in the past, the irrational elements should not be continued in the present, if the member is to cope with such experiences constructively. Such strong feelings toward the worker are more noticeable in therapy and socialization groups of children than in educational or behavioral groups because the former place more emphasis on self-understanding and affect than the latter.

The development of intimacy began in the preceding stage of development as members came to know each other better, worked out certain conflicts, and learned to trust the worker and each other. Mutual acceptance and shared self-disclosure are essential ingredients of intimacy. In this stage, the members come to share more and more of themselves in the group, but they often reflect ambivalence about the search for intimacy. Valerian Derlega points out that there are realistic risks to full disclosure.[2] Members may fear that others will discover all that is wrong with them and abandon them. They may fear that confidentiality will be violated, that what they say will be used against them, that they will lose control of their own destructive impulses as these come to awareness, that they will lose their individuality, or that they will become engulfed by or enmeshed with other members. The ability to develop intimacy is essential to effective adult psychosocial functioning. L. M. Horowitz reports that failure to develop intimate relationships has been found to be the most common reason for seeking outpatient psychotherapy.[3] Without intimate relationships, people feel lonely, isolated, and alienated. The group modality has the potential for the achievement of desired intimacy.

Membership

Usually, members have become invested in the group; they feel that be-longing is important to them and they know who belongs. The social worker has a responsibility to maintain members in the group when the group can be beneficial to them; this is done through follow-up of absences and pro-vision of support in the form of encouragement when resistance or ambiv-alence recurs. Members tend to feel threatened by the entry of newcomers to the group but are generally able to face and work through the problem. The newcomer upsets the steady state, including the norms and patterns of relationships. Additions of new members to an ongoing group dilutes and interferes with the progressive deepening of feelings between the members until the newcomer is accepted by the group.

Turnover in membership detracts from orderly movement. New members need to become oriented to the group, develop relationships with other members, and test the mutuality of perceptions of goals and expectations; they are in the initial phase of treatment. The older members need to adapt their roles and contributions to the group to take into account the needs of the newcomer who may have difficulty in accepting other members or the group's norms and process. When intimate relationships have been achieved, a newcomer can feel great discomfort in trying to become a part of the group. The usual anxieties about entering a new situation are aggra-vated by the sense of intruding into an existing system of relationships.

Newcomers to a cohesive group are in a difficult position. They have the feelings typical of entry into any new group situation, but, in addition, they need to become socialized into the member role in a group that has devel-oped its own patterns of goals, relationships, communication, and norms. In many cases, new members are left with the responsibility of finding their place in the group; the old members may not willingly share responsibility with them. One example of the difficulty for an individual and a group in adapting to a new member concerns a young adult therapy group in which most members had been together for several months. No members had been added since the end of the first few sessions. The group had developed a sense of togetherness and had been engaged in discussions of intimate re-lationships.

One afternoon, just as the group was beginning, a stranger arrived, saying she had been referred to this group. The worker entered the group at about the same time the stranger appeared. She had not prepared the group for this event but welcomed Genevieve and introduced her to each member. The members were polite and made efforts to include her in the discussion. At the worker's suggestion, they returned to the discussion that had started earlier, but the content was superficial and there was almost no sharing of deep concerns.

Genevieve attempted to give advice to the others about their problems, which is typical behavior for the first stage. After the session ended, Genevieve left, but the other members lingered. When the worker indicated that they might be upset about the new member, each one expressed much anger toward the worker for having permitted this to happen and for not letting them participate in making the decision. Jack said, with sadness, that it had taken them so long to be able to trust the worker and themselves. Sally agreed and said it would be hard for her to really share herself again. The worker said she had no idea they would feel this way; she just thought that a group experience would be good for Genevieve. She thought the group was ready and should be able to work it out. The members left, without saying goodbye. In a conference with Genevieve, the worker learned that it had been a devastating experience for her. She felt the members' great discomfort and hostility and just couldn't seem to fit into what was going on.

Such experiences are not uncommon when there has been inadequate preparation of both the newcomer and the group and when the timing of entry is inappropriate. They can be used for the benefit of all concerned, but that requires great sensitivity to the emotional interplay between the members and the readiness of people to learn from them.

Assimilation into the group is dependent upon learning to take roles, to perceive oneself in relation to others, and to acquire the commonly shared frames of reference. The nucleus group already has a culture of norms that may, however, have become so much a part of the members that they cannot readily be verbalized.[4] The new person needs to discover these and test them out before finding a place in the group. In the case of disturbed persons, the process may be prolonged and fraught with hesitating and belabored efforts to find acceptance.

Preparation of the group for the arrival of a new member helps the group to maintain its cohesion even while adapting to a new person. Through discussion of changes in membership, some members may recall their own feelings concerning entering the group and generalize about what makes it easy or difficult to find one's place in a group. Assimilation of new members seems to be easier in open groups with frequent turnover of members than in relatively closed ones, but it should be remembered that the developmental process in open groups tends to be slower.

The timing of the entry of newcomers is important. They may at one time bring in desirable new stimulation. At other times, they may seriously disrupt the stability of the group. Although there are no clear rules, the best time to admit members is usually after the group has worked through a conflict or completed its work on a particular task or issue and is ready to move on to a new theme or activity. It is also necessary at times to admit a new member when someone drops out, in order to maintain a sufficient number of members in the group. Changes in membership provide opportunities for bringing new inputs into the group and for solving problems of acculturating new members, breaking affectional ties with departing members, and realigning roles and friendship alliances. It is the workers' responsibility to prepare the group for the entry of new members as well as to prepare the newcomer for the group. Workers prepare the group by informing the members that a new person has been referred to the group, seeking a response to this announcement, and answering appropriate questions about the entry of a new person. They ask the members to recall some of their own feelings and experiences in their first meeting and what they think can be done to help the newcomer.

When the group has been prepared for a new person, the members can be very helpful to that person. An example of the successful entry of a new member took place on a ward of a mental hospital in which a group of young adults had been meeting for three months.

I went to the ward to gather up the group and introduced Betty, a new person, to each of the members. They had been prepared for her coming in the preceding two meetings. When I introduced Betty to Martha, Martha smiled and said, "Oh, I know Betty; she eats at my table with me." As we walked off the ward, Martha walked with Betty arm in arm.

As we walked to the store, Martha told me that she had seen Joan, a former member, at the laundry. Jane interrupted Martha to tell me that she didn't go the dance last night. When Martha asked why not, Jane said, "I just decided not to." Sarah said she wanted to get the next issue of a magazine she was carrying with her. She's reading a continued story and "just can't wait to see how it ends." She asked Betty if she ever read stories that she enjoyed. Betty said she hadn't read for a long time, but she'd like to try. Then she began asking questions about the group, which Sarah and Martha answered very accurately, a sign of their great progress. Betty asked me about my age, marital status, and other personal questions. Before I had a chance to answer, Sarah said, "Betty, there are some things that people just don't tell and we don't ask Miss J. such personal questions." I said that it was perfectly all right and natural that she should want to know something about me and things about the other members and the group, too. Joan said, "Yes, you can ask her." I added that we would try to help her fit into the group. She said, "You have already, and so has Martha and Sarah . . . and all of you."

Discontinuance of members from closed or semiclosed groups is not frequent during this stage. Some members cannot, however, accept the increasing demands of the group for give and take, or they cannot tolerate dealing with the subject matter of the group. They become anxious and resistant. Feelings about exposure of self in the group may recur as its content touches upon more areas of the life experiences of its members. It is crucial that the person come to "have confidence that his real self can be understood and accepted by others in the group."[5] Until the point is reached in which there is openness and acceptance of self and others, some members may seek to withdraw from the group. Workers need to support such persons in staying, by making very clear that they want them to remain in the group. It is hoped that the other members can reassure the ambivalent members that they have a place in the group. Departure of a member stirs up varied reactions: a sense of loss, fear that the group will disintegrate, or ambivalence about wanting the person in the group, with accompanying guilty feelings.

Positive Motivation and Resistance

Identification with the social worker and feelings of trust and mutual acceptance provide powerful motivation for continuing in the group. In such an atmosphere, anxieties and fears are lessened and hopefulness is increased. People are not likely to remain in groups if they believe that some positive

changes in themselves or their situations are not possible. They need to have
and to believe that they have the power to achieve some change. In an earlier
chapter, it was noted that there must be hope that relief from discomfort,
pain, or dissatisfaction with the current situation can occur. There must be
enough discomfort with what is that a person desires some further development or change in the situation. Thus, the worker needs to work to maintain a balance between discomfort and hope as the members try to change
in some way. Mastery of skills and situations strengthens the ego and success
tends to build on success. What might have been a vicious cycle of hope-
lessness-failure-greater hopelessness gets replaced with a cycle of hopeless-
ness-success-hopefulness.[6]

Even within a general atmosphere in which individual and group motivation is high, there will be times when apathy or discouragement sets in.
Particular members resist efforts by the worker or by other members to help
them work on difficulties or obstacles to goal achievement. In this stage of
group development, resistance is often mobilized by anxiety about the helping process itself. Members may fear disclosing certain secrets or highly
charged experiences or become aware of feelings and ideas that have been
suppressed as these break into consciousness. Facing things in themselves
that they find difficult to accept upsets the steady state. When anxiety increases beyond a tolerable level, persons defend themselves: they resist. Resistance often represents an effort to hold on to the familiar, fears of intimacy,
and fears of trying out alternative ways of feeling, thinking, and doing. According to Nathan Ackerman, "it reflects the patient's need to place a fence
around the most vulnerable areas of self in an attempt to immunize the self
against the danger of reopening old psychic wounds."[7] But resistance does
not occur only because of the feelings and needs of the members. It may be
a reasonable response to the workers' part in the process, as when workers
are late to meetings, when they confront members in a punitive manner and
without conveying empathy, or when their interpretations are too many
and too threatening. The resistance of some members may also be due to
their interactions with other members when they are attacked or devalued
or when member-to-member confrontations and interpretations are inappropriate.

The following example is taken from the record of a group of adult men
and women with problems in social relationships in an adult psychiatric
clinic.

About halfway through the tenth session, the subject turned to religion. There was very little personal investment in the subject by any of the members, and it seemed to be a device to avoid talking about their fears. I asked, "Do you remember that, in our last meeting, you shifted away from talking about yourselves to talking about general things that didn't really seem to involve you much: aren't you starting to do the same thing again today?" There was an uncomfortable silence. I said, "It's been different in this group for the last two sessions." There was another uncomfortable silence. Allen broke the silence. "Who's holding back?" Everyone laughed.

Shirley said she came to this group because she was putting all her own problems on her children. I said, "Yes, and you and the others have not been working on those kinds of problems recently. What accounts for that?" There was another uncomfortable silence. Shirley broke the silence. "You don't want to bring out the real, deep problems that are bothering you."

Leon: "It's hard to even put your finger on the real problem—I'm mixed up about that." Allen: "It's easier to talk about religion than about what I really feel. I guess it's a cover-up." Leon cracked a joke and the mood changed. The other members laughed and Leon told another joke.

I said, "Let's look at what's been going on right now. Shirley said it's hard to share the real problems, Leon that he's not sure what these are, Allen that he needs a cover-up for what he really feels, and Susan, Barbara, and Carl haven't said a thing. Some of you were just getting close to talking about things that matter when Leon cracked a joke to take the focus off yourselves. It may feel scary to delve deeper into the feelings and relationships that contribute to your troubles." Shirley said, "I have to agree with that." Susan said, "Me, too. What will happen to me if I tell too much? But I'm willing to try." The members, including the usually silent ones, continued to discuss this matter.

In this example, the worker confronted the group, asked the members to illuminate the group process, and then made an interpretation that was accepted by the members. As with this group, confrontation is used quite frequently in this stage, tending to arouse anxiety. What is to be communicated is not condemnation but a direct statement that something is blocking the members' abilities to move ahead in problem solving. Confrontation that strips defenses is harmful. Workers need to allow time to provide support to members, as they try to understand the meaning of the message to them. Interpretation often follows confrontation. The most helpful interpretations are those offered by members, but when that does not occur the worker intervenes.

Statements about the meaning of behavior may be resisted, or they may be readily accepted. They may be resisted because the worker has expressed a truth that the members are not yet ready to recognize or because the worker has misunderstood the meaning of the situation and the interpretation is inaccurate. It is hard for anyone to face the intensity of deep feelings, and it is no wonder that members defend themselves against such understanding until they have developed enough self-esteem to accept these aspects of themselves. Secrecy leads to resistance. When members keep a secret from the group, they are making it impossible for others to help. When a worker withholds information from a group, the members are deprived of a source of help. Pallassana Balgopal and R. F. Hull explain how in therapeutic groups resistance often occurs because there are secrets between one or more members and the worker that are not revealed or discussed in group sessions. These areas of secrecy create barriers.[8]

The specific interventions of social workers in overcoming resistance are as varied as the reasons for the resistance. But, to be worked with, the members must be supported as the resistance is acknowledged and brought to the group's attention. Workers may comment that they have noticed a particular thing has happened. They bring to conscious awareness the expectations, disappointments, or anxieties that work against continuation of effort. Their next move depends upon the response from one or more members. They may invite ventilation of the feelings of anxiety, hopelessness, or fear that create the stalemate, provide support in the form of realistic reassurance to reduce threat, universalize the problem, acknowledging that it is natural to be uncertain about the consequences of efforts toward change or that distrust is often realistic owing to times when trust has not been earned, engage the individual or group in exploration of the situation, and, at times, use confrontation to disrupt the steady state in order to overcome apathy, denial, or avoidance of a particular issue. They may offer facts that have not been recognized or encourage the members to search for facts on which to base a decision about moving into a feared area, through the use of comments to illuminate the process. When workers feel secure in their interpretation of what the problem is or how it developed, they can share these observations with the group in a way that invites members to respond to them.

Influencing Group Structure and Process

Roles and Subgroups

During the preceding stages, the members assumed or were assigned to roles in the group, and a leading task for both the worker and the members was to identify and work through dysfunctional roles. Some stereotyping of members may continue that prevents the use of the group in a flexible manner, according to the needs of the members. Some workers use many skills in addressing the roles of members in the group, as discussed in chapter 10.

Subgroups can generally be accommodated by the group and can contribute to the group as a whole. This does not mean that no subgroups will be inimical to the welfare of individuals and the group. Indeed unhealthy pair relations may develop or continue from the earlier stages that indicate problems in interpersonal relationships, and their modification becomes an important goal for those members. It is natural that transitory negative relationships will develop within the group as the members try to solve the many individual and group problems.

Norms

A group culture was developed in the last stage, consisting of norms that are recognized, understood, and generally accepted by the members. The worker's efforts were directed toward influencing the nature of the code. If this has been successful, differences are now perceived as being potentially useful, although they may create discomfort. Individual differences and talents are acknowledged, used, and viewed as valuable. As Pallassana Balgopal and Thomas Vassil have noted, "An overriding principle is that the potential for change in groups is enhanced when differences are harnessed for work through interdependent efforts. Individual differences are not lost in the process but are expanded to the end that the members' goals have been reached."[9] Prestige is now attached to members' efforts to express themselves and to work on problems. The members recognize that conflict can be used constructively toward the achievement of purposes.

During this stage of group development, social workers continue to help members to recall and act in accordance with the norms in the group and some of the underlying values. They accredit and support the norms that are positive to the achievement of goals, openly question changes that are negative in the influence they have on the group, encourage the examination of existing norms and the consideration of alternative ones, and continue to help the group to find an appropriate balance between control and freedom in feeling and behaving. It is a temptation for a practitioner to overstress group loyalty and group standards to strengthen the impact of the group on its members; the crucial consideration is that the code of standards approve and support flexibility, experimentation, and individuation. Edgar Schein points out that, otherwise, there is danger the group will become "so stable in its approach to its environment that it loses its ability to adapt, innovate, and grow.[10]

Behavior that deviates from the norms of the group poses a threat to the stability of the group. The other members tend to respond with efforts to control the deviator. The deviator's failure to conform to the group's expectations makes life difficult for all concerned. An example is of an activity group for older adults in a community center. The activity was baking. The group had established a particular structure for working together in triads, with each person responsible for some part of the whole, and had established rules for sharing equipment and ingredients. During the midstage of the group, a new member, Helen, entered the group. Unfortunately, she had not had adequate pregroup preparation, and the group had not been prepared for her entry. Helen was an excellent baker and a hard worker, but her interactions with the old members were stormy. Her efforts to help others resulted in rejection, partly because of her controlling manner and negative attitudes toward others and partly because of the rigidity of the group's system of work. As time went on, Helen became more angry and upset with the others, and they with her, as indicated by the following excerpt from the group record.

Helen said to Dorothea, "What are you doing there? That's all wrong. Let me show you." Sally said, "Dorothea's doing all right." Helen said, "No, it's not mixing—what's the matter—she doesn't hear me." Dorothea said, "I hear you, but this is my job. You don't have to tell me." Helen took the sugar, before Dorothea had a chance to measure out what she needed. Dorothea said, "You're grabbing things before anyone else has a chance to finish. Stop that." Sally said to Sue, "See, Helen thinks she knows everything." Anger was mounting. I said, "OK, time out. I'm wondering what's going on among you."

The other members cannot count on the deviator—in this case, a newcomer—so they tend to respond by penalizing her in order to influence her toward conformity to the expectations of the group. This is essential to the group's ability to continue its activities. But the deviator has expectations, too, which need to be taken into account, and by doing so the group may find better ways of accomplishing its tasks. The worker's task is to assess the contributions that all members make to the conflict and to work toward mutuality of understanding. The major set of techniques in such situations is illumination of the group process.

Communication and Conflict

Patterns of communication appropriate to the purpose of the group were established earlier. There is now greater ease in communication about feelings, problems, and opinions and greater spread of communication between the members. Conflict continues, however, to be present and serves as a dynamic for change. Many intrapersonal and intragroup conflicts concerning power and acceptance were worked out during the preceding stage. But resolution of major interpersonal and intrapersonal conflicts usually cannot occur until the group has developed a basic consensus that provides strength to face and weather serious differences. When the social climate of the group is marked by mutual acceptance and support, members are more willing to risk exposure of themselves and their ideas than in the earlier stages, when they were more uncertain of their acceptance and the consequences of self-expression. They recognize that expression of difference need not mark the end of the relationship. In the words of Georg Simmel:

It is by no means the sign of the most genuine and deep affection never to yield to occasions for conflict. . . . On the contrary, this

behavior often characterizes attitudes which lack the ultimate unconditional devotion. . . . The felt insecurity concerning the basis of such
relations often moves us to the avoidance of every possible conflict.
Where, on the other hand, we are certain of the irrevocability and
unreservedness of our feeling, such peace at any price is not necessary.
We know that no crisis can penetrate to the foundation of the relationship.[11]

There are numerous sources of conflict. Conflict often has its source in
the intrapersonal drives and needs of the members—their differential needs
for control, affection, and inclusion, as these interact with the needs of other
members. Intrapsychic conflicts often get displaced onto the group. Members work out their sibling rivalries and relationships with parents and others
within the arena of the group. Members bring with them into the group the
values and norms from their primary reference groups. Many subcultural
and idiosyncratic differences within American culture influence the way
people shape their goals, perceive other people, and influence their attitudes
toward the process and content of the group. As these differences become
acknowledged, people become defensive and tend to promulgate their own
points of view. Or they have different knowledge about and experiences with
issues. The external situation and differential perceptions of that situation
are another frequent source of conflict. For example, awareness of ethnic
and political differences is very intense at times, and different population
groups vary in regard to how they view the services of community organizations. It is not one of these, but the interaction between them, that creates
conflict. Generally, the group has developed means for the resolution and
management of conflict that are appropriate to the members' capacities.
More frequently, conflict is resolved through means of consensus, acknowledgment of the right to differ, or integration rather than elimination of some
members or subjugation of some by others. This subject is discussed more
fully in chapter 9.

Cohesion

Cohesion is generally present to a great extent in that the members are
mutually attracted to each other and to the group. The degree of cohesion
is, however, relative. It is dependent upon the members' common interests
and goals and their abilities to enter into collaborative and intimate relations

with others. It is unlikely, for example, that patients with severe mental illness will develop into as cohesive a group as persons with greater competence in interpersonal relations. But the group has come to have meaning to the members. As the members become more secure in their own relationships, and in the identity of their group, they become more able to relate to other groups in an effective manner. The worker continues to pay attention to the development of the dimensions of group structure and process in order to maintain the group as a viable modality for the achievement of the goals of its members.

In this stage of development, groups exert their greatest influence on the members, owing at least in part to the fact that the group has become attractive to its members. It is sufficiently cohesive that the mutual aid process predominates, even though some members are more attracted to the group than are others. Irvin Yalom has summarized the evidence from research on the importance of a high degree of cohesion in the interpersonal learning process.[12] He reports that findings from seven studies support the proposition that group cohesion is an important determinant of positive outcome, both in encounter and therapy groups. Cohesive groups are characterized by mutual trust and acceptance. They also permit greater development and expression of hostility and conflict. When unexpressed hostility and hidden conflicts exist, open and honest communication is impossible. When members of groups have come to mean enough to each other, their relationships are not permanently disrupted, and they can, with help, work through the conflict. Highly cohesive groups also have better attendance and less turnover of membership than those with low degrees of cohesion.[13]

Achievement of Goals

During this stage, the predominant focus of the content is on the needs of the members as these are connected with those of others and with the general purpose of the group. Considerable emphasis is given to discussion of problems of individuals, with other members contributing their ideas, as elaborated by Dominique Steinberg.[14] General themes of concern to members are often discussed, with progression from the general concern to a specific problem or from a specific concern to the general. These themes vary with the particular goals of the members and with their strengths and limitations at a given time.

Successful outcome usually involves

1. acquisition of essential knowledge about behavior, situations, and problems;
2. improvement in affective and cognitive understanding of oneself in relation to others, referred to as interpersonal understanding;
3. development of capacity to cope with stress, including transitions and crises;
4. development of competence in performing social roles, and changing maladaptive relationships and communication;
5. use of social resources and removal of environmental obstacles.

Acquisition of Knowledge

A major theme in this stage is education to increase common understanding of problematic situations and their meaning for the functioning of the members and their families. Members often need considerable information about the issue at hand. For example, a group of adolescent girls needed accurate knowledge about sexuality to correct the many myths they had about their bodies, the connection between menstruation and pregnancy and its cause, birth control methods, and the psychosocial consequences of early parenthood. Patients with AIDS and their families cope more effectively with the disease if they have adequate and accurate knowledge of the medical situation and its impact on their lives. A nurse or physician may present the medical material. It is essential, however, to go beyond the giving of information to recognizing and emphasizing the strengths of the members and helping them find sources of support in addition to that provided in the group.

Knowledge given by members is often more effective than that provided by practitioners. Andrew Malekoff provides an excellent example of the power of information offered by a member.[15] In a group of adolescent boys in a child guidance center, the boys traded information about sexually transmitted diseases (STDs). There was a "curious combination of fact and fiction, not unlike typical conversations of natural groups of teens."

——————

It turned out that, in a roundabout way, they were also seeking information about how to get tested for HIV. The worker tried to inform them about the local testing site and procedures. They all talked over him, effectively short-circuiting anything of value that he might have to say. That is, all except for one of the boys who made fleeting eye contact with the worker and seemed to be responding in concert with him, obviously familiar with the information he was trying to impart. The worker, recognizing that the group was not focused on him, remembered that he wasn't the only one available to provide help to the members. He asked, on a hunch, "Has anyone here ever been tested for STDs?" The boy who seemed to be responding, Frank, raised his hand high, obviously anxious to share some information with the group. He started off quickly, as if in a race to get to the finish line.

The worker stopped him momentarily, to help him help the others, and suggested that he start from the beginning. The worker coached him as follows: "OK, you walk into the clinic and then what happens, travel us through it, take your time." He was able to take this direction and did a masterful job of carefully explaining the testing process from beginning to end. There wasn't a single interruption. He had succeeded where the worker had not—that is, until it dawned on the worker that success didn't rest upon him being the central helping person.

In this group, as in many others, the problem was a lack of accurate and adequate information about an embarrassing subject. Learning from other members and giving to other members—the mutual aid process—has value beyond the specific knowledge obtained. Knowledge needs to be followed by exploration of its meaning to the members and then the use of that information in their daily lives. Understanding is more than cognitive: affect and behavior are also involved. As John Dewey, the progressive educator, expressed it, "Amid all uncertainties there is one permanent frame of reference; namely, the organic connection between education and personal experience."[16]

Interpersonal Understanding

Understanding of oneself and others often helps people to cope with stress and problems. Striving for self-understanding is based on the theoretical assumption that if people can understand how the values, emotions, patterns of behavior, and prior experiences have contributed to the current problems, they become able to distinguish which attitudes and behaviors best serve their goals. It is assumed that the more accurate the perception of inner and outer reality, the firmer the foundation for effective social functioning. More accurate perception of other significant persons may lead to changes in attitudes and behavior toward them. In the group, it must be remembered that interaction between the members is the primary instrument of change. Mutual aid is a powerful means of influencing changes in feelings, thought, and action. As members interact with each other, they become aware of themselves in their relationships with others. They can test out their assumptions not only against those of a professional helper but also, and more important, against those of their peers. They not only develop cognitive understanding but also integrate that with their feelings and learn about the effects on their behavior. They develop explanations to account for the particular patterns of behavior. They may come to a better understanding of their feelings and attitudes, their patterns of behavior in relation to what they are doing with other people, the reasons for the behavior, and, in some instances, the influence of the past on current functioning.

When people are anxious, they tend to cling to the familiar and avoid risking further upsets in the steady state. Change is threatening, resulting in the use of maladaptive coping strategies. What is required is that the group worker use supportive techniques and adequate exploration of the situation to assist the members to enter into reflective discussion of the situation and their parts in it. Acquiring self-understanding requires that persons disclose aspects of self that may be frightening and painful and that they fear will be unacceptable to the worker and to other members. Some members can, however, gain a great deal from listening to others and silently integrating the knowledge. But they do not gain the benefits from receiving feedback on their own feelings and ideas. The worker needs to differentiate between a healthy need for private contemplation and compulsive secrecy. Some members, on the other hand, reveal too much too soon. Experimentation with different ways of behaving requires wading in unknown waters. To venture into this arena requires that a relationship of trust has been developed between the participants. Research indicates that an adequate amount of self-disclosure is positively related to successful outcomes in various forms of groups.[17]

The attitudes toward the self with which the worker deals most frequently are the closely interrelated ones of identity and self-esteem. The sense of identity involves knowledge about and acceptance of oneself. As it develops through the life cycle, it incorporates more broadly and fully many aspects that define who a person is, what she can do, and what she will become. Often, members of groups feel stigmatized by the nature of their illnesses or handicapping conditions, for example, mental illness, mental retardation, cancer, AIDS, delinquency, or even the "bad mother" or "bad child" label. Feelings that people have about their sociocultural backgrounds often interfere with the development of positive self-esteem. A sense of self-esteem is closely related to, indeed, may be a part of, identity.

Certain events threaten the self-esteem of even healthy persons. Report cards, civil service examinations, work evaluations, or comparisons of development between children arouse fears of failure and worries about adequacy. These events force people to find out how their performance stands in relation to their own and others' expectations. Sexual adequacy is a recurrent theme in groups of adolescents and adults, related to the underlying theme of sexual identity. For aged persons, forced retirement and loss of relatives and friends through death are threats to their identity and self-esteem. Conflicts in identity also often come to the fore with clarity as members come to feel some success in their achievements. One typical example is the struggles of delinquent adolescents as they realize that, in order to achieve certain goals, they need to give up their identification with a gang or friendship group. Whether members approach an experience with competence and hope or a devastating sense of inadequacy with its accompanying hopelessness is of deep concern to the social worker.

In interpersonal learning, observation and clarification of nonverbal behavior is an essential skill of the social worker. An example is of a group of parents in a child guidance clinic. The meeting opened with listening to a tape on parent-child relationships.

During the time the tape was being played, Mr. D. appeared to be fully involved. Hands, eyes, posture, body movement, and absence of whispering to others reflected his involvement. Since he had not been this intense before the tape, something was affecting him deeply. When the tape was over, he sat back for only a second, but it was long enough for a discussion to get going about children's problems. Every time he tried to get into the discussion, someone else got in first. His finger tapping, leg crossing, and squirming seemed to indicate growing anxiety. By the time he got into the discussion, the topic was only distantly related to the tape.

Mr. and Mrs. A. were talking about their nephew's difficulty in cub scouts. Mr. D. stated that, since he is a den master, he could help the boy, if they would like. After some further discussion of children's problems in clubs, I said to Mr. D., "I bet you really enjoy helping the cub scouts—it does seem to strengthen parent-child relations . . . but, you know what? I have a feeling you would like to talk about something else and just haven't been able to get it into the discussion. It seemed like parts of that tape had a lot of meaning for you." Everyone perked up when Mr. D. said, "Yes, they did. There was a lot of me in that tape. I could see myself in it." All of a sudden, the members seemed to realize that in their excitement to talk about how the tape related to their children, they overlooked how the content might relate directly to themselves. The members were very supportive of Mr. D. as he shared some emotionally powerful experiences. That, in turn, led to discussion of other members' parts in the problems of relationships in their families.

The skills in practice reflected in this brief excerpt include sensitive observation of nonverbal as well as verbal behavior, support of Mr. D's positive abilities in Boy Scouting, the nonthreatening use of interpretation based on observation and sensitive listening, demonstration of an empathic response to anxiety, and a refocusing of the content to the primary needs of the members. With a worker who supports the group process, the ventilation and discussion of feelings by one member evoke greater self-disclosure on the part of the others also. As members listen to the story of one, they reflect on its meaning to them. They ask themselves such questions as "Have I ever been in such a situation?" or "I wonder how I'd feel," reflecting on the ways that their own experiences are like or unlike those of the presenter. In such ways, they deepen understanding of themselves as well as of others.

Adequate exploration of the person-group-situation configuration is an essential foundation for reflective discussion used to enhance understanding of self in interaction with varied situations. Adequate ventilation and sharing of feelings to ascertain the similar and different ones between the members are often essential, too. One example is taken from Judith Lee and Danielle Park's record of a group of adolescent girls in foster homes.[18] Considerable time was spent in exploring their feelings about being foster children, requiring support and empathy from the worker in sharing such feelings as "Being foster is like being a piece of garbage" or "You're just something somebody tossed out."

Carin, who had been reading, lifted her head, put her hands flat on the table, and said, "I got one for the group—what would you do if you thought you were going crazy?" There was a silence, and the members looked at one another. I asked Carin if she was talking about herself. She said yes, and the girls appeared to freeze. I asked if she could tell us what this going crazy feeling feels like. After thinking, she said seriously, "It feels like nothing matters to me anymore." Kenya asked her what about school, and she unfolded her story. I let them know it wasn't so crazy to feel that way with a life like Carin's.

In this and other situations, as feelings and experiences are revealed and understood by self and others, the members can move next to desired changes in feelings, relationships, and behavior. It is necessary to state the reality that a person like Carin is not mentally ill, in spite of the feelings, and to offer realistic hope that things will get better.

The group process can be very effective in helping members acknowledge feelings and problems in relationships. A short-term group of young adults in a psychiatric clinic had as its purpose the improvement of interpersonal relationships, primarily with members of their families. Joseph, age twenty-four, tended to deny his mixed feelings toward his wife's parents. Marjorie, age twenty-three, had expressed anger at her mother's need to control her. The following interchange occurred in the fifth meeting.

MARJORIE: I am afraid Mother will collapse if I disagree with her. The few times I did express myself, she acted oh so hurt. It just made me feel very guilty.
JOSEPH: You feel mortgaged?
MARJORIE: (acknowledges Joseph's insight) When I go home for the weekends, mother treats me like a special guest. But when we discuss almost anything, I just have to restrain myself from saying anything, since our values are so far apart. And I mean far apart. (She makes

further comments and several members point to difficulties with their parents, also.)

WORKER: You seem to be listening intently, Joseph.

JOSEPH: Yes . . . (*silence*). I'm really with what Marge says.

MARJORIE: How?

JOSEPH: Well—it's just like me and my in-laws. They give us all kinds of material goods, but if I don't like them . . . wow! I get so upset. I feel trapped.

WORKER: Trapped? Feeling mortgaged as you thought Marjorie felt?

JOSEPH: Absolutely.

MARJORIE: Like me! Definitely.

JOSEPH: (Goes on to explain situation. He often gets angry with his in-laws, with whom he lives. After a pause, he said, "But angry with myself, too.")

KEVIN: Yeah, I'll bet you feel guilty like Marge said she did. Is there nothing we can do to not feel so mortgaged at home?

The members had become able to express empathy for each other and identify with the common underlying feelings in spite of different family situations. The movement is from ventilating feelings, recognizing their nature, blaming others, and beginning to want to make some changes.

Sharing of feelings often produces mitigation of fear, guilt, hopelessness, or other strong emotions. Members often talk about situations in which they have been unable to express their feelings because they did not have the words to symbolize the feelings, were afraid of offending other persons, felt guilt about feelings, or were fearful of the consequences of acknowledging the feelings. The ventilation and discussion of feelings by some members evoke similar or different responses from the other members. The following incident occurred in a group of parents in a child guidance clinic. The purpose of the group is to help the members to cope more effectively with their emotionally disturbed children, who are enrolled in the clinic's pre-grade school. Most of the parents are not emotionally disturbed, but two members, one of them Mrs. J., has been diagnosed as borderline. Mrs. J. has been in the group for five months. She was divorced shortly after the birth of her only child, Jonathon, who is now five years old. She is head of the household, has a meager income, and is the sole support of herself and her son. The case study gives evidence that Mrs. J. is very dependent on the child for love and support, but she has not previously revealed the extent of her dependence on the boy.

During one session, the members were discussing how angry and disgusted they felt about being parents of disturbed children. Mrs. S. said, "Sometimes I feel like I could just give Tommy away—get rid of him—because he isn't getting any better." Mrs. J. responded loudly, "Oh, no! I could never give my Jonathon away, because he is my life—he is my life. If I did not have Jonathon I would have had a nervous breakdown." There was silence. The members' eyes were riveted on me. I responded, "I think those must be painful feelings—can you tell us more about the feelings, Mrs. J.?" She said, "They are terrible and terrifying." Mrs. B. nodded and said she guessed they had all had some terrifying feelings. Mr. P. said, "You're suffering—but I'm curious about what makes you feel you could have a nervous breakdown." The tears came to Mrs. J.'s eyes as she said simply, "I just know it—Jonathon means everything to me." Her voice began to crack and there were facial twitches as she continued, "I'm afraid to be without him—I'd feel so all alone." One member, feeling uncomfortable, changed the subject. I said, "It's hard for some of you to listen to Mrs. J., isn't it, but could we stick with the subject a while longer?" Mrs. J. became calmer and the tears stopped. She asked, "Have none of you ever felt so all alone that you thought you'd go crazy?" Mrs. B. said, "I really think I know the feeling." That remark led to a new level of sharing feelings about their relationships with their children and a desire to understand these feelings.

Looking back at this record, it is essential that the worker refer the group back to Mrs. S.'s distress. Her feelings seemed to get lost in responses to Mrs. J's more dramatic story.

Members of groups often need assistance in disclosing information about themselves. When members find it difficult to express their concerns, comments from the leader or another member that mention the universality of certain feelings and problems often release inhibitions. Examples would be a statement that it is normal to feel unhappy about being a foster child, for teenagers to feel rebellious against their parents at times, or to have frightening feelings about sex. Those things that people are often ashamed of, or are embarrassed about, are also of deep concern to them, for example, sexual attitudes and experiences, racial differences, failures at school or work, and fear of permanent disability or even death.

In today's multiethnic societies, groups often deal with the issue of racism when the group is sufficiently cohesive for members to disclose their feelings. They may then become able to confront and understand their own attitudes toward others. Support accompanies confrontation. An example is that of a worker's use of herself with a group of black girls, all with problems in high school and from low-income families. Frequent topics of discussion were feelings of being discriminated against and feelings of prejudice toward others. The sensitivity of these girls created frequent outbreaks of emotion in the group.

At first, the worker supported the expression of feelings about the girls' race and toward others, then gradually worked toward clarification of what part was the reality and what was displacement and projection of feelings onto others. When a teacher, also black, asked the girls to be less noisy, one member screamed, "Oh, I hate her; she is just prejudiced. She doesn't even stick up for her own race." Others joined in the ventilation of feelings against teachers and white students, who were perceived as being discriminatory. Gross distortions were evident, one complaint being that no black student had ever been an officer of the student organization.

When the worker expressed understanding of the members' feelings but confronted them with the reality of the situation, including the fact that the president of the student organization was a black boy, the girls stopped to ponder the statement. One grudgingly admitted, "That's true, but I just hate white kids." Later, the worker commented that the members seemed to feel at one about this. All agreed. The worker asked, "And there are no exceptions?" Two teachers were mentioned as being all right, but the expressions of hatred continued. To the two girls who expressed most of the feelings, the worker commented, "You seem to be full of hate today." The response was, "Well, yes, we've a right to." The worker acknowledged that sometimes there were reasons to feel hatred. Gradually, the members themselves began to confront each other with the facts. One girl said, "After all, Mrs. G. (the worker) is white, too." The most vociferous of the members looked startled, and said, "Oh, no," and broke into tears, then added, "But, but, I like you." From that point, the girls began to individualize people, with more realistic evaluation of people and situations.

Social workers need to remember that one of the characteristics of a non-racist practitioner is the ability to confront members when they distort the intentions and behavior of others.[19]

When members confront each other, the worker needs to understand whether the intent of the confronter was to hurt or to help, the influence of the confrontation on the members toward whom it was directed and on the other members, and the needs and readiness of the group to use it. An example of a group's confrontation of one of its members occurred in a group of couples with marital problems.

One couple was engaged in unproductive and prolonged accusations of each other's part in threatening the marriage. The worker confronted them with the observation that, although both of them had said they wanted to make the marriage work, they had not yet tried to make it work. The husband, Ben, said he was willing to open up communication with Alice, his wife. Then, he said angrily, "But will you promise to do that, too?" Alice's response was to leap from the chair, hysterically shouting that she saw no point in staying here to be the object of abuse and insensitivity from Ben—she was leaving. Tom, another member, said quickly and sternly, "Don't leave, Alice. I have something to say to you both." Alice didn't sit down, but remained in the room, leaning her arms against the back of the chair. Tom said that both of them should stop fighting right now. Both looked taken aback. Tom told them they were acting like two children, just like the kids that he works with at school. He related an episode of a fight between two kids, neither of whom would admit what happened and each blaming the other for the fight. He said that's exactly what Alice and Ben were doing. Each blamed the other, and neither would tell each other what it was all about. He went on to explain the relationship as he saw it. There was a dead silence in the room. Ben said, "Well, I'm willing to try," but then asked Alice in an angry way, "Are you willing, too?" Jane shouted, "My God, Ben, you didn't take in a single thing that Tom was telling you." Steve said, "For God's sake, Ben, what's the matter with you?" Elaine shouted, "There you go again." Ben was silent, looking as if he had been hit. I wondered what message Ben got from the group. He said, "I got the word clearly, and I will try." This time he did not add angrily that Alice should do this, too.

When it was time to end the meeting, I commented that the free expression of conflict had been hard for all — especially for Alice and Ben. Elaine said, "You can say that again, but we learned through it." She got up from her chair, and the others followed. Ben went over to Alice and helped her to put her coat on. As they were leaving, Tom said to Alice, "You and Ben are coming for coffee, aren't you?" They said they would like to do that.

On the basis of an on-the-spot assessment of the situation, the worker supports or does not support the efforts of the confronter, encourages the members to continue dealing with the issue, and works with them to summarize the learnings and generalize from a particular situation. Gradually, the members become more able to empathize with each other and thereby become more helpful than hurtful in the intent and nature of their confronting comments.

According to their understanding of the needs of the members and their motivation and capacity to deal with personal and interpersonal problems, workers help the members to focus on clarification of patterns of behavior that are helpful or destructive to them. There seems to be a natural progression from recognition of the behavior in the situation to elaboration of the situation more fully in its many facets — the feelings about it, the behavior patterns and the situations in which they occur, and the consequences of the behavior. In some situations, such understanding is sufficient; in others, further work is desirable to clarify the meaning of the situation or behavior.

Social workers' major efforts build on and support the use of the members' positive motivations and capacities and encourage members to support or to question the comments and behavior of each other. For example, in a group of adolescent boys, one member asked Pete directly about school. Pete, aged seventeen, replied that he had quit. One member said it was stupid to have done that. The other members agreed. One member commented, "We'd better stop jumping Pete and find out what happened." Here, the worker supported, through purposeful silence, the group's work in understanding one of its members and then helping him to face his behavior more realistically.

Within the protection of the group, the worker may create an awareness among members of the discrepancy between their private attitudes and behavior and their earlier statements to the group. He may do this by encouraging a member with high status in the group to tell the group about his feelings and behavior that deviate from his earlier public expressions. One example is of a group in which a high-status older adolescent revealed that his earlier exaggerations concerning his sexual conquests and his sexual security were not true; that he really felt very uncomfortable with girls. Following their expressions of surprise at this admission, the other members openly expressed their fears and anxieties. The facade of sexual adequacy gave way to efforts to achieve more adequate masculine identification. Thus, instead of continuing to support each other's denials, the members could move toward support of efforts to change attitudes and behavior. Arthur Blum says that, when possible, the selection of a member with high status is deliberate; if such revelation emanates from a member with low status, there is danger that he will become a scapegoat. Such a member is also less likely to be able to influence the behavior of the other members.[20]

Irrational beliefs about oneself are forms of lack of self-knowledge. Low self-esteem or lack of positive identity leads many clients to deprecate themselves and engage in self-defeating patterns of behavior. "I am not loved," "I'm really ugly," "If you really knew me, you'd know how rotten I am" are messages that often convey irrational beliefs about oneself. Such beliefs about who one is develop through relationships and experiences with other people who confirm or contradict the beliefs. Responses from others interact with one's own perceptions.

In a group of hospitalized patients with mental illness, Mr. M. started a discussion of the possibility of getting a job when he is ready to go home. Mr. R., the newest member of the group, mentioned his fears about being able to get a job, and all the members, except Mr. D., who is still not able to participate very much, laughed and said they all had those fears. After further discussion, I said that it really was a worry not to be sure about a job, wasn't it? Mr. M. and Mr. R. both said I was right, and other members seemed to agree through nonverbal nods. Mr. R. then said that was not his biggest worry: he had a really big worry, but he did not want the members to know about it. He asked me if I knew what it was. I said I knew whatever was in his record. I reassured the members that they could express whatever they wanted to in this group, but they did not have to talk about things until they were ready to do so. Mr. M. said that the group is here for us to talk about our problems. Mr. R. then started to talk in a very general way about sex, but it was difficult to follow what he was saying. The others listened quietly to his efforts. I said that if he could try to be a little more specific, perhaps other members could help him with the problem. Mr. R. asked if I would explain his "big problem" to the others. I merely said in a questioning way, "You want me to tell the group for you?" He nodded. Mr. M. said he gathered that the problem had to do with sex. Mr. R. said that was it and thanked him for saying it.

Mr. M. said, "Well, go ahead and discuss it; that is what the group is for—to talk about problems like that." Mr. R. looked at me, and I assured him that it was all right to talk about those things. He said then that his problem was that he was in love with somebody. Finally, Mr. M. asked him if he was talking about women, and Mr. R. said he was not. Mr. M. then said, "Oh, you're talking about being gay, then." Mr. R. said that was it—he didn't want people to know about it, but he thought they could tell just by looking at him. The other members told him that this was not so. Mr. R. then said he guessed he should talk about this with me alone, because I had training and understood these things. Mr. M. supported this proposal. I said that I needed to disagree; it would be better for them to work on such problems here in the group. I said I thought other members had their own feelings about this subject and perhaps we could work on those, too. Mr. M. and Mr. O. said they were gay, too. I said we could talk about that next time.

It was almost time to close the meeting and Mr. R. said, "You can tell me to get out of this group and not come back." I said he must be afraid that we would kick him out because we thought that being gay was bad. He said, "How did you know?" and added that was exactly what he was feeling. First Mr. M. and then each other member said something to reassure him that they did not think worse of him for what he had shared here. I asked if he wanted to tell us anything else about his feelings about sharing with us. He said that part of a big load was off his mind, but he had another one now, knowing that others also shared his problem. I hoped his fears would not get so bad that he would not want to come back to the group. He said firmly, "Oh, no—I will be here." I said I would be on the ward tomorrow morning so any of them could see me if they wanted to. After the meeting, Mr. R. shook hands with me and thanked me for helping him to tell the group about himself.

In this example, the newest member opened up a subject that the group had avoided but was almost ready to discuss. In light of the reality that many people have homophobic attitudes, Mr. R. was appropriately cautious of and fearful about the responses to the self-disclosure. He tested the assumption that if the members knew about his sexual orientation, they would reject him. In the group, however, a process of mutual acceptance and capacity for empathy was operating that made it possible for Mr. R. to share his deep concern with the others and open up a hitherto taboo topic.

The social worker can provide conditions, through the relationship, that allow clients to test the validity of their beliefs about their self-esteem and identity. When possible, a worker can use external realities to correct distortions in perception of self. In a group of married couples, for example, the worker said to a wife, "John just said that he loves you very much—didn't you hear him say that?" John said, "And I meant it—I do love you and want us to be happy together." Another member said, "And I think he really means it." Others nodded in agreement. Groups offer a broader arena for such testing than is true of one-worker-one-client relationships.

As discussed in chapter 11, activities may often be used for the express purpose of stimulating reflection on feelings and concerns. Many children will pour out their feelings and ideas on toy telephones, tape recorders, role playing, or through puppets, for such communication is one step removed from face-to-face communication with the leader and other members. As members progress in treatment, the nonverbal behavior becomes less prominent and there is more moving back and forth between action and talking. In work with adults, movies, tape recordings, books, and pictures are often used to stimulate discussion of the event and then to move to discussion of how it is related to the experiences of the members.

In this stage of development, support, exploration, guidance, and education continue to be important, but clarification and interpretation also become major skills in helping members to understand themselves in relation to others, as indicated in some of the previous examples. Explanations and interpretations need to be attuned to the particular perspectives of the members and timed in accordance with their readiness. That is a general principle, applicable to all groups.

Whatever the major purpose of the group, some work on enhancing understanding of self, other people, and social situations is relevant. Skills are used differentially according to the major goals of the group and the needs of the members. In counseling and therapy groups, particularly, there is greater focus on interpretation than is usually true for groups in which the greatest emphasis is on cognitive learning, behavioral modification, or social action.

Coping with Stress

Some groups are established for the primary purpose of helping individuals or families to reduce unbearable stress by coping effectively with crises in their lives. Crises, according to Gerald Caplan, are "limited time periods of upset in the psychosocial functioning of individuals, precipitated by current exposure to environmental stressors." He explains, "The basic thesis is that individuals exposed to a particular level of stress, who concomitantly benefit from a high level of social support, have less risk of subsequent mental and physical illness than do similar individuals exposed to similar stress who do not have such support."[21] Groups provide a highly supportive environment and also help members to find and use other supports in the community.

A crisis is precipitated by a hazardous event occasioned by (1) difficult transitions to new roles or statuses, such as in divorce, retirement, or a change in school or work, (2) acute situational distress occasioned by traumatic experiences such as death of a loved one, loss of health, rape, or physical assault, or (3) community disruptions or natural disasters, such as riots, floods, or tornadoes. The hazardous event may be perceived as a threat to important life goals, security, or affectional needs. When people are in a state of crisis, they are especially susceptible to well-timed and well-focused help. The intensification of stress often enhances motivation to find new ways of coping with the problem. Two major goals of crisis intervention are to relieve anxiety and other symptoms of distress and to mobilize capacities for coping adaptively with the effects of stress on the person, family, or group.[22]

An example is of a group composed of five- to seven-year-old boys and girls who had suffered a recent loss in their families. There is substantial research to indicate that the death of a family member creates emotional turmoil for members of the family.[23] Even young children can benefit from a group experience in which the relationship with the social worker and members reduces anxiety, helps the children to understand the nature of the illness, and provides support during a trying time.

The children were playing house. Two of them had volunteered to be mother and father and asked Jenny to be a child. Jenny said, "Nooo, I can't play. I have no mommy; she went to heaven." The playing stopped. Kathy asked, "Why did she die?" Jenny, with tears in her eyes, slowly said, "Cancer. She had little bugs that were biting her." "How sad," said Simon. "Oh, no," cried Megan, "that's not right, is it? It does not eat you up." I listened, feeling the pathos of the children over the loss of someone dear to them. Slowly, I said, "Cancer is a word that scares us. Many people who have it get well, but some do die." I observed the children, noting their nonverbal behavior, trying to decide what to say next. Tommy interrupted the silence, saying that his brother died of leukemia (he had difficulty pronouncing it), but he did not have bugs on him. I responded, "No, one does not have bugs that bite." I moved close to Jenny. "But there are what we call cells in the body that get out of control and make people sick. That may remind us of bugs, but they are not bugs." Jenny said, "Oh, maybe my mommy did not have bugs." Tommy said, "My brother did not either." Betty asked, "Who takes care of you, Jenny?" "Oh, my daddy takes good care of me." Alan said, "Let's play house now." Taking the mother out of the play house, he said to Jenny, "Now you can play. I'll be your daddy."

In addition to crisis intervention groups, crises are bound to occur in any group. Crises faced by members outside the group may be brought into the content of the group. The group, with its potential for support and stimulation, may be an effective aid in helping the person resolve the problem. Members of some groups are faced with crises over and over again, precipitated by lack of water and heat due to nonpayment of bills, suspensions from school, arrests, interpersonal violence, and illness. This is particularly true of low-income families with multiple situational problems and of persons with character disorders. Crises may occur also within the internal system of the group. The absence of a worker from a group of severely disturbed children, the transfer of the group to another worker, the death of a member, or any other sudden change in the group may be perceived as a crisis by the members. Such situations may stir up suppressed feelings about prior separations, so that the event itself is magnified beyond the reality of the situation. Within the climate of acceptance that tends to pervade the group during this stage, conflict between members or subgroups may be severe enough to constitute a crisis for the group.

As exemplified in the children's group, crises that are most amenable to treatment through groups seem to be those in which members share the same precipitating event. The sense of a common fate is a strong force for mutual identification, support, and mutual aid in finding effective means of coping with the problem. An example is taken from the record of a group for survivors of rape.

Sara, twenty-five-years old from a working class family, was the most troubled of the group of six survivors of rape. Her symptoms were the most severe: she was extremely fearful, nervous, and depressed. Having been, according to her own account, a sociable person, she was now leading a lonely, isolated life. She was able to work only part time and was angry with her parents, who were divorced, paid no attention to her, blamed her, and offered no emotional support. The violent attack haunted her day and night. She was at work alone in the evening when two men broke into the office; they taped her face and arms, ransacked the office, and then took her into the bathroom, where each one raped her before locking her in. She had managed to get out eventually, called the police, who treated her politely but who were never able to find and arrest the men.

At this time, all members had attended at least three prior sessions. They had described and achieved some understanding of the nature of rape, ventilated their feelings, and discussed the positive and negative reactions of families and friends to the event. The content of the group was now on how members were coping with their feelings and with other people, making efforts to find acceptance and understanding from families and friends. Sara was presenting information about the fact that she is alienated from her family. She kept repeating her story, with the result that several members became impatient.

———

Recognizing her great sense of loneliness, I said, "Sara, it seems to me, as I have listened to you, that I hear something from you that I don't hear so much from the others. The other members seem to have found friends and family to confide in, but you seem to have few people just now to whom you can turn. Do you feel that you are very much alone with your fears and troubles?"

Sara was silent for a moment and there were tears in her eyes as she replied that she was lonely and that, except for the group, there was no one to turn to. At this point, other members turned to Sara and assured her of their concern for her. Then Ellen questioned her about her reluctance to turn to anyone for comfort and company. Lois said that Sara seems so independent, but she needs help now. Sara replied, "I can't ask people. I can't do that. I don't want to be a little girl again. I've always been able to tough it out and that's what I want to do this time." Kathy said, "But, Sara, it doesn't mean you're weak because you ask other people for help." When there was a pause, I said, "You know, maybe you are ashamed to let anyone outside of this group see that you feel badly and need help."

Lois picked this up and said that, until she had broken down with some of her friends, none of them had been able — or had dared — to offer help. Esther told the group how she had suffered after her father died, and the rape brought up a lot of those painful memories. But she has learned to challenge her mother and stepfather when they hurt her, and they are more respectful of her as a result. Alicia, a nun, said she had begun to discover new friends in her order, to whom she was beginning to open up about the rape and in whom she was learning to trust. Turning to Sara, she said, "I want you to listen to me. My dearest friend and I had a long talk about what had happened to me. It took me a long time to tell her because, as you know, I'm not a blabbermouth about myself. Anne said to me afterward that she was happy that I had confided in her and that she was able to help. I'm much stronger now because I know I can depend on someone else without giving up my integrity." Others shared their experiences in confiding in friends. Sara explained why she couldn't do that. She had told one old friend about the assault recently, but "I can't wake her up at two in the morning, when I feel most depressed." Esther said, "You're not listening to us: you can call me and any of us any time." Sara gulped and nodded. There was an exchange of phone numbers, and Lois asked, "Why didn't we think of this before? We can call each other." I said I was very glad they had thought of this idea, and then asked Sara, "Do you know now that you have a good circle of supporters here?" She answered, "I do know that now."

The group is a temporary support system, but people in a state of crisis need to find others in the wider environment who will not blame them, who will listen to them, and who will provide opportunities to develop or reestablish relationships that have been cut off. In a research study, two-thirds of the rape victims who were interviewed listed the need for support and understanding as most important.[24] The victim must deal not only with her own emotions and reactions but also with the reactions of other people, who, too often, blame the victim. Thus, the victim's efforts to cope are compounded by the reactions of others. Working with people in a state of crisis makes full use of the problem-solving process in a time-limited treatment. Successful intervention requires

1. rapid assessment of the nature and extent of the stress, the impact of the hazardous event on the member and significant others, emotional reactions to the event, the member's adaptive capacities, and available sources of support;
2. exploration of feelings that have been stirred up by the event and acceptance of such feelings as anger, hopelessness, guilt, or remorse; such exploration helps members to master their own emotions but also the reactions of other people who, too often, blame the victim;
3. education and clarification concerning the nature and severity of the precipitating event;
4. consideration of alternative means of coping with the problems that are associated with the hazardous event and selection of one or more that might best fit the person's needs and situation;
5. discovery and use of appropriate resources in the form of emotional support or health and welfare services in the community.

In the group, the members, as well as the worker, are expected to provide support, sensitive listening, suggestions for alternative means of problem solving, and hope that comes from perceiving that others have successfully risked new ways of coping and changing. Through such means, stress is reduced and social functioning is restored.

Competence in Role Functioning

In this stage of development, many opportunities arise to help the members to learn adaptive behavior in carrying their social roles. Adaptation is a dynamic process that involves mastery of tasks and situations, as well as appropriate use of defenses and coping efforts. Social competence is the ability to perform roles in ways that are personally satisfying and that meet reasonable expectations of significant persons, such as spouses, parents, employers, teachers, police, or friends. The theoretical assumption underlying work to achieve social competence is that the ego is strengthened and personal power achieved when persons have confidence in their abilities to perform desired social roles effectively. According to a report on research by Don Fuchs and Theresa Costes, empowerment involves changes toward positive perceptions of oneself, involvement in healthy and satisfying relationships with others and, then, toward interactions with other people and organizations in the community. The authors refer to this process as participatory competence.[25] To become competent, people need considerable understanding of themselves and others and a network of skills, knowledge, and talents that enable them to interact effectively with their environments.

Knowledge about the tasks typical of stages of development in the life cycle, as described in chapter 2, is useful to the practitioner in locating common needs and concerns, provided that the worker assesses individual differences and group deviations from such norms. Unresolved problems from earlier stages may be brought into the group. Differences in lifestyle concerning such matters as orientation to time, patterns of child rearing, stereotypes of gender role, group associational patterns, and educational and vocational aspirations need to be included in the worker's assessment of the adequacy of the members' performance of roles. The fact that most members have achieved satisfaction in their roles as members of the group enhances their readiness to examine their performance in other roles in which they have difficulty or the variables that seem to account for greater success in one role than in others.

The development of skills necessary for improved performance in selected roles may comprise a considerable portion of the content of the group. Using communication skills, securing information, rehearsing behavior, preparing budgets, practicing ways to make friends, and learning activities that are expected of a person of a given age and gender are but a few examples of specific content in this area. Reports of progress or successes in meeting expectations of roles outside the group become more frequent as the group progresses. The worker's focus is not limited to the content of specific roles but is also on the development of affective and cognitive styles or processes of acquiring mastery over oneself and the environment. Understanding is not sufficient: there is need for action—for successful doing.

Effective communication is one of the most important social skills. During earlier meetings, in order for the group to have formed, some satisfactory channels for communication were developed, and communication between members was adequate to achieve the tasks typical of those stages. The members now tend to use the group for help in working through problems in communication with such persons as their parents, children, siblings, employers, teachers, or colleagues.

An example concerns Maria, aged fifteen, who announced that she had been "kicked out of school." The worker suggested that this was a good place to talk about it. Maria replied, "Oh, no. I never could." There followed considerable ventilation of negative feelings about school and empathy with Maria. But when she felt the worker's and the group's acceptance, she told the group about the situation. When another member asked if the suspension were final, it developed that Maria could be reinstated only if her mother would go to school. Her mother had refused to do this when her brother had been in similar trouble. Maria brought out much anger toward school and a feeling of hopelessness about her mother's lack of cooperation. Another member said, "Then there's just nothing that can be done." The worker said she did not think the situation was hopeless and suggested that the group could act out the situation to try to find ways that Maria might talk to her mother. She knew that the members were ready and able to help with the problem and that, as they worked on it, they would also learn more effective ways of communicating with their own parents.

Decision making. One frequent type of competence is successful decision making. Members often have difficulty in making, evaluating, and implementing decisions. In social work practice with groups, the worker's emphasis is on helping the members to learn how to use a problem-solving process in arriving at a decision. The decision may focus on resolving a problem of a member or a problem in the group structure and interaction.

As the group progresses through time, its decisions now extend from those about the group's purpose, structure, norms, and process to those about the life of its members outside the group. The worker helps the group work toward decisions applicable to the life situations of the members. It is not realistic to hope that if members learn how to make decisions about their group life, this ability can be transferred automatically to other situations. The members need to recognize the carryover to other areas of social functioning. Thus, the focus on problems in the interaction between individuals and the social environment needs to be maintained. It is important that the participants experience the relevance between what they do in the group and what they can do in their families and the community.

Participation in planning and decision-making processes is often a means through which members of groups gain in social competence. How difficult this is for some people is often underemphasized.

During the sixth month of service to a group of very disturbed boys, aged twelve to fourteen, in a residential treatment center, the boys requested a trip to an amusement park. The worker, assessing that the boys were ready for it, engaged them in detailed planning for the trip. One of the first steps was to consider the nature of the decisions to be made: where to go, how to get there, how much money was needed, what to bring, and so forth. The tension became almost unbearable as the group decided that Billy, one of the oldest members, should make a phone call to get information about the amusement park. All of the boys tried to instruct Billy on how to use the phone and what questions to ask. None really knew how to do this. What a great sense of accomplishment the boys experienced when Billy was able to get at least some of the desired information.

As in that example, successful performance of a complex task often leads to increased self-esteem and a sense of competence. Andrew Malekoff illustrated the use of a project in which a group of nine- and ten-year-old boys painted a room in a community mental health center.[26] The boys had been referred by school personnel for problems of low self-esteem, poor judgment, and immaturity.

Recognizing that the room needed a coat of paint, the social worker decided to solicit the members to do the job. He wrote, "There was spontaneous unanimity in their decision to perform the task. As a result, discussion was slowly transformed into an activity that was intended to support the group's sense of competency and autonomy." To do the job, several steps were required: planning, decision making, pricing and purchasing materials, developing skills, committing time, and planning a schedule. "The job itself, which lasted roughly six hours, was completed with great care. The worker, who was present during the job, intervened minimally and primarily to 'inspect' the work in progress and to praise the boys' effort and skill."

This project demonstrated "the integration of discussion and activity to promote a sense of belonging, build ego strengths, and enhance the self esteem of young adolescent boys. As each group member's mastery of the new situation grew, so grew the competence of the group, and the members' sense of pride in one another as well as their parents' pride in what they had accomplished." Malekoff gives other illustrations of using projects for developing competence.

Arriving at a decision is in and of itself not necessarily helpful. It is crucial that alternative solutions be considered and the consequences of each alternative explored thoroughly. To look at alternative modes of behavior and act on the basis of such examinations tends to enhance social competence.

In a group of delinquent boys on probation, John exploded that his father was angry and had had enough of him. Tom asked about the trouble. John said he had been forbidden to use the car, but some of his friends insisted, so he gave in. Later that evening, he was arrested for speeding. Then he grumbled about his father for a long time. Brian said, "But you're in double trouble—with the cops and with your dad." Tom said, "You sure messed up." The worker commented that John seemed caught between two pulls: his father and his friends. He suggested that the members go back to the time when John made the decision to take his father's car and think about other ways that John might have dealt with the problem.

In the discussion that followed, the worker helped the boys to understand conflicting desires and pressures, weigh circumstances, and make decisions based on what solutions bring satisfaction and have utility. Then, the group content turned to what John could do now. This decision-making process focused on one member, yet it provided a valuable experience for the others as well. It contributed to enhanced understanding of themselves in relation to situations. As they learn to be helpful to each other, people become more confident in their own capacities to face issues and make decisions.

Once implemented, decisions need to be reviewed, evaluated, and often modified on the basis of experience. Thus, there is a recurrent cycle of problem identification, decision making, and action on the part of an individual or of the group as a unit. Such problem-solving activities can enhance the members' general competence to make decisions that are based on understanding of one's own motives and the demands of the situation.

A variety of activity-oriented experiences, as well as discussion, may be used to enhance decision-making capacities. As part of the problem-solving process, members may be helped to carry out decisions through rehearsal. Rehearsal is useful in work with certain persons, regardless of their age, to clarify situations and plan how to face difficult situations. How to tell the teacher that one needs help, apply for a job, communicate effectively with parents or spouse, talk with a probation officer or employer, or behave when challenged to fight are common situations that can be discussed and rehearsed in the group. Follow-up of what happened when efforts were made to apply learning from the group to situations outside the group provides opportunity for evaluation and, when necessary, stimulates further efforts to solve the problem.

The problem-solving process can be used to help members with problems in their functioning in particular roles. Members can be encouraged to report incidents of problematic situations, explore the situation, and consider alternative means of dealing with the situation more effectively. Other members who have observed or been involved in similar situations can be effective in correcting each other's false perceptions of the situation or of their own behavior and in proposing alternative coping methods. When decisions have been made about the modes of behavior and means of achieving desired objectives, the worker suggests ways they can be put into practice between meetings. Through such means, persons can learn that new efforts are worthwhile, and progress becomes more rapid. Role-playing may be used to recreate the stressful encounters and to test out alternative solutions. As new roles are explored, the members gain experience with different attitudes and a clearer perception of both the dynamics behind the action and the ways in which others perceive them. Such activities may be effective as practice for dealing with situations in the environment.

Activities in the environment expand the horizons and experiences of the members and provide the group with opportunities for learning and problem solving in their lives outside the group. Such work in the environment can assure that the helping process does not become disengaged from the social environment. Within the group, too, it is essential that attention be given to the transfer of learning from the group to situations at home, work, play, school or associations with other people.[27]

To become competent in the performance of social roles requires that a person have knowledge about and ability to use resources and supportive networks. Depending upon the purpose of the group and the members' situations, the content of the group may include information about and skills in identifying and using resources through discussion, sharing of experiences, bringing resource persons into the group, and considering referrals. The members of groups are thereby linked to other people and services in the community in a manner that enhances their self-esteem, and competence. Members' participation in the process is extensive; workers offer their knowledge and expertise to them.

Altruism is a dynamic positive force for change. Concern with dependency-interdependency conflicts and the concomitant need to both give and take are prevalent with many members of groups. With people in hospitals and other residential settings, particularly, there is necessary dependence on many staff members. A sign of maturity in relationships is to be able to give as well as to receive. The group itself fosters interdependency between members, but often a need also exists to give to others outside the group, within the institution or the wider community. The ego-enhancing opportunities to give to others, in terms of contribution of time, ideas, or material things, should not be underestimated.

The opportunities are many. A group of mothers of hospitalized children, toward the end of their experience in a group, used the last session to plan and carry out special holiday programs for all the children and staff in the hospital. A group of physically handicapped children were enthralled when, instead of only being entertained and given to at a community party, the members could contribute cookies and take responsibility for registering guests. A group composed of patients with mental illness sent representatives to a meeting that was held to plan a community action program on mental health. A group of black adolescent girls, following discussion of their own feelings about experiences with discrimination, initiated and participated in a social action project directed toward making a recreational activity available to people of all races. A parent education group, in cooperation with a church, developed a playground for young children and volunteered to supervise it. Low-income parents, previously fearful of approaching school personnel, became active in a parent-teachers association and thereby helped to achieve a school lunch program.[28] Interdependence, then, is important, not only within the group but also between the group and the community.

The worker progressively extends the experience of the members to other areas of community life. Expectations for members are raised gradually, as they show the capacity to achieve certain tasks and as they indicate readiness for more complex activities. Through broadening the experience of members and evaluating, with them, their responses to new situations, members develop the power to become able to handle a greater variety of experiences in an adequate manner. Soon they will be ready to leave the group.

Interviews with Individuals

Conferences with individuals are an integral part of the social worker's practice with groups. The worker's use of self in interaction with the group is, in one sense, the essence of social work practice with groups. Yet workers are extremely limited if they view this as the only means of help. They often work directly, on a one-to-one basis, with some members or with a parent, spouse, or other person of importance in the life of the member.

There are brief interviews between the worker and a member within the group, which Fritz Redl refers to as life space interviews.[29] Such interviews are held immediately before, after, or even during a group session. The member may seek out the worker or the conference may be initiated by the worker, usually when a particular concern about a member is not likely to be brought into the orbit of the group session itself.

Sometimes conflict between a member and other members of the group becomes so intense and the group is so unready to handle it that private conferences may be necessary.

In a group in a community center, Janice complained about the recreational staff; she thought they picked on her, disliked her, and blamed her for things that were not her fault. Kathy criticized Janice for not being able to say anything good about anybody, and other members agreed with Kathy. Janice angrily turned her chair to the wall, sat there for awhile, and then left the room, slamming the door behind her. The other members were very upset. The worker acknowledged with them some of their feelings. She suggested the group continue its planning with the assistant leader while she went to see if Janice was still in the building so she could talk with her and help her return to the group. She found Janice sitting in the lobby, crying. In a brief conference, the worker said she knew that Janice was troubled about a number of things that seemed to make it hard for her to get along in the group. After some discussion, Janice responded to the worker's suggestion that she return to the group to try to work things out there. This was done.

———

The important skill is to use such brief interviews to meet the immediate needs of the person yet not detract from the group itself as the primary means of service. A great deal of analytical judgment is necessary to decide wisely whether to deal with the concern privately with the member or to encourage the person to bring the concern into the group. The skilled worker can often find ways to relate what seems like a unique problem to the concerns of the group, through searching for likeness in seemingly unlike situations.

Interviews with members of the group, or other persons in their behalf, often take place in privacy, usually by appointment. Such interviews are used for several purposes. One is to orient and prepare new members for making a satisfactory initial entry into an open-ended group. Another purpose is to help a member to cope more effectively with a pressing problem that seems unsuitable for discussion within the group at a particular time, owing either to the situation in the group or to the fact that, at the time, the person cannot bear to express feelings and thoughts or to present a problem to the group. A conference may enable the person to bring it into the group or may indicate that individual or family treatment is necessary. In groups in which certain responsibilities have been assigned to officers or committees, a conference may be used to aid such persons to fulfill their responsibilities as effectively as possible.

Referrals

Members of groups often need to be referred to other services in the community that cannot be provided through the group or the agency, or they may need special support as they get connected with other services. Knowledge of social, health, and educational organizations in the community is necessary for effective referrals—knowledge of their functions, auspices, concepts of service, and interrelationships. Referrals to employment services, social clubs, work training programs, health and medical care, or religious organizations should be part of treatment if members are to be helped to function at or nearer to their full capacities. When members have enough confidence and skill to handle the situation, the worker supports them in doing this, for the principle is that the worker supports people's ego functioning by strengthening their ability to handle their own affairs. Sometimes the worker needs to mediate between the client and the desired services so that the client does not get lost between slots of agency functions and policies. It may mean explaining the member's goals, problems, capacities, and special needs to appropriate staff in the new organization. It may mean giving considerable assistance to help a member to understand the intake procedures and to make concrete plans for the first encounter. Successful referral involves clarification of the specific needs or problems, motivation to initiate an application, and follow-through procedures. Whatever the worker does, it is done with the informed consent and active participation of the members—that is ethical behavior.

Guidelines for Practice

In this stage of group development, members engage in a process of mutual aid to enhance social skills and cope with personal, interpersonal, and environmental problems that are related to the group's purpose. As they seek for intimacy and differentiation, they are more able to accept and empathize with one another. Their relationships with the worker tend to be close, but subject to distortions in the form of transference and identification. Within a generally supportive climate, members are usually motivated but may, at times, resist working toward their goals. The norms of the group support acceptance of differences. Communication is free and easy, with appropriate means of self-disclosure. A group has developed that is cohesive enough for the mutual aid process to work effectively.

In helping the members to work toward achievement of their goals, social workers continue to help the group develop into a growth-promoting system in which individual and group goals are pursued. The workers' tasks are to

1. continue to reflect on their part in the process, understanding how their own feelings, opinions, and experiences promote or interfere with effective work with individuals and the group;
2. continue to assess each member's participation in the group, the roles they have acquired, and their motivation and capacity to acquire knowledge and skills and to cope with problems and also assess the development of the group as a need-meeting system and the opportunities and obstacles in the environment;
3. strengthen supportive relationships, offering appropriate forms of support, recognizing needs, influencing roles, and using confrontation to deal with dysfunctional behaviors;
4. recognize conflict as it occurs and view it as a dynamic for constructive change by helping the members to use the problem-solving process to reduce or eliminate the conflict;
5. conduct interviews with individuals, as needed, to help them participate more effectively in the group, cope with problems that do not fit within the focus of content at a given time, or refer them to resources outside the group;
6. provide a focus for content of the group that is relevant to the purpose of the group; typical themes of content include (1) acquiring essential knowledge about behavior, problems, or environment, (2) improving interpersonal understanding, (3) learning to cope with stress, including life transitions and crises, (4) developing competence in the performance of social roles, and (5) developing or using appropriate health, welfare, recreational, and educational resources, expanding or changing social networks, and making efforts to reduce environmental obstacles.

Within a caring, accepting, and empathic relationship, social workers make use of all of the categories of intervention. Confrontation, clarification, and interpretation are more frequently used in this stage of group development than in the preceding stages. Whether the content is primarily discussion or activities, the interventive skills are used selectively to achieve a particular result.

15 Stage IV: Separation-Termination

Termination is a dynamic and vital process in social work. It is more than a symbol of the end of treatment: it is an integral part of the process. If properly understood and managed, it becomes an important force in integrating changes in feeling, thinking, and doing. In the ending stage, the predominant socioemotional issue concerns members' separation from the social worker and usually also from each other. The predominant task is termination of a member or the group in such a way that the gains made through the group experience will carry over to everyday relationships and achievements. The role of the social worker is to evaluate the readiness of the members for termination, understand and help members to cope with their reactions, maintain beneficial changes, help members transfer the gains made in the group to daily living, and seek out and use new services and experiences when appropriate.[1]

Social work services are always time limited. The intent of treatment, said Gordon Hamilton, "is always to help the person return as soon as possible to natural channels of activity with strengthened relationships."[2] Professional help beyond the point that the person's natural growth can be resumed may interfere with the natural potential for growth and lead to continuing dependency. If members are helped to face the meaning of the group experience and to leave it with a sense of achievement, they should be able to use what they have learned in the group in their relationships and roles in the community. They may be more able to cope with other separations that occur throughout their lives. As Irvin Yalom said, "termination is thus more than an extraneous event in the group; it is the microcosmic representation of some of the most crucial and painful issues of all."[3]

Ending an experience needs to be done in such a way that social work values are implemented. Ideally, members belonged to a group in which they have been helped to achieve their goals, have felt that they were treated with acceptance and respect, and have been encouraged to participate actively in the process, with due regard for the welfare of self and others. An interdependent and intimate relationship has been achieved with the social worker and other members of the group. The members have found mutual acceptance and respect and have participated actively in a process of mutual aid. Now the termination of a member or the breaking up of a group needs to be done in such a way that the ending becomes a dynamic growth-producing experience.

The decision to terminate and the process of ending make use of the knowledge essential to effective practice. A group has been formed and sustained for achieving particular goals. Now, the knowledge about biopsychosocial functioning is used to help the members to leave the worker and each other. Particularly useful are perspectives on growth and development that incorporate the concepts of loss and separation related to the significance of social relationships to people in each phase of development and that explain the ways the ego defends itself against, copes with, and masters the experience. Erik Erikson, Henry Maas, and Constance Shapiro have such a perspective.[4] When faced with loss or separation, the steady state is upset. The members react with a variety of emotional and behavioral reactions to the loss of a member or worker and to the threat of termination. The nature and intensity of the reactions to termination depend upon many circumstances, such as the structure of the group, the length of service, reasons for termination, past experiences with losses and separations, and the extent of meaningful relationships and supports in the environment.

Characteristics of the Group

Pallassana Balgopal and Thomas Vassil point out that the termination stage is marked by a transition from the rhythm of work to disengagement and preparation for the future. Earlier themes of loss, dependency, and ambivalence are revisited and coexist with feelings of satisfaction and recognition of limited but worthy accomplishments. As members look backward and forward, the group experience is memorialized and affirmed as a reference point for negotiating the future.[5]

As the group moves toward readiness for termination, the socioemotional issues become separation and coming to terms with the meaning that the group experience has had for the members. The members exhibit anxiety about separation and ambivalence about the loss of relationships with the social worker and other members. They mobilize their defenses against facing termination. Although they accept each other, there is a movement toward the breaking of interpersonal ties as members find satisfaction in relationships outside the group. Exceptions are family units or natural peer groups that continue after the ending of the social work service. And, in formed groups, some members may have become close friends, continuing their relationship after the group ends.

The goals that members have for themselves and for each other have been partially achieved, although movement in the group may have been faster for some than for others, and some may be more satisfied with the progress made than others. Members generally talk about some of the changes that have taken place in themselves and in the group. Future plans become prominent topics of discussion, and there is greater readiness for new relationships and experiences in the community. Attendance may become irregular, unless the worker makes special efforts to motivate members to continue until the final session. Some members may feel ready to terminate before the time set for the group; others may want to drop out owing to insecurity, feeling they have been left behind by members who have made more rapid progress. The structure tends to become more flexible, for example, by the giving up of official roles within the membership or by changes in time, place, and frequency of meetings. The norms of members have become more nearly in harmony with those of appropriate socially desirable segments of the community where the members live or of which they are a part. The members' norms evidence some degree of confidence in the future. Communication tends to be free and easy, although sometimes obstacles to open communication arise. Group controls are lessened, and an increase in inner controls occurs on the part of the members. Cohesion weakens as the members begin to find satisfactions and new relationships outside the group.

Termination of Individuals

Termination occurs for a number of reasons, some of them planned as an integral part of service and some of them unplanned or unanticipated. Ideally, termination occurs when the members no longer need the professional service. The social worker is required to make a judgment that there has been sufficient progress to enable persons to continue to consolidate the gains they have made without the help of the worker and often also without the group. All people have problems, but usually they can cope with them with the support and help of families, friends, and nonprofessional community resources. It is unrealistic to continue service until the members have achieved their fullest potential; the question rather is whether there has been sufficient progress to assume that the members can continue to improve without the group.

Early Terminations

Too often, termination occurs that is not the natural outcome of a plan for one or more members of the group. Changes in the interests and situations of members often result in premature termination from a group, for example, a move away from the locale in which the group meets, a change in the work or school schedule of a member, an illness, the removal of a child from a group by the parent, lack of continued eligibility for public assistance, or other situations over which the worker has no control. Whenever a member drops out, both the member who leaves and the remaining members have varied feelings about the event.

Here is an example of a group in which one member discloses that he is going to leave the group. The members of the group have severe coronary artery disease and are in different stages of recovery. The goals of the group were to enhance the members' understanding of their condition, reduce the isolation they all felt, lessen anxiety through the ventilation of feelings, reduce reliance on unhealthy defenses, develop an awareness of the patterns of behavior that influence health, and deal with the practical realities of daily living. The group had been meeting for several months when faced with the loss of one of its members, Ben. Seven members were present.

Ben was very quiet throughout the meeting. When there was a pause in the discussion, he announced that this would be his last time in the group. He was moving up North to a new home. He invited the members to visit him there when he got settled. He wrote down the address and phone numbers so that the members could copy it. He said he was sad to leave in a way: he did not think he could have made it without the group. He said this feeling was a dramatic change from the beginning when he really did not think the group would be worth much, but he learned differently.

It was very quiet. All the members sat with arms crossed and heads down. I said that I would miss Ben. I appreciated his openness and friendliness. Ed looked up and said he would miss him, too. He said he had always felt comfortable with Ben. Jerry just shook his head, unable to say anything. Gloria made light of it, saying in a teasing way, "If I come to see you, do I have to bring my husband?" Ben joked with her about this, but there was a sense of mutual caring in the banter. Jim said he admired Ben for all he had done and wished him the best—he wished he had the guts to do what Ben had done. Jerry got up, went over to Ben, and said, "We've been here since the group started—both of us—it's hard to see you go." Mary said she never dreamed he would leave like this, and Janet looked sad but said nothing.

Ben told of leaving the group in a calm and gentle manner, but the group felt betrayed and let down. Although he had mentioned his intention to move much earlier, the group thought he meant some time in the distant future, and none of the members was prepared for his leaving now.

The members were able to make use of the group process to express their feelings about one member leaving; the worker intervened actively only to open up discussion through sharing his own feelings about the loss and through nonverbal support of the members' interactions.

Problems in Participation

Another major reason for early termination is the dropout's problems in group participation. When members drop out, they tend not to share their intention to do so with the worker or the other members. They stop coming to the meetings. The stress of belonging to the group may be too much for them. They fear intimacy or the demands for self-disclosure, they are unable to share with others, they get inadequate support, they lack a sense of compatibility with others, or they do not see the group's purpose and procedures as relevant to their particular needs and situations. These problems in participation often result from errors in the planning process or from inadequate preparation for the group experience.[6] Dropouts may be dissatisfied with the worker or the group in some way, and the worker may not have helped them to explore these dissatisfactions. The worker or other members may have threatened their defenses, so they cope by fleeing the group. The worker may not have given adequate attention to helping the person find solutions to the problems of group participation.

Follow-up of absences is essential to understand the reason for withdrawal, to assess the member's needs and situation, and, when indicated, to help the person return to the group. After all, people cannot be helped if they do not attend. Some highly competent practitioners almost never have dropouts, because they have skill in the planning process and in preparing prospective members for the group; they also have confidence about the value of the group, and this gets transmitted to the members. They have skill in selecting and using the appropriate supportive or challenging skills at a given time.

Planned Terminations

In many groups, the plan is that members may terminate at different times. In open-ended groups, a member leaves a group that is going to continue without him. Even in relatively closed membership groups, some members may be ready to leave before the termination of the group itself. The termination of one member poses both special problems and opportunities for the worker and the members. In some instances, the fact that a member is ready for termination provides both hope and stimulation toward change for the other members. In other instances, it points up the slower progress of the others and is reacted to with a sense of failure or discouragement. It may arouse feelings of rivalry and competition between the members. Those members who remain may feel apprehensive about what new members will come to fill the place of the departing one. They have to adapt to a changed group. When a new person enters the group, both the old members and the newcomer worry about whether they will be acceptable to each other. If these feelings are not recognized and dealt with, the old members tend to project onto the new arrival the anger left over from the experience of losing a valued member of the group.

Time needs to be devoted to preparing an individual for termination and to helping the remaining members with their reactions to the person who is leaving and to the change in the composition and dynamics of the group occasioned thereby. The worker tries to use this change for the benefit of all. If the members do not bring up the subject of the loss of a member, a collective denial may be operating. The worker needs to introduce the subject and explore its meaning to the members. A universalizing comment is often effective, for example, that people usually feel sad when someone is leaving, followed by asking the members to discuss this topic. Usually, members are relieved when the issue is brought out into the open. Such discussion is invaluable to the terminating member, who perceives the meaning that leaving has for self and for others. Some members with long histories of damaged self-esteem find it difficult to imagine they have really helped other members and contributed to the group. The painful disruption of relationships during termination is eased when they understand not only that they are ready to leave but also that they will be missed.

Termination of Worker

Social workers may be the ones who terminate their relationship with a group, particularly in groups that meet for many months as contrasted with short-term groups. Too often, the worker leaves when the group is in the early part of the goal achievement stage. The members have developed trust in and affection for the worker and may be in the very midst of working on interpersonal problems. The reasons for the worker's termination tend to be such situational factors as a change in work assignments, a long illness, change of job, or the planned end of an assignment, as when interns complete their field work.

When a worker leaves before the group is ready to terminate, the desirable situation is a planned transfer to another worker. The amount of time it takes to accomplish a successful transfer depends upon the nature of the group. One example of a transfer of a group to a new worker is taken from the record of a group of fourteen- and fifteen-year-old girls who had been referred by their school's principal to a community agency that specialized in services to adolescents with severe problems in school and in the community. The worker, a second-year student in a graduate school of social work, was to complete her assignment at the time of graduation. The group was well into the third stage of development. She introduced the topic of her leaving several weeks before the event.

In the next meeting, Sally asked if I meant it when I said I would be leaving them in June. Opal protested that she still needed me "real badly," and Sally said, "We all do, honestly." I said I thought I understood that they really wanted me to stay with the group, but I could not do so. I had to leave because I was completing my internship—I was taking a full-time job—but another social worker from our agency would meet with them for another six months. Ann said, "That's not the same," and the others nodded agreement with her. I acknowledged that it would not be the same, but that I felt confident the group could continue and have a good experience with another worker. Opal said she didn't want "a fat social worker from the welfare department." I said it would be one of the workers from this agency and helped them to express some of their fears about what the new worker would be like.

Next meeting. Jan said that all this talking made her hungry and wondered if we could go to the hot dog stand in the station wagon. I asked if the others wanted to do this, and they all agreed they did. On the way, we talked again about my leaving. I said we had four more meetings and the last meeting would be on June 14. Sally protested that she didn't realize it would be so soon. The others echoed this statement. Ann said she wanted to cry because she did not want me to leave. Jan said she guessed they would all cry when I left. I told the girls that it would be hard for me to leave them also. When they asked who the new social worker would be, I said I would give them a definite answer next week.

Next meeting. As we were driving in the station wagon, I said that I wanted to tell them that Mrs. D. would be their new social worker. They said it would be hard to get used to somebody new—just as they got used to somebody, she left them. I said I guess it felt as if I were deserting them. Opal said, "That's exactly it—you are." Most of the girls then expressed a little anger at me. Opal wanted to know if Mrs. D. was Caucasian or black. I said she was Caucasian, but wondered why she asked that question. Opal said they just wanted to know. I wondered what they would prefer. Ann asked, "What are you?" I said I was Caucasian, and Opal said, "Then, that's what we want." Sally said she didn't care what color the new worker was, whether she was pink, purple, yellow, white, or black, so long as she was someone they could get along with. I asked what she meant by "get along with." She said someone who could understand them and was kind and considerate. Ann added, "Someone we can talk to and won't try to tell us what to do." When Gladys said, "And someone who can help us with our problems like you do," Ann said, "We'll all buy that." And Kay added, "But not too serious—we need some fun, too."

I said that, although it would be hard at first, I'm sure they will become able to get along well with Mrs. D. I said that Mrs. D. had asked me to ask them what meeting she should come to before I leave so that they could become acquainted. After some discussion and further protest of the fact that the end would come too soon, they agreed she should come to the next-to-last meeting. They wanted to be able to tell me if they liked her at the last meeting.

Back in the center, as the girls were eating corn chips and cookies, Opal brought up the question of Jenny's infection: they expressed concern about her. Opal asked what it meant if you had a discharge. I said it could mean different things, ranging from something very minor to something quite serious. Opal said she guessed they all better go back to the clinic. We talked about their experiences at the clinic. Opal and Kay said their reports were negative. Helen said that her and Mary's reports had been positive until last time, which was a great relief. The discussion turned quite naturally to the subject of pregnancy. I answered their questions and said they seemed to have deep concerns about the matter. They said they did. I said this was one thing we could work on in the remaining time we had together, and then Mrs. D. could also work with them on their concerns if even more help was needed. I said I had told Mrs. D. about each of them and about what the group had been doing. They said they were glad that I had done that—it would make it easier for them to get acquainted with her.

Next meeting. The girls expressed concern about whether Mrs. D. would let them be noisy at times as I had. I said I was sure she would understand that there were times when they needed to blow off a little steam—the agency does not forbid them from doing it. Again, we talked about their fear of having a new worker, and I repeated exactly how we would work out the transfer of leadership. They seemed to take some comfort from knowing what would happen and that I would be present when they meet Mrs. D.

Next-to-the-last meeting. Mrs. D. and I arrived at the center a little early. All of the girls were already there, dressed in their best clothes. There was an air of excitement in the room. At my suggestion, the members all participated in telling Mrs. D. something about the group. I shared what the members had told me about what they wanted in their next worker, asking them if I had got it right. They nodded their approval. Mrs. D. said they expected a lot from her, but she would do her best in working with them. There was a very positive tone, until Mrs. D. said she was sure they could work out some of the problems they had mentioned before the group would end in December. Although I had told them twice that we thought the group would be continued for six months more, the girls became very resistant and defensive, saying that if we really cared about them we would not throw them out like that. Sally said she didn't expect her problems to be gone by December, and besides, "We like the group." The other members supported Sally by grumbling assent to her remarks, although they became silent and sullen for most of the meeting.

Mrs. D. left about 5:30, and the rest of the meeting was spent in helping the girls to express their feelings of hostility and frustration. They questioned whether they even wanted to continue in the group. I said this was certainly their choice to make and I thought they probably had mixed feelings about it. Opal commented that Mrs. D. was "too serious" for us. Ann said this was probably because she was "nervous." I suggested that they might also have felt nervous. This met with an emphatic positive response. They said they had wanted to make a good impression on Mrs. D. and wanted her to like them. I expressed my confidence in their ability to get along with her and in her ability to like and care for them. I reminded them that the decision to plan for the group to last for six more months resulted from the progress they had made and that they should feel pride in the fact that we think they can get along without therapy after that time. Mrs. D. can help them find other groups to which they would like to belong or interests they would like to pursue in the community. They will not have to give up the friendships they have made in the group. They seemed to take some comfort from these comments and even began to talk about how different they were now than when they first came to the group.

Last meeting. The girls had planned a surprise party for me and took a great deal of pride in what they had done. They were pleased with my surprise and delight in the party. There was some discussion of the next week and their relationship with Mrs. D. It was much more positive than last week. Sally was able to say she was looking forward to getting to know Mrs. D. and the other girls seemed to support this idea.

Toward the end of the meeting, I asked them to share their impressions of how each of them had made progress this year, and I shared my own impressions with them. I mentioned that we had worked on many individual and shared problems and that they could continue to help each other and get help from Mrs. D. with those that were still most troublesome. I let them know that it was difficult for me to have to say good-bye to them, for they had taught me how to be a better social worker, and I liked and cared about each of them. There was a thoughtful silence, broken by Sally's saying, "We'll sure miss you," echoed by the others.

I took pictures of each girl with my Polaroid camera and also gave each girl a turn at deciding what kind of picture of the group she wanted. Giving the pictures to the girls served as a fitting closing ritual. I drove each of the girls home and went to say good-bye to the families and to each girl in turn.

Note that the social worker had established a close relationship with the members and they with her and with each other. She accepted and clarified the girls' feelings about her leaving and the new worker's coming. She gave the members accurate information, reviewed and supported the progress they had made, engaged them in making decisions about priorities for work during the remaining time together, prepared them for the next experience with a new worker, supported their efforts to cope with the situation, and ended her relationship with them. She did not forget the importance of the girls' families to the success of the group and took time to terminate with them.

The loss of a worker, especially in groups of persons with serious psychosocial problems, may be a traumatic event unless handled with empathy and skill. Successful working through of separation from workers can have beneficial outcomes in the members' learning to cope more effectively with the many separations that people face in their lives. But, too often, the termination of a worker unnecessarily disrupts progress toward the agreed-upon goals for each member and the group as a whole. Inadequate time is given to preparation and consideration of the consequences of the loss of a worker to the group. Too often, the too early loss of a worker occurs in groups led by students who are on an academic year calendar, which often does not coincide with the needs of clients. If initial planning for groups were more thorough, these situations could be anticipated and means developed to minimize the negative consequences of worker turnover.

A planned duration for a group that coincides with the planned time available for the practitioner may be an effective alternative to continuous groups with frequent changes of workers and members. The goals would be sufficiently specific and clear that the members could feel satisfaction in their progress in the group. When such help was insufficient, the members could be assigned to new groups with revised goals to meet their specific needs. The existing group could be reorganized with some new and some old members and a new worker with a new working agreement. In light of the evidence from research that services of planned and fairly limited duration are at least as effective as long-term help, there should be compelling reasons for continuing groups from month to month or from year to year.[7] Social workers have a responsibility to make efforts to change organizational polices and procedures that create obstacles to the successful termination of individuals and the group.

Termination of Groups

The purposeful nature of social work implies that from time to time it is necessary to assess the desirability of continuing the group. One criterion for termination is that progress toward the achievement of goals has been sufficient and further help is not necessary, so the group should be terminated. In addition to the achievement of specific goals, there should be an expectation that the members will be able to function without the group but will use appropriate resources in the community for meeting their needs. Workers have anticipated termination from the beginning of their work with a group and have clarified with the members its possible duration, so that the goals and the means of achieving them have been related to plans for both individuals and the group. Sometimes the nature of the service itself determines the approximate number of sessions, planned and understood from the beginning. That form of termination is typical of family life edu-

cation groups, task-centered practice, crisis intervention, and services to patients who are hospitalized for a fairly predictable period of time.

When the members have made little progress and there seems to be little
potential for changing the situation, the service may need to be terminated.
But every effort should be made then to find a more suitable form of service
for the members. There are times, too, when entropy takes over; the group
disintegrates owing to the loss of members or unresolvable problems in the
relationships between the members or in the group's structure and processes.
In such instances, the social work goals have not been achieved. If it is too
late for the worker to help the members to work through the problems, then
there is no choice but to terminate the group. Nazneen Mayadas and Paul
Glasser postulate that neither task nor treatment groups will survive unless
there is a high level of both task interdependence and socioemotional attraction between the members.[8] Attraction to both the tasks and to the relationships results in the members' satisfaction with the group.

Duration of Groups

Some groups are established for a particular period of time, and the members have known this fact since the time of the initial interview. Ideally,
planning for the length of service was related to the agency's purpose of
offering the group service. Knowledge about the duration of the group has
been an important factor in the determination of specific goals by the members and of the content and focus of the group.

Some groups of predetermined duration are time-limited ones, consisting
of from one to approximately sixteen sessions. They are used for such purposes as orientation, preparation for a new experience, coping with crises,
support during a period of transition, or the resolution of specific situational
problems. The limited duration of the group does not mean that it has been
less meaningful to its members than if it had been of longer duration. The
greater specificity of the shared problems or the crisis situations may indeed
have influenced the development of intensive relationships between the
members and with the worker and a deep sense of accomplishment. A short-
term group moves through all the stages of development, but in a condensed
manner. Knowledge of the duration of the group has, to some extent, eased
the trauma of leaving a meaningful experience. But the members of such a

group still have many ambivalent reactions to the reality of the group's termination, similar to those of members of continued service groups.

Informing the Group

In groups without a preset date for termination, there is a tendency to delay making decisions about the group's ending. Workers need to search for clues that the group should be terminated. The initial clues often come from the members themselves. The content of the group tends to include more reports from members about their successful efforts to try new things or to modify their patterns of behavior outside the group. Workers are alert to such a development in the group. They respond to these cues, if their own evaluation of progress confirms the members' views, by introducing the possibility of termination of the group in the near future. The responses of the members indicate whether the subject should be pursued further or await developments. But practitioners cannot wait for the group to introduce the matter of termination to make a decision about it. When it does not come from the group, they are responsible for introducing the reality of termination and for shifting toward preparing the members for it.

A short-term group without a preset duration was started for assisting severely disabled women patients to accept and plan for their discharge from a rehabilitation hospital. During the past two months, the group had made great progress and become very cohesive. The first few meetings were devoted to clarifying group purpose, developing mutual expectations, and ventilating hostility toward being discharged. Then the group considered what alternatives were available to them for future living and made some realistic decisions and plans. The group members became able to help each other a great deal and had changed from narcissistic attitudes to mutual concern for each other.

The worker opened this meeting by stating that the group would soon end, as all of them would be moving into nursing homes of their choice. She said that each one had made progress and had been able to help others, too. She then asked if the members would like to discuss their progress. One by one, the women reported how much they felt they had accomplished. It was obvious that the group had been a meaningful experience for each of them. The worker encouraged and supported each in her evaluation of the group meetings. Then, the focus was on the dates the members would leave the hospital.

MRS. G: I don't care when they set the date for me to leave. If I have to leave, I'll just go on and leave. I don't want to be in anybody's way. If the doctors are through with me here, and there's nothing else they can do for me, and if they don't want me here, then I'll just go ahead and leave. But they promised me an electric wheelchair, and as soon as I get my chair, I'll just go on and go.

WORKER: You feel they don't want you here?

MRS. G: Well, they must not—they're sending us out.

WORKER: Does anyone want to respond to Mrs. G.'s feelings about being sent out? (*No response.*) Do any of the rest of you have feelings like that?

MRS. C: All I want is for them to give me time to have my sister come out and help me get my things together. But I still have some problems getting my shoes on—maybe that swelling will hold me back.

MRS. A: (*Started to say something when interrupted by Mrs. T.*)

MRS. T: I don't want to go—I want to stay here—but they won't let me.

WORKER: It's not easy to leave a place where you have lived for so long, it it?

MRS. T: (*looked wistfully and said softly*) No.

MRS. C: It won't be easy—I'll feel very sad, but I'm ready.

WORKER: Mrs. A., you seem to have wanted to say something earlier but didn't have a chance.

MRS. A: The way I feel about it is that since we have had these wonderful meetings, it has brought out many things and thoughts we wanted to express. You've all done wonderful work with us. I don't believe, like Mrs. G. said, that they don't want us here. It's just that there are new patients coming in every day and this is rehabilitation. After they have done all they can for us, they are trying to find us a better place to go if we don't have a home to go to.

MRS. G: I didn't mean that they don't want us here, but rather that they are ready for us to go, and they have done all they can for us. I'm sure they would want us here if they could do more for us. We just have to go where we can be peaceful, and I think the doctor does want us to go where we can get the care we need.

MRS. C: We really have been treated well here, and you (*looking at the worker*) have helped us so much.

WORKER: The group seems to have had a lot of meaning for many of you.

The worker then turned the discussion toward how the group could help them until they leave the hospital. The discussion focused primarily on the choice of nursing homes and the things they could do for themselves now.

In the last two meetings, there were further discussions of sadness at leaving the worker, each other, and the hospital, and still some anger about being pushed out. The predominant feelings, however, were those of pride in having made enough progress to leave and to prepare for a new life in a nursing home.

The need for termination should be discussed in advance of the termination date to allow sufficient time to make of it a positive experience for the members. But if termination is discussed too early, anxiety and hostility may be aroused that detract from motivation to use the group fully toward goal achievement. The time span between the initial information about termination and the final meeting of the group will vary with many factors, including the group's purpose, the length of time that members have been together, the problems and progress of the members, their anticipated reactions to termination, and the press of environmental circumstances on them. If a tentative date for termination is set, work can proceed with that time in mind, yet it is hoped there can be flexibility in changing the date if circumstances warrant it.

Reactions of Members to Termination

A group experience may feel so good and be so gratifying to the members that they want to continue, even though they have made many positive gains and could probably maintain these in the community. The conflict between the acknowledgment of improvement and movement away from social work help, and the fear of the loss of the worker's special attention and the support of the group, lead to varied reactions to termination on the part of members.[9] In groups in which intimacy and interdependence have been prominent and in which members have disclosed their feelings and problems, the members need help to work through their ambivalence about termination. The members' ambivalence may be expressed through reawakening of dependency needs, excluding the worker from discussion or activity, regressive behavior to prove that the group is still needed, devaluation of the group experience, or flight—leaving the group before its ending.

The major theme is separation and loss.[10] That theme is addressed both in terms of feelings between the members and in terms of opportunities to work on old conflicts about loss and separation. As Paul Bywaters describes it, "Closure is an opportunity to choose, face, and accept separation and to experience the survival of loss and evidence of new strength and mastery.[11]

To the extent that a worker or a member of a group becomes loved and valued by one of the members, that member will feel a deep sense of loss and will need to mourn the loss. Thus, as John Bowlby indicates, "Separation anxiety is the inescapable corollary of attachment behavior."[12] The learned capacity to deal with separation and other aspects of the group experience may be carried over to more effective coping with later losses in life, according to Baruch Levine.[13]

When members of groups have achieved a sense of closeness, termination is especially difficult, as exemplified by a therapy group in an adult psychiatric clinic in which the members had been together weekly for six months to work on their maladaptive patterns of interpersonal relationships. About halfway through the session, the focus shifted from discussion of sexual matters to termination.

———

Shirley said she thought the group really understood her situation. Maria casually commented that now that she finally felt understood by us, the group is going to finish. She added that when this group finishes, she is going to have to go back to something stronger (meaning drugs). What will we do?

WORKER: What about when this group finishes? (Response is confusion).
SAM: I wanted to ask about that.
SHEILA: Do we get thrown out with the garbage?

WORKER: Thrown out with the garbage? That's how you feel about terminating?

SHEILA: I feel, yeah, like where do I turn? Cause I look forward to it so much all week. To me, this is my everything. And to think by next month, you know, I don't know what happens. What will happen then?

MARIA: That's what I was trying to ask.

WORKER: Might we talk now about what's going on with us in thinking about parting. What are you feeling now?

SHEILA: It's been on my mind for some time. You said something about next month being the end and that's been bothering me ever since. (After some other discussion).

MARIA: I think we are getting closer. I think everyone feels like they want more, and then all of a sudden, there's nothing to get together.

SHIRLEY: Even if we find another group, it won't be the same. (Each member of the group expressed similar feelings of regret about the end of the group, and Maria reiterated, "And just as we're really getting close!")

WORKER: It may be that what Maria is talking about is really what is happening. Somehow, in spite of all our fighting and carrying on back and forth, there is a feeling of closeness.

MARIA: Yes, we know each other.

WORKER: And the feeling that something has happened here.

TERRY: Yes, yes.

SHEILA: Yes, definitely. And it feels so good.

WORKER: Is closeness not the heart of the problem? Everybody needs to be close to people, and yet you fight against it all the time. And suddenly the thought that whatever you're sharing here is blowing apart makes you feel terrible.

SHEILA: That's right—definitely! I've been thinking. What am I going to do?

SAM: I had that feeling before, when a worker at the child agency left. She left.

WORKER: What's the feeling when a person gets left?

SAM: You feel lost . . . or . . . well, that's the way I felt.

SHIRLEY: I remember the feeling, but I can't put it into words.

SAM: The feeling is lost.

SHEILA: And frightened.

SHIRLEY: And, oh, so lonely

SHEILA: All of these—lost, frightened, lonely.

TERRY: That's it. All of them.

Terry shared an experience when he felt lost and lonely, followed by stories from several other members. The group continued with this level of intensity for the remainder of the session. I shared my feelings of loss regarding termination, also. There was a reluctance to end the session when the time was up. I said that we still had two more weeks together and we can try to make the most of them.

The worker recognized that she needed to encourage ventilation of the ambivalent feelings, clarify them, and connect the feelings to the issue of intimacy and other losses in the members' lives. The interacting skills are primarily support, exploration, and clarification.

Termination is viewed with ambivalence by almost all members of groups and by the social worker, for that matter. In a group of adult women, the worker commented that people usually have mixed feelings about ending with a group and asked if some of them could express their feelings about termination. Mrs. B. spoke up, saying that she knows she still needs to come—she is not ready to leave. The worker wondered if she was feeling pushed out, to which Mrs. B. replied, "That's exactly what I feel," and elaborated on these feelings. Mrs T. and Mrs. G. said they also felt that way. Mrs. J. said she would miss the group, but she would feel good to be able to manage on her own. Mrs. T. said that she was being pushed out too soon; then, after a silence, "But I feel I've gained a lot, too."

Expression of ambivalent feelings about termination makes it more possible for the members to evaluate the experience realistically rather than have it clouded by unrecognized feelings. If ambivalence is worked through, the members' ego capacities are released for other purposes. Doubt, hesitancy, and unresolved tugs between positive and negative feelings are characteristic of this stage of development. Members recognize the progress they have made and want to move on to new relationships and new activities, yet they also want to continue to receive the gratifications provided by the worker and the sense of belonging to the group. They may mobilize a variety of defenses to cope with the ambivalence. The strength of the dependency needs, the nature of the relationships in the group, and the amount of improvement that has been made will influence how a particular member will respond. The diversity of reactions set off by the confrontation that the group will definitely terminate is reminiscent of the range of maneuvers displayed during the time when the group was forming. Anxiety similar to that experienced over coming together is felt now in relation to moving apart and breaking the bonds that have been formed. Some members do not know their feelings and are bewildered by them. James Garland, Hubert Jones, and Ralph Kolodny point out that many maneuvers are employed by the members both to avoid and to forestall termination and to face and accomplish it.[14]

Sadness

It is certainly natural to feel sad when one has completed an experience and is separating from others if the experience has had deep meaning for the person. The sadness is aggravated by the fact that one separation often reactivates feelings of loss from other life experiences. When members face the reality of their feelings about the loss that is inherent in termination, they react with expressions of sadness and engage in reflective thinking about the situation. Such reflective thinking and acceptance of the separation are major sources of therapeutic gain.

Anxiety

Although anxiety is often directed toward the loss of the worker, a study by Saul Scheidlinger and Marjorie Holden found that the major separation anxiety was expressed in regard to the threatened loss of the group as an entity rather than to the loss of the worker.[15] As one member of a prerelease group in a mental hospital expressed it, "I came to say good-bye to you [the worker] again. It's hard to do this and hard to leave the hospital after such a long time. But leaving our group is the hardest of all." Then, following the worker's comment, "Yes, I know," the patient continued, "But it's easier knowing others are facing the same thing, trying to make a go of life outside." A member of a group of adults in a family service agency said it this way, "I feel that the group is the family I never had," associating separation from the group with the family situation. The group that is being dissolved is usually a meaningful reference group and vehicle for social gratifications for the members, which fact creates additional anxieties and resistances concerning termination.

Denial

Members resist termination in numerous ways. Denial that the group is terminating is one typical reaction. Denial serves as a defense against facing the impending separation and the feelings of loss and anxiety associated with it. The members refuse to accept the notion of termination, behave as though it were not going to happen, and forget that the worker has explained the plan for the duration of the group and its termination. Sometimes denial is more subtle. Some evidences of denial may be long atypical silences when termination is mentioned, numerous references to loss scattered throughout the discussion, or changing the subject when the worker tries to explore the meaning of separation with the members. A variation of the usual denial maneuvers may be exaggerated independence that is not an accurate reflection of the person's level of functioning. A person may act stoical and need to appear strong when confronted with the loss. The denial may also be expressed through superficially greater cohesiveness than before: the group strengthens its bonds against the threat of the worker or agency.

Anger

Angry reactions often overlap with denial. Clients may react with anger to what they perceive as abandonment, rejection, or punishment. There may be what Sheldon Schiff calls the "unspoken rebuke" aimed at the worker for leaving.[16] Anger may be expressed in such phrases as "So, you're kicking us out," "I guess you never did care," "It doesn't matter," "The group is no good anyhow," or a simple "So what?" An example is from a group of young children, reflecting the depth of their feelings.

Toward the end of the meeting, the worker said she wanted to bring something up for the members to think about so they can talk about it more fully at the next meeting. Jane asked, "What is it?" "Yes, what is it?" asked Johnny. The worker said, "I think we should talk about the group ending when school vacation begins." Jane asked, with distress in her voice, "B-b-but—why?" All of the children were very quiet. The worker said they had been talking about how much better things were for all of them now—they'll soon be able to get along fine without the group. "Oh, no," screamed John. "No," added Jane, and then, after a silence, "So. . . you're no good for us any way." Then, Jane said, "To think I thought you really cared." She then cried.

The expression of anger may often begin with indirect or displaced expressions directed toward the worker, each other, or people outside the group. Members may talk about their anger at other people who have disappointed them, such as parents, teachers, employers, friends, or lovers. This ventilation of anger serves as a catharsis and needs to be accepted by the worker for a time. If workers recognize these expressions as symbolic of the members' feelings and accept them, they may then move to making comments or asking questions that connect these expressions of hostility to the group's termination.

Regression

Apparent regression is another frequent response to the need to terminate: the members return to earlier patterns of behavior. These actions may be in the form of inability to cope with situations and tasks that had apparently been mastered earlier or in the reactivation of conflicts between members. The members may become increasingly dependent on the worker's leadership and on routines. They may repeat earlier patterns of scapegoating, susceptibility to contagion, and impulsivity. Sometimes the members behave in ways that are dramatically reminiscent of earlier developmental phases, reflecting a desire to begin all over again. It is not unusual for a group to face the fact of termination in an explosion of behavior that says, in effect, "You thought we were better or more able, but you were wrong. We really are not. We still need you and the group." There is an increase in bringing up problems that were previously worked on.

In an open-ended couples group in a family service agency, Walt and Jane announced that they had been getting along very well for the past few weeks. As they described how they had handled some upheavals in their lives, it appeared that they had developed ways of coping with their conflicts and also were able to enjoy intimacy with each other. The other members and the worker expressed their feelings and reactions to the prospect of Walt and Jane's leaving the group. Walt and Jane then decided they would come to two more sessions just to make sure they were ready to get along without the group. When they returned the next week, they said things were very bad; they were back to where they were at the beginning; they had not made any positive changes after all. Several members commented that Jane and Walt were certainly not ready to leave. The worker explored with them what the major problems were and recalled their prior experiences with similar problems. In the ensuing discussion, Walt and Jane were able to cope with the problem with a minimum of help from the worker and other members. The worker then suggested that last week the focus had been on their readiness to leave, but they had not dealt with their mixed feelings about the group and what it meant to them. Walt and Jane decided to come back twice more to talk about this matter. By that time, they were really ready to leave.

It is important that the worker not interpret these incidents as actual regression or agree that the members are back at the beginning. Rather, it is necessary to understand the acts as the members' way of coping with ambivalence about ending. In some instances, the negative behavior expresses anxiety that the worker will put the members out before they are ready to leave. The flare-up may be an indication of difficulty in leaving relationships and experiences that have been important. Such members need the worker's assurance that they will not leave until they are ready.

Flight

Flight is another pattern of behavior. Some members may be so fearful of being left that they are compelled to break off the relationship precipitously, as if to say, "I'll leave you before you leave me." People who have never experienced much trust in parents and others in positions of authority are particularly fearful of the intimacy of the social work relationship. Through the many hurts of their life experiences, they are easily triggered to withdraw if they have a glimmer that they might be hurt again and fearful that they will not be able to deal with the actual separation. The impulse to flee from the warm group climate may be great. With such a problem, the worker's activities need to be geared to helping the members to stay in the group until its official ending or until a member has been prepared for termination.

Rejection

Feeling rejected by the social worker is another typical reaction to termination. The feelings of rejection are often accompanied with anger. As aptly put by Schiff, "The therapist has been a big liar. What good parent would throw his child out?"[17] Or, as members of one group said, "Why don't you just drive us back to the housing project and forget you ever knew us?" Some members may react through denying the positive meaning of the experience for them to prove that the worker never really did care for them. Some may feel that the group is terminating as a punishment for their unacceptable behavior. To this end, the members exhibit a variety of rejecting and rejection-provoking behavior toward the worker. They may be absent, leave the group, or express verbally their feelings of being rejected by the worker or of rejecting the worker.

Accepting Termination

Not all reactions to the group's termination are related to inability to accept it. Another set is concerned with accepting and making constructive moves toward separating from the worker and often from the other members, too.

The literature places heavy emphasis on the painful feelings and problematic behavior that tend to accompany work toward termination. There is always, perhaps, some sense of loss in leaving an experience that has been helpful in important ways or to which a person has contributed much of himself and his skills. William Schwartz has suggested that, in groups, "the resistance to endings seems to be marked by a general reluctance to tear down a social structure built with such difficulties, and to give up intimacies so hard to achieve."[18] It is to be remembered that there is also the positive side of the ambivalence and that this side predominates in some situations.[19]

There may be happy anticipation of the ending, as is true of certain other experiences in life such as graduation or leaving the parental home. Some members have highly positive reactions to termination, such as "I really feel I'm ready," "I never thought a group could be so great—I'll miss you all—but I'm ready to try on my own." There may be high motivation to use the remaining sessions to complete unfinished business. Feeling competent to cope more effectively with life's challenges and having confidence in one's ability to do so are richly rewarding and are accompanied by feelings of satisfaction and hope. These feelings and reactions are often the outcome of having achieved the goals, accepting the positive and negative feelings about ending, and making constructive moves toward new experiences and relationships. Realizing that the positive changes have come from a process of mutual aid—the dynamic force of altruism—gives the members a sense of pride in having helped themselves and others as well.

A combination of varied reactions tends to occur, with modifications in tendency and duration, in most groups that have continued with sustained attendance over a significant period of time. There is a tendency for reactions to occur in flashes and in clusters, even within the space of a single session. Over a period of time, there seems to be a certain progression in rationality among the reactions, for example, from denial or reactivation of symptoms to review and evaluation. Nevertheless, the actual emergence is not always in sequence. It is not uncommon for members to evaluate their experience together in a reflective manner and later explode into mutual recriminations over responsibility for unacceptable behavior that occurred some time ago.

Variations in Reactions

It was noted earlier that feelings and reactions toward termination vary from person to person, depending upon the intensity of the relationships between the members and the members' prior experiences with separation. Carel Germain and Alex Gitterman note that "the intensity of feeling associated with a relationship and with its ending depends upon its duration and its quality of mutual regard, respect, and reciprocity."[20] The termination process has been described as especially intense and prolonged in groups of elderly patients in nursing homes, in groups of adolescents in residential treatment, and in groups of hard-to-reach adolescents in community agencies.[21]

Other factors also influence the termination process. One is the purpose of the service. Therapeutic services are apt to be more intense and more permeated with problems in relationships than educational services or those that aim to enhance the social competence of people who do not usually have serious problems. In the latter instances, members are more able to anticipate and work through termination without intense emotion and with fewer negative reactions. In task-oriented groups, the fact that the participants are there to work toward some defined tasks that are achieved outside the group means that somewhat less emphasis is placed on the socioemotional dynamics of the experience.[22] This does not mean that there is not a sense of loss of relationships at ending such an endeavor. It does not mean that feelings of satisfaction or dissatisfaction are not stirred up, including the possibility of anger at the worker or group that more was not accomplished.

In some models of social work practice with groups, the focus is limited to the acquisition of knowledge, particular skills or changes in overt behavior. In such groups, attachment is usually only moderate in intensity.[23] The practice is behavioral or cognitively oriented instead of psychosocial, which takes into account socioemotional as well as cognitive and behavioral issues. Nazneen Mayadas and Paul Glasser, for example, regard some models of practice as focused too much on "sentimental nostalgia" rather than on highlighting satisfactory learning and as a point of reference for the initiation and assessment of other challenges.[24] If group members have not developed close relationships and worked on problems of interpersonal and group relationships, reactions to termination may be less intense.

General agreement is found in the literature on both socialization and psychosocial treatment groups that emotional reactions to termination occur. The findings come from analysis of process records or tape recordings of practice. Research was conducted by Benjamin Lewis, who studied fourteen treatment and ten socialization groups, predominantly of adolescents but also including a few groups for children and adults. The groups met weekly for an average of one year and were led by social workers with graduate degrees. The purpose of the study was to test the characteristics of the termination stage as formulated by Garland and associates. The study confirmed the presence of the major categories of emotional reactions in the groups, although not all groups were characterized by all reactions.[25] In another research study, Mary Lackey confirmed the presence of multiple emotional reactions to termination,[26] as did Sidney Kramer, who found that feelings of loss were most prevalent.[27] Anne Fortune's research on termination found that almost all clients had some negative reactions, but there were more positive than negative reactions.[28]

The duration of the service influences the content of the ending process to some extent. Generally, short-term services of up to three months are offered to persons whose problems are less chronic than the problems of clients are who are offered long-term treatment. Hence, the impact of termination will usually be less upsetting to these members than to those in longer-term treatment. But some short-term groups have deep meaning for their members and develop close worker to individual and worker to group relationships. An example by Joseph Carosella concerned a group for "worried well" gay men who did not have AIDS, but were concerned about getting the illness.[29] The plan was for the group to meet for four weeks. The goals were (1) to help lessen anxiety about AIDS, (2) to educate members about the disease, its transmission, treatment, and safe sex practices, (3) to discuss good health care, and (4) to explore safe areas of socialization. The group dealt with such themes as death, suicide, illness, homophobia, guilt, anger, and isolation. In the last session, there was exploration of feelings and evaluation of the experience. One member summarized his experience this way, "AIDS has always been a nightmare for me. I would try not to think about it, but it was pushing me around and making me crazy. Here, with the group's help, I've been able to look at AIDS under a bright and friendly light. We've been able to take AIDS and put it in the center of the room and look at it. It's a lot less frightening now. I feel that I can act rather than react to AIDS." That was the consensus of the group.

In crisis intervention, which is by definition a brief service, the resolution of the crisis or at least a return to a previous state of functioning provides a natural time for termination, which has been built in from the beginning. Little attention has been given by writers to the ending phase of crisis intervention. Lydia Rapoport, however, emphasizes that "in brief treatment, termination needs to be dealt with explicitly."[30] Since the length of treatment is discussed in the initial interview, the ending process is anticipated from the beginning. Because of the partialized and specifically defined goals and the assumption that the state of crisis is a time-limited phenomenon, the minimum goal is achieved within a period of several weeks. It must be remembered, however, that clients in an acute state of crisis do not always grasp the idea of brief service. People are bound to have feelings toward a worker and members of a group who have helped them to overcome unbearable anxiety, confusion, and uncertainty. An example is from the record of a crisis intervention group in a community mental health agency. The six members of the group are between the ages of nineteen and twenty-three and are middle-class white women. The group is open-ended; members attend for six or seven sessions.

Sara, age twenty, came to the clinic with an unwanted pregnancy, resolving the immediate crisis by planning for and obtaining an abortion, which, in turn, engendered another crisis. In addition, she resolved the masochistic relationship with the child's father by ending it, and thus creating another loss. During the period of treatment, she gained some understanding of the dynamics that led to the presenting crisis, namely, a six-month self-destructive and chaotic period following the simultaneous loss of her fiancé and rejection by her parents. She has now established a new and more healthy relationship with her parents.

Individual treatment supplemented the group modality because it was necessary to connect Sara with other resources. Brief interviews and telephone consultations were frequent. Sara became very dependent on me, since we had developed a more intense relationship than is usual with group members. As termination approached, Sara denied the impending separation and reached out to me for more, rather than less, individual attention. During the last week, she telephoned me twice, insisting that she would "crack up" if I did not have another interview with her. I saw her, but used the interview to remind her of the impending separation from me and the group and the importance of new ways of dealing with loss. But her denial continued. She did not want to attend the group meeting or acknowledge her investment in the group. I worked with her to help her understand that really dealing with saying good-bye to the group was essential if she wanted to maintain the gains she had made with us and if she was to be free to enter into a new therapeutic relationship. She finally accepted this and agreed to come to the group, but she had not yet accepted her ambivalent feelings.

Hoping to see me alone before the group, Sara arrived early. Since the receptionist did not inform me of her presence, I saw Sara only briefly before the meeting. After my co-therapist had worked on some other matters in the group session, I suggested that Sara might want to say good-bye to the group. Earlier in the meeting, she had seemed calm and participated only minimally. In response to my comment, she seemed stunned, gazed at me for a moment with a strained expression on her face, and then burst into tears, her face in her hands. One of the members handed her the tissue box, a symbol of support and concern when a member is having a hard time. Sara accepted the tissue, fiddled with it for a moment as she still looked down, then looked at me and, in a broken voice, said how much I had helped her, how she felt she would never again find anyone who would care so much about her. Then she turned toward the other members and said, "And you've helped me, also." Leaning forward in my chair, I said softly that she had made a great many gains in our time together, but she had done much of the growing herself. The group and I had helped her to help herself. I then said, "It's hard to leave people you've grown close to, isn't it?" to which she replied, "It sure is," with more tears.

The members of the group had been very quiet and listened intently to our conversation. I asked if they could respond to Sara. Each, in a different way, said she felt close to her and would miss her. Greta said she thought the group was helping them to get in touch with their feelings and that seemed to help. Sara had helped her to do this. There was nodding of heads all around. Sara said it was hard to talk about how you felt inside, but now that it was over, it didn't feel so scary. Then she said, "Mrs. G. did help me enormously, but you in the group will never know how much you helped, too." There was a warm feeling in the room. I said that we had gone way overtime today, but I thought it had been important to do so. All agreed, either verbally or through nods. I said I thought we should still take time to say goodbye to Sara and for Sara to say goodbye to us. As the group ended, I put my hand on Sara's shoulder, and we said goodbye to each other.

One of the powerful dynamics in crisis intervention is the experience that there are people available—a professional worker and a group—who reach out to help at a time when one's own coping capacities are inadequate. Thus, the relationships between worker and member and member and member are very meaningful. Since many crises, as with Sara, involved loss of some kind, it is essential that members learn better ways to handle the loss of the worker and the group. Working through the difficulties of terminating can thus contribute to competence in facing and coping with future losses.

In open-ended groups in which membership changes frequently, it has been implied that intensity of relationships and strong cohesion tend not to develop. If this is true, it would be expected that termination would be less

imbued with strong emotions in open than in closed groups. Crisis intervention groups are certainly exceptions to that generalization. The important
point is that social workers have the sensitivity and the knowledge to make
an accurate judgment about the meaning of endings to the members and
the group and that they use this understanding in the termination process,
whether the service has been brief or long or in an open-ended or closed
group.

Interventions of the Social Worker

Self-awareness on the part of the social worker and an ability to control
emotional reactions are essential. The social worker is not immune from
feelings about terminating with members of the group. It is natural that
workers will often feel pleased about the progress of a group and their part
in it. It is natural, too, that they will feel some sense of loss. It is essential
that they be able to share these feelings with the members. The feelings
expressed must be genuine, not phony. An example follows:

Four weeks before the planned termination day, the worker reminded a
group of high school girls that there were only two more meetings before
school was out and the group would end. The members protested that
they did not know time would go so fast—they wanted to continue. After
the meeting closed, the girls insisted upon staying. They gathered in a
corner of the hall. Later, they went to the worker's office to give her a
letter in which they expressed their feelings about leaving her. The worker
read it and said she was very touched by it and commented that it would
be hard for her to leave them also. One girl asked, "You really mean it?"
The worker assured them that she really did mean it; she would miss
each of them and miss working with the group. Betty exclaimed, "She
really means it—I can tell." Clarise said, "See, we like her and she likes
us—we'll never forget what she did for us." The girls all clapped spontaneously. The worker reminded them that they would still be together
for two more meetings and engaged the girls in making decisions about
priorities for those meetings.

It is natural that social workers will have strong emotional reactions to the feelings expressed by the members. When the members express hostility toward or rejection of these, workers may take those statements personally rather than accept them as part of the process. They may react with anger, may respond to apparently regressive behavior by agreeing that the members really are back at the beginning and that no progress has been made, and by feeling that they are a failure, or they may resist termination by forgetting to remind the group of the approaching deadline or by continuing discussions or activities as though the group would go on forever. When one is in the midst of a group process in which there is anger and reactivation of unacceptable behavior, it is easy to forget that these behaviors are typical of the ending phase and blame oneself for creating the chaos or hostility.

If a group has been particularly difficult for a worker, there may be a great sense of relief that it is ending. As one student exclaimed, "Thank God, it's over—I never thought I'd see the day." On further reflection, however, he realized how much he had learned from the experience and could observe quite realistically that every member had made some progress. Some workers may expect perfection from their clients and be dissatisfied with their progress. Or they may feel that surely their clients cannot live without them; they get overattached to some of the members, so they cannot support them in going on to new experiences without them. Termination also stirs up feelings about the quality of the worker's performance, for example, certain guilt feelings for not having had the time or the skill to have been more helpful to more members. Workers may have doubts about the nature and permanence of the gains made by the members, leading to a desire to hang on to the group. If they are to use their own feelings in a helpful rather than a hurtful way, workers need to acknowledge them and renew their faith in the members' capacities to continue to grow after their relationship with them is terminated.

Preparatory to working with the members on issues of termination, social workers need to make a decision concerning when to initiate the process. The goals, preferably clear and mutually agreed upon, serve as a basis for the decision. The worker needs to be clear about what criteria are being used for initiating a termination process: preset time limits for the duration of the group, the achievement of goals, or forced termination due to an unforeseen circumstance. Once the group has been informed of the impending end, the workers' efforts become centered on helping the members cope with the stressful situation of ending.

If termination is to be a growth-producing experience, the social worker has a number of important instrumental goals to achieve during the final stage of service. These are to help the members to (1) prepare for termination in a timely manner, (2) explore and clarify their feelings about termination and resolve the ambivalence about leaving the worker and often, except for natural groups, the other members as well, (3) review, evaluate, and support the progress the members have made, acknowledge the realistic gains, identify the needs that still exist, and evaluate the effectiveness of the group, (4) set priorities for work on unfinished problems or tasks that are clearly relevant to the members' progress and work toward stabilizing and generalizing from the gains that have been made, and (5) make transitions toward new experiences, such as follow-up sessions or referrals, as indicated.[31] The social worker uses all the categories of skills in carrying out these tasks to help the members work toward successful termination.

Once social workers have reminded the group of the impending end, their efforts become centered on helping the members cope with the stressful situation. Workers face a complexity of feelings: the separate reactions of each individual, which may be like or different from those of the other members. But, through mutual influence, a group feeling or mood emerges to which attention needs to be directed. Supportive techniques are used to facilitate the ventilation of ambivalent feelings toward termination, convey acceptance of the feelings, universalize them to the extent possible, and communicate empathy. If a reaction is one of feeling abandoned or rejected, additional support is needed. At times, workers need to help the members identify and understand their feelings. They may need to interpret how the present reactions are similar to modes of dealing with other problematic situations. They may reach out to confront gently those members who attempt to flee, requesting that they try to work out their feelings in the group rather than run away from them. They recognize that, unless the group is to continue as a unit, the feelings tend to revolve around the loss of the group as well as the loss of the worker.

Evaluation of Gains

One common focus during the last meetings is a review with the members of the group's purpose and individual goals and the extent to which the members perceive the achievement of these goals. Social workers accept differences in progress made. They may need to work with the group to help bring about acceptance of differences or give special help to a particular member of the group who feels disappointed at not having made as much progress as hoped for. They have a responsibility to share their observations of progress and their confidence in the growing ability of the members to get along without the group. As the group evaluates its experience together, workers need to be secure enough to accept and elicit evaluations of things that could have been done differently as well as of those things that they did that were most useful and satisfying to the members. They seek to learn to which aspects of the group the members attribute the satisfactions and gains that have been made, which of the dynamic change mechanisms seemed most important to the members, and what they liked and did not like about the group.

Acknowledging Progress

Members need to have ample time to ventilate and come to understand their feelings about termination. But one important task for the social worker is to move the members from prolonged preoccupation with feelings to a recognition that they are approaching the completion of a group experience through which at least some of their goals have been achieved. While missing the group, they are ready to find new satisfactions in the community. Their feelings often get in the way of recognizing positive gains that have been made. In a last group session, for example, one man said, "I'd rather not stop, it's hard for me to let go, to end things. I just want to stay there, stay there, stay there. Each session that we've gotten together has become more profitable—my feeling is that it's getting better and better. I'm worried about ending." He has moved from expression of feelings toward evaluation.

Setting Priorities and Stabilizing Gains

Once workers have engaged the members in an evaluation of their progress and of the group's effectiveness, they anticipate and plan for making use of the remaining sessions. An important challenge is to keep the members working toward goal achievement, even as they deal with the issue of separation. Otherwise, the group will lose its effectiveness too early, and the last meetings will not be productive. As the members engage in a preliminary evaluation process, they tend to identify needs still unmet. Workers can use this review to help the members set priorities for what they still want to work on during the time that remains. Awareness of a limited amount of time may enhance motivation to use that time effectively. But workers need to beware of the danger of trying to get everything possible accomplished at the last minute. The priorities set should be realistic in terms of the members' capacities and readiness and the constraints of time.

The major priorities are often to engage in talk and activities that test out the skills that have been learned, first in different situations in the group and then in situations in the community. In these ways, the skills are stabilized and generalized to new situations. These activities are a natural progression from those in the preceding stage of development. They tend to be oriented to the community, as, for example, in visits to schools or employment offices or participation in sophisticated social experiences that test the members' capacities for adaptive behavior in relevant situations. Sometimes, the members desire to repeat earlier experiences, either those that were gratifying or those in which they failed in some way. Through such repetition, the members confirm their judgment that they are more able to deal with problematic situations now than previously. They have developed competence.

Social workers support the members' efforts to move away from the group, to develop new relationships outside the group, and to find their place in the usual activities of the community. Their activity is pinpointed on helping the members transfer the skills learned in the group to other experiences; they thereby instill hope for future satisfactory performance. They help members develop their own identity apart from the group, a natural extension of earlier work on problems of identity and differentiation. The members need now to be able to get along without the group, to have further help in integrating the gains, and to make decisions about their own futures. Workers accredit the members' developing interests in other things and are pleased when other interests come to take precedence over group meetings. Hamilton said it this way: "The painful aspects of terminating a helpful relationship are diminished by the clients' own growing sense of strength as they are able to extend their interests and social relationships into the community."[32]

Social workers facilitate the members' consideration of and use of health, welfare, recreation, and educational resources in the agency or elsewhere in the community. All members can benefit from information about and discussion of how to seek additional services, if they should be needed. They can benefit, too, from knowledge of community resources for the enrichment of their lives, including other forms of social support, informal educational groups, and opportunities to develop hobbies or occupational skills. Some members may need referral for help with psychosocial problems that were not addressed adequately in the group. Workers need also to indicate and clarify the nature of any continuing relationship they may have with individuals, their families, or with the group. When feasible, they make plans to be available to the members if problems are encountered, to follow up with interviews for the purpose of evaluating how members are getting along later, or to have reunions with the group. It is the social worker's ethical responsibility to ensure, to the extent possible, that members are not left to fend for themselves when they clearly need additional help.

In time-limited groups, a decision may be made to continue the group for an additional period of time or to reorganize it to meet new or continuing needs of members. Although most members may be ready to leave, others should continue. In such instances, a new working agreement needs to be negotiated about the plan, with clarity about the goals to be sought and the duration of the reorganized group.

The tasks of facilitating the expression of feeling and resolving the ambivalence about ending, continuing work on unresolved problems, stabilizing changes, evaluating progress and process, and making transitions to new experiences seldom occur in that order but are interwoven into the last meetings of the group. One example is of a group of couples with serious marital conflicts that threatened the continuation of their marriages. It was a planned time-limited group of four months' duration. In the next to the last session, the members had worked toward stabilizing gains they had made in communicating with each other and with other family members and in making important decisions that affected their marital relationships and families. They had considered what they would try to do to make further gains before the final session. They had been reminded of the reality of the group's ending, with a tendency to deny it or to express mild feelings of sadness and unreadiness to give up the group. They had been given information about the agency's crisis intervention services that would be available to them if they should require them and about resources in the community to meet some of the members' or their children's needs for vocational testing, tutoring, family planning, and recreation.

Members of the group had earlier ventilated many feelings about ending. Now they were engaged in evaluating the progress they had made. While they recognized gains, they also identified unresolved problems. As Katherine told about a recent fight with her husband, she blurted out, "The trouble with this whole therapy is just that it isn't long enough. Why in hell can't these sessions go on: here we are right in the midst of our problems and the whole thing is going to end soon." I said that Katherine was certainly feeling that she was not ready for the group to end and that she is still very angry about it and asked how the others felt. All said, in different ways, that I just did not care about helping them anymore. I said that most of them seemed to feel I was abandoning them in their time of need. "I sure do" and "That's what you are doing" were typical responses. I said that I, too, wished the group could meet for a little longer, but that is not possible. I reminded them that we had agreed to meet for fifteen sessions, and that time is up next week. There was silence. I also reviewed briefly what each had said earlier about how things were better for them now and said I had confidence that they could continue to work on their problems outside the group. What they had learned here could be carried over to their discussions with each other and with their families.

Esther changed the mood with a statement that while she still has a long way to go, this group had helped her and her husband more than earlier therapy had. When Katherine asked her about this, she replied, "Well, it's something when six people land on you at one time; boy, that really made an impression on me; it was a painful process and I wouldn't want to go through it again. But I lived through it because you all seemed to like me and care about me." Her husband said that he agreed—it was good to be able to talk things over with people who had marital problems, too, even though not identical with theirs. There was further discussion of the ways the group had helped them. There was also presentation of things that were not going well, so that ventilation of feelings, problem-solving, and review and evaluation were interspersed during this meeting and during the final one. By the end of that session, positive feelings toward the group's ending predominated, because the members had seen how they could continue to use what they had learned in facing problems, communicating about their feelings and perceptions of the difficulties, and trying to make decisions that would not create too much conflict.

When group members have had a particularly satisfying experience in working together, they may resist completion of the work if relationships between them have been more satisfying than the achievement of the agreed upon goals. Members may delay completing the work in order to prolong the relationships. Some groups desire to continue on a friendship basis after the original purpose has been achieved. Such a decision is often not realistic; it represents a resistance to facing termination and moving out into new experiences in the community. Rather than accede to the members' demands, the need is to face the group with the problem and help them work it through.

A decision to reestablish a group usually means that it has changed its purpose to that of a social, self-help or support group that continues, often without the assistance of a social worker. Wilma Greenfield and Beulah Rothman refer to a transformation stage beyond termination.[33] Although the members remain together, they still need to face the changes and deal with the separation from the worker and also often from the sponsoring organization. Many self-help and support groups have started with some members who participated in a therapeutic or psychoeducational group and then desired to maintain relationships with people with whom they have shared a particular need. The social worker's role in such groups is to help the members plan for the group and, in some instances, to continue as a consultant or advisor to the group.

In many situations, it is not sufficient that the worker notify and prepare the members of the group for termination and follow-up. In work with children, parents need to participate in the review and evaluation of the child's progress in the group and in the decisions concerning any follow-up services to be provided by the agency or referrals elsewhere. In serving groups within an institutional setting, other staff members who have responsibilities to the members need either to be notified about or to participate in the actual decision to terminate the group service, depending on circumstances. When group work is one part of a constellation of services to a member, the other personnel within the agency or the community need to be involved in the follow-up plans for the member. A group is not an island unto itself: its members are parts of other social systems that may be affected by its discontinuance.

The Ending

The actual termination occurs during the last session of the group. Often, a final ritual symbolizes the members' internalization of the experience. In one group of patients with mental illness, there was an exchange of statements of hope that each would be able to get along well and a statement by one member, in behalf of the group, of the meaning the experience had to them and of their appreciation of the help given by the worker. A group of parents brought elaborate refreshments and a thank-you card for the worker to symbolize the ending of that group. In such instances, the worker accepts graciously the members' expressions of appreciation for help given.

The policies of organizations vary concerning follow-up activities. In the actual final disengagement, social workers make clear that the door is open if agency policy allows it, that they will be available to the members if they feel it necessary to contact them. They assure the members of their continued interest in them, even though they are leaving. The worker's concern for the members does not stop on the last day, and the members need to know this. Hope is held out that the new strengths and outlooks gained through the group experience will provide a base for each member's continued coping with the problems of daily living.

Guidelines for Practice

The socioemotional issues for the members in the final stage of group development are a sense of loss in separating from the worker and other members and in receiving help from the group. In coping with these losses, members express a variety of feelings concerning the ending of the group experience. They mobilize their defenses against facing the reality of termination. Gradually, they move toward breaking ties in the group as they find satisfaction in relationships outside the group. Emotional reactions to termination vary with the needs of individuals, the progress made, and the purpose and type of group. They tend to be more intense in therapeutic and support groups than in educational or task-centered ones. The group, however, does more than deal with reactions to termination. It continues to work on tasks and to resolve problems in the psychosocial functioning of the members.

Achieving successful terminations is a complex process, requiring depth of knowledge about human behavior, groups, and environments, and how to help people to cope successfully with the many terminations in their lives. The successful practitioner will

1. be aware of and try to cope with one's own emotions related to separations and to accept and understand the range of emotions exhibited by the members;
2. continue to model acceptance, empathy, and genuineness as members struggle with their feelings of loss and success or failure;
3. assess the readiness of each member for termination, recognizing differences in the nature and degree of progress and in external circumstances that influence transfer of learnings from the group to other situations;
4. prepare members for termination of the group or of an individual from an ongoing group in a timely manner; sufficient time needs to be allowed to achieve the essential tasks;
5. explore, support, and clarify the expression of a variety of emotional reactions to termination and help the group to resolve ambivalence about separation and the achievement of outcomes;
6. review, evaluate, and support the progress that members have made, acknowledging gains and identifying the needs that still exist; set priorities for work on unfinished tasks, activities, or unresolved problems;
7. stabilize the gains that have been made and generalize learning from the group to situations in the environment; support the members' efforts to develop new relationships or give up destructive relationships;
8. facilitate the members' use of resources and services in the agency or community that will enrich their lives;
9. communicate with significant others, including families, about the ending of the group or a particular member's termination and, when appropriate, involve them in making decisions about additional services for the member.

In all the worker's activities with individuals and the group, the members are full participants in a mutual aid process in which they help each other to move toward successful termination.

Termination is a dynamic and vital process, not just an end point. If properly understood and managed, it becomes an important force in integrating changes in feeling, thinking, and behaving. In this final stage, knowledge about human behavior and skills of treatment are used to help the group to terminate in a way that benefits the members. If done successfully, the social worker has prepared the members for other experiences with loss and separation that they will face in the future. When workers feel that their service has been successful, they will have grown too. In a sense, they benefit as much as the members. The members teach them how to be better social workers. What is learned from serving a particular group should make it possible for them to give better service to the next group. How could it be otherwise? We are all parts of dynamic interacting systems of people who influence and are influenced by each other. We are not islands unto ourselves.

16   Evaluation

Evaluation is an ongoing process that includes appraisal of the members' use of the group and the quality of the service. A basic ethical principle asserts that social workers are accountable for what they do and the way they do it. They are expected to provide a reasonable standard of help to their clients. They are expected to evaluate their own practice and to hold themselves accountable for their choice of models of practice and interventions. They share responsibility with members for the results related to the agreed upon goals.

The evaluation is based upon the plan of service and the contract established between the worker and the individuals and group. As Roselle Kurland and Andrew Malekoff wrote, "Without agreement among group members and between the worker and the members about what needs a group will attempt to meet, without clarity in regard to group purpose and individual goals, the effectiveness of a group cannot begin to be measured or evaluated."[1] The process of evaluation follows ethical principles of confidentiality, informed consent, and the responsible use of the information that workers have about individuals and the group. The use of any theoretical approach to practice ought to be appropriate to the needs, culture, capacities, and problems of the members of the group.

Research on outcomes is important, but evaluation should also be regarded as an integral part of practice. Workers are responsible for using the best available knowledge that has been developed through research and analysis of experience. There is a considerable body of knowledge about successful work with groups that can guide practitioners. Major contributions from research have been reported throughout this book. They include, for example:

1. the relationship of clarity of purpose and expectations with successful outcomes;
2. the crucial importance of relationships between the worker and each member and between the members, characterized by acceptance or nonpossessive warmth, empathy, authenticity, and caring;
3. the development of a model of planning that alerts workers to decisions that are essential to successful formation of groups;
4. the therapeutic or helpful dynamics within the group process;
5. identification of techniques or skills of intervention, their use, and relative effectiveness;
6. the importance of positive motivation and hope related to the continuance of members in the group;
7. the impact of differences in culture, race, age, social class, gender, and health on group participation;
8. the emotional reactions of members to termination of individuals and the group;
9. the outcome of groups in achieving mutually agreed upon goals, including comparative studies of individual, family, and group modalities.

What is sorely needed is a thorough review of the research that has been done and the organization of findings in such a way that their relevance to competent practice is clear.

Use of Records

In evaluating their practice with a particular group, practitioners need to have some appropriate means for collecting data to ascertain the group's operation, the members' use of the group, and the worker's contribution to the gains or losses made.

Process Records

Process records serve important uses in the evaluation of individuals, the group, and the worker.[2] In these records, workers describe what they remember about what occurred in the group meeting from beginning to end. The goal is to secure information about the verbal and nonverbal behavior of members, the relationships and interactions between the members, the worker's interventions, and the members' responses to what the worker did. To evaluate each member's participation in the group, it is useful to add thumbnail sketches of each member. That also makes it possible for workers to alert themselves to the behavior of the more quiet members and those with special needs.

In writing records, workers learn to sharpen their skills in observation and analysis to learn about their practice as they reflect on the meaning of the content and use that understanding to enhance their competence and to plan for the next session. The process record usually includes

1. date, place, and time of session,
2. names of present and absent members,
3. contacts with members or other persons in their behalf since the last meeting,
4. the process recording,
5. notes on each member's participation and its meaning in relation to the agreed upon goals,
6. analysis of the session, including the worker's interventions.

Process records continue to have important uses in the evaluation of individuals, the group, and the worker. Through content analyses, they may contribute to understanding the group process and interventions for particular purposes. They also have value in teaching and learning practice. They are time consuming, however, so various forms of summaries and measurements serve useful purposes.

Individual Summaries

The ultimate test of the effectiveness of practice is the extent to which the members have made positive changes toward achieving the goals set with them. To evaluate the progress of members, suitable records are essential. Social workers are held accountable for their work: demands for accountability to the public are increasing. The increase of third-party payers and managed care organizations requires that practitioners act in accordance with the policies of insurance agencies, health maintenance organizations, Medicare, and Medicaid. A suitable system of recording is essential to meet these demands.

Evaluation is an ongoing process, involving a capacity to make sound judgments in relation to the purpose of the group. The progress or regression of a member is appropriately made in relation to the person's particular characteristics, background, problems, and strengths, rather than in relation to fixed or uniform standards. In some instances, notably work with families or other groups that will continue to exist when the group work service is terminated, the concern is with changes in the structure and interacting processes of the group, as well as changes in the individuals who comprise it.

Evaluation of the progress of members is made more precise and easier for the worker if some plan is developed for tracing changes in attitudes, relationships, and behavior periodically during the course of the group experience. Perhaps, minimally, summary reports should be made at the end of the first meeting, toward the end of the second stage of group development and before termination is being considered.

The first report would include

1. a brief description of the plan for the group, with special attention to its purpose and goals;
2. identifying information about the member in terms of age, gender, ethnicity, race, occupation or education, and family constellation;
3. assessment of the member, including needs, problems, and strengths in psychosocial functioning, mental and physical health (as well as, when necessary, any diagnosis of mental disorder or illness), the impact of the group on that functioning, and environmental obstacles and opportunities;
4. description and evaluation of the member's participation in the group.

As changes occur, these can be summarized from week to week or periodically. The movement of each member is evaluated in relation to the trend of changes in the group and the impact of environmental influences on it.

Individual and process records can be useful in ascertaining the suitability of a particular model of practice for achieving specific goals for particular populations. An example is the article by Karen Subramanian, Sylvia Hernandez, and Angie Martinez, who developed a psychoeducational group for low-income, monolingual, Latina mothers who were HIV infected. The article presents clear information about the planning process, using assessment of the prospective members, with special emphasis on the women's ethnicity and socioeconomic status combined with knowledge of AIDS and its impact on individual and family functioning. It describes a clear rationale for the selection of the group modality, based on the available evidence concerning the effectiveness of groups with persons having HIV infections and with persons of color. The purpose and goals of the group are clearly stated, as is the content of sessions throughout the group's development.

In addition to knowledge about the members' use of the group, the authors summarize the lessons they learned from the group's experience:

1. Low-income monolingual mothers with a precarious medical condition and heavy child care responsibilities will attend a short-term psychoeducational group.
2. Successful attendance and participation depend in part on how well the group model integrates respect for their language and provides rationales for treatment that are based on congruence with the women's own cultural beliefs about health and illness and their role as women within the Latino culture.
3. Leaders should encourage a comfortable, cooperative atmosphere that upholds cultural values such as respecto and dignidad.
4. Child care and transportation problems must be adequately addressed.
5. Between-group contact is necessary to encourage attendance and spot crises before they become exacerbated.
6. Many of the women possess an extremely low level of information about health, nutrition, child care, and sexual issues.
7. The women's partners must be included in some fashion because a woman may be reluctant or even unable in some cases to consider and/or request alternative sexual practices without enlisting the cooperation of her partner, especially if she is economically

dependent on him. (This component was not included in the first trial of this group).[3]

The authors make suggestions of outcome measures that can be used for formal evaluations of such groups. Such careful descriptions and evaluation of models of practice make it possible for other practitioners to adopt the model, while adapting it to the needs of particular clients. Such work should be a preliminary step to formal research evaluations.

Evaluation is complex. According to Robert Chin, "Evaluation studies of goal achievement or outcome are of limited importance unless the evaluation study also tries to pinpoint the components which 'cause' the degree of attainment or hindrance of goals."[4] Thus, both progress and process must be studied, as must changes in the client's external relationships and conditions. Workers engage the members themselves and significant others in a mutual process of review of the working agreement and the members' views of whether and, if so, to what extent they have reached their goals.

Social workers with groups who keep such records will have the information necessary for informal evaluation of outcome and for meeting the usual requirements for peer review and quality assurance. The information in the records should be as factual and relevant as possible. Workers should keep in mind the fact that the members and others may have legitimate access to records. These may include consultants, members of interdisciplinary teams, family members, third-party payers, attorneys, and the court.

Use of Measurements

Social workers' evaluations of the outcomes for members of their groups may be enhanced through the use of instruments that do not interfere with the service being given. Individualized rapid assessment tools, unlike standardized scales, are especially appropriate for use in group work because they can accurately portray a particular member's goals and problems. They can be constructed quickly and used easily. Erich Coché presents a core battery of outcome measures for use with groups.[5] It consists of a spectrum of measures to assure its applicability to a wide variety of members and groups. Several of the measures are useful in ongoing practice without making changes in the operation of the group or the interventions of the worker.

Among appropriate measures of outcome:

Goal attainment scaling. In this measure, members are asked to list the three most important goals they would like to achieve.[6] After the group has terminated, members are asked to rate the extent to which goals have been achieved on a seven-point scale, ranging from worse to total improvement. Such a scale tends to make more precise the changes that members have made in relation to the agreed upon goals.

Client satisfaction. These measure are in the form of interviews or questionnaires for securing the members' opinions about the practice and outcome.

The Global Assessment Scale (GAS). This scale consists of personality descriptions given for every ten point space on a 100-point scale dealing with adequacy or impairment in functioning. The practitioner assigns a simple numerical rating at the beginning of treatment and again at termination. The scale takes only about one minute to complete.[7]

In addition to measuring outcomes, it is useful to have measures of group process. One example of these measures follows.

The Group Climate Questionnaire. This assesses key dimensions of group process, rated on a seven-point scale.[8] Twelve items measure interpersonal behavior perceived by members within a session of the group. The results indicate how the environment of the group influences behavior and alerts practitioners to emerging trends in group interaction as perceived by the members.

Numerous other measure have been developed for evaluating outcome and process. Of particular relevance is Walter Hudson's scale to measure the severity of problems with peer relationships and self-esteem.[9] Charles Garvin describes instruments that can be used to evaluate changes in individuals, group conditions, and the environment.[10] Irene Waskow and Morris Parloff and Ronald Toseland and Robert Rivas also present some useful measures.[11] The measures selected should be those that are clearly relevant to the predetermined goals, are not intrusive, do not interfere with the ongoing group process, and are used with the full knowledge and informed consent of the participants.

Formal Research Evaluation

The focus of this book is on evaluation as a component of practice as contrasted with formal research that proves outcomes, usually experimental in nature. Practitioners, however, often participate in research on the effectiveness of practice or provide consultation to researchers who are engaged in evaluating their clients. In these roles, they are responsible for making sure that the research procedures pose almost no risk for members and that they are conducted with respect for confidentiality and informed consent. The criteria used for measuring outcomes should be clearly relevant to the group purpose, the goals for particular members, and the plan for the group. Practitioners benefit greatly from the knowledge that comes from such research.

Studies of Effectiveness

There is growing evidence from research that groups tend to be effective for achieving their purposes, but much more needs to be done. In Ronald Toseland and Max Siporin's major review of research,[12] thirty-two studies were discovered that compared individual and group treatment and that met the author's criteria of using classic experimental designs with control groups, standardized measurement instruments, and face-to-face contacts between practitioners and clients. The results of the service were positive for both individual and group treatment, but in eight of the studies group treatment was found to be significantly more effective than individual treatment. Fewer dropouts also occurred in groups. No clear pattern emerged concerning what types of clients or problems were best suited to treatment in groups. Other factors, such as the theoretical approach used, the competence of the worker, and characteristics of the group's structure and process, may have influenced the findings.

Other reviews of research on outcome tend to confirm the findings of Toseland and Siporin. Mary Russell's review of evaluative research demonstrated that a variety of theoretical approaches were used, with treatment and therapy preeminent.[13] Positive findings were found, particularly in groups with a social support or mutual aid function, and in structured groups in which specific problems or deficits were addressed. In another review, Robert Dies concluded, "The results clearly support the efficacy of group treatment."[14]

In a recent study of clinical social work practice with overwhelmed clients, June Hopps, Elaine Pinderhughes, and Richard Shankar reported that, although agencies preferred the one-to-one approach, group work offered strong potential for changing the norms and behavior of overwhelmed clients, particularly youth and young adults. When groups were used, there was "success in overall functioning as demonstrated by movements in self-esteem, self-mastery, competence, and enhanced differentiation."[15] They were effective in helping clients to focus action on urgent and pressing problems, such as drugs and violence in their neighborhoods. The authors present reports of other studies that deal with the values of group interaction.

But not all people are helped through group experience. Casualties do occur in groups, as Maeda Galinsky and Janice Schopler found in their research.[16] Practitioners are responsible for preventing casualties to the extent that it is humanly possible to do so.

Evaluation of Social Workers

The outcome for members of the group is dependent, at least in part, on the worker's competence in providing appropriate and skillful services. Assessment of the worker's part in the group's development and process contributes to understanding the members' experience in the group and its influence on their progress or lack of progress in achieving their goals. The following guidelines are offered for workers' self-evaluations of the group and their participation in it.

1. **Planning.**

What needs did the members have that would suggest the group as the modality of choice?

What did you want to help the members to achieve? Were the group's purpose and the members' goals congruent? Were the goals revised, if and when this seemed to be indicated by the situation?

To what extent was the composition of the group functional or dysfunctional to the achievement of goals?

How suitable was the structure of the group to the needs of the members?

2. **Initial Stage.**

To what extent did you create an environment for the group that was maximally beneficial?

To what extent and how did you orient the members to the group?

How well did the members understand what was expected of them?

What norms developed in the group and what did you do to influence their development? What type of authority seemed to be required of you (permissive, laissez-faire, democratic-facilitative, directive-authoritative, flexible)? How did you help this authority to change during the life of the group?

Did the content of the initial meetings seem appropriate to the needs of the group?

3. Ongoing Assessment of Individuals and Group.

To what extent did you demonstrate ongoing understanding of each member's needs, problems, and strengths?

How aware were you of problems in the functioning of the group as a system?

To what extent did you take into account environmental influences on each member's progress and that of the group?

To what extent did you make appropriate use of cultural values and norms as they influence individuals and the group?

4. Use of Relationship.

What seems to be the nature and quality of your relationship with each member? Consider the qualities of empathy, acceptance, genuineness, adherence to ethical principles, ability to accept and respond to positive and negative feelings expressed toward you and between the members, and transference and countertransference reactions that are evident.

To what extent have you been able to facilitate interpersonal relationships between the members, appropriate to each stage of group development?

What forms of emotional support did you provide and to what extent were you able to help members to support each other?

5. Use of Categories of Intervention.

To what extent did you select and use appropriately the major skills of intervention, keeping in mind the needs and readiness of each member and the group? Consider support, structuring, advice and guidance, exploration, education, clarification, confrontation, and interpretation.

How did you help the members to use these skills with each other, when appropriate?

6. Effective Use of Group Structure and Interactional Processes.

How successful were you in helping members to participate in the group's decisions and activities?

To what extent did you help the members use norms for participation related to the dynamic forces in groups?

To what extent were you alert to opportunities to give individuals and the group as much power as possible to make choices, within their capacities?

To what extent were you able to help the members search for and find common ground, when appropriate, to tie needs and contributions of one individual to those of others?

To what extent and how were you able to help members to accept and respect the differences between them?

When giving suggestions, information, explanations, or interpretations to one member or a subgroup, were you able to help others make connections to the content?

How successful were you in dealing with problems in the functioning of the group, such as difficulties in communication, resistance, dysfunctional member roles, instability of membership, maladaptive self-disclosure, interpersonal and group conflict, or malfunctioning problem-solving processes?

To what extent were you able to promote a sense of continuity and sequence appropriate to the needs of the members?

To what extent did you help the members to select and use appropriate activity-oriented experiences, discussion, and problem-solving to achieve the goals?

To what extent was the content of the group—discussion and activities— relevant to the achievement of goals?

How, and to what extent, did you help the members to translate learning from the group experience to their lives outside the group?

7. **Evaluation of Service and Termination.**

How many dropouts were there? For what reasons did these occur?

To what extent were you able to help members to evaluate the experience and progress made?

To what extent were you aware of the movement of each member and the group as a whole through the major stages of group development?

To what extent did you adequately prepare each member and the group as a whole for termination?

Reviewing one's practice with groups leads to competence, which is the performance of roles with integrity, knowledge, and skill. In Gordon Hearn's words:

To act with professional integrity is to act consistently within a framework of values, a framework that is shared generally by members of the profession; to act with knowledge is to act with an awareness of the rationale for and probable consequences of our actions; and to act with skill is to exercise such control that our actions more closely approximate our intentions.[17]

The use of guidelines for the analysis of skill can be useful in helping workers assess their own practice and then use supervision, consultation, and study to further enhance their competence.

Ben Orcutt suggests that competence "evolves out of commitment, curiosity, and the thirst for knowledge—a creative, imaginative search to know."[18] The practitioner has an ethical responsibility to practice within the realm of the accumulated theoretical base and tested interventions. It can be exhilarating to perceive that one has achieved success and know why that has happened. That sense of accomplishment can lead to making major contributions to one's chosen profession.

Notes

1. Groups in Social Work Practice

1. Tocqueville, *Democracy in America*, p. 107.
2. Wilson, "From Practice to Theory," pp. 1–15.
3. Commager, "Preface" to Addams, *Twenty Years at Hull House*.
4. Konopka, "The Generic and Specific in Group Work Practice," p. 14.
5. Richmond, "Some Next Steps in Social Treatment," p. 250.
6. Richmond, "What Is Social Case Work?" pp. 222–23.
7. Sheffield, *Creative Discussion*.
8. Coyle, "Group Work in Psychiatric Settings," p. 18.
9. Follett, *The New State*, p. 23.
10. Dewey, *Democracy and Education*; Dewey, *How We Think*.
11. Newstetter, Feldstein, and Newcomb, *Group Adjustment*.
12. Coyle, *Group Work with American Youth*, p. 253.
13. Hartford, "The Contributions of Grace Coyle," pp. 91–110.
14. Hearn, ed. *The General Systems Approach*. For a more recent application of social systems concepts, see Greene, "General Systems Theory."
15. Boyd, "Group Work Experiments in State Institutions."
16. Konopka, *Social Group Work*, pp. 7–9.
17. For major contributions of these writers, see the bibliography.
18. For proceedings of these conferences, see Trecker, *Group Work in the Psychiatric Setting*; NASW, *Use of Groups in the Psychiatric Setting*.
19. Frey, *Use of Groups in the Health Field*.

20. Northen, "Social Work Practice with Groups in Health Care."
21. Williamson, *The Social Worker in Group Work.*
22. Newstetter, "What is Social Group Work?" pp. 296–97.
23. Kaiser, *Objectives of Group Work.*
24. Bartlett, "Toward Clarification and Improvement of Practice: The Working Definition," pp. 3–9. See also Bartlett, *The Common Base of Social Work Practice.*
25. Hartford, "Working Papers."
26. Murphy, *The Social Group Work Method in Social Work Education.*
27. Garvin, "Group Theory and Research."
28. Papell and Rothman, "Social Group Work Models."
29. Roberts and Northen, *Theories of Social Work with Groups.*
30. Wilson, *Group Work and Case Work,* p. 3. See also American Association of Group Workers, *Group Work–Case Work Cooperation.*
31. Committee on Practice, *The Psychiatric Social Worker as Leader of a Group.*
32. Pinamonti, "Caseworkers' Use of Groups."
33. Reynolds, *Learning and Teaching,* p. 5; Hathway, "Twenty-Five Years of Professional Education"; Johnson, "Development of Basic Methods."
34. Johnson, "Development of Basic Methods," p. 111.
35. For a description of this development, see Northen, "Social Work Practice at USC: Its Roots and Branches," pp. 243–70.
36. See bibliography for first editions of books by Hearn, 1958, 1968; Whittaker, 1974; Siporin, 1975; Germain and Gitterman, 1980; Shulman, 1979; Northen, 1982; Falck, 1988; Middleman and Goldberg Wood, 1990. Since then, new editions of several of these books have been published.
37. Smalley, *Theory for Social Work Practice,* pp. 294–95.
38. Goldberg, "Beliefs and Attitudes About the Group Therapies," "Group Work and Group Treatment."
39. Falck, "The Management of Membership."
40. Konopka, *Social Group Work,* p. 27.
41. Woods and Hollis, *Casework,* p. 6.
42. Perlman, "Social Work Method: A Review," p. 169.
43. Montagu, *The Cultured Man,* p. 13.
44. Silberman, "A New Strain for Social Work," p. 9.
45. Konopka, "All Lives Are Connected to Other Lives."
46. For further information, see Devore and Schlesinger, *Ethnic-Sensitive Social Work Practice;* Solomon, *Black Empowerment.*
47. Pray, *Social Work in a Revolutionary Age,* p. 278.
48. See Northen, "Ethical Dilemmas in Social Work with Groups"; also see Houston-Vega and Nuehring, with Daquio, *Prudent Practice.*
49. Maas, *People and Contexts,* p. 3.

50. Cook, "Population," p. 42.
51. Dies, *Man's Nature and Nature's Man*, p. 23.
52. Northen and Northen, *Ingenious Kingdom*, p. 17.
53. *The Creative Use of the Social Process* is the subtitle of Wilson and Ryland, *Social Group Work Practice*.
54. Turner, *Social Work Treatment*, p. 84.
55. Coyle, "Some Basic Assumptions," p. 89.
56. Simon, *The Empowerment Tradition in American Social Work*.
57. Solomon, *Black Empowerment*, p. 6.
58. Lee, *The Empowerment Approach*.
59. Pernell, "Empowerment in Social Group Work."
60. Kaiser, "Characteristics of Social Group Work," p. 157.
61. Eubank, *The Concepts of Sociology*, p. 163.
62. Homans, *The Human Group*, p. 3.
63. Davidson, "The Case for Uncommon Sense," pp. 7–8.
64. See Schopler, Abell, and Galinsky, "Technology-Based Groups," pp. 193–208.
65. Schutz, *Interpersonal Underworld*, p. 1.
66. Corsini and Rosenberg, "Mechanisms of Group Psychotherapy," pp. 406–11.
67. Yalom, *The Theory and Practice of Group Psychotherapy*.
68. Yalom, *Inpatient Group Psychotherapy*, p. 45.
69. Yalom, *The Theory and Practice of Group Psychotherapy*, 2d ed.
70. Marks, "Group Psychotherapy for Emotionally Disturbed Children," pp. 70–77.
71. National Association of Social Workers, *Use of Groups in the Psychiatric Setting*.
72. Primary references for this list are as follows: Bloch, Crouch, and Reibstein, "Therapeutic Factors in Group Psychotherapy," pp. 519–26; Corsini and Rosenberg, "Mechanisms of Group Psychotherapy"; Couch, *Joint and Family Interviews*; Goldstein, *Social Learning and Change*; Hill, "Further Considerations of Therapeutic Mechanisms"; NASW, *Use of Groups in the Psychiatric Setting*; Northen, "Selection of Groups," pp. 19–34; Northen, *Clinical Social Work*, pp. 198–200; Rohrbaugh and Bertels, "Participants' Perceptions of Curative Factors," pp. 430–56; Shulman, *The Skills of Helping Individuals, Families, and Groups*; Yalom, *The Theory and Practice of Group Psychotherapy*; and Yalom, *Inpatient Group Psychotherapy*.
73. Goldstein, *Social Learning and Change*, p. 102.
74. Hartford, "Working Papers," p. 70.
75. Abels and Abels, "Social Group Work's Contextual Purposes," p. 154.
76. Goldstein, *Social Learning and Change*, p. 185.
77. Caple, "Preventive Social Work Practice."
78. Gitterman and Shulman, *Mutual Aid Groups*; Hartford, "Group Methods and Generic Practice," pp. 145–74; Golan, *Passing Through Transitions*; Golan, *The*

Perilous Bridge; Henry, *Group Skills in Social Work*; Northen, *Clinical Social Work*.

79. McBroom, "Socialization Through Small Groups," pp. 268–303.
80. Germain and Gitterman, *The Life Model of Social Work Practice*.
81. Solomon, *Black Empowerment*, pp. 322–23.
82. Parad, Selby, and Quinlan, "Crisis Intervention with Families and Groups," pp. 304–30.

2. The Knowledge Base for Practice

1. Somers, "The Small Group in Learning and Teaching," p. 160.
2. Goldstein, *Ego Psychology and Social Work Practice*; Hartmann, *Ego Psychology and the Problem of Adaptation*; Greene and Ephross, *Human Behavior Theory*; Greene, "Eriksonian Theory."
3. Goldstein, "Cognitive Approaches to Direct Practice," pp. 534–55.
4. Vaillant, *The Wisdom of the Ego*, p. 248.
5. Erikson, *Childhood and Society* and *Identity, Youth, and Crisis*.
6. Erikson, "Identity and the Life Cycle," p. 162.
7. American Psychiatric Association, *Task Force on DSM IV*, *Diagnostic and Statistical Manual*.
8. Solomon, *Black Empowerment*, p. 45.
9. Garvin and Reed, "Gender Issues in Social Group Work."
10. Gutiérrez and Lewis, *Empowering Women of Color*, p. 5.
11. For reviews of literature, see Hartford, *Groups in Social Work*; Garvin, "Group Theory and Research," pp. 682–96.
12. Lewin, *Field Theory in Social Science*, pp. 239–40.
13. Moreno, *Who Shall Survive?* Jennings, *Leadership and Isolation*.
14. Bales, *Interaction Process Analysis*.
15. Homans, *The Human Group*.
16. Douglas, *Group Processes in Social Work*.
17. Shaw, *Group Dynamics*, pp. 135–38.
18. Balgopal and Vassil, *Groups in Social Work*, pp. 27–28.
19. For a fuller discussion, see Hartford, *Groups in Social Work*, pp. 139–58.
20. Berelson and Steiner, *Human Behavior*, p. 352; Shaw, *Group Dynamics*, pp. 326–36.
21. For references on affective ties and interpersonal relations, see Coyle, *Group Work with American Youth*, pp. 91–132; Durkin, *The Group in Depth*; Hartford, *Groups in Social Work*; Jennings, *Leadership and Isolation*; Scheidlinger, *Psychoanalysis and Group Behavior*, pp. 131–45.
22. Phillips, *Essentials of Social Group Work Skill*, p. 93.

23. Falck, "Aspects of Membership"; Kohut, *The Restoration of the Self*; Mahler, Pine, and Bergman, *The Psychological Birth of the Human Infant*.

24. Major references on status and role are Coyle, *Group Work with American Youth*, pp. 91–132; Hartford, *Groups in Social Work*, pp. 208–18; Merton, *Social Theory and Social Structure*, pp. 281–386; Shaw, *Group Dynamics*, pp. 241–47; Stein and Cloward, *Social Perspectives on Behavior*, pp. 171–262.

25. Bronfenbrenner, *The Ecology of Human Development*, p. 85.

26. Stein and Cloward, *Social Perspectives on Behavior*, p. 174.

27. Merton, *Social Theory and Social Structure*, pp. 369.

28. For an excellent book on the development of norms, see Edgar H. Schein, *Organizational Culture and Leadership*.

29. Thibaut and Kelley, *Social Psychology of Groups*, p. 130.

30. Cooley, *Social Process*, p. 39.

31. Buckley, "Society as a Complex Adaptive System," p. 500.

32. For further explanation of constructive conflict, see Bernstein, "Conflict and Group Work," pp. 72–106; Coser, *Functions of Social Conflict*; Deutsch, *The Resolution of Conflict*; van de Vliert, "Conflict in Prevention and Escalation," pp. 521–51.

33. Sanford, *Self and Society*, p. 33.

34. For other definitions of group cohesion, see Cartwright and Zander, *Group Dynamics*, p. 72; Douglas, *Group Processes in Social Work*, p. 58; Hartford, *Groups in Social Work*, pp. 245–60; Henry, *Group Skills in Social Work*, p. 15; Levy, "Group Cohesion," pp. 28–36; Stokes, "Toward an Understanding of Cohesion."

35. Garvin, Reid, and Epstein, "A Task-Centered Approach," pp. 264; Levy, "Group Cohesion," pp. 80–97; Lieberman, Yalom, and Miles, *Encounter Groups*, pp. 302–13; Shaw, *Group Dynamics*, pp. 200–30; Stokes, "Toward an Understanding of Cohesion"; Yalom, *The Theory and Practice of Group Psychotherapy*, 3d ed., pp. 52–56.

36. For a summary of the social work literature citing evidences of group cohesion, see Levy, "Group Cohesion," pp. 37–50.

37. Evans and Servis, "Group Cohesion," pp. 359–70; Levy, "Group Cohesion," pp. 98–104.

38. Homans, *The Human Group*, p. 453.

39. Tuckman, "Developmental Sequence," pp. 284–99.

40. Bales, *Interaction Process Analysis*.

41. Wilson and Ryland, *Social Group Work Practice*, p. 71.

42. Garland, Jones, and Kolodny, "A Model for Stages of Development," pp. 17–71.

43. Cohen and Smith, *The Critical Incident in Growth Groups*, pp. 209–10.

44. Lacoursiere, *The Life Cycle of Groups*.

45. Schiller, "Stages of Development in Women's Groups," pp. 117–38.
46. Ibid., p. 122, 137.
47. Zamudio, "Stages of Group Development."
48. MacKenzie and Livesley, "A Developmental Model," pp. 101–16.
49. Berman-Rossi and Kelly, "Advancing Stages of Group Development Theory"; Levine, *Group Psychotherapy*, p. 68; Glassman and Kates, "Authority Themes," pp. 33–52; Berman-Rossi, "Empowering Groups Through Stages," pp. 239–56; O'Connor, "Small Groups."
50. Galinsky and Schopler, "Developmental Patterns," pp. 99–120.
51. Ephross and Vassil, *Groups That Work*, pp. 65–73.
52. Mondros and Berman-Rossi, "The Relevance of Stages of Group Development Theory," pp. 43–58.
53. Kemp, Whittaker, and Tracy, *Person-Environment Practice*, p. 85.
54. Bronfenbrenner, *The Ecology of Human Development*, pp. 21–22.
55. Coyle, *Social Process in Organized Groups*, p. 27.
56. Shimer, *This Sculptured Earth*, p. 1.
57. See, for example, Davis and Proctor, *Race, Gender, and Class*; Delgado, *Social Services in Latino Communities*; Gutiérrez and Lewis, *Empowering Women of Color*; Jung, *Chinese Americans in Family Therapy*; Lum, *Social Work Practice and People of Color*; Pinderhughes, *Understanding Race, Ethnicity, and Power*; Solomon, *Black Empowerment*; Takaki, *Strangers from a Different Shore*.
58. Sotomayor, "Language, Culture, and Ethnicity."
59. Longres, *Human Behavior in the Social Environment*, pp. 149–52.
60. Major classifications of social class are by Hollingshead and Redlich; Warner; Devore and Schlesinger.
61. Pinderhughes, "Power, Powerlessness, and Practice."
62. Kemp, Whittaker, and Tracy, *Person-Environment Practice*, p. 68.
63. Glasser and Garvin, "An Organizational Model," p. 111.
64. Pierce, Sarason, and Sarason, "Integrating Social Support Perspectives," p. 173.
65. Northen, *Clinical Social Work*, p. 298.
66. Tracy, "Identifying Social Support Resources," p. 354.
67. Caplan, *Support Systems and Community Mental Health*.
68. Tracy, "Identifying Social Support Resources."
69. Pierce, Sarason, and Sarason, "Integrating Social Support Perspectives."

3. Relationships: The Heart of Practice

1. Richmond, *Social Diagnosis*, p. 4.
2. Perlman, *Relationship*, pp. 2–3.
3. Fischer, *To Dwell Among Friends*, p. 28.

4. Bowlby, "Separation Anxiety."
5. Gilligan, "Adolescent Development Reconsidered," p. 8.
6. Konopka, *Social Group Work*, p. 37.
7. Lewis and Rosenblum, *Friendship and Peer Relations*, p. 7. See also Grunebaum and Solomon, "Toward a Peer Group Theory," and "On the Development and Significance of Peers and Play."
8. Whittaker, "A Developmental-Educational Approach," p. 180.
9. Lynch, *The Broken Heart*, p. 16.
10. Gilligan, "Adolescent Development Reconsidered," pp. 7–11.
11. Ibid., p. 5.
12. Konopka, *The Adolescent Girl in Conflict*; Whittaker, "Causes of Childhood Disorders," pp. 91–96.
13. Mor-Barak, *Social Networks and Health*.
14. Schutz, *Interpersonal Underworld*.
15. Bronfenbrenner, *The Ecology of Human Development*.
16. Weiss, "The Provisions of Social Relationships."
17. For a discussion of transference in groups, see Durkin, *The Group in Depth*, pp. 139–70 and pp. 183–97; Levine, *Group Psychotherapy*, pp. 160–64; Scheidlinger, *Psychoanalysis and Group Behavior*, pp. 80–85; Yalom, *The Theory and Practice of Group Psychotherapy*, pp. 199–212.
18. Anna Freud, *The Ego and the Mechanisms of Defense*, pp. 117–31.
19. Overton and Tinker, *Casework Notebook*, p. 162.
20. Hartford, *Groups in Social Work*, pp. 202–8.
21. Ibid., pp. 195–97.
22. Ibid., p. 196.
23. Phillips, *Essentials of Social Group Work Skill*, p. 93.
24. Coyle, "Some Basic Assumptions," p. 100.
25. Kutchins, "The Fiduciary Relationship," pp. 106–13.
26. Rogers, "The Necessary and Sufficient Conditions," pp. 95–103.
27. Levine, *Group Psychotherapy*, p. 282.
28. Woods and Hollis, *Casework*, p. 25.
29. Katz, *Empathy: Its Nature and Uses*, p. 1.
30. Rogers, "The Necessary and Sufficient Conditions."
31. Berger, *Clinical Empathy*, p. 5.
32. Woods and Hollis, *Casework*, p. 26.
33. Keefe, *Empathy*, and "Empathy Skill and Critical Consciousness."
34. Scheidlinger, "The Concept of Empathy."
35. Raines, "Empathy in Clinical Social Work," pp. 57–72.
36. Schiller and Zimmer, "Sharing the Secrets," pp. 215–38.
37. Cousins, *Head First*, p. 34.
38. Dies, "Clinical Implications of Research on Leadership," pp. 32–34.

39. Ripple, Alexander, and Polemis, *Motivation, Capacity, and Opportunity*, pp. 66–67; Sainsbury, *Social Work with Families*; Beck and Jones, *Progress in Family Problems*, p. 8; Mullen, "Casework Communication."
40. Schwartz, "Behavior and Psychodynamics," p. 374.
41. Russell, *Clinical Social Work*, p. 53.
42. Coady, "The Worker-Client Relationship Revisited," pp. 291–300.
43. Young and Poulin, "The Helping Relationship Inventory."
44. Lieberman, Yalom, and Miles, *Encounter Groups*; Larsen and Hepworth, "Skill Development."
45. Perlman, *Relationship*, p. 163.
46. Garvin, *Contemporary Group Work*, 3d ed.
47. Lieberman, "Culturally Sensitive Intervention," p. 106. See also Maki, "Countertransference with Adolescent Clients"; Durst, "Understanding the Client–Social Worker Relationship," pp. 29–42.
48. Pinderhughes, *Understanding Race, Ethnicity, and Power*, pp. 147–48.
49. Konopka, *Social Group Work*, p. 94.
50. Pigors, *Leadership or Domination*, p. 401.
51. Flanzer, "Conintegration."
52. Dana, "The Collaborative Process," p. 193.

4. Intervention in Groups

1. Group for the Advancement of Psychiatry, *The Process of Child Therapy*, pp. 2–3.
2. Anderson, *Social Work with Groups*, p. 81.
3. Fatout, "A Comparative Analysis of Practice Concepts"; Furness, "Some Factors of Similarity and Difference"; Peirce, "A Study of the Methodological Components"; Videka-Sherman, "Meta Analysis of Research."
4. Balgopal and Vassil, *Groups in Social Work*; Carlton, *Clinical Social Work*; Ephross and Vassil, *Groups That Work*; Gitterman, *Handbook of Social Work Practice and Vulnerable Populations*.
5. Bertcher, *Group Participation*; Middleman and Goldberg Wood, *Skills for Direct Practice*; Shulman, *The Skills of Helping*.
6. Horowitz, "Worker Interventions."
7. Gordon, "Toward a Social Work Frame of Reference."
8. Kemp, Whittaker, and Tracy, *Person-Environment Practice*; Garvin, *Contemporary Group Work*, pp. 109–11.
9. For further information, see Hall, *The Hidden Dimension*; Hartford, *Groups in Social Work*, pp. 173–84; Seabury, "Arrangement of Physical Space," pp. 48–49.

10. Fatout, "Using Limits and Structures."
11. Middleman and Goldberg Wood, *Skills for Direct Practice*, pp. 104–8.
12. Duck, "Communication of Social Support," p. 175.
13. Pierce, Sarason, and Sarason, "Integrating Social Support Perspectives," p. 173.
14. Tracy, "Identifying Social Support Resources of At-Risk Families, p. 354.
15. Northen, "Social Relationships and Support," pp. 4–5.
16. Ibid., pp. 5–7.
17. Bertcher, *Group Participation*, pp. 31–41; Middleman and Goldberg Wood, *Skills for Direct Practice*, pp. 53–58.
18. Hopps, Pinderhughes, and Shankar, *The Power to Care*.
19. Gitterman, "The President's Pen," pp. 1–3.
20. Ephross and Vassil, *Groups That Work*; Toseland and Rivas, *Introduction to Group Work Practice*.
21. Yalom, *The Theory and Practice of Group Psychotherapy*, 2d ed., pp. 19–44.
22. From Christ and Flomenhaft, eds., *Psychosocial Family Interventions*.
23. Solomon, *Black Empowerment*, pp. 301–8.
24. Schwartz, "The Social Worker in the Group," pp. 146–71.
25. Kane, "Editorial," p. 2.
26. Reid and Epstein, *Task-Centered Practice*, p. 172.
27. Lieberman, Yalom, and Miles, *Encounter Groups*, pp. 371–73.
28. Sainsbury, *Social Work with Families*.
29. Davis, "Advice-Giving in Parent Counseling," pp. 343–47.
30. Overton and Tinker, *Casework Notebook*, p. 68.
31. Solomon, *Black Empowerment*, p. 313.
32. Brown, "Feedback in Family Interviewing," pp. 52–59.
33. Heine, "A Comparison of Patients' Reports."
34. Middlemen and Wood, *Skills for Direct Practice*, pp. 82–83; Toseland and Rivas, *Introduction to Group Work Practice*, p. 101.
35. Hutten, "Short Term Contracts IV," p. 617.
36. Yalom, *The Theory and Practice of Group Psychotherapy*.
37. Fatout, "Physically Abused Children," pp. 83–97.
38. Konopka, "Significance of Social Group Work," p. 128.
39. Coyle, "Social Group Work," p. 29.
40. Brown, "The Technique of Ascription," p. 73.
41. Lee and Park, "A Group Approach to the Depressed Adolescent Girl," pp. 516–27.
42. Konopka, *Social Group Work*, p. 104.
43. Brown, "Feedback in Family Interviewing," pp. 52–59.
44. Dies, "Clinical Implications of Research on Leadership," p. 50.
45. Lieberman, Yalom, and Miles, *Encounter Groups*.

5. Planning

1. Kurland, "Planning," p. 173.
2. Siporin, *Introduction to Social Work Practice*, p. 39.
3. See, for example, Bartlett, "Toward Clarification and Improvement," pp. 5–8; Boehm, "The Nature of Social Work," pp. 10–18; Coyle, *Social Process in Organized Groups*, p. 28.
4. For example, Hartford wrote about private and public pregroup phases that occurred prior to the actual conduct of a group, *Groups in Social Work*, pp. 67–74; Northen discussed the planning and intake processes, including such elements as group purpose, structure, and diagnosis, *Social Work with Groups*, 1st ed., pp. 86–115; Levine, *Fundamentals of Group Treatment*, pp. 4–40; and Sarri and Galinsky, "A Conceptual Framework for Group Development," also identified a phase of origin in which the social worker's actions included determination of group purpose and composition, establishment of a contract, and determination of structural elements such as time, place, and frequency of group meetings.
5. See, for example, Brown, *Groups for Growth and Change*, pp. 143–60; Ephross and Vassil, *Groups That Work*, pp. 56–74; Garvin, *Contemporary Group Work*, pp. 50–75; Gitterman, "Developing A New Group Service," pp. 59–80; Henry, *Group Skills in Social Work*, pp. 43–69; Shulman, *The Skills of Helping*, pp. 319–42; and Toseland and Rivas, *Introduction to Group Work Practice*, pp. 145–72.
6. In separate studies, Briar and Lieberman found that persons are more apt to continue service when they and their workers share similar expectations of such service. Briar, "Family Services," pp. 25–26; Lieberman, "Clients' Expectations, Preferences, and Experiences," p. 174.
7. Garvin, "Complementarity of Role Expectations in Groups," p. 191.
8. Main, "Selected Aspects of the Beginning Phase," p. 114.
9. Kurland and Salmon, *Teaching a Methods Course in Social Work with Groups*, pp. 32–33.
10. Kurland, "A Model of Planning for Social Work with Groups."
11. Falck, *Social Work: The Membership Perspective*.
12. A great deal has been written about cultural and racial beliefs and their relation to group work. See, for example, Bentelspacher, De Silva, Chuang, and La Rowe, "A Process Evaluation of the Cultural Compatibility;" Bilides, "Race, Color, Ethnicity, and Class"; Chau, "Needs Assessment for Group Work with People of Color"; Delgado and Humm-Delgado, "Hispanics and Group Work"; Liu, "Towards Mutual Aid in a Chinese Society"; Waites, "The Tradition of Group Work and Natural Helping Networks"; Sistler and Washington, "Serenity for African American Caregivers."

13. For good articles on this subject, see Miller and Solomon, "The Development of Group Services for the Elderly," pp. 74–106; and Cohen, "Who Wants to Chair the Meeting?" pp. 71–87.

14. For further information, see Lonergan, *Group Intervention*; Klein, "Some Problems of Patient Referral," pp. 229–39.

15. See Gitterman, "Developing a New Group Service," pp. 59–77. See also Germain and Gitterman, *The Life Model of Social Work Practice*, pp. 297–342; Brager and Holloway, *Changing Human Service Organizations.*

16. This material is adapted from Northen, *Clinical Social Work*, pp, 67–74.

17. Germain and Gitterman, *The Life Model of Social Work Practice*, pp. 77–136; Golan, *Passing Through Transitions*; Golan, *The Perilous Bridge.*

18. Parad, Selby, and Quinlan, "Crisis Intervention," pp. 304–30.

19. For good discussions, see Rothman, "Analyzing Issues in Race," pp. 24–37; Solomon, *Black Empowerment*; Chau, "A Model of Practice"; Brown and Mistry, "Group Work with Mixed Membership Groups"; Glasgow and Gouse-Sheese, "Themes of Rejection and Abandonment"; Van Den Bergh, "Managing Biculturalism at the Workplace."

20. Derlega, *Communication, Intimacy, and Close Relationships.*

21. Orcutt, "Family Treatment of Poverty Level Families," p. 92.

22. For elaboration of these ideas, see Hartford, *Groups in Social Work*, pp. 139–58; Lowy, "Goal Formulation in Social Work Groups," pp. 116–44; Schopler and Galinsky, "Goals in Social Work Practice," pp. 140–58; Brager, "Goal Formation," pp. 2–36; and Steinberg, *The Mutual-Aid Approach to Working with Groups*, pp. 52–60.

23. For a good discussion of support groups, see Schopler and Galinsky, "Expanding Our View," pp. 3–10.

24. Cohen and Mullender, "The Personal in the Political."

25. For a good example, see Malekoff, "Pink Soap and Stall Doors," pp. 219–20.

26. Little has been written about when group membership is preferred and when it might be contraindicated. One article that does address this subject is Northen, "Selection of Groups as the Preferred Modality of Practice," pp. 19–33. See also Galinsky and Schopler, "Negative Experiences in Support Groups," pp. 77–95.

27. Redl, "The Art of Group Composition," pp. 76–96.

28. See Bertcher and Maple, "Elements and Issues in Group Composition," pp. 180–202.

29. See Schwartz, "Between Client and System," pp. 171–97; Tropp, "A Developmental Theory," pp. 198–237.

30. Redl, "The Art of Group Composition."

31. Levine reports evidence from research to support this position in *Group Psychotherapy*, p. 13.

32. Schiller, "Stages of Development in Women's Groups," pp. 117–38.

33. Daley and Koppenaal, "The Treatment of Women," pp. 343–57.

34. Garvin and Reed, "Gender Issues in Social Group Work," pp. 3–19.

35. Yalom, *Theory and Practice of Group Psychotherapy*, p. 237.

36. Kadushin, *The Social Work Interview*, pp. 254–60.

37. Solomon, *Black Empowerment*, pp. 299–313.

38. One entire issue of the journal *Social Work with Groups*, vol. 3, no. 4, addresses the issues of co-leadership. Each author presents many references on the subject. For an excellent analysis of positive and negative aspects of co-leadership, see Galinsky and Schopler, "Structuring Co-Leadership," pp. 51–63.

39. See Nosko and Wallace, "Female/Male Co-Leadership in Groups," pp. 3–16; Reed, "Women Leaders in Small Groups," pp. 35–42.

40. MacLennan, "Co-Therapy," pp. 154–66. Summarizing five studies on co-leadership in therapy groups, Dies's conclusions were similar. He found that "co-leadership may complicate the group therapeutic process and actually precipitate problems that are not evident in groups with one leader." See Dies, "Clinical Implications of Research on Leadership," p. 59.

41. A study of fifty therapists in conjoint family therapy found somewhat similar feelings among experienced therapists. They gradually reached a point of diminishing returns in satisfaction with co-therapy and came to prefer work as the sole therapist because they considered this to be a more effective way to serve clients. See Rice, Fey, and Kepecs, "Therapist Experience and Style," pp. 1–12.

42. Hartford, *Groups in Social Work*, p. 162. For other research on size of groups, see Hare, Borgatta, and Bales, *Small Groups*, pp. 495–510; Thomas and Fink, "Effects of Group Size," 525–35; Berelson and Steiner, *Human Behavior*, pp. 358–59.

43. Yalom, *The Theory and Practice of Group Psychotherapy*, 3d ed., p. 283.

44. Large groups may benefit from tighter organization. See Goldberg and Simpson, "Challenging Stereotypes," pp. 79–94.

45. Bales et al., "Structure and Dynamics of Small Groups," p. 394.

46. A number of articles have been published about single-session groups, many in medical settings. See Bloom and Lynch, "Group Work in a Hospital Waiting Room," pp. 48–63; Block, "On the Potentiality and Limits of Time," pp. 516–26; Weisberg, "Single Session Group Practice in a Hospital," pp. 99–112; Rotholz, "The Single Session Group," pp. 143–46. Waldron, Whittington, and Jensen looked at the use of single-session groups with children of military families in which parents are being deployed. See Waldron, Whittington, and Jensen, "Children's Single Session Briefings," pp. 101–9.

47. Yalom, *Inpatient Group Psychotherapy*, pp. 74–82.

48. See Hartford, *Groups in Social Work*, pp. 167–81; Seabury, "Arrangement of Physical Space," pp. 43–49; Siporin, *Introduction to Social Work Practice*, pp. 177–78.
49. Taken from Kurland, *Group Formation*, pp. 14–17.
50. Dewey, *Experience and Education*, pp. 57–58.

6. Pregroup Contact: Selection and Preparation of Members

1. For an example of such an insufficient approach to recruitment and outreach, see Kurland and Salmon, "Self-Determination: Its Use and Misuse," pp. 113–15.
2. Both Cloward and Gouldner see informal entry procedures and lack of bureaucratic procedures and what is perceived as red tape as facilitating the acceptance of social work services by low-income persons. See Cloward, "Agency Structure as a Variable," pp. 30–44; Gouldner, "Red Tape as a Social Problem," pp. 410–18.
3. Siporin, *Introduction to Social Work Practice*, p. 224.
4. For fuller information on assessment, see Northen, "Assessment in Direct Practice," pp. 171–83.
5. Richmond, "Some Next Steps in Social Treatment," p. 487.
6. Frances, Clarkin, and Perry, *Differential Therapeutics in Psychiatry*.
7. Schwartz, "Between Client and System," pp. 171–97.
8. For excellent material on how this concept applies to residential settings, see Maier, "Social Group Work Method," pp. 26–44.
9. A growing body of group work literature addresses issues of race and ethnicity. See, for example, Chau, "Needs Assessment," pp. 53–66; Davis, *Ethnicity in Social Group Work Practice*; Davis, "Group Work Practice with Ethnic Minorities of Color"; Chau, *Ethnicity and Biculturalism*.
10. A similarly expanding body of group work literature addresses issues of gender and sexual orientation. See, for example, Ball and Lipton, "Group Work with Gay Men," pp. 259–77; Englehardt, "Group Work with Lesbians," pp. 278–94; Garvin and Reed, "Sources and Visions for Feminist Group Work"; Gottlieb, Burden, McCormick, and Nicarthy, "The Distinctive Attributes of Feminist Groups"; Lewis, "Regaining Promise," pp. 271–84; Travers, "Redefining Adult Identity," pp. 103–18.
11. Compton and Galaway, eds., *Social Work Processes*; Goldstein, *Social Work Practice*; Pincus and Minahan, *Social Work Practice*; Siporin, *Introduction to Social Work Practice*; Toseland and Rivas, *Introduction to Group Work Practice*.
12. Toseland and Rivas, *Introduction to Group Work Practice*; Wilson and Ryland, *Social Group Work Practice*.

13. Somers, "Problem-Solving in Small Groups," pp. 331–67; Perlman, "The Problem-Solving Model in Social Casework," pp. 129–81.
14. Lewis, *The Intellectual Base of Social Work Practice.*
15. Solomon, *Black Empowerment*, p. 306.
16. Lewis, *The Intellectual Base of Social Work Practice.*
17. Siporin, *Introduction to Social Work Practice*, pp. 239–41.
18. Meadow, "The Effects of a Client-Focused Pregroup Preparation Interview," pp. 52–134; Meadow, "The Preparatory Interview," pp. 35–45.
19. Yalom, *The Theory and Practice of Group Psychotherapy*, 3d ed., pp. 295–96.
20. Piper and Pennault, "Pretherapy Preparation for Group Members," pp. 17–34.
21. Levine, *Group Psychotherapy*, pp. 45–48.
22. Boatman, "Caseworkers' Judgements of Client's Hope"; Fanshel, "A Study of Caseworkers' Perceptions," pp. 543–51; Ripple, "Factors Associated with Continuance," pp. 87–94; Yalom, *The Theory and Practice of Group Psychotherapy*, 2d ed., pp. 6–7; Zalba, "Discontinuance During Social Service Intake."
23. Hannah, "Preparing Members for the Expectations of Social Work with Groups."
24. Dewey, *Democracy and Education*, p. 104.

7. Purpose

1. Steinberg, *The Mutual-Aid Approach to Working with Groups*, p. 56.
2. Siporin, *Introduction to Social Work Practice*, p. 258.
3. Schmidt, "The Use of Purpose in Casework Practice," p. 80.
4. Ibid, pp. 77–84.
5. Raschella, "An Evaluation of the Effect of Goal Congruence."
6. Garvin, "Complementarity of Role Expectations in Groups," pp. 127–45.
7. In her research, Hartford found that workers frequently failed to make group purposes explicit and that this contributed to the failure of group formation. See Hartford, "The Social Worker and Group Formation."
8. See Kurland and Salmon, "Self-Determination: Its Use and Misuse," pp. 105–21.
9. This material was taken from a 1997 paper, "The Evolution of Group Purpose," by Elena Epstein for a course on group work at the Hunter College School of Social Work. It was originally included in Kurland and Salmon, "Purpose," pp. 5–17.

8. The Problem-Solving Process

1. For an historical discussion of how problem-solving evolved in social work, see Somers, "Problem-Solving in Small Groups," pp. 331–68.

2. Dewey, *How We Think.*
3. The importance of a clearly defined and mutually understood problem is emphasized by Toseland and Rivas, *An Introduction to Group Work Practice,* pp. 320–21.
4. Perlman, *Social Casework,* p. 91.
5. Compton and Galaway, *Social Work Processes,* p. 50.
6. Mutual aid has long been recognized as central to social group work. An important influence in its use in social work is the 1908 work of the social scientist Kropotkin, *Mutual Aid: A Factor of Evolution,* in which he recognized that *mutual support* is far more effective than *mutual contest* in the progressive development of humankind.
7. Steinberg, *The Mutual-Aid Approach to Working with Groups,* p.xv.
8. Hartford, "Groups in Human Services," p. 23.
9. Middleman, "Returning Group Process to Group Work," pp. 16, 22.
10. This material is taken from Kurland and Salmon, "Group Work vs. Casework in a Group," pp. 3–14.
11. An emphasis on the strengths of group members and the expectation of mutual aid has always been basic to social work with groups. More recently, a strengths perspective has been emphasized in work with individuals and families. See Maluccio, *Learning From Clients*; and Weick, Rapp, Sullivan, and Kisthardt, "A Strengths Perspective for Social Work Practice," pp. 332–37.
12. Breton, "Learning from Social Group Work Traditions," pp. 3–25.
13. Brown, *Groups for Growth and Change,* p. 86.

9. Conflict

1. For further discussion of conflict, see Bernstein, "Conflict and Group Work," pp. 72–106; Coser, *Functions of Social Conflict*; Deutsch, *Resolution of Conflict*; van de Vliert, "Conflict in Prevention and Escalation," pp. 521–51.
2. Steinberg, "Some Findings from a Study," pp. 23–39.
3. Baxter, "Conflict Management," p. 38.
4. Wilson and Ryland, *Social Group Work Practice,* p. 53.
5. Deutsch, *Resolution of Conflict,* p. 352.
6. Herrick, "Perception of Crisis," pp. 15–30.
7. Follett, *Dynamic Administration,* p. 35.
8. Overton and Tinker, *Casework Notebook,* p. 68.
9. Solomon, *Black Empowerment,* pp. 299–313.
10. For discussion of self-determination, see Kurland and Salmon, "Self-Determination: Its Use and Misuse," pp. 105–21; Bernstein, "Self-Determination: King or Citizen," pp. 3–8; Freedberg, "Self-Determination: Historical Perspectives,"

pp. 33–38; Perlman, "Self-Determination: Reality or Illusion?" pp. 65–89; Rothman, "Client Self-Determination: Untangling the Knot," pp. 598–612.

11. The issue of mandated reporting, especially when it concerns the use of excessive corporal punishment, is a murky area. Uncertainty about when to report causes considerable anxiety. It is generally acknowledged that a worker must use reasonable professional judgment in determining when to make a report. For further discussion, see Levine and Doueck, *The Impact of Mandated Reporting on the Therapeutic Process*, pp. 46–49; Myers, *Legal Issues in Child Abuse and Neglect*, pp. 102–3.

12. Malekoff, *Group Work with Adolescents*, pp. 190–91.

13. Brown and Mistry, "Group Work with 'Mixed Membership' Groups," p. 8.

14. Ibid., pp. 5–21.

15. Pinderhughes, *Understanding Race, Ethnicity, and Power*.

10. Roles of Members

1. Shaw, *Group Dynamics*, pp. 246–47.

2. Bales and Slater, "Functional Roles of Group Members," pp. 259–306; Benne and Sheats, "Functional Roles of Group Members," pp. 41–49; Coyle, *Group Work with American Youth*, pp. 91–132.

3. Radin and Feld, "Social Psychology for Group Work Practice," pp. 50–69.

4. Hartford, *Groups in Social Work*, p. 218.

5. Ibid.

6. Shulman has written extensively on the role of scapegoat. See Shulman, "Scapegoats, Group Workers, and Pre-emptive Intervention," pp. 37–43; Shulman, *The Skills of Helping Individuals, Families, Groups, and Communities*, pp. 476–495. See also Colman, *Up from Scapegoating*; Douglas, *Scapegoats: Transferring Blame*; Anstey, "Scapegoating in Groups," pp. 51–63; Garland and Kolodny, "Characteristics and Resolution of Scapegoating," pp. 55–74.

7. Shulman, in particular, cautions workers about being overprotective of the scapegoat. See Shulman, "Scapegoats, Group Workers, and Pre-emptive Intervention," pp. 37–43.

11. The Use of Activity

1. A comprehensive description of the place of activity in group work has been developed by Middleman in *The Non-Verbal Method*, pp. 25–63.

2. Coyle, "Social Group Work in Recreation," pp. 202–3.

3. Coyle, *Group Work with American Youth*, pp. 169–216.

4. Murphy, *The Social Group Work Method in Social Work Education*, p. 39.

5. For references on the benefits of activity see Balgopal and Vassil, *Groups in Social Work*, pp. 143–48; Heap, *Process and Action in Work with Groups*; Henry, *Group Skills in Social Work*; Middleman, *The Non-Verbal Method*; Whittaker, "Program Activites," pp. 217–50; Wilson and Ryland, *Social Group Work Practice*, chapter 5 and part 2; Shulman, "Program in Group Work," pp. 221–40.

6. For references on role playing, see Etcheverry, Siporin, and Toseland, "Uses and Abuses of Role Playing"; Klein, *Role Playing in Leadership Training*; Middleman, *The Non-Verbal Method*, p. 102.

7. For examples, see Sheridan, "Talk Time for Hospitalized Children," pp. 40–45.

8. Waldron, Whittington, and Jensen, "Children's Single Session Briefings," pp. 101–9.

9. Decker, "Puppets Help Children."

10. Malekoff explores the use of activity with adolescents in his book, *Group Work with Adolescents*, pp. 146–65.

11. Schnekenburger, "Waking the Heart Up," pp. 19–40; Potocky, "An Art Therapy Group," pp. 73–82; Lynn and Nisivoccia, "Activity-Oriented Group Work with the Mentally Ill," pp. 95–106; Pollio, "Hoops Group," pp. 107–22; Waite, "Drama Therapy in Small Groups," pp. 95–108.

12. This example is adapted from Fatout, "Group Work with Severely Abused and Neglected Latency Age Children: Special Needs and Problems," Unpublished paper, November 1986.

13. Heap, *Process and Action in Work with Groups*, p. 93.

14. Collins, "How Do You Spell Hippopotamus?" pp. 61–75.

15. This example is adapted from Wright, "The Use of Purpose in On-Going Activity Groups."

16. Rae-Grant, Gladwin, and Bower, "Mental Health, Social Competence, and the War on Poverty."

17. Schnekenburger, "Waking The Heart Up," pp. 28–29.

18. Heap, *Process and Action in Work with Groups*, p. 93.

19. Maier, *Group Work as Part of Residential Treatment*, p. 28.

20. Goldstein, *Social Work Practice*, p. 101.

21. Wright, "The Use of Purpose in On-Going Activity Groups."

22. Pinderhughes, "Empowerment for Our Clients," pp. 331–38; Solomon, *Black Empowerment*.

23. Lubell, "Living with a Lifeline," pp. 283–96.

24. Berman-Rossi, "The Fight Against Homelessness," pp. 385–412.

25. Lipton and Malter, "The Social Worker as Mediator on a Hospital Ward."

26. Lee, "No Place to Go," pp. 245–62.

27. Germain and Gitterman, *Life Model of Social Work Practice*, p. 316.

28. Garvin, *Contemporary Group Work*, 2 nd ed., pp. 176–87.

29. Pernell, "Empowerment in Social Group Work," pp. 107–18; Solomon, *Black Empowerment*.
30. Bittner, "Therapeutic Mother-Child Groups," pp. 154–61.
31. Delgado, "Activities and Hispanic Groups," pp. 85–96.
32. Edwards, Edwards, Davies, and Eddy, "Enhancing Self-Concept and Identification," pp. 309–18.
33. Marsiglia, Cross, and Mitchell-Enos, "Culturally Grounded Group Work," pp. 89–102.
34. For discussion of activity in different stages of group development, see Henry, *Group Skills in Social Work*; Middleman, *The Non-Verbal Method*, pp. 113–29; Ross and Bernstein, "A Framework for the Therapeutic Use of Group Activities," pp. 627–40.
35. Wright, "The Use of Purpose in On-Going Activity Groups," pp. 33–57.
36. Ibid.
37. Ibid.
38. See, for example, Fluegelman, *The New Games Book*; Fluegelman, ed., *More New Games*; Orlick, *The Cooperative Sports and Games Book*; Orlick, *The Second Cooperative Games Book*; Rohnke, *Silver Bullets*; Spolin, *Theater Games for the Classroom*; Middleman, *The Non-Verbal Method*, pp. 174–258; Wilson and Ryland, *Social Group Work Practice*, pp. 197–346; Brandler and Roman, *Group Work*, pp. 295–324.
39. For helpful material on the use of activity, see Vinter, "Program Activities," pp. 233–43; and Brandler and Roman, *Group Work*, pp. 135–78.

12. Stage I: Inclusion-Orientation

1. Coyle, *Group Work with American Youth*, p. 45.
2. Schwartz, "Between Client and System," pp. 186–88.
3. Williams, "Limitations, Phantasies, and Security Operations," pp. 15–62.
4. Goffman, *Behavior in Public Places*, p. 16.
5. Garland, Jones, and Kolodny, "A Model for Stages of Development."
6. Brandler and Roman, *Group Work*, p. 18.
7. Solomon, *Black Empowerment*, p. 308.
8. Cooper, "A Look at the Effect of Racism," p. 76; For other important references, see Chau, *Ethnicity and Biculturalism*; Davis, "Group Work Practice with Ethnic Minorities," pp. 324–45; Delgado and Humm-Delgado, "Hispanics and Group Work," pp. 85–96; Fong and Mokuau, "Not Simply Asian Americans"; Gutiérrez and Lewis, *Empowering Women of Color*; Jung, *Chinese American Family Therapy*; Ho, "Social Group Work with Asian Pacific Americans," pp. 49–61; Lum, *Social Work Practice with People of Color*.

9. Velasquez, Vigil, and Benavides, "A Framework for Establishing Social Work Relationships," pp. 197–203.
10. Aguilar, "Initial Contacts with Mexican-American Families," pp. 66–77.
11. Hammond, "Cross-Cultural Rehabilitation," pp. 34–36.
12. Nakama, "Japanese Americans' Expectations of Counseling."
13. Kadushin, "The Racial Factor in the Interview," pp. 88–98.
14. Solomon, *Black Empowerment*, p. 324–25.
15. Maas, "Group Influences on Client-Worker Interaction," pp. 70–79; Aronson and Overall, "Treatment Expectations of Patients," pp. 35–41.
16. Parloff, Waskow, and Wolfe, "Research on Therapist Variables," p. 262.
17. Ibid, p. 273.
18. Garvin and Reed, "Gender Issues in Social Group Work," pp. 3–14.
19. Osborn, "Some Factors of Resistance," pp. 1–14.
20. Bounous, "Study of Client and Worker Perceptions," pp. 94–95; Siporin, *Introduction to Social Work Practice*, p. 208.
21. Yalom, *Theory and Practice of Group Psychotherapy*, pp. 115–34.
22. Brown, "Social Workers' Verbal Acts."
23. Garvin, "Complementarity of Role Expectations in Groups," pp. 127–29.
24. Briar, "Family Services," pp. 14–15 and 21–27.
25. Schein, *Organizational Culture and Leadership*, pp. 224–26.
26. Lee and Park, "A Group Approach to Depressed Adolescent Girls," pp. 516–27.
27. Kurland and Salmon, "Not Just One of the Gang."
28. Rosen and Lieberman, "Experimental Evaluation of Interview Performance," pp. 395–412.
29. Gentry, "Initial Group Meetings."
30. Glassman and Kates, *Group Work*, p. 30.
31. For a fuller discussion, see Brandler and Roman, "Uncovering Latent Content in Groups"; and Brandler and Roman, *Group Work*, pp. 165–67.
32. Shyne, "What Research Tells Us," pp. 223–31; Stark, "Barriers to Client-Worker Communication," pp. 177–83.
33. Polansky and Kounin, "Clients' Reactions to Initial Interviews," pp. 237–64.
34. Worby, "Adolescents' Expectations," pp. 19–59.
35. Slocum, "A Survey of Expectations," p. 40.
36. Mayer and Rosenblatt, "The Client's Social Context," pp. 511–18.
37. Maluccio and Marlow, "The Case for the Contract," pp. 28–36.
38. Tsang and Bogo, "Engaging with Clients Cross-Culturally," pp. 73–91.
39. Garvin, "Complementarity in Role Expectations," p. 128.

13. Stage II: Uncertainty-Exploration

1. Garland, Jones, and Kolodny, "A Model for Stages of Development," pp. 41–45.

2. Schiller, "Stages of Development in Women's Groups," pp. 117–38.
3. Solomon, *Black Empowerment*, pp. 28–29; see also Konopka, "Formation of Values," pp. 86–96.
4. Berman-Rossi, "Tasks and Skills of the Social Worker," pp. 69–81.
5. Sullivan, "Who Owns the Group?" pp. 15–32.
6. Berman-Rossi, "The Tasks and Skills," pp. 69–81.
7. For a fuller discussion, see Kurland and Salmon, "Not Just One of the Gang."
8. Thompson and Kahn, *The Group Process*, p. 63.
9. Levine, *Group Psychotherapy*, p. 75.
10. From Lee and Park, "A Group Approach to the Depressed Adolescent Girl," pp. 516–27; see also Levine and Schild, "Group Treatment of Depression," pp. 49–52.
11. Zamudio, "Stages of Group Development."
12. Bilides, "Reaching Inner-City Children," pp. 129–44.
13. Clemenger, "Congruence Between Members and Workers."
14. Main, "Selected Aspects of the Beginning Phase."
15. Paradise, "The Factor of Timing," pp. 524–30.
16. Lasater and Montalvo, "Understanding Mexican-American Culture," pp. 23–25.
17. Velasquez, Vigil, and Benavides, "A Framework for Establishing Social Work Relationships," p. 239.
18. Rice, "Premature Termination of Group Therapy," pp. 5–23.
19. Hartford, "The Social Group Worker and Group Formation."
20. Lonergan, *Group Intervention*, p. 7.
21. Hartford, "The Social Group Worker and Group Formation."
22. Lonergan and Manuele, "A Group for Relatives," pp. 357–59.
23. Maier, "Play Is More than a Four-Letter Word," pp. 65–74.
24. Garvin, "Complementarity of Goal Expectations," p. 145.
25. Brown, "Social Workers' Verbal Acts."
26. Yalom, Houts, Newell, and Rand, "Preparation of Patients for Group Therapy," p. 426.
27. Cartwright and Zander, *Group Dynamics*, 3d ed., p. 426.
28. Gitterman, "Building Mutual Support," pp. 5–21; Steinberg, *The Mutual-Aid Approach*.

14. Stage III: Mutuality and Goal Achievement

1. Garland, Jones, and Kolodny, "A Model for Stages of Development."
2. Derlega, "Self Disclosure in Intimate Relationships," pp. 1–9.

3. Horowitz, "Cognitive Structure of Interpersonal Problems," pp. 5–15.
4. Schein, *Organizational Culture and Leadership.*
5. Powdermaker and Frank, *Group Psychotherapy*, p. 433.
6. Perley, Winget, and Placci, "Hope and Discomfort as Factors," pp. 557–63.
7. Ackerman, *Treating the Troubled Family*, p. 88.
8. Balgopal and Hull, "Keeping Secrets," pp. 334–36.
9. Balgopal and Vassil, *Groups in Social Work*, p. 129.
10. Schein, *Organizational Culture and Leadership*, p. 206.
11. Simmel, *Conflict*, p. 46.
12. Yalom, *The Theory and Practice of Group Psychotherapy*, 3d ed., pp. 52–55.
13. Ibid., p. 67.
14. Steinberg, *The Mutual-Aid Approach*, pp. 111–32.
15. Malekoff, *Group Work with Adolescents*, pp. 127–29.
16. Dewey, *Experience and Education*, p. 12.
17. Yalom, *The Theory and Practice of Group Psychotherapy*, pp. 361–62.
18. Lee and Park, "A Group Approach to the Depressed Adolescent Girl," p. 522.
19. Solomon, *Black Empowerment*, pp. 311–13.
20. Blum, "The A-ha Response as a Therapeutic Goal," pp. 47–56.
21. Caplan, "Recent Developments in Crisis Intervention," p. 7.
22. For references on crisis intervention in groups, see Aguilera, *Crisis Intervention*, pp. 29–59; Bell, "Traumatic Event Debriefing," pp. 36–43; Parad, Selby, and Quinlan, "Crisis Intervention," pp. 304–30; Allgeyer, "Resolving Individual Crises"; Allgeyer, "The Crisis Group"; Berger, "Crisis Intervention: A Drop-in Group"; Buckley, "The Use of the Small Group."
23. Ell and Northen, *Families in Health Care*, pp. 175–77.
24. Williams and Holmes, *The Second Assault*, pp. 87–89.
25. Fuchs and Costes, "Building on Strengths," pp. 200–1.
26. Malekoff, *Group Work with Adolescents*, pp. 149–51.
27. Vinter and Galinsky, "Extragroup Relations."
28. DelValle and Alexander, "Project Enable," pp. 633–38.
29. Redl, "Strategy and Techniques for the Life Space Interview," pp. 1–18.

15. Stage IV: Separation-Termination

1. Garvin, *Contemporary Group Work*, chapter 10; Hess and Hess, "Termination in Context," pp. 489–97.
2. Hamilton, *Theory and Practice of Social Case Work*, p. 236.
3. Yalom, *The Theory and Practice of Group Psychotherapy*, 3d ed., p. 373.
4. Erikson, *Identity, Youth, and Crisis*, pp. 99–141; Maas, *People and Contexts*; Shapiro, "Termination," pp. 13–19.

5. Balgopal and Vassil, *Groups in Social Work*, p. 212.
6. Yalom, *The Theory and Practice of Group Psychotherapy*, 3d ed., pp. 230–44; Kurland, "Planning," pp. 173–78.
7. See Beck and Jones, *Progress in Family Problems*; Kerns, "Planned Short-Term Treatment," pp. 340–46; Epstein, "Brief Group Therapy," pp. 33–48; Reid and Shyne, *Brief and Extended Casework*.
8. Mayadas and Glasser, "Termination," p. 253.
9. See Fox, Nelson, and Bolman, "The Termination Process," pp. 53–63; Garland, Jones, and Kolodny, "A Model for Stages of Development," pp. 17–71; Germain and Gitterman, *Life Model*, pp. 28–78; Hartford, *Groups in Social Work*, pp. 87–93; Hellenbrand, "Termination in Direct Practice," pp. 765–69; Henry, *Group Skills in Social Work*, pp. 87–93; Lackey, "Termination"; Northen, *Clinical Social Work*, pp. 320–28; Shulman, *Skills of Helping*, pp. 278–91.
10. Garland, Jones, and Kolodny, "A Model," pp. 57–58; Northen, *Clinical Social Work*, p. 321.
11. Bywaters, "Ending Casework Relationships," p. 337.
12. Bowlby, "Separation Anxiety," p. 102.
13. For a more thorough discussion of separation crises, see Levine, *Group Psychotherapy*, pp. 224–40.
14. Garland, Jones, and Kolodny, "A Model," pp. 57–58.
15. Scheidlinger and Holden, "Group Therapy of Women," pp. 174–89.
16. Schiff, "Termination of Therapy," p. 80.
17. Ibid.
18. Schwartz, "Between Client and System," p. 192.
19. In a content analysis of four adult groups, Lackey found many expressions of positive feelings about termination. See Lackey, "Termination." See also Hess and Hess, "Termination in Context."
20. Germain and Gitterman, *Life Model*, p. 258.
21. Bolen, "Easing the Pain of Termination," pp. 519–27; Casey and Cantor, "Group Work with Hard-to-Reach Adolescents," pp. 9–22; Eklof, "The Termination Phase," pp. 55–71.
22. For a task-centered approach to work with groups, see Garvin, Reid, and Epstein, "A Task-Centered Approach," pp. 238–67.
23. Hess and Hess, "Termination in Context," pp. 491–92.
24. Mayadas and Glasser, "Termination," p. 252.
25. Lewis, "Examination of the Final Phase," pp. 507–14.
26. Lackey, "Termination."
27. Kramer, "The Termination Process," pp. 526–31.
28. Fortune, "Grief Only?" pp. 159–71.
29. From Carosella, "AIDS Anxiety—Techniques and Skills."
30. Rapoport, "Crisis Intervention," p. 236.

31. For similar formulations of tasks, see Garvin, *Contemporary Group Work*, pp. 208–9; Toseland and Rivas, *Introduction to Group Work Practice*, pp. 333–41; Malekoff, *Group Work with Adolescents*, pp. 168–69.
32. Hamilton, *Theory and Practice*, p. 81.
33. Greenfield and Rothman, "Termination or Transformation," pp. 51–66.

16. Evaluation

1. Kurland and Malekoff, "From the Editors," pp. 1–3.
2. Wilson and Ryland, *Social Group Work Practice*, pp. 76–80. See also Ames, "Social Work Recording." For a good review of the use of records, see Graybeak and Ruff, "Process Recording."
3. Subramanian, Hernandez, and Martinez, "Psychoeducational Group Work for Low Income Latina Mothers," pp. 53–64.
4. Chin, "Evaluating Group Movement," p. 42.
5. Coché, "Change Measures," pp. 79–99.
6. Kiresuk and Sherman, "Goal Attainment Scaling," pp. 443–53.
7. Luborsky, "Clinicians' Judgments of Mental Health," pp. 407–17.
8. MacKenzie, "Measurement of Group Climate," pp. 287–96.
9. Hudson, *The Clinical Measurement Package*, p. 16; see also Leavitt and Reid, "Rapid Assessment Instruments."
10. Garvin, *Contemporary Group Work*, pp. 162–88.
11. Waskow and Parloff, *Psychotherapy Change Measures*; Toseland and Rivas, *An Introduction to Group Work Practice*, pp. 162–88.
12. Toseland and Siporin, "When to Recommend Group Treatment," pp. 171–206.
13. Russell, *Clinical Social Work*, pp. 111–21.
14. Dies, "Bridging the Gap Between Research and Practice," p. 5.
15. Hopps, Pinderhughes, and Shankar, *The Power to Care*, p. 165.
16. Galinsky and Schopler, "Warning: Groups May Be Dangerous," pp. 89–94; Schopler and Galinsky, "When Groups Go Wrong," pp. 424–29.
17. Hearn, *Theory Building in Social Work*, p. 25.
18. Orcutt, *Science and Inquiry*, pp. 56–57.

Bibliography

Abels, Sonia Leib and Paul Abels. "Social Group Work's Contextual Purpose." In Sonia Leib Abels and Paul Abels, eds., *Proceedings, 1979 Symposium on Social Work with Groups*, pp. 146–60. Louisville, Ky.: Committee for the Advancement of Social Work with Groups, 1979.

Ackerman, Nathan. *Treating the Troubled Family*. New York: Basic, 1966.

Addams, Jane. *Twenty Years at Hull House*. New York: MacMillan, 1910.

Aguilar, Ignacio. "Initial Contacts with Mexican American Families." *Social Work* 17, no. 3 (May 1972): 66–70.

Aguilera, Donna. *Crisis Intervention: Theory and Methodology*. 6th ed. St. Louis: Mosby, 1990.

Allgeyer, Jean M. "Resolving Individual Crises Through Group Methods." In Howard J. Parad, H. L. P. Resnik and Libbie G. Parad, eds., *Emergency and Disaster Management*, pp. 159–67. Bowie, Md.: Charles, 1976.

——— "The Crisis Group: Its Unique Usefulness to the Disadvantaged." *International Journal of Group Psychotherapy* 20, no. 3 (April 1970): 235–40.

American Association of Group Workers. *Group Work—Casework Cooperation*. New York: Association, 1946.

American Psychiatric Association. *Diagnostic and Statistical Manual of Mental Disorders IV*. Washington, D.C.: Association, 1997.

——— *Task Force on DSM IV*. Washington, D.C.: Association, 1991.

Ames, Natalie. "Social Work Recording: A New Look at an Old Issue." *Journal of Social Work Education* 35, no. 2 (Spring/Summer 1999): 227–37.

Anderson, Joseph. *Social Work with Groups: A Process Model.* New York: Longman, 1997.

Anstey, Mark. "Scapegoating in Groups: Some Theoretical Perspectives and a Case Record of Intervention." *Social Work with Groups* 5, no. 3 (Fall 1982): 51–63.

Aronson, H. and B. Overall. "Treatment Expectations of Patients in Two Social Classes." *Social Work* 11, no. 1 (January 1966): 35–41.

Bales, Robert F. *Interaction Process Analysis: A Method for the Study of Small Groups.* Cambridge, Mass.: Addison-Wesley, 1950.

Bales, Robert F. and Philip E. Slater. "Functional Roles of Group Members." In Talcott Parsons and Robert F. Bales, eds., *Family: Socialization and Interaction Process.* Glencoe, Ill.: Free, 1955.

Bales, Robert F. et al. "Structure and Dynamics of Small Groups: A Review of Four Variables." In Joseph Gittler, ed., *Review of Sociology: Analysis of a Decade.* New York: Wiley, 1957.

Balgopal, Pallassana R. and R. F. Hull. "Keeping Secrets: Group Resistance for Patients and Therapists." *Psychotherapy: Theory, Research, and Practice* 10, no. 4 (Winter 1973): 334–36.

Balgopal, Pallassana R. and Thomas V. Vassil. *Groups in Social Work: An Ecological Perspective.* New York: Macmillan, 1983.

Ball, Steven and Benjamin Lipton. "Group Work with Gay Men." In Geoffrey L. Greif and Paul H. Ephross, eds., *Group Work with Populations at Risk.* New York: Oxford University Press, 1997.

Bartlett, Harriet M. *The Common Base of Social Work Practice.* New York: National Association of Social Workers, 1970.

—— "Toward Clarification and Improvement of Social Work Practice: The Working Definition." *Social Work* 3, no. 2 (April 1958): 3–9.

Baxter, Leslie A. "Conflict Management: An Episodic Approach." *Small Group Behavior* 13, no. 1 (February 1982): 23–42.

Beck, Dorothy Fahs and Mary Ann Jones. *Progress in Family Problems.* New York: Family Service Association of America, 1973.

Bell, Janet L. "Traumatic Event Debriefing: Service Delivery Designs and the Role of Social Work." *Social Work* 40, no. 1 (January 1995): 36–43.

Bentelspacher, Carl E., Evelyn De Silva, Terrence Leng Chuang, and Karl D. La Rowe. "A Process Evaluation of the Cultural Compatibility of Psychoeducational Family Group Treatment with Ethnic Asian Clients." *Social Work with Groups* 19, nos. 3/4 (1996): 41–55.

Benne, Kenneth D. and Paul Sheats. "Functional Roles of Group Members." *Journal of Social Issues* 4, no. 2 (Spring 1948): 41–49.

Berelson, Bernard and Gary A. Steiner. *Human Behavior: An Inventory of Scientific Findings.* New York: Harcourt, Brace and World, 1964.

Berger, David M. *Clinical Empathy.* Northvale, N.J.: Aronson, 1987.

Berger, Jeanne M. "Crisis Intervention: A Drop-in Group For Cancer Patients and Their Families." *Social Work in Health Care* 10, no. 2 (Winter 1984):81–92.

Berman-Rossi, Toby. "Empowering Groups Through Stages of Group Development." *Social Work with Groups* 15, nos. 2/3 (1992): 239–56.

—— "The Fight Against Homelessness and Despair: Institutionalized Aged." In Alex Gitterman and Lawrence Shulman, eds., *Mutual Aid Groups and the Life Cycle*, pp. 385–412. 2d ed. New York: Columbia University Press, 1994.

—— "The Tasks and Skills of the Social Worker Across Stages of Group Development." *Social Work with Groups* 16, nos. 1/2 (1993): 69–81.

Berman-Rossi, Toby and Timothy B. Kelly. "Advancing Stages of Group Development Theory." Paper presented at the 44th Annual Symposium, Association for the Advancement of Social Work with Groups, 1998.

Bernstein, Saul. "Conflict and Group Work." In Saul Bernstein, ed., *Explorations in Group Work*, pp. 72–106. Boston: Boston University School of Social Work, 1965.

—— "Self-Determination: King or Citizen in the Realm of Values." *Social Work* 5, no. 1 (1962): 3–8.

Bernstein, Saul, ed., *Explorations in Group Work*. Boston: Boston University School of Social Work, 1965; rpr. Milford House, 1973.

—— *Further Explorations in Group Work*. Boston: Milford House, 1973.

Bertcher, Harvey J. *Group Participation: Techniques for Leaders and Members*. Beverly Hills: Sage, 1979.

Bertcher, Harvey J. and Frank Maple. "Elements and Issues in Group Composition." In Martin Sundel, Paul Glasser, Rosemary Sarri, and Robert Vinter, eds., *Individual Change Through Small Groups*, pp. 180–202. 2d ed. New York: Free, 1985.

Bilides, David G. "Race, Color, Ethnicity and Class: Issues in Biculturalism in School-Based Adolescent Counseling Groups." *Social Work with Groups* 13, no. 4 (1990): 43–58.

—— "Reaching Inner-City Children: A Group Work Program Model for Public Middle Schools." *Social Work with Groups* 15, nos. 2/3 (1992): 129–44.

Bittner, Ruth. "Therapeutic Mother-Child Groups: A Developmental Approach." *Social Casework* 65, no. 3 (March 1984): 154–61.

Bloch, Sidney, Erik Crouch, and Janet Reibstein. "Therapeutic Factors in Group Psychotherapy." *Archives of General Psychiatry* 38, no. 5 (May 1981): 516–26.

Block, Lisa Rae. "On the Potentiality and Limits of Time: The Single Session Group and the Cancer Patient." *Social Work with Groups* 8, no. 2 (Summer 1985): 81–110.

Bloom, Naomi D. and Joseph G. Lynch. "Group Work in a Hospital Waiting Room." *Health and Social Work* 4, no. 3 (August 1979): 48–63.

Blum, Arthur. "The 'Aha' Response as a Therapeutic Goal." In Henry W. Maier, ed., *Group Work as Part of Residential Treatment*, pp. 47–56. New York: National Association of Social Workers, 1965.

Boatman, Frances Louise. "Caseworkers' Judgments of Clients' Hope: Some Correlates Among Client-Situation Characteristics and Among Workers' Communication Patterns." D.S.W. dissertation, Columbia University, 1975.

Boehm, Werner W. "The Nature of Social Work." *Social Work* 3, no. 2 (April 1958): 10–18.

Bolen, Jane K. "Easing the Pain of Termination for Adolescents." *Social Casework* 53, no. 9 (November 1972): 519–27.

Bounous, Ronald C. "A Study of Client and Worker Perceptions in the Initial Phase of Casework Marital Counseling." Ph.D. dissertation, University of Minnesota, 1965.

Bowlby, John. "Separation Anxiety." *International Journal of Psychoanalysis* 4, no. 2 (March-June 1960): 89–113.

Boyd, Neva. "Group Work Experiments in State Institutions in Illinois." *Proceedings, National Conference of Social Work*, p. 344. Chicago: University of Chicago Press, 1935.

Brager, George. "Goal Formation: An Organizational Perspective." In National Association of Social Workers, *Social Work with Groups*, pp. 22–36. New York: Association, 1960.

Brager, George and Stephen Holloway. *Changing Human Service Organizations.* New York: Free, 1978.

Brandler, Sondra and Camille P. Roman. *Group Work: Skills and Strategies for Effective Intervention.* 2d ed. Binghamton, N.Y.: Haworth, 1999.

———— "Uncovering Latent Content in Groups." In Roselle Kurland and Robert Salmon, eds., *Group Work Practice in a Troubled Society: Problems and Opportunities*, pp. 19–32. Binghamton, N.Y.: Haworth, 1995.

Breton, Margot. "Learning from Social Group Work Traditions." *Social Work with Groups* 13, no. 3 (1990): 21–45.

Breton, Margot and Anna Nosko. "Group Work with Women Who Have Experienced Abuse." In Geoffrey L. Greif and Paul H. Ephross, eds., *Group Work with Populations at Risk*, pp. 134–46. New York: Oxford University Press, 1997.

Briar, Scott. "Family Services." In Henry S. Maas, ed., *Five Fields of Social Service: Reviews of Research*, pp. 9–50. New York: National Association of Social Workers, 1966.

Bronfenbrenner, Urie. *The Ecology of Human Development: Experiments by Nature and Design.* Cambridge: Harvard University Press, 1979.

Brown, Allan and Tara Mistry. "Group Work with 'Mixed Membership' Groups: Issues of Race and Gender." *Social Work with Groups* 17, no. 3 (1994): 5–21.

Brown, June H., Wilbur Finch, Helen Northen, Samuel Taylor, and Marie Weil. *Child/Family/Neighborhood: A Master Plan for Social Service Delivery.* New York: Child Welfare League of America, 1982.

Brown, Leonard N. *Groups for Growth and Change*. New York: Longman, 1991.

———— "Social Workers' Verbal Acts and the Development of Mutual Expectations with Beginning Client Groups." D.S.W. dissertation, Columbia University, 1971.

Brown, Robert A. "Feedback in Family Interviewing." *Social Work* 18, no. 5 (September 1973): 52–59.

———— "The Technique of Ascription." D.S.W. dissertation, University of Southern California, 1971.

Buckley, Lola Elizabeth. "The Use of the Small Group at a Time of Crisis: Transition of Girls from Elementary to Junior High School." D.S.W. dissertation, University of Southern California, 1970.

Buckley, Walter. "Society as a Complex Adaptive System." In Walter Buckley, ed., *Modern Systems Research for the Behavioral Scientist*. Chicago: Aldine, 1968.

Burleson, B. R., T. L. Albrecht, and I. G. Sarason. *Communication of Social Support*. Newbury Park, Calif.: Sage, 1994.

Bywaters, Paul. "Ending Casework Relationships (1)." *Social Work Today* 6, no. 10 (August 1975): 301–4.

———— "Ending Casework Relationships (2)." *Social Work Today* 6, no. 11 (September 1975): 336–38.

Caplan, Gerald. "Recent Developments in Crisis Intervention and the Promotion of Support Services." *Journal of Primary Prevention* 10, no. 1 (Fall 1984): 3–26.

———— *Support Systems and Community Mental Health*. New York: Behavioral, 1974.

Caple, Frances. "Preventive Social Work Practice: A Generic Model for Direct Service on Behalf of Children." Ph.D. dissertation, University of Southern California, 1982.

Carlton, Thomas Owen. *Clinical Social Work in Health Settings: A Guide to Professional Practice with Exemplars*. New York: Springer, 1984.

Carosella, Joseph R. "AIDS Anxiety: Techniques and Skills: The Worried-Well Group." Paper presented at the Annual Symposium, Association for the Advancement of Social Work with Groups, 1986.

Cartwright, Dorwin and Alvin Zander, eds. *Group Dynamics: Research and Theory*. 3d ed. Evanston, Ill.: Row Peterson, 1960.

Casey, Richard D. and Leon Cantor. "Group Work with Hard-to-Reach Adolescents: The Use of Member-Initiated Program Selection." *Social Work with Groups* 6, no. 1 (Winter 1983): 9–22.

Chau, Kenneth L. "A Model of Practice with Special Reference to Ethnic Minority Populations." In Marie Weil, Kenneth L. Chau, and Dannia Southerland, eds., *Theory and Practice in Social Group Work: Creative Connections*. Binghamton, N.Y.: Haworth, 1992.

———— "Needs Assessment for Group Work with People of Color: A Conceptual Formulation." *Social Work with Groups* 15, nos. 2/3 (1992): 53–66.

Chau, Kenneth L. ed. *Ethnicity and Biculturalism: Emerging Perspectives of Social Work*. Binghamton, N.Y.: Haworth, 1991.

Chin, Robert. "Evaluating Group Movement and Individual Change." In National Association of Social Workers, ed., *Use of Groups in the Psychiatric Setting*, pp. 34–45. New York: Association, 1960.

Christ, Adolph E. and Kalman Flomenhaft, eds. *Psychosocial Family Interventions in Chronic Pediatric Illness*. New York: Plenum, 1982.

Clemenger, Florence. "Congruence Between Members and Workers on Selected Behaviors of the Role of the Social Group Worker." D.S.W. dissertation, University of Southern California, 1965.

Cloward, Richard. "Agency Structure as a Variable in Service to Groups." In National Conference on Social Welfare, *Group Work and Community Organization*. New York: Columbia University Press, 1956.

Coady, Nick. "The Worker-Client Relationship Revisited." *Families in Society* 74 (1993): 291–300.

Coché, Erich. "Change Measures and Clinical Practice in Group Psychotherapy." In Robert R. Dies and K. Roy MacKenzie, eds., *Advances in Group Psychotherapy*, pp. 79–100. New York: International Universities Press, 1983.

Cohen, Arthur M. and R. Douglas Smith. *The Critical Incident in Growth Groups: A Manual for Group Workers*. La Jolla: University Associates, 1976.

Cohen, Marcia B. "Who Wants to Chair the Meeting? Group Development and Leadership Patterns in a Community Action Group of Homeless People." *Social Work with Groups* 17, nos. 1/2 (1994): 71–87.

Cohen, Marcia B. and Audrey Mullender. "The Personal in the Political: Exploring the Group Work Continuum from Individual to Social Change Goals." *Social Work with Groups* 22, no. 1 (1999): 13–31.

Collins, Lainey. "How Do You Spell Hippopotamus? The Use of Group Work in After-School Tutoring Programs." *Social Work with Groups* 21, nos. 1/2 (1998): 61–75.

Colman, Arthur D. *Up From Scapegoating: Awakening Consciousness in Groups*. Wilmette, Ill.: Chiron, 1995.

Commager, Henry S. "Preface." In Jane Addams, *Twenty Years at Hull House*. New York: Signet/New American Library, 1961.

Committee on Practice, Psychiatric Social Work Section, National Association of Social Workers. *The Psychiatric Social Worker as Leader of a Group*. New York: Association, 1956.

Compton, Beulah R. and Burt Galaway. *Social Work Processes*. 6th ed. Pacific Grove, Calif.: Brooks/Cole, 1999.

Cook, Robert C. "Population: Some Pitfalls of Progress." In Sylvan Kaplan and Everlyn Kivy-Rosenberg, eds., *Ecology and the Quality of Life*. Springfield, Ill.: Thomas, 1973.

Cooley, Charles. *Social Process*. New York: Scribner's, 1918.

Cooper, Shirley A. "A Look at the Effect of Racism on Clinical Work." *Social Casework* 54, no. 2 (February 1973): 76–84.

Corsini, Raymond J. and Bina Rosenberg. "Mechanisms of Group Psychotherapy: Process and Dynamics." *Journal of Abnormal and Social Psychology* 51, no. 4 (1955): 406–11.

Coser, Lewis A. *The Functions of Social Conflict*. Glencoe, Ill.: Free, 1956.

Couch, Elsbeth Herzstein. *Joint and Family Interviews in the Treatment of Marital Problems*. New York: Family Service Association of America, 1969.

Cousins, Norman. *Head First: The Biology of Hope*. New York: Dutton, 1989.

Coyle, Grace L. "Group Work in Psychiatric Settings: Its Roots and Branches." In National Association of Social Workers, *Use of Groups in the Psychiatric Setting*, pp. 12–22. New York: Association, 1960.

—— *Group Work with American Youth*. New York: Harper, 1948.

—— "Social Group Work: An Aspect of Social Work Practice." *Journal of Social Issues* 8, no. 1 (1952): 21–35.

—— "Social Group Work in Recreation." In *Proceedings of the National Conference of Social Work*, pp. 195–208. New York: Columbia University Press, 1946.

—— *Social Process in Organized Groups*. New York: Smith, 1930.

—— "Some Basic Assumptions About Social Group Work." In Marjorie Murphy, ed., *The Social Group Work Method in Social Work Education*, pp. 88–105. New York: Council on Social Work Education, 1959.

—— *Studies in Group Behavior*. New York: Harper, 1937.

Daley, Barbara Sabin and Geraldine Suzanne Koppenaal. "The Treatment of Women in Short-Term Women's Groups." In Simon H. Budman, *Forms of Brief Therapy*, pp. 343–57. New York: Guilford, 1981.

Dana, Bess. "The Collaborative Process." In Rosalind S. Miller and Helen Rehr, eds., *Social Work Issues in Health Care*, pp. 181–220. Englewood Cliffs, N.J.: Prentice-Hall, 1983.

Davidson, Mark. "The Case for Uncommon Sense." *Transcript* (June 1983): 7–8. Los Angeles: University of Southern California.

Davis, Inger P. "Advice-Giving in Parent Counseling." *Social Casework* 56, no. 6 (June 1975): 343–47.

Davis, Larry E. "Group Work Practice with Ethnic Minorities of Color." In Martin Sundel, Paul Glasser, Rosemary Sarri, and Robert Vinter, eds., *Individual Change Through Small Groups*, pp. 324–44. New York: Free, 1985.

Davis, Larry E., ed. *Ethnicity in Social Group Work Practice* (special issue), *Social Work with Groups* 7, no. 3 (1984).

Davis, Larry E. and Enola Proctor. *Race, Gender, and Class: Guidelines for Practice with Individuals, Families, and Groups*. Englewood Cliffs, N.J.: Prentice Hall, 1989.

Decker, Kathleen. "Puppets Help Children Shed Horrors of Abuse." *Los Angeles Times*, April 1985.

Delgado, Melvin. "Activities and Hispanic Groups: Issues and Suggestions." *Social Work with Groups* 6, no. 1 (Spring 1983): 85–96.

——— *Social Services in Latino Communities: Research and Strategies.* Binghamton, N.Y.: Haworth, 1998.

Delgado, Melvin and Denise Humm-Delgado. "Hispanics and Group Work: A Review of the Literature." *Social Work with Groups* 7, no. 3 (Fall 1984): 85–96.

Del Valle, Alline and Felton Alexander. "Project Enable: Effects of the Project on Family Service Agencies and Urban Leagues." *Social Casework* 48, no. 1 (December 1967): 633–38.

Derlega, Valerian J. "Self-Disclosure in Intimate Relationships." In Valerian J. Derlega, ed., *Communication, Intimacy, and Close Relationships*, pp. 1–9. Orlando, Fla.: Academic, 1984.

Derlega, Valerian J., ed. *Communication, Intimacy, and Close Relationships.* Orlando, Fla.: Academic, 1984.

Deutsch, Morton. *The Resolution of Conflict.* New Haven: Yale University Press, 1973.

Devore, Wynetta and Elfrieda G. Schlesinger. *Ethnic-Sensitive Social Work Practice.* St. Louis: Mosby, 1981.

Dewey, John. *Democracy and Education.* New York: Ethical Culture Society, 1938; rpr. Free, 1966.

——— *Experience and Education.* New York: Macmillan, 1938.

——— *How We Think.* Boston: Heath, 1910.

Dies, Lee P. *Man's Nature and Nature's Man: The Ecology of Human Communication.* Ann Arbor: University of Michigan Press, 1955.

Dies, Robert R. "Bridging the Gap Between Research and Practice in Group Psychotherapy." In Robert R. Dies and K. Roy MacKenzie, eds., *Advances in Group Psychotherapy*, pp. 1–26. New York: International Universities Press, 1983.

——— "Clinical Implications of Research on Leadership in Short-Term Group Psychotherapy." In Robert R. Dies and K. Roy MacKenzie, eds., *Advances in Group Psychotherapy*, pp. 27–78. New York: International Universities Press, 1983.

Douglas, Tom. *Group Processes in Social Work: A Theoretical Synthesis.* New York: Wiley, 1979.

——— *Scapegoats, Transferring Blame.* London: Routledge, 1995.

Duck, Steve. "Communication of Social Support." In B. R. Burleson, T. L. Albrecht, and I. G. Sarason, eds., *Communication of Social Support*, p. 175. Newbury Park, Calif.: Sage, 1994.

Durkin, Helen. *The Group in Depth.* New York: International Universities Press, 1964.

Durst, Douglas. "Understanding the Client—Social Worker Relationship in a Multicultural Setting: Implications for Practice." *Journal of Multicultural Social Work* 3, no. 4 (1994): 29–42.

Edwards, E. Daniel, Margie E. Edwards, Geri M. Davies, and Francine Eddy. "Enhancing Self-Concept and Identification with Indianness of American Indian Girls." *Social Work with Groups* 1, no. 3 (Fall 1978): 309–18.

Eklof, Mona. "The Termination Phase in Group Therapy: Implications for Geriatric Groups." *Small Group Behavior* 15, no. 4 (November 1984): 565–71.

Ell, Kathleen and Helen Northen. *Families and Health Care: Psychosocial Practice.* New York: de Gruyter, 1990.

Englehardt, Bonnie. "Group Work with Lesbians." In Geoffrey L. Greif and Paul Ephross, eds., *Group Work with Populations at Risk*, pp. 278–94. New York: Oxford University Press, 1997.

Ephross, Paul H. and Thomas Vassil. *Groups That Work: Structure and Process.* New York: Columbia University Press, 1988.

Epstein, Norman. "Brief Group Therapy in a Child Guidance Clinic." *Social Work* 15, no. 3 (July 1970): 33–48.

Erikson, Erik H. *Childhood and Society.* 2d ed. New York: Norton, 1963.

—— "Identity and the Life Cycle." In *Psychological Issues*, pp. 18–164. New York: International Universities Press, 1959.

—— *Identity, Youth, and Crisis.* New York: Norton, 1968.

Etcheverry, Roger, Max Siporin, and Ronald W. Toseland. "The Uses and Abuses of Role Playing." In Paul H. Glasser and Nazneen S. Mayadas, eds., *Group Workers at Work: Theory and Practice in the Eighties.* Totowa, N.J.: Rowman and Littlefield, 1986.

Eubank, Earle E. *The Concepts of Sociology.* Boston: Heath, 1932.

Evans, Nancy and Paul A. Servis. "Group Cohesion: A Review and Revaluation." *Small Group Behavior* 11, no. 4 (November 1980): 359–70.

Falck, Hans S. "Aspects of Membership: On The Integration of Psychoanalytic Object-Relations Theory and Small Group Service." *Social Thought* (Winter 1980): 17–26.

—— *Social Work: The Membership Perspective.* New York: Springer, 1988.

—— "The Management of Membership: Social Group Work Contributions." *Social Work with Groups* 12, no. 3 (1989): 19–32.

Fanshel, David. "A Study of Caseworkers' Perceptions of Their Clients." *Social Casework* 39, no. 10 (December 1958): 543–51.

Fatout, Marian F. *Children in Groups.* Westport, Conn.: Auburn House, 1996.

—— "A Comparative Analysis of Practice Concepts Described in Selected Social Work Literature." D.S.W. dissertation, University of Southern California, 1975.

—— "Physically Abused Children: Activity as a Therapeutic Medium." *Social Work with Groups* 16, no. 3 (1993): 83–97.

——— "Using Limits and Structures for Empowerment of Children in Groups." *Social Work with Groups* 17, no. 4 (1995): 55–69.

Fischer, Claude S. *To Dwell Among Friends: Personal Networks in Town and City.* Chicago: University of Chicago Press, 1982.

Flanzer, Jerry. "Conintegration: The Concurrent Integration of Treatment Modalities in Social Work Practice." D.S.W. dissertation, University of Southern California, 1973.

Fluegelman, Andrew, ed. *The New Games Book.* New York: Doubleday-Dolphin, 1976.

——— *More New Games.* New York: Doubleday-Dolphin, 1981.

Follett, Mary Parker. *Dynamic Administration.* New York: Harper, 1942.

——— *The New State.* New York: Longmans Green, 1926.

Fong, Rowena and Noreen Mokuau. "Not Simply Asian Americans: Periodical Literature Review on Asians and Pacific Islanders." *Social Work* 39, no. 3 (May 1994): 298–305.

Fortune, Anne E. "Grief Only? Client and Social Worker Reactions to Termination." *Clinical Social Work Journal* 15, no. 2 (Summer 1987): 159–71.

Fox, Evelyn, Marion Nelson, and William Bolman. "The Termination Process: A Neglected Dimension in Social Work." *Social Work* 14, no. 4 (October 1969): 53–63.

Frances, Allen, John F. Clarkin, and Samuel Perry. *Differential Therapeutics in Psychiatry: The Art and Science of Treatment Selection.* New York: Brunner/Mazel, 1984.

Freedberg, Sharon. "Self-Determination: Historical Perspectives and Effect on Current Practice." *Social Work* 34, no. 1 (1989): 33–38.

Freud, Anna. *The Ego and the Mechanisms of Defense.* New York: International Universities Press, 1946.

Frey, Louise A. "Support and the Group: Generic Treatment Form." *Social Work* 7, no. 3 (October 1962): 35–42.

Frey, Louise A., ed. *Use of Groups in the Health Field.* New York: National Association of Social Workers, 1966.

Friedlander, Walter A., ed. *Concepts and Methods of Social Work.* Englewood Cliffs, N.J.: Prentice-Hall, 1958.

Fuchs, Don and Theresa Costes. "Building on Strengths of Family and Network Ties for the Prevention of Child Maltreatment: A Group Work Approach." In David Fike and Barbara Rittner, eds., *Working from Strengths: The Essence of Group Work,* pp. 200–19. Miami: Center for Group Work Studies, 1992.

Furness, Anne-Marie. "Some Facets of Similarity and Difference Between the Social Work Methods of Casework and Group Work." D.S.W. dissertation, University of Southern California, 1971.

Galinsky, Maeda J. and Janice H. Schopler. "Developmental Patterns in Open-Ended Groups." *Social Work with Groups* 12, no. 2 (1989): 99–120.

———— "Negative Experiences in Support Groups." *Social Work in Health Care* 20, no. 1 (1994): 77–95.

———— "Structuring Co-Leadership." *Social Work with Groups* 3, no. 4 (1980): 51–63.

———— "Warning: Groups May Be Dangerous." *Social Work* 22, no. 2 (March 1977): 89–94.

Garland, James A. and Louise A. Frey. "Application of Stages of Group Development to Groups in Psychiatric Settings." In Saul Bernstein, ed., *Further Explorations in Group Work*, pp. 1–33. Boston: Milford House, 1973.

Garland, James A., Hubert E. Jones, and Ralph L. Kolodny. "A Model for Stages of Development in Social Work Groups." In Saul Bernstein, ed., *Explorations in Group Work*, pp. 17–71. Boston: Boston University School of Social Work, 1965; Milford House, 1973.

Garland, James A. and Ralph Kolodny. "Characteristics and Resolution of Scapegoating." In Saul Bernstein, ed., *Further Explorations in Group Work*, pp. 55–74. Boston: Milford House, 1973.

Garvin, Charles D. "Complementarity of Role Expectations in Groups: The Member-Worker Contract." In National Conference on Social Welfare, *Social Work Practice*, pp. 127–45. New York: Columbia University Press, 1969.

———— *Contemporary Group Work*. 2d ed. Englewood Cliffs, N.J.: Prentice-Hall, 1987.

———— *Contemporary Group Work*. 3d ed. Boston: Allyn and Bacon, 1997.

———— "Group Theory and Research." *Encyclopedia of Social Work I*. Washington, D.C.: National Association of Social Workers, 1987.

Garvin, Charles D. and Beth Glover Reed. "Gender Issues in Social Group Work: An Overview." *Social Work with Groups* 6, no. 3 (Fall/Winter 1983): 3–19.

———— "Sources and Visions for Feminist Group Work: Reflective Processes, Social Justice, Diversity, and Correction." In Nan Van Den Bergh, ed., *Feminist Visions for Social Work*. Silver Springs, Md.: National Association of Social Workers, 1995.

Garvin, Charles D., William J. Reid, and Laura Epstein. "A Task-Centered Approach." In Robert W. Roberts and Helen Northen, eds., *Theories of Social Work with Groups*, pp. 238–67. New York: Columbia University Press, 1976.

Gentry, Martha. "Initial Group Meetings: Member Expectations and Information Distribution Process." Ph.D. dissertation, Washington University, 1974.

Germain, Carel and Alex Gitterman. *The Life Model of Social Work Practice*. New York: Columbia University Press, 1980.

Getzel, George. "AIDS." In Alex Gitterman, ed., *Handbook of Social Work Practice with Vulnerable Populations*, pp. 35–64. New York: Columbia University Press, 1991.

———— "Group Work Services to People with AIDS During a Changing Pandemic."

In Geoffrey L. Greif and Paul H. Ephross, eds., *Group Work with Populations at Risk*, pp. 42–56. New York: Oxford University Press, 1997.

Gibbs, Jewelle Taylor. "Treatment Relationships with Black Clients: Interpersonal vs. Instrumental Strategies." In Carel B. Germain, ed., *Advances in Clinical Social Work Practice*, pp. 184–95. Washington, D.C.: National Association of Social Workers, 1985.

Gilligan, Carol. "Adolescent Development Reconsidered." St. Paul, Minn.: Center for Youth Development and Research and School of Social Work, University of Minnesota, 1987.

Gitterman, Alex. "Building Mutual Support in Groups." *Social Work with Groups* 12, no. 2 (1989): 5–21.

Gitterman, Alex. "Developing a New Group Service: Strategies and Skills." In Alex Gitterman and Lawrence Shulman, eds., *Mutual Aid Groups, Vulnerable Populations, and the Life Cycle*, pp. 59–80. New York: Columbia University Press, 1994.

——— "Introduction: Social Work Practice with Vulnerable Populations." In Alex Gitterman, ed., *Handbook of Social Work Practice with Vulnerable Populations*, pp. 1–34. New York: Columbia University Press, 1991.

——— "The President's Pen." *Social Work with Groups Newsletter.* August 1998.

Gitterman, Alex and Lawrence Shulman, eds., *Mutual Aid Groups, Vulnerable Populations and the Life Cycle.* 2d ed. New York: Columbia University Press, 1994.

Glasser, Paul and Charles Garvin. "An Organizational Model." In Robert W. Roberts and Helen Northen, eds., *Theories of Social Work with Groups.* pp. 331–67. New York: Columbia University Press, 1976.

Glasgow, Godfrey F. and Janice Gouse-Sheese. "Themes of Rejection and Abandonment in Group Work with Caribbean Adolescents." *Social Work with Groups* 17, no. 4 (1995): 3–24.

Glassman, Urania and Len Kates. "Authority Themes and Worker-Group Transactions: Additional Dimensions to the Stages of Group Development." *Social Work with Groups* 6, no. 2 (Summer 1983): 33–52.

Glassman, Urania and Len Kates. *Group Work: A Humanistic Approach.* Newbury Park, Calif.: Sage, 1990.

Goffman, Erving. *Behavior in Public Places.* New York: Free, 1963.

Golan, Naomi. *Passing Through Transitions: A Guide for Practitioners.* New York: Free, 1981.

——— *The Perilous Bridge: Helping Clients Through Mid-Life Transitions.* New York: Free, 1986.

Goldberg, Elisa Valladares and Thomas Simpson. "Challenging Stereotypes in Treatment of the Homeless Alcoholic and Addict: Creating Freedom Through Structure in Large Groups." *Social Work with Groups* 18, nos. 2/3 (1995): 79–94.

Goldberg, Ted. "Beliefs and Attitudes About the Group Therapies by Group Workers." Paper presented at the 14th Symposium, Association for the Advancement of Social Work with Groups, October 1992.

——— "Group Work and Group Treatment: A Preliminary Analysis." Paper presented at the 13th Symposium, Association for the Advancement of Social Work with Groups, October 1991.

Goldstein, Eda G. *Ego Psychology and Social Work Practice*. New York: Free, 1984.

Goldstein, Howard. "Cognitive Approaches to Direct Practice." *Social Service Review* 56, no. 4 (December 1982): 539–55.

——— *Social Learning and Change*. Columbia, S.C.: University of South Carolina Press, 1981.

——— *Social Work Practice: A Unitary Approach*. Columbia, S.C.: University of South Carolina Press, 1973.

Gordon, William E. "Toward a Social Work Frame of Reference." *Journal of Education for Social Work* 1, no. 2 (Fall 1965): 19–26.

Gottlieb, Naomi, Dianne Burden, Ruth McCormick, and Ginny Nicarthy. "The Distinctive Attributes of Feminist Groups." *Social Work with Groups* 6, nos 3/4 (1983): 81–93.

Gouldner, Alvin W. "Red Tape as a Social Problem." In Robert K. Merton, Alisa P. Gray, Barbara Hockey, and Hanan C. Selvin, eds., *Reader in Bureaucracy*, pp. 410–18. Glencoe, Ill.: Free, 1952.

Graybeak, Clay and Elizabeth Ruff. "Process Recording: It's More Than You Think." *Journal of Social Work Education* 3, no. 2 (Spring/Summer 1995): 169–81.

Greene, Roberta R. "Eriksonian Theory: A Developmental Approach to Ego Mastery." In Roberta R. Greene and Paul H. Ephross, eds., *Human Behavior Theory and Social Work Practice*, pp. 79–104. New York: de Gruyter, 1991.

——— "General Systems Theory." In Roberta R. Greene and Paul H. Ephross, eds., *Human Behavior Theory and Social Work Practice*, pp. 227–60. New York: de Gruyter, 1991.

Greenfield, Wilma L. and Beulah Rothman. "Termination or Transformation? Evolving Beyond Termination in Groups." In Joseph Lassner, Kathleen Powell, and Elaine Finnegan, eds., *Social Group Work: Competence and Values in Practice*, pp. 51–66. New York: Haworth Press, 1987.

Greif, Geoffrey and Paul H. Ephross, eds., *Group Work with Populations at Risk*. New York: Oxford University Press, 1997.

Group for the Advancement of Psychiatry. *The Process of Child Therapy*. New York: Brunner/Mazel, 1982.

Grunebaum, Henry and Leonard Solomon. "Toward a Peer Group Theory of Group Psychotherapy, I." *International Journal of Group Psychotherapy* 30, no. 1 (January 1980): 23–50.

Grunebaum, Henry and Leonard Solomon. "On the Development and Significance of Peers and Play." *International Journal of Group Psychotherapy* 32, no. 3 (July 1982): 283–308.

Gutiérrez, Lorraine M. and Edith A. Lewis. *Empowering Women of Color*. New York: Columbia University Press, 1999.

Hall, Edward T. *The Hidden Dimension*. Garden City, New York: Doubleday, 1966.

Hamilton, Gordon. *Theory and Practice of Social Case Work*. 2d ed. New York: Columbia University Press, 1951.

Hammond, D. Corydon. "Cross-Cultural Rehabilitation." *Journal of Rehabilitation* 37, no. 5 (September-October 1977): 34–36.

Hannah, Patricia. "Preparing Members for the Expectations of Social Work with Groups: An Approach to the Preparatory Interview." *Social Work with Groups* 22, no. 4 (2000).

Hare, A. Paul, Edgar F. Borgatta, and Robert F. Bales, eds., *Small Groups: Studies in Social Interaction*. New York: Knopf, 1955.

Harrison, Diane F., Bruce A. Thyer, and John S. Wodarski, eds. *Cultural Diversity and Social Work Practice*. 2nd ed. Springfield, Ill.: Thomas, 1996.

Hartford, Margaret E. "Group Methods and Generic Practice." In Robert W. Roberts and Helen Northen, eds., *Theories of Social Work with Groups*, pp. 45–74. New York: Columbia University Press, 1976.

—— "Groups in Human Services: Some Facts and Fancies." *Social Work with Groups* 1, no. 1 (1978): 7–13.

—— *Groups in Social Work*. New York: Columbia University Press, 1971.

—— "The Contributions of Grace Coyle and the Faculty of Sociology of the School of Applied Social Sciences of Western Reserve University to Group Practice Theory." In Sonia Leib Abels and Paul Abels, eds., *Social Work with Groups*, Proceedings 1979 Symposium, pp. 91–110. Louisville, Ky.: Committee for the Advancement of Social Work with Groups, 1981.

—— "The Social Group Worker and Group Formation." Ph.D. dissertation, University of Chicago, 1962.

Hartford, Margaret. ed., "Working Papers Toward a Frame of Reference for Social Group Work." New York: National Association of Social Workers, 1964.

Hartmann, Heinz. *Ego Psychology and the Problem of Adaptation*. New York: International Universities Press, 1958.

Hathway, Marion E. "Twenty-Five Years of Professional Education for Social Work—and a Look Ahead." *Compass* 27, no. 5 (June 1946): 13–18.

Heap, Ken. *Process and Action in Work with Groups: The Preconditions for Treatment and Growth*. New York: Pergamon, 1979.

Hearn, Gordon. *Theory Building in Social Work*. Toronto: University of Toronto Press, 1958.

Hearn, Gordon, ed., *The General Systems Approach: Contributions Toward a Holistic Conception of Social Work*. New York: Council on Social Work Education, 1968.

Heine, R. W. "A Comparison of Patients' Reports on Psychotherapeutic Experience with Psychoanalytic, Nondirective, and Adlerian Therapists." Ph.D. dissertation, University of Chicago, 1950.

Hellenbrand, Shirley C. "Termination in Direct Practice." In National Association of Social Workers, *Encyclopedia of Social Work*, pp. 765–69. 18th ed. Silver Spring, Md.: NASW, 1987.

Henry, Sue. *Group Skills in Social Work: A Four-Dimensional Approach.* 2d ed. Piedmont, Calif.: Brooks/Cole, 1992.

Hepworth, Dean H. and Jo Ann Larsen. *Direct Social Work Practice: Theory and Skills.* Homewood, Ill.: Dorsey, 1982.

Herrick, James C. "The Perception of Crisis in a Modified Therapeutic Community." D.S.W. dissertation, University of Southern California, 1966.

Hess, Howard and Peg McCartt Hess. "Termination in Context." In Beulah R. Compton and Burt Galaway, eds., *Social Work Processes*, 6th ed. Pacific Grove, Calif.: Brooks/Cole, 1999.

Hill, William F. "Further Considerations of Therapeutic Mechanisms in Group Therapy." *Small Group Behavior* 6, no. 4 (November 1975): 421–29.

Ho, Man Keung. "Social Group Work with Asian/Pacific Americans." *Social Work with Groups* 7 (1984): 49–61.

Hollingshead, August B. and Frederick C. Redlich. *Social Class and Mental Illness: A Community Study.* New York: Wiley, 1958.

Homans, George. *The Human Group.* New York: Harcourt-Brace, 1950.

Hopps, June Gary and Elaine Pinderhughes. *Group Work with Overwhelmed Clients.* New York: Free, 1999.

Hopps, June Gary, Elaine Pinderhughes, and Richard Shankar. *The Power to Care.* New York: Free, 1995.

Horowitz, Gideon. "Worker Interventions in Response to Deviant Behavior in Groups." Ph.D. dissertation, University of Chicago, 1968.

Horowitz, L. M. "Cognitive Structure of Interpersonal Problems Treated in Psychotherapy." *Journal of Consulting and Clinical Psychology* 47, no. 5 (1979): 5–15.

Houston-Vega, Mary Kay and Elaine Nuehring with Elisabeth R. Daquio. *Prudent Practice: A Guide for Managing Malpractice Risk.* Washington, D.C.: NASW, 1997.

Hudson, Walter. *The Clinical Measurement Package.* Homewood, Ill.: Dorsey, 1982.

Hutten, Joan M. "Short-Term Contracts IV, Techniques: How and Why To Use Them." *Social Work Today* 6, no. 20 (August 1976): 614–18.

—— *Short-Term Contracts in Social Work.* London: Routledge and Kegan Paul, 1977.

Jenkins, Shirley. *The Ethnic Dilemma in Social Services.* New York: Free, 1981.

Jennings, Helen Hall. *Leadership and Isolation: A Study of Personality in Interpersonal Relations.* New York: Longmans Green, 1950.

Johnson, Arlien. "Development of Basic Methods of Social Work Practice and Education." *Social Work Journal* 36, no. 3 (July 1955): 109–13.

Jung, Marshall. *Chinese Americans in Family Therapy*. San Francisco: Jossey-Bass, 1998.

Kadushin, Alfred. "The Racial Factor in the Interview." *Social Work* 17, no. 3 (May 1972): 88–98.

———— *The Social Work Interview*, New York: Columbia University Press, 1972.

Kaiser, Clara. "Characteristics of Social Group Work." In National Conference of Social Work, *The Social Welfare Forum*. New York: Columbia University Press, 1957.

———— "Objectives of Group Work: A Commission Report," National Association for the Study of Group Work, 1936.

———— *The Group Records of Four Clubs at the University Settlement Center*. Cleveland: School of Applied Social Sciences, Western Reserve University, 1930.

Kane, Rosalie. "Editorial: Thoughts on Parent Education." *Health and Social Work* 6, no. 1 (February 1981): 1–4.

Katz, Robert L. *Empathy: Its Nature and Uses*. New York: Free, 1963.

Keefe, Thomas. "Empathy: The Critical Skill." *Social Work* 21, no. 1 (January 1976): 10–15.

Keefe, Thomas. "Empathy Skill and Social Consciousness." *Social Casework* 61 (September 1980): 387–93.

Kemp, Susan P., James K. Whittaker, and Elizabeth M. Tracy. *Person-Environment Practice: The Social Ecology of Interpersonal Helping*. New York: de Gruyter, 1997.

Kerns, Elizabeth. "Planned Short-term Treatment: A New Service to Adolescents." *Social Casework* 51, no. 6 (June 1970): 340–46.

Kiresuk, Thomas J. and Robert E. Sherman. "Goal Attainment Scaling: A General Method for Evaluating Comprehensive Community Mental Programs." *Community Mental Health Journal* 4 (1968): 443–53.

Klein, Alan F. "Role Playing in Leadership Training and Group Problem Solving." New York: Association, 1956.

Klein, Robert H. "Some Problems of Patient Referral for Outpatient Group Psychotherapy." *American Journal of Group Psychotherapy* 33, no. 2 (April 1983): 29–39.

Kohut, Heinze. *The Restoration of the Self*. New York: International Universities Press, 1977.

Konopka, Gisela. *The Adolescent Girl in Conflict*. Englewood Cliffs, N.J.: Prentice-Hall, 1966.

———— "All Lives are Connected to Other Lives: The Meaning of Social Group Work." In Marie Weil, Kenneth L. Chau, and Dannia Southerland, eds., *Theory and Practice in Social Group Work: Creative Connections*. Binghamton, N.Y.: Haworth, 1992.

———— "Formation of Values in the Developing Person." *American Journal of Orthopsychiatry* 43, no. 1 (January 1973): 86–96.

———— "The Generic and Specific in Group Work Practice in the Psychiatric Setting." *Social Work* 1, no. 1 (January 1956): 72–80.

———— *Group Work in the Institution: A Modern Challenge.* New York: Whiteside, Morrow, 1954.

———— "The Significance of Social Work Based on Ethical Values." *Social Work with Groups* 1, no. 2 (Summer 1978): 123–31.

———— *Social Group Work: A Helping Process.* 3d ed. Englewood Cliffs, N.J.: Prentice-Hall, 1983 [1963].

———— *Therapeutic Group Work with Children.* Minneapolis: University of Minnesota Press, 1949.

Kramer, Sidney A. "The Termination Process in Open-Ended Psychotherapy: Guidelines for Clinical Practice." *Psychotherapy* 23 (1986): 526–31.

Kropotkin, Petr. *Mutual Aid: A Factor of Evolution.* Montreal: Black Rose, 1989 [1903].

Kurland, Roselle. *Group Formation: A Guide to the Development of Successful Groups.* Albany, N.Y.: Continuing Education Program, School of Social Welfare, State University of New York at Albany and United Neighborhood Centers of America, 1982.

———— "Planning: The Neglected Component of Group Development." *Social Work with Groups* 1, no. 2 (Summer 1978): 173–78.

Kurland, Roselle and Andrew Malekoff. "From the Editors." *Social Work with Groups* 18, nos. 2/3 (1995): 1–3.

Kurland, Roselle and Robert Salmon. "Group Work vs. Casework in a Group: Principles and Implications for Teaching and Practice." *Social Work with Groups* 15, no. 4 (1992): 3–10.

———— "Not Just One of the Gang. Group Workers and Their Role as an Authority." *Social Work with Groups* 16, nos. 1/2 (1993): 153–67.

———— "Purpose: A Misunderstood and Misused Keystone of Group Work Practice." *Social Work with Groups* 21, no. 3 (1998): 5–17.

———— "Self-Determination: Its Use and Misuse in Group Work Practice and Social Work Education." In David F. Fike and Barbara Rittner, eds., *Working from Strengths: The Essence of Group Work,* pp. 105–21. Miami: Center for Group Work Studies, Barry University, 1992.

———— *Teaching a Methods Course in Social Work with Groups.* Alexandria, Va.: Council on Social Work Education, 1998.

Kutchins, Herb. "The Fiduciary Relationship: The Legal Basis for Social Workers' Responsibilities to Clients." *Social Work* 36, no. 2 (March 1996): 106–13.

Lackey, Mary Beit-Hallahmi. "Termination: The Critical Stage of Social Work." D.S.W. dissertation, University of Southern California, 1981.

Lacoursiere, Roy B. *The Life Cycle of Groups: Group Development Stage Theory.* New York: Human Sciences, 1980.

Larsen, JoAnn and Dean H. Hepworth. "Skill Development through Competency-Based Education." *Journal of Education for Social Work* 14 (1978): 73–81.

Lasater, Tonia Tash and Frank F. Montalvo. "Understanding Mexican-American Culture: A Training Program." *Children Today* 11, no. 3 (May-June 1982): 23–25.

Lassner, Joseph, Kathleen Powell, and Elaine Finnegan, eds. *Social Group Work: Competence and Values in Practice.* New York: Haworth, 1987.

Leavitt, John L. and William J. Reid. "Rapid Assessment Instruments in Social Work Practice." *Social Work Research and Abstracts* 17, no. 1 (Spring 1981): 13–20.

Lee, Judith A. B. *The Empowerment Approach to Social Work Practice.* New York: Columbia University Press, 1994.

———— "No Place to Go: Homeless Women." In Alex Gitterman and Lawrence Shulman, eds., *Mutual Aid Groups and the Life Cycle*, pp. 245–62. Itasca, Ill.: Peacock, 1986.

Lee, Judith A. B. and Danielle N. Park. "A Group Approach to the Depressed Adolescent Girl in Foster Care." *American Journal of Orthopsychiatry* 48, no. 3 (July 1978): 516–27.

Levine, Baruch. *Fundamentals of Group Treatment.* Chicago: Whitehall, 1967.

———— *Group Psychotherapy. Practice and Development.* Englewood Cliffs, N.J.: Prentice-Hall, 1979.

Levine, Baruch and Judith Schild. "Group Treatment of Depression." *Social Work* 14, no. 4 (October 1969): 46–52.

Levine, Murray and Howard J. Doueck. *The Impact of Mandated Reporting on the Therapeutic Process.* Thousand Oaks, Calif.: Sage, 1995.

Levy, Alan J. "A Community-Based Approach to Clinical Services for Children of Substance Abusers." *Child and Adolescent Social Work Journal* 11, no. 3 (June 1994): 221–233.

Levy, Avraham. "Group Cohesion." Ph.D. dissertation, University of Southern California, 1984.

Lewin, Kurt. *Field Theory in Social Science.* New York: Harper and Row, 1951.

Lewis, Benjamin F. "An Examination of the Final Phase of a Group Development Theory." *Small Group Behavior* 9, no. 4 (December 1978): 507–17.

Lewis, Elizabeth. "Regaining Promise: Feminist Perspectives for Social Work Practice." *Social Work with Groups* 15, nos. 2/3 (1992): 271–84.

Lewis, Harold. *The Intellectual Base of Social Work Practice: Tools for Thought in a Helping Profession.* New York: Haworth, 1982.

Lewis, M. and L. A. Rosenblum. *Friendship and Peer Relations.* New York: Wiley, 1975.

Lieberman, Alicia F. "Culturally Sensitive Intervention with Children and Families." *Child and Adolescent Social Work* (1990): 101–19.

Lieberman, Florence. "Clients' Expectations, Preferences and Experiences of Initial Interviews in Voluntary Social Agencies," D.S.W. dissertation, Columbia University, 1968.

Lieberman, Morton A., Irvin D. Yalom, and Matthew B. Miles. *Encounter Groups: First Facts*. New York: Basic, 1973.

Lipton, Harold and Sydney Malter. "The Social Worker as Mediator on a Hospital Ward." In William Schwartz and Serapio R. Zalba, eds., *The Practice of Group Work*. pp. 97–121. New York: Columbia University Press, 1971.

Liu, Fanny W. C. L. "Towards Mutual Aid in a Chinese Society." In Roselle Kurland and Robert Salmon, eds., *Group Work Practice in a Troubled Society: Problems and Opportunities*, pp. 89–100. Binghamton, N.Y.: Haworth, 1995.

Lonergan, Elaine Cooper. *Group Intervention: How to Begin and Maintain Groups in Medical and Psychiatric Settings*. Northvale, N.J.: Jason Aronson, 1982.

Lonergan, Elaine Cooper and Gaetana M. Manuele. "A Group for Relatives and Friends of Patients Hospitalized in an Acute Care Service." In Max Rosenbaum, ed., *Handbook of Short-Term Therapy Groups*. pp. 357–79. New York: McGraw-Hill, 1983.

Longres, John F. *Human Behavior in the Social Environment*. Itasca, Ill.: Peacock, 1990.

Lowy, Louis. "Goal Formulation in Social Work Groups." In Saul Bernstein, ed., *Further Explorations in Group Work*, pp. 116–44. Boston: Milford House, 1973.

Lubell, Derryl. "Living with a Lifeline: Peritoneal Dialysis Patients." In Alex Gitterman and Lawrence Shulman, eds., *Mutual Aid Groups and the Life Cycle*, pp. 283–97. New York: Peacock, 1986.

Luborsky, L. "Clinicians' Judgments of Mental Health." *Archives of General Psychiatry* 7 (1962): 407–17.

Lum, Doman. *Social Work Practice and People of Color: A Process-Stage Approach*. 3d ed. Pacific Grove, Calif.: Brooks/Cole, 1996.

Lynch, James J. *The Broken Heart: The Medical Consequences of Loneliness*. New York: Basic, 1977.

Lynn, Maxine and Danielle Nisivoccia. "Activity-Oriented Group Work with the Mentally Ill: Enhancing Socialization." *Social Work with Groups* 18, nos. 2/3 (1995): 95–106.

Maas, Henry S. "Group Influences on Client-Worker Interaction." *Social Work* 9, no. 2 (April 1964): 70–79.

——— *People and Contexts. Social Development from Birth to Old Age*. Englewood Cliffs, N.J.: Prentice-Hall, 1984.

McBroom, Elizabeth. "Socialization Through Small Groups." In Robert W. Roberts and Helen Northen, eds., *Theories of Social Work with Groups*, pp. 268–303. New York: Columbia University Press, 1976.

MacKenzie, K. Roy. "Measurement of Group Climate." *International Journal of Group Psychotherapy* 31 (1981): 287–95.

———— "Time Limited Group Psychotherapy." *International Journal of Group Psychotherapy* 46, no. 1 (1996): 41–60.

MacKenzie, K. Roy and W. John Livesley. "A Developmental Model for Brief Group Therapy." In Robert R. Dies and K. Roy MacKenzie, eds., *Advances in Group Psychotherapy*, pp. 101–16. New York: International Universities Press, 1983.

MacLennen, Beryce W. "Co-Therapy." *International Journal of Group Psychotherapy* 13, no. 2 (April 1965): 154–66.

Mahler, Margaret S., Fred Pine, and Ani Bergman. *The Psychological Birth of the Human Infant*. New York: Basic, 1975.

Maier, Henry W. "Play Is More than a Four-Letter Word: Play and Playfulness in the Interaction of People." In Paul Glasser and Nazneen Mayadas, eds., *Group Workers at Work: Theory and Practice in the 80s*, pp. 65–74. Totowa, N.J.: Rowman and Littlefield, 1986.

———— "The Social Group Work Method and Residential Treatment." In Henry W. Maier, ed., *Group Work as Part of Residential Treatment*, pp. 236–44. New York: National Association of Social Workers, 1965.

Maier, Henry W., ed. *Group Work as Part of Residential Treatment*. New York: National Association of Social Workers, 1965.

Main, Marjorie White. "Selected Aspects of the Beginning Phase of Social Group Work." Ph.D. dissertation, University of Chicago, 1964.

Maki, Mitchell T. "Counter-Transference with Adolescent Clients of the Same Ethnicity." *Child and Adolescent Social Work Journal* 7, no. 2 (April 1990): 135–46.

Malekoff, Andrew. *Group Work with Adolescents: Principles and Practice*. New York: Guilford, 1997.

———— "Pink Soap and Stall Doors." *Families in Society* (May-June 1999): 219–20.

Maluccio, Anthony N. *Learning from Clients: Interpersonal Helping as Viewed by Clients and Their Workers*. New York: Free, 1979.

Maluccio, Anthony N. and Wilma Marlow. "The Case for the Contract." *Social Work* 19, no. 1 (January 1974): 28–36.

Marks, Malcolm. "Group Psychotherapy for Emotionally Disturbed Children." In National Conference of Social Work, *Group Work and Community Organization*, pp. 70–77. New York: Columbia University Press, 1956.

Marsiglia, Flavio, Suzanne Cross, and Violet Mitchell-Enos. "Culturally Grounded Group Work with Adolescent American Indian Students." *Social Work with Groups* 21, nos. 1/2 (1998): 89–102.

Mayadas, Nazneen and Paul Glasser. "Termination: A Neglected Aspect of Social Group Work." *Social Work with Groups*, no. 4 (Spring/Summer 1981): 193–204.

Mayer, John E. and Aaron Rosenblatt. "The Client's Social Context: Its Effect on Continuance in Treatment." *Social Casework* 45, no. 4 (November 1964): 511–18.

Meadow, Diane A. "The Preparatory Interview: A Client-Focused Approach with Children of Holocaust Survivors." *Social Work with Groups* 4, nos. 3/4 (Fall/Winter 1981): 135–45.

Meadow, Diane A. "The Effects of a Client-Focused Pregroup Preparation Interview on the Formation of Group Cohesion and Members' Interactional Behavior." Ph.D. dissertation, University of Southern California, 1992.

Merton, Robert K. *Social Theory and Social Structure.* Glencoe, Ill.: Free, 1949.

Middleman, Ruth R. *The Non-Verbal Method in Working with Groups.* New York: Association Press, 1968.

——— "Returning Group Process To Group Work." *Social Work with Groups* 1, no. 1 (Winter 1978): 15–26.

——— "The Use of Program: Review and Update." *Social Work with Groups* 3, no. 3 (1980): 5–23.

Middleman, Ruth R. and Gale Goldberg Wood. *Skills for Direct Practice in Social Work.* New York: Columbia University Press, 1990.

Miller, Irving and Renee Solomon. "The Development of Group Services for the Elderly." *Journal of Gerontological Social Work* 2, no. 3 (Spring 1980): 241–58.

Mondros, Jacqueline and Toby Berman-Rossi. "The Relevance of Stages of Group Development Theory to Community Organization Practice." *Social Work with Groups* 14, no. 3/4 (1991): 203–22.

Mondros, Jacqueline, Richard Woodrow, and Lois Weinstein. "The Use of Groups to Manage Conflict." *Social Work with Groups* 15, no. 4 (1992): 43–58.

Montagu, Ashley. *The Cultured Man.* Cleveland: World, 1958.

Mor-Barak, Michal. *Social Networks and Health of the Frail Elderly.* New York: Garland, 1991.

Moreno, Jacob L. *Who Shall Survive? A New Approach to the Problem of Human Interaction.* Washington, D.C.: Nervous and Mental Disease, 1934.

Mullen, Edward J. "Casework Communication." *Social Casework* 49, no. 6 (November 1968): 546–51.

Murphy, Marjorie, ed. *The Social Group Work Method in Social Work Education: A Project Report of the Curriculum Study.* Vol. 11. New York: Council on Social Work Education, 1959.

Myers, John E.B. *Legal Issues in Child Abuse and Neglect.* Newbury Park, Calif.: Sage, 1992.

Nakama, George. "Japanese-Americans' Expectations of Counseling: An Exploratory Survey." D.S.W. dissertation, University of Southern California, 1980.

National Association of Social Workers. *Code of Ethics.* Washington, D.C.: Association, 1993.

National Association of Social Workers. *The Psychiatric Social Worker as Leader of a Group.* New York: Association, 1959.

National Association of Social Workers. *Use of Groups in the Psychiatric Setting.*
New York: Association, 1960.

Newstetter, Wilber I. "What Is Social Group Work?" *Proceedings, National Conference of Social Work,* pp. 291–99. Chicago: University of Chicago Press, 1935.

Newstetter, Wilber I., Mark J. Feldstein, and Theodore M. Newcomb. *Group Adjustment—A Study in Experimental Sociology.* Cleveland: Western Reserve University, 1938.

Northen, Helen. "Assessment in Direct Practice." In National Association of Social Workers, *Encyclopedia of Social Work,* pp. 171–83. 18th ed. Silver Spring, Md.: 1987.

―――― *Clinical Social Work Knowledge and Skills.* 2d ed. New York: Columbia University Press, 1995.

―――― "Ethical Dilemmas in Social Work with Groups." *Social Work with Groups* 21, nos. 1/2 (1998): 5–18.

―――― "Psychosocial Practice in Small Groups." In Robert W. Roberts and Helen Northen, eds., *Theories of Social Work with Groups,* pp. 116–52. New York: Columbia University Press, 1976.

―――― "Selection of Groups as the Preferred Modality of Practice." In Joseph Lassner, Kathleen Powell, and Elaine Finnegan, eds., *Social Group Work: Competence and Values in Practice,* pp. 19–34. New York: Haworth, 1987.

―――― "Social Relationships and Support: Multidisciplinary Studies." Los Angeles: Emeriti Center, University of Southern California, 1995.

―――― "Social Work Practice at USC: Its Roots and Branches." In Frances L. Feldman, ed., *The Evolution of Professional Social Work Education, Scholarship, and Community Service at the University of Southern California,* Los Angeles: School of Social Work, University of Southern California, 1996.

―――― "Social Work Practice with Groups in Health Care." *Social Work with Groups* 12, no. 4 (1989): 7–26.

―――― "Social Work with Groups in Health Settings: Promises and Problems." In Gary Rosenberg and Helen Rehr, eds., *Advancing Social Work Practice in the Health Care Field,* pp. 107–21. New York: Haworth, 1983.

Northen, Henry and Rebecca Northen. *Ingenious Kingdom: The Remarkable World of Plants.* Englewood Cliffs, N.J.: Prentice-Hall, 1970.

Nosko, Anna and Robert Wallace. "Female/Male Co-Leadership in Groups." *Social Work with Groups* 20, no. 2 (1997): 3–16.

O'Connor, Gerald G. "Small Groups: A General System Model." *Small Group Behavior* 11, no. 2 (May 1980): 145–74.

Orcutt, Ben A. "Family Treatment of Poverty Level Families," *Social Casework* 58, no. 2 (February 1976): 92–100.

―――― *Science and Inquiry in Social Work Practice.* New York: Columbia University Press, 1990.

Orlick, Terry. *The Cooperative Sports and Games Book: Challenge Without Competition.* New York: Pantheon, 1978.

—— *The Second Cooperative Sports and Games Book.* New York: Random House, 1982.

Osborn, Hazel. "Some Factors of Resistance Which Affect Group Participation." In Dorothea Sullivan, ed., *Readings in Group Work.* New York: Association, 1952.

Overton, Alice and Katherine Tinker. *Casework Notebook.* St. Paul, Minn.: Greater St. Paul Community Chests and Councils, 1957.

Papell, Catherine P. and Beulah Rothman. "Social Group Work Models: Possession and Heritage." *Journal of Education for Social Work* 2, no. 2 (Fall 1966): 66–77.

Parad, Howard J., Lola G. Selby, and James Quinlan. "Crisis Intervention with Families and Groups." In Robert W. Roberts and Helen Northen, eds., *Theories of Social Work with Groups*, pp. 304–30. New York: Columbia University Press, 1976.

Paradise, Robert. "The Factor of Timing in the Addition of New Members to Established Groups." *Child Welfare* 47, no. 9 (November 1968): 524–30.

Parloff, Morris B., Irene E. Waskow, and Barry E. Wolfe. "Research on Therapist Variables in Relation to Process and Outcome." In Sol Garfield and Allen Bergin, eds., *Handbook of Psychotherapy and Behavior Change*, pp. 233–82. New York: Wiley, 1978.

Parnes, Marvin, ed. *Innovations in Social Group Work: Feedback from Practice to Theory.* New York: Haworth, 1986.

Peirce, Francis J. "A Study of the Methodological Components of Social Work with Groups." D.S.W. dissertation, University of Southern California, 1966.

Perley, Janice, Carolyn Winget, and Carlos Placci. "Hope and Discomfort as Factors Influencing Treatment Continuance." *Comprehensive Psychiatry* 12, no. 6 (November 1971): 557–63.

Perlman, Helen Harris. "The Problem-Solving Model in Social Casework." In Robert W. Roberts and Robert H. Nee, eds., *Theories of Social Casework.* pp. 129–80. Chicago: University of Chicago Press, 1970.

—— *Relationship, the Heart of Helping People.* Chicago: University of Chicago Press, 1979.

—— "Self-Determination: Reality or Illusion?" In F. F. McDermott, ed., *Self-Determination in Social Work*, pp. 65–89. London: Routledge and Paul Kegan, 1975.

—— *Social Casework: A Problem-Solving Process.* Chicago: University of Chicago Press, 1957.

—— "Social Work Method: A Review." *Social Work* 10, no. 4 (1965): 166–78.

Pernell, Ruby B. "Empowerment in Social Group Work." In Marvin Parnes, ed., *Innovations in Social Group Work: Feedback from Practice to Theory*, pp. 107–118. New York: Haworth, 1986.

Phillips, Helen U. *Essentials of Social Group Work Skill.* New York: Association, 1957.

Pierce, Gregory A., Barbara R. Sarason, and Irvin G. Sarason. "Integrating Social Support Perspectives: Working Models, Personal Relationships, and Situational Factors." In Steve Duck and R. C. Silver, eds., *Personal Relationships and Social Support.* Newbury Park, Calif.: Sage, 1990.

Pigors, Paul. *Leadership or Domination.* New York: Houghton-Mifflin, 1935.

Pinamonti, Guido. "Caseworkers' Use of Groups in Direct Practice." D.S.W. dissertation, University of Southern California, 1961.

Pincus, Allen and Anne Minahan. *Social Work Practice: Model and Method.* Itasca, Ill.: Peacock, 1973.

Pinderhughes, Elaine. "Empowerment for Our Clients and for Ourselves." *Social Casework* 64, no. 6 (June 1983): 331–36.

Pinderhughes, Elaine B. "Power, Powerlessness, and Practice." In Sylvia Sims Gray, Ann Hartman, and Ellen Saalberg, eds., *Empowering the Black Family.* Ann Arbor: National Child Welfare Training Center, University of Michigan, School of Social Work, 1985.

—— *Understanding Race, Ethnicity, and Power: The Key to Efficacy in Clinical Practice.* New York: Free, 1989.

Piper, W. E. and E. L. Pennault. "Pretherapy Preparation for Group Members." *International Journal of Group Psychotherapy* 39, no. 1 (1989): 17–34.

Polansky, Norman A. and Jacob Kounin. "Clients' Reactions to Initial Interviews: A Field Study." *Human Relations* 9 (1956): 237–64.

Pollio, David E. "Hoops Group: Group Work with Young 'Street' Men." *Social Work with Groups* 17, nos. 2/3 (1995): 107–22.

Potocky, Miriam. "An Art Therapy Group for Clients with Chronic Schizophrenia." *Social Work with Groups* 16, no. 3 (1993): 73–82.

Powdermaker, Florence B. and Jerome D. Frank. *Group Psychotherapy: Studies in Methodology of Research and Therapy.* Cambridge: Harvard University Press, 1953.

Pray, Kenneth L. M. *Social Work in a Revolutionary Age.* Philadelphia: University of Pennsylvania Press, 1949.

Radin, Norma and Sheila Feld. "Social Psychology for Group Work Practice." In Martin Sundel, Paul Glasser, Rosemary Sarri, and Robert Vinter, eds., *Individual Change Through Small Groups*, pp. 50–69. 2d ed. New York: Free, 1985.

Rae-Grant, Quentin A. F., Thomas Gladwin, and Eli M. Bower. "Mental Health, Social Competence, and the War on Poverty." *American Journal of Orthopsychiatry* 36, no. 4 (July 1966): 652–64.

Raines, James C. "Empathy in Clinical Social Work." *Clinical Social Work Journal* 18, no. 1 (Spring 1990): 57–72.

Rapoport, Lydia. "Crisis Intervention as a Mode of Brief Treatment." In Robert W.

Roberts and Robert H. Nee, eds., *Theories of Social Casework*, pp. 267–311. Chicago: University of Chicago Press, 1970.

Raschella, Gerald. "An Evaluation of the Effect of Goal Congruence Between Client and Therapist on Premature Client Dropout from Therapy." Ph.D. dissertation, University of Pittsburgh, 1975.

Redl, Fritz. "The Art of Group Composition." In Suzanne Schulze, ed., *Creative Group Living in a Children's Institution*, pp. 76–98. New York: Association, 1953.

—— "Diagnostic Group Work." *American Journal of Orthopsychiatry* 14, no. 1 (January 1944): 53.

—— "Strategy and Technique of the Life Space Interview." *American Journal of Orthopsychiatry* 29, no. 1 (January 1959): 1–18.

Redl, Fritz and David Wineman. *Children Who Hate*. Glencoe, Ill.: Free, 1951.

—— *Controls from Within: Techniques for the Treatment of the Aggressive Child*. Glencoe, Ill.: Free, 1952.

Reed, Beth Glover. "Women Leaders in Small Groups: Social-Psychological, Psychodynamic, and Interactional Perspectives." *Social Work with Groups* 6, nos. 3/4 (Fall/Winter 1983): 35–42.

Reid, William J. and Laura Epstein, eds. *Task-Centered Practice*. New York: Columbia University Press, 1977.

Reid, William J. and Barbara L. Shapiro. "Client Reactions to Advice." *Social Service Review* 43, no. 2 (June 1969): 165–73.

Reid, William J. and Ann W. Shyne. *Brief and Extended Casework*. New York: Columbia University Press, 1969.

Reynolds, Bertha C. *Learning and Teaching in the Practice of Social Work*. New York: Farrar and Rinehart, 1942.

Rice, Cecil A. "Premature Termination of Group Therapy: A Clinical Perspective." *International Journal of Group Psychotherapy* 46, no. 1 (June 1996): 5–23.

Rice, David G., William F. Fey, and Joseph G. Kepecs. "Therapist Experience and Style as Factors in Co-Therapy." *Family Process* 11, no. 1 (March 1971): 1–12.

Richmond, Mary. *Social Diagnosis*. New York: Russell Sage, 1917.

—— "Some Next Steps in Social Treatment." *The Long View*. New York: Russell Sage, 1930.

—— *What Is Social Casework?* New York: Russell Sage, 1922.

Ripple, Lilian. "Factors Associated with Continuance in Casework Service." *Social Work* 2, no. 1 (January 1957): 87–94.

Ripple, Lilian, Ernestina Alexander, and Bernice W. Polemis. *Motivation, Capacity, and Opportunity: Studies in Casework Theory and Practice*. Chicago: School of Social Service Administration, University of Chicago, 1964.

Roberts, Robert W. and Robert H. Nee, eds. *Theories of Social Casework*. Chicago: University of Chicago Press, 1970.

Roberts, Robert W. and Helen Northen, eds. *Theories of Social Work with Groups*. New York: Columbia University Press, 1976.

Rogers, Carl R. "The Necessary and Sufficient Conditions of Therapeutic Personality Change." *Journal of Consulting Psychology* 21 (1957): 95–103.

Rohnke, Karl. *Silver Bullets: A Guide to Initiative Problems, Adventure Games, Stunts, and Trust Activities*. Hamilton, Mass.: Project Adventure, 1984.

Rohrbaugh, Michael and Bryan D. Bartels. "Participants' Perceptions of Curative Factors in Therapy and Growth Groups." *Small Group Behavior* 6, no. 4 (November 1975): 430–56.

Rosen, Aaron and Dina Lieberman. "The Experimental Evaluation of Interview Performance of Social Workers." *Social Service Review* 46, no. 3 (September 1972): 395–412.

Ross, Andrew L. and Norman D. Bernstein. "A Framework for the Therapeutic Use of Group Activities." *Child Welfare* 55, no. 9 (November 1976): 627–40.

Rotholz, Tryna. "The Single Session Group: An Innovative Approach to the Waiting Room." *Social Work with Groups* 8, no. 2 (Summer 1985): 143–46.

Rothman, Jack. "Analyzing Issues in Race and Ethnic Relations." In Jack Rothman, ed., *Issues in Race and Ethnic Relations*, pp. 24–37. Itasca, Ill.: Peacock, 1977.

———— "Client Self-Determination: Untangling the Knot." *Social Service Review* 63, no. 4 (December 1989): 598–612.

Russell, Mary Nomme. *Clinical Social Work: Research and Practice*. Newbury Park, Calif.: Sage, 1990.

Sainsbury, Eric. *Social Work with Families*. London: Routledge and Kegan Paul, 1975.

Sanford, Nevitt. *Self and Society: Social Change and Individual Development*. New York: Atherton, 1966.

Sarri, Rosemary C. and Maeda J. Galinsky. "A Conceptual Framework for Group Development." In Martin Sundel, Paul Glasser, Rosemary Sarri, and Robert Vinter, eds., *Individual Change Through Small Groups*, pp. 71–88. New York: Free, 1974.

Scheidlinger, Saul. *Psychoanalysis and Group Behavior*. New York: Norton, 1952.

Scheidlinger, Saul. "The Concept of Empathy in Group Psychotherapy." *International Journal of Group Psychotherapy* 16, no. 4 (October 1966): 413–24.

Scheidlinger, Saul and Marjorie A. Holden. "Group Therapy of Women with Severe Character Disorders: The Middle and Final Phases." *International Journal of Group Psychotherapy* 16, no. 2 (April 1966): 174–88.

Schein, Edgar H. *Organizational Culture and Leadership*. San Francisco: Jossey-Bass, 1985.

Schiff, Sheldon K. "Termination of Therapy: Problems in a Community Psychiatric Outpatient Clinic." *Archives of General Psychiatry* 6, no. 1 (January 1962): 77–82.

Schiller, Linda Yael. "Stages of Development in Women's Groups: A Relational Model." In Roselle Kurland and Robert Salmon, eds., *Group Work Practice in a Troubled Society: Problems and Opportunities*, pp. 117–38. Binghamton, N.Y.: Haworth, 1995.

Schiller, Linda Yael and Bonnie Zimmer. "Sharing the Secrets: Women's Groups for Sexual Abuse Survivors." In Alex Gitterman and Lawrence Shulman, eds., *Mutual Aid Groups, Vulnerable Populations, and the Life Cycle*, pp. 215–38. 2d ed. New York: Columbia University Press, 1994.

Schmidt, Julianna. "The Use of Purpose in Casework Practice." *Social Work* 4, no. 1 (January 1969): 77–84.

Schnekenburger, Erica. "Waking the Heart Up: A Writing Group's Story." *Social Work with Groups* 18, no. 4 (1995): 19–40.

Schopler, Janice H. and Maeda J. Galinsky. "Expanding Our View of Support Groups as Open Systems." In Maeda Galinsky and Janice H. Schopler, eds., *Support Groups: Current Perspectives on Theory and Practice*, pp. 3–10. New York: Haworth, 1995.

——— "When Groups Go Wrong." *Social Work* 26, no. 5 (September 1981): 424–29.

Schopler, Janice H., Melissa D. Abell, and Maeda J. Galinsky. "Technology-Based Groups: A Review and Conceptual Framework for Practice." *Social Work* 43, no. 3 (May 1998): 193–208.

Schopler, Janice H., Maeda J. Galinsky and Mark D. Alicke. "Goals in Social Group Work Practice: Formulation, Implementation, and Evaluation." In Martin Sundel, Paul Glasser, Rosemary Sarri, and Robert Vinter, eds., *Individual Change Through Small Groups*, pp. 340–58. 2d ed. New York: Free, 1985.

Schutz, William C. *Interpersonal Underworld*. Palo Alto: Science and Behavior, 1966.

Schwartz, Arthur. "Behaviorism and Psychodynamics." *Child Welfare* 56, no. 6 (June 1977): 368–79.

Schwartz, William. "Between Client and System: The Mediating Function." In Robert W. Roberts and Helen Northen, eds., *Theories of Social Work with Groups*, pp. 171–97. New York: Columbia University Press, 1976.

——— "The Social Worker in the Group." In *The Social Welfare Forum, 1961*, pp. 146–71. New York: Columbia University Press, 1961.

Schwartz, William and Serapio R. Zalba, eds. *The Practice of Group Work*. New York: Columbia University Press, 1971.

Seabury, Brett A. "Arrangement of Physical Space in Social Work Settings." *Social Work* 16, no. 4 (October 1971): 43–49.

Shapiro, Constance Hoenk. "Termination: A Neglected Concept in the Social Work Curriculum." *Journal of Education for Social Work* 16, no. 2 (Summer 1980): 13–19.

Shaw, Marvin E. *Group Dynamics: The Psychology of Small Group Behavior.* 3d ed. New York: McGraw-Hill, 1981.

Sheffield, Alfred. *Creative Discussion.* New York: Association, 1926.

Sheridan, Mary E. "Talk Time for Hospitalized Children." *Social Work* 20, no. 1 (January 1975): 40–45.

Shimer, John A. *This Sculptured Earth: The Landscape of America.* New York: Columbia University Press, 1959.

Shulman, Lawrence. " 'Program' in Group Work: Another Look." In William Schwartz and Serapio Zalba, eds., *The Practice of Group Work*, pp. 221–40. New York: Columbia University Press, 1971.

——— "Scapegoats, Group Workers, and Pre-emptive Intervention." *Social Work* 12, no. 2 (1967): 37–43.

——— *The Skills of Helping Individuals, Families, and Groups.* 3d ed. Itasca, Ill.: Peacock, 1992.

——— *The Skills of Helping Individuals, Families, Groups, and Communities.* 4th ed. Itasca, Ill.: Peacock, 1999.

Shyne, Ann W. "What Research Tells Us About Short-Term Cases in Family Agencies." *Social Casework* 38, no. 5 (May 1957): 223–31.

Silberman, Samuel. "A New Strain for Social Work." Paper presented at the Annual Meeting of the Group for the Advancement of Doctoral Education, October 1982.

Simmel, Georg. *Conflict.* Trans. Kurt H. Wolfe. Glencoe, Ill.: Free, 1955.

Simon, Barbara Levy. *The Empowerment Tradition in American Social Work: A History.* New York: Columbia University Press, 1994.

Siporin, Max. *Introduction to Social Work Practice.* New York: Macmillan, 1975.

Sistler, Audrey and Kimberly S. Washington. "Serenity for African American Caregivers." *Social Work with Groups* 22, no. 1 (1999): 49–62.

Slocum, Yolanda. "A Survey of Expectations About Group Therapy Among Clinical and Non-Clinical Populations." *International Journal of Group Psychotherapy* 37, no. 1 (January 1987): 39–54.

Smalley, Ruth. *Theory for Social Work Practice.* New York: Columbia University Press, 1967.

Solomon, Barbara Bryant. *Black Empowerment: Social Work in Oppressed Communities.* New York: Columbia University Press, 1976.

Somers, Mary Louise. "Problem-Solving in Small Groups." In Robert W. Roberts and Helen Northen, eds., *Theories of Social Work with Groups*, pp. 331–67. New York: Columbia University Press, 1976.

——— "The Small Group in Learning and Teaching." In Bureau of Family Services, Welfare Administration, *Learning and Teaching in Public Welfare.* Washington, D.C.: U.S. Department of Education and Welfare, 1963.

Sotomayor, Marta. "Language, Culture, and Ethnicity in the Developing Self-Concept." *Social Casework* 58, no. 4 (April 1977): 195–203.

Spolin, Viola. *Theater Games for the Classroom: A Teacher's Handbook*. Evanston, Ill.: Northwestern University Press, 1986.

Stark, Frances B. "Barriers to Client-Worker Communication at Intake." *Social Casework* 40, no. 4 (April 1959): 177–83.

Stein, Herman D. and Richard A. Cloward, eds. *Social Perspectives on Behavior: A Reader in Social Science for Social Work and Related Professions*. Glencoe, Ill.: Free, 1958.

Steinberg, Dominique Moyse. *The Mutual-Aid Approach to Working with Groups*. Northvale, N.J.: Jason Aronson, 1997.

—— "Some Findings from a Study on the Impact of Group Work Education on Social Work Practitioners' Work with Groups." *Social Work with Groups* 16, no. 3 (1993): 23–39.

Stokes, Joseph Powell. "Toward an Understanding of Cohesion in Personal Change Groups." *International Journal of Group Psychotherapy* 33, no. 4 (October 1983): 449–67.

Subramanian, Karen, Sylvia Hernandez, and Angie Martinez. "Psychoeducational Group Work for Low-Income Latina Mothers with HIV Infection." *Social Work with Groups* 18, nos. 2/3 (1995): 53–64.

Sullivan, Nancy. "Who Owns the Group? The Role of Worker Control in the Development of a Group: A Qualitative Research Study of Practice." *Social Work with Groups* 18, nos. 2/3 (1995): 15–32.

Sundel, Martin, Paul Glasser, Rosemary Sarri, and Robert Vinter, eds. *Individual Change Through Small Groups*. 2d ed. New York: Free, 1985.

Takaki, Robert R. *Strangers from a Different Shore: A History of Asian Americans*. Boston: Little, Brown, 1989.

Thibaut, John W. and Harold H. Kelley. *The Social Psychology of Groups*. New York: Wiley, 1959.

Thomas, Edwin and Clinton Fink. "Effects of Group Size." In A. Paul Hare, Edgar F. Borgatta, and Robert F. Bales, eds., *Small Groups: Studies and Social Interaction*. New York: Knopf, 1955.

Thompson, Sheila and J. H. Kahn. *The Group Process as a Helping Technique*. Oxford: Pergamon, 1970.

Tocqueville, Alexis de. *Democracy in America*. Vol. 2. New York: Dearborn, 1838.

Toseland, Ronald W. and Robert F. Rivas. *An Introduction to Group Work Practice*. 3d ed. Boston: Allyn and Bacon, 1998.

Toseland, Ronald W. and Max Siporin. "When to Recommend Group Treatment: A Review of the Clinical and Research Literature." *International Journal of Group Psychotherapy* 36, no. 2 (April 1986): 171–206.

Tracy, Elizabeth M. "Identifying Social Support Resources of At-Risk Families." *Social Work* 35, no. 3 (1990): 252–58.

Travers, Anna. "Redefining Adult Identity: A Coming Out Group for Lesbians." In

Benj. L. Stempler and Marilyn Glass, eds., *Social Group Work: Today and Tomorrow*, pp. 103–18. Binghamton, N.Y.: Haworth, 1996.

Trecker, Harleigh B. *Social Group Work—Principles and Practices*. Rev. ed. New York: Whiteside, 1973.

Trecker, Harleigh B., ed. *Group Work in the Psychiatric Setting*. New York: Whiteside and Morrow, 1956.

Tropp, Emanuel. "A Developmental Theory." In Robert W. Roberts and Helen Northen, eds., *Theories of Social Work with Groups*, pp. 198–237. New York: Columbia University Press, 1976.

Tsang, A. Ka Tat and Marilyn Bogo. "Engaging with Clients Cross-culturally: Towards Developing Research Based Practice." *Journal of Multicultural Social Work* 6, nos. 3/4 (1997): 73–91.

Tsui, Philip and Gail L. Schultz. "Ethnic Factors in Group Process: Cultural Dynamics in Multi-Ethnic Therapy Groups." *American Journal of Orthopsychiatry* 58, no. 1 (January 1988): 136–42.

Tuckman, Bruce W. "Developmental Sequence in Small Groups." *Psychogical Bulletin* 63, no. 6 (June 1965): 384–99.

Tuckman, Bruce W. and M. A. C. Jensen. "Stages of Small Group Development Revisited." *Group and Organizational Studies* 2, no. 1 (January 1977): 419–27.

Turner, Francis J., ed. *Social Work Treatment: Interlocking Theoretical Approaches.* 2d ed. New York: Free, 1979.

Vaillant, George E. *The Wisdom of the Ego*. Cambridge: Harvard University Press, 1993.

Van Den Bergh, Nan. "Managing Biculturalism at the Workplace: A Group Approach." *Social Work with Groups* 13, no. 4 (1990): 71–84.

van de Vliert. "Conflict in Prevention and Escalation." In Pieter J. Drenth, ed., *Handbook of Work and Organizational Psychology*, pp. 521–55. New York: Wiley, 1984.

Velasquez, Joan, Marilyn Vigil, and Eustalio Benavides. "A Framework for Establishing Social Work Relationships Across Racial Ethnic Lines." In Beulah Roberts Compton and Burt Galaway, eds., *Social Work Processes*, pp. 197–203. 6th ed. Homewood, Ill.: Dorsey, 1999.

Videka-Sherman, Lynn. "Meta Analysis of Research on Social Work Practice in Mental Health." *Social Work* 33, no. 4 (July/August 1988): 325–38.

Vinter, Robert D. "Program Activities: An Analysis of Their Effects on Participant Behavior." In Martin Sundel, Paul Glasser, Rosemary Sarri, and Robert Vinter, eds., *Individual Change Through Small Groups*, pp. 226–36. 2d ed. New York: Free, 1985.

Vinter, Robert D. and Maeda J. Galinsky. "Extra-Group Relations and Approaches." In Martin Sundel, Paul Glasser, Rosemary Sarri, and Robert Vinter, eds. *Individual Change Through Small Groups*, pp. 266–76. 2d ed. New York: Free, 1985.

Waite, Lesley Meirovitz. "Drama Therapy in Small Groups with the Developmentally Disabled." *Social Work with Groups* 16, no. 4 (1993): 95–108.

Waites, Cheryl. "The Tradition of Group Work and Natural Helping Networks in the African American Community." In David F. Fike and Barbara Rittner, eds., *Working From Strengths: The Essence of Group Work*, pp. 220–35. Miami Shores: Center for Group Work Studies, 1992.

Waldron, Jane A., Ronaele Whittington, and Steve Jensen. "Children's Single Session Briefings: Group Work with Military Families Experiencing Parents' Deployment." *Social Work with Groups* 9, no. 2 (Summer 1985): 101–9.

Warner, W. Lloyd. *Life in America: Dream and Reality.* New York: Harper, 1952.

Waskow, Irene E. and Morris B. Parloff, eds. *Psychotherapy Change Measures.* Washington, D.C.: National Institute of Mental Health, U.S. Government Printing Office, 1975.

Weick, Ann, Charles Rapp, W. Patrick Sullivan, and Walter Kisthardt. "A Strengths Perspective for Social Work Practice." *Social Work* 34, no. 4 (July 1989): 350–54.

Weisberg, Alma. "Single Session Group Practice in a Hospital." In Joseph Lassner, Kathleen Powell, and Elaine Finnegan, eds., *Social Group Work: Competence and Values in Practice*, pp. 99–112. Binghamton, N.Y.: Haworth.

Weiss, Robert S. "The Provisions of Social Relationships." In Z. Rubin, ed., *Doing Unto Others.* Englewood Cliffs, N.J.: Prentice-Hall, 1974.

Whittaker, James K. "A Developmental-Educational Approach to Child Treatment." In Francine Sobey, ed., *Changing Roles in Social Work Practice.* pp. 176–96. Philadelphia: Temple University Press, 1977.

——— "Causes of Childhood Disorders: New Findings." *Social Work* 21, no. 2 (March 1976): 91–96.

——— "Program Activities: Their Selection and Use in a Therapeutic Milieu." In Martin Sundel, Paul Glasser, Rosemary Sarri, and Robert Vinter, eds., *Individual Change Through Small Groups*, pp. 217–50. 2d ed. New York: Free, 1985.

——— *Social Treatment: An Approach to Interpersonal Helping.* Chicago: Aldine, 1974.

Williams, Joyce E. and Karen A. Holmes. *The Second Assault: Rape and Public Attitudes.* Westport, Conn.: Greenwood, 1981.

Williams, Meyer. "Limitations, Phantasies, and Security Operations of Beginning Group Therapists." *International Journal of Group Psychotherapy* 16, no. 2 (April 1966): 15–62.

Williamson, Margaretta. *The Social Worker in Group Work.* New York: Harper, 1929.

Wilson, Gertrude. "From Practice to Theory: A Personalized History." In Robert W. Roberts and Helen Northen, eds., *Theories of Social Work with Groups*, pp. 1–44. New York: Columbia University Press, 1976.

——— *Group Work and Case Work: Their Relationship and Practice.* New York: Family Welfare Association of America, 1941.

Wilson, Gertrude and Gladys Ryland. *Social Group Work Practice.* Boston: Houghton-Mifflin, 1949.

Woods, Mary E. and Florence Hollis. *Casework: A Psychosocial Therapy.* 4th ed. New York: McGraw Hill, 1990.

Worby, Marsha. "The Adolescents' Expectations of How a Potentially Helpful Person Will Act." *Smith College Studies in Social Work* 26 (1955): 29–59.

Wright, Whitney. "The Use of Purpose in On-Going Activity Groups: A Framework for Maximizing the Therapeutic Impact." *Social Work with Groups* 22, nos. 2/3 (1999): 33–57.

Yalom, Irvin D. *Inpatient Group Psychotherapy.* New York: Basic Books, 1983.

————— "A Study of Group Therapy Drop-Outs." *Archives of General Psychiatry* 14 (1966): 393–414.

————— *The Theory and Practice of Group Psychotherapy.* New York: Basic, 1970.

————— *The Theory and Practice of Group Psychotherapy.* 2d ed. New York: Basic, 1975.

————— *The Theory and Practice of Group Psychotherapy.* 3d ed. New York: Basic, 1985.

Yalom, Irvin D., P. S. Houts, G. Newell, and K. H. Rand. "Preparation of Patients for Group Therapy." *Archives of General Psychiatry* 17 no. 4 (1967): 416–27.

Young, Thomas M. and John E. Poulin. "The Helping Relationship Inventory: A Clinical Appraisal." *Families in Society* 79, no. 2 (March/April 1998): 123–38.

Zalba, Serapio R. "Discontinuance During Social Service Intake." Ph.D. dissertation, Western Reserve University, 1971.

Zamudio, Sylvia. "Stages of Group Development in Children's Bereavement Groups." Paper presented at the 20th Annual Symposium, Association for the Advancement of Social Work with Groups, October 1998.

Index